Frederick Marryat

Snarleyyow: or,

The dog fiend

Frederick Marryat

Snarleyyow: or,
The dog fiend

ISBN/EAN: 9783337814922

Printed in Europe, USA, Canada, Australia, Japan

Cover: Foto ©ninafisch / pixelio.de

More available books at **www.hansebooks.com**

NEW YORK YACHT CLUB EDITION

SNARLEYYOW

OR

THE DOG FIEND

BY
CAPTAIN MARRYAT

NEW YORK
CROSCUP AND COMPANY
MDCCCXCVI

Contents

		PAGE
Chapter I	. . . .	1
Chapter II	. . . .	7
Chapter III	. . . .	11
Chapter IV	. . . .	16
Chapter V	. . . .	20
Chapter VI	. . . .	28
Chapter VII	. . . .	33
Chapter VIII	. . . .	37
Chapter IX	. . . .	43
Chapter X	. . . .	56
Chapter XI	. . . .	66
Chapter XII	. . . .	71
Chapter XIII	. . . .	77
Chapter XIV	. . . .	86
Chapter XV	. . . .	96
Chapter XVI	. . . .	101
Chapter XVII	. . . .	109
Chapter XVIII	. . . .	120
Chapter XIX	. . . .	124

Contents

	PAGE
Chapter XX	133
Chapter XXI	145
Chapter XXII	153
Chapter XXIII	164
Chapter XXIV	172
Chapter XXV	185
Chapter XXVI	191
Chapter XXVII	197
Chapter XXVIII	204
Chapter XXIX	215
Chapter XXX	226
Chapter XXXI	241
Chapter XXXII	249
Chapter XXXIII	260
Chapter XXXIV	266
Chapter XXXV	275
Chapter XXXVI	283
Chapter XXXVII	290
Chapter XXXVIII	296
Chapter XXXIX	301
Chapter XL	311
Chapter XLI	318
Chapter XLII	326
Chapter XLIII	331
Chapter XLIV	340
Chapter XLV	349
Chapter XLVI	357
Chapter XLVII	365

Contents

CHAPTER XLVIII	372
CHAPTER XLIX	380
CHAPTER L	386
CHAPTER LI	392
CHAPTER LII	397
CHAPTER LIII	404
CHAPTER LIV	409
CHAPTER LV	415

List of Etchings

SMALLBONES SOON MADE HIS APPEARANCE	*Frontispiece*
	PAGE
SNARLEYYOW APPEARED ON THE FORECASTLE, AND MADE A RUSH AT SMALLBONES	65
THE BODY HALF RAISED ITSELF FROM ITS KNEES WITH A STRONG MUSCULAR ACTION, AND THEN TOPPLED OVER	119
"MERCY, WOMAN!" EXCLAIMED VANSLYPERKEN, "DO NOT HARM THE POOR DOG"	184
"TE TOG'S TAIL, MYNHEER," REPLIED THE CORPORAL, GRAVELY	288
"OUT OF MY HOUSE, YOU VILLAIN!"	348

Drawn and Etched by J. AYTON SYMINGTON.

Prefatory Note

THE DOG FIEND, OR SNARLEYYOW is the earliest of the three novels, *The Phantom Ship* and *The Privateersman* being the other two, in which Marryat made use of historical events and attempted to project his characters into the past. The research involved is not profound, but the machinations of Jacobite conspirators provide appropriate material for the construction of an adventure plot and for the exhibition of a singularly despicable villain. Mr Vanslyperken and his acquaintances, male and female, at home and abroad, are all—except perhaps his witch-like mother—thoroughly life-like and convincing: their conduct is sufficiently probable to retain the reader's attention for a rapid and exciting narrative.

The numerous escapes of the vile cur, after whom the novel is christened, and of his natural enemy Peter Smallbones are not all equally well contrived, and they become a little wearisome by repetition; but a general atmosphere of *diablerie* is very effectively produced by their means. Some such element of unreality is absolutely demanded to relieve the sordid and brutal details by which the main plot is worked out; and it must be admitted that in certain passages—the death-struggle between Smallbones and the lieutenant's mother, the discovery of the woman's body, and the descriptions of kisses between Corporal Van Spitter and the Frau Vandersloosh—Marryat's habitual literalness becomes unpleasantly coarse. The offensive touches, however, are incidental, and the execution of the two villains, Vanslyperken and Snarleyyow, with its dash of genuine pathos, is dramatic and impressive :—"They were damnable in their lives, and in their deaths they were not divided."

As usual the interest of the novel depends almost entirely upon men, but on the character of Mrs Corbett, *née* Nancy Dawson, Marryat has expended considerable care with satisfactory results. Barring the indecorous habit of regretting her past in public, which is not perhaps untrue to nature, she is made attractive by her wit and sincere repentance, without becoming unnaturally refined. The song in her honour referred to on p. 107 is not suitable for reproduction in this place. She was an historic character in the reign of William III., but must not be confounded with her more celebrated namesake (1730-1767) of Sadler's Wells, Covent Garden, and Drury Lane, who danced a horn-pipe in *The Beggar's Opera* to the air of "Nancy Dawson," which is mentioned in the epilogue of *She Stoops to Conquer*, and survives in our nurseries as "Here we go round the Mulberry Bush."

The greater part of *Snarleyyow* was first printed in *The Metropolitan Magazine*, 1836 and 1837; but on reaching Chapter xl., just as the novel had appeared in book form, the editor—not then Marryat himself—told his readers that it was not his intention to give an extended review of this work, as they had already "ample means of forming their own opinion of its varied merits :"—"We shall therefore content ourselves with a few remarks, in announcing its publication and giving a brief outline of the termination of the story from our last number." At the close of the said extracts he writes :—

"And so ends Snarleyyow, with as much quaintness, spirit, and character as it commenced."

The book was evidently written in haste, and few of the minor characters retained one Christian name throughout its pages. It is here reprinted, with the corrections of such slips as those just mentioned, from the first edition in three volumes. Henry Colburn, 1837.

R. B. J.

Snarleyyow

Chapter I

Introduction of divers parties and a red-herring.

It was in the month of January, 1699, that a one-masted vessel, with black sides, was running along the coast near Beachy Head, at the rate of about five miles per hour. The wind was from the northward and blew keenly, the vessel was under easy sail, and the water was smooth. It was now broad daylight, and the sun rose clear of clouds and vapour; but he threw out light without heat. The upper parts of the spars, the hammock rails, and the small iron guns which were mounted on the vessel's decks, were covered with a white frost. The man at the helm stood muffled up in a thick pea-jacket and mittens, which made his hands appear as large as his feet. His nose was a pug of an intense bluish red, one tint arising from the present cold, and the other from the preventive checks which he had been so long accustomed to take to drive out such an unpleasant intruder. His grizzled hair waved its locks gently to the wind, and his face was distorted with an immoderate quid of tobacco which protruded his right cheek. This personage was second officer and steersman on board of the vessel, and his name was Obadiah Coble. He had been baptised Obadiah about sixty years before; that is to say if he had been baptised at all. He stood so motionless at the helm, that you might have imagined him to have been frozen there as he stood, were it not that his eyes occasionally wandered from the compass on the binnacle to the bows of the vessel, and that the breath from his mouth, when it was thrown out into the clear frosty air, formed a smoke like to that from the spout of a half-boiling tea-kettle.

The crew belonging to the cutter, for she was a vessel in the service of his Majesty, King William the Third, at this time employed in protecting his Majesty's revenue against the importation of alamodes and lutestrings, were all down below at their breakfasts, with the exception of the steersman and lieutenant-commandant, who now walked the quarter-deck, if so small an extent of plank could be dignified with such a name. He was a Mr Cornelius Vanslyperken, a tall, meagre-looking personage, with very narrow shoulders and very small head. Perfectly straight up and down, protruding in no part, he reminded you of some tall parish pump, with a great knob at its top. His face was gaunt, cheeks hollow, nose and chin showing an affection for each other, and evidently lamenting the gulf between them which prevented their meeting. Both appeared to have fretted themselves to the utmost degree of tenuity from disappointment in love: as for the nose, it had a pearly round tear hanging at its tip, as if it wept. The dress of Mr Vanslyperken was hidden in a great coat, which was very long, and buttoned straight down. This great coat had two pockets on each side, into which its owner's hands were deeply inserted, and so close did his arms lie to his sides, that they appeared nothing more than as would battens nailed to a topsail yard. The only deviation from the perpendicular was from the insertion of a speaking-trumpet under his left arm, at right angles with his body. It had evidently seen much service, was battered, and the clack Japan worn off in most parts of it. As we said before, Mr Vanslyperken walked his quarter-deck. He was in a brown study, yet looked blue. Six strides brought him to the taffrail of the vessel, six more to the bows, such was the length of his tether—and he turned, and turned again.

But there was another personage on the deck, a personage of no small importance, as he was all in all to Mr Vanslyperken, and Mr Vanslyperken was all in all to him; moreover, we may say, that he is the hero of the TAIL. This was one of the ugliest and most ill-conditioned curs which had ever been produced:—ugly in colour; for he was of a dirty yellow, like the paint served out to decorate our men-of-war by his Majesty's dockyards:—ugly in face; for he had one wall-eye, and was so far under-jawed as to prove that a bull-dog had had something to do with his creation:—ugly in shape; for although larger than a pointer, and strongly built, he was coarse and shambling in his make, with his forelegs bowed out. His ears and tail had never been docked, which was a pity, as the more you curtailed his proportions, the better looking the cur would have been. But his ears, although not cut, were torn to ribbons by the various encounters with dogs on shore, arising from the acidity of his temper. His tail had lost its hair from an inveterate mange, and reminded you of the same appendage to a rat. Many parts of his body were bared from the same disease. He carried his head and tail low, and had a villanous sour look. To the eye of a casual observer, there was not one redeeming quality that would warrant his keep; to those who knew him well, there were a thousand reasons why he should be hanged. He followed his master with the greatest precision and exactitude, walking aft as he walked aft, and walking forward with the same regular motion, turning when his master turned, and moreover, turning in the same direction; and, like his master, he appeared to be not a little nipped with the cold, and, as well as he, in a state of profound meditation. The name of this uncouth animal was very appropriate to his appearance, and to his temper. It was Snarleyyow.

At last, Mr Vanslyperken gave vent to his pent-up feelings. "I can't, I won't stand this any longer," muttered the lieutenant, as he took his six strides forward.

At this first sound of his master's voice the dog pricked up the remnants of his ears, and they both turned aft. "She has been now fooling me for six years;" and as he concluded this sentence, Mr Vanslyperken and Snarleyyow had reached the taffrail, and the dog raised his tail to the half cock.

They turned, and Mr Vanslyperken paused a moment or two, and compressed his thin lips—the dog did the same. "I will have an answer, by all that's blue!" was the ejaculation of the next six strides. The lieutenant stopped again, and the dog looked up in his master's face; but it appeared as if the current of his master's thoughts was changed, for the current of keen air reminded Mr Vanslyperken that he had not yet had his breakfast.

The lieutenant leant over the hatchway, took his battered speaking-trumpet from under his arm, and putting it to his mouth, the deck reverberated with, "Pass the word for Smallbones forward." The dog put himself in a baying attitude, with his forefeet on the coamings of the hatchway, and enforced his master's orders with a deep-toned and measured bow, wow, wow.

Smallbones soon made his appearance, rising from the hatchway like a ghost; a thin, shambling personage, apparently about twenty years old—a pale, cadaverous face, high cheek-bones, goggle eyes, with lank hair very thinly sown upon a head, which, like bad soil, would return but a scanty harvest. He looked like Famine's eldest son just arriving to years of discretion. His long lanky legs were pulled so far through his trousers, that his bare feet, and half way up to his knees, were exposed to the chilling blast. The sleeves of his jacket were so short, that four inches of bone above his wrist were bared to view—hat he had none—his ears were very large, and the rims of them red with cold, and his neck was so immeasurably long and thin, that his head appeared to topple for want of support. When he had come on deck, he stood with one hand raised to his forehead, touching his hair instead of his hat, and the other occupied with a half-roasted red-herring. "Yes, sir," said Smallbones, standing before his master.

"Be quick!"—commenced the lieutenant; but here his attention was directed to the red-herring by Snarleyyow, who raised his head and snuffed at its fumes. Among other disqualifications of the animal, be it observed, that he had no nose except for a red-herring, or a post by the way side. Mr Vanslyperken discontinued his orders, took his hand out of his great coat pocket, wiped the drop from off his nose, and then roared out, "How dare you appear on the quarter-deck of a king's ship, sir, with a red-herring in your fist?"

"If you please, sir," replied Smallbones, "if I were to come for to go to leave it in the galley, I shouldn't find it when I went back."

"What do I care for that, sir? It's contrary to all the rules and regulations of the service. Now, sir, hear me——"

"O Lord, sir! let me off this time, it's only a *soldier*," replied Smallbones, deprecatingly; but Snarleyyow's appetite had been very much sharpened by his morning's walk; it rose with the smell of the herring, so he rose on his hind legs, snapped the herring out of Smallbones' hand, bolted forward by the lee gangway, and would soon have bolted the herring, had not Smallbones bolted after him and overtaken him just as he had laid it down on the deck preparatory to commencing his meal. A fight ensued; Smallbones received a severe bite in the leg, which induced him to seize a handspike, and make a blow with it at the dog's head, which, if it had been well aimed, would have probably put an end to all further pilfering. As it was, the handspike descended upon one of the dog's fore toes, and Snarleyyow retreated, yelling, to the other side of the forecastle, and as soon as he was out of reach, like all curs, bayed in defiance.

Smallbones picked up the herring, pulled up his trousers to examine the bite, poured down an anathema upon the dog, which was, "May you be starved, as I am, you beast!" and then turned round to go aft, when he struck against the spare form of Mr Vanslyperken, who, with his hands in his pocket, and his trumpet under his arm, looked unutterably savage.

"How dare you beat *my* dog, you villain?" said the lieutenant at last, choking with passion.

"He's a-bitten my leg through and through, sir," replied Smallbones, with a face of alarm.

"Well, sir, why have you such thin legs, then?"

"'Cause I gets nothing to fill 'em up with."

"Have you not a herring there, you herring-gutted scoundrel? which, in defiance of all the rules of the service, you have brought on his Majesty's quarter-deck, you greedy rascal, and for which I intend——"

"It ar'n't my herring, sir, it be yours—for your breakfast—the only one that is left out of the half-dozen."

This last remark appeared somewhat to pacify Mr Vanslyperken.

"Go down below, sir," said he, after a pause, "and let me know when my breakfast is ready."

Smallbones obeyed immediately, too glad to escape so easily.

"Snarleyyow," said his master, looking at the dog, who remained on the other side of the forecastle; "O Snarleyyow, for shame! Come here, sir. Come here, sir, directly."

But Snarleyyow, who was very sulky at the loss of his anticipated breakfast, was contumacious, and would not come. He stood at the other side of the forecastle, while his master apostrophised him, looking him in the face. Then, after a pause of indecision, he gave a howling sort of bark, trotted away to the main hatchway, and disappeared below. Mr Vanslyperken returned to the quarter-deck, and turned, and turned as before.

Chapter II

Showing what became of the red-herring.

SMALLBONES soon made his re-appearance, informing Mr Vanslyperken that his breakfast was ready for him, and Mr Vanslyperken, feeling himself quite ready for his breakfast, went down below. A minute after he had disappeared, another man came up to relieve the one at the wheel, who, as soon as he had surrendered up the spokes, commenced warming himself after the most approved method, by flapping his arms round his body.

"The skipper's out o' sorts again this morning," said Obadiah, after a time. "I heard him muttering about the woman at the Lust Haus."

"Then, by Got, we will have de breeze," replied Jansen, who was a Dutch seaman of huge proportions, rendered still more preposterous by the multiplicity of his nether clothing.

"Yes, as sure as Mother Carey's chickens raise the gale, so does the name of the Frau Vandersloosh. I'll be down and get my breakfast, there may be keel-hauling before noon."

"Mein Got—dat is de tyfel."

"Keep her nor-east, Jansen, and keep a sharp look out for the boats."

"Got for dam—how must I steer the chip and look for de boats at de same time?—not possible."

"That's no consarn o' mine. Those are the orders, and I passes them—you must get over the unpossibility how you can." So saying, Obadiah Coble walked below.

We must do the same, and introduce the reader to the cabin of Lieutenant Vanslyperken, which was not very splendid in its furniture. One small table, one chair, a mattress in a standing bed-place, with curtains made of bunting, an open cupboard, containing three plates, one tea-cup and saucer, two drinking glasses, and two knives.

More was not required, as Mr Vanslyperken never indulged in company. There was another cupboard, but it was carefully locked. On the table before the lieutenant was a white wash-hand basin, nearly half full of burgoo, a composition of boiled oatmeal and water, very wholesome, and very hot. It was the allowance, from the ship's coppers, of Mr Vanslyperken and his servant Smallbones. Mr Vanslyperken was busy stirring it about to cool it a little, with a leaden spoon. Snarleyyow sat close to him, waiting for his share, and Smallbones stood by, waiting for orders.

"Smallbones," said the lieutenant, after trying the hot mess before him, and finding that he was still in danger of burning his mouth, "bring me the red-herring."

"Red-herring, sir?" stammered Smallbones.

"Yes," replied his master, fixing his little grey eye sternly on him, "the red-herring."

"It's gone, sir!" replied Smallbones, with alarm.

"Gone!—gone where?"

"If you please, sir, I didn't a-think that you would have touched it after the dog had had it in his nasty mouth; and so, sir—if you please, sir——"

"And so what?" said Vanslyperken, compressing his thin lips.

"I ate it myself—if you please—O dear—O dear!"

"You did, did you—you gluttonous scarecrow—you did, did you? Are you aware that you have committed a theft—and are you aware of the punishment attending it?"

"O sir—it was a mistake—dear sir," cried Smallbones, whimpering.

"In the first place, I will cut you to ribbons with the cat."

"Mercy, sir—O sir!" cried the lad, the tears streaming from his eyes.

"The thief's cat, with three knots in each tail."

Smallbones raised up his thin arms, and clasped his hands, pleading for mercy.

"And after the flogging—you shall be keel-hauled."

"O God!" screamed Smallbones, falling down on his knees, "mercy—mercy!"

But there was none. Snarleyyow, when he saw the lad go down on his knees, flew at him, and threw him on his back, growling over him, and occasionally looking at his master.

"Come here, Snarleyyow," said Mr Vanslyperken. "Come here, sir, and lie down." But Snarleyyow had not forgotten the red-herring; so in revenge, he first bit Smallbones in the thigh, and then obeyed his master.

"Get up, sir," cried the lieutenant.

Smallbones rose, but his temper now rose also; he forgot all that he was to suffer, from indignation against the dog: with flashing eyes, and whimpering with rage, he cried out, as the tears fell, and his arms swung round, "I'll not stand this—I'll jump overboard—that I will: fourteen times has that ere dog a-bitten me this week. I'd sooner die at once, than be made dog's-meat of in this here way."

"Silence, you mutinous rascal, or I'll put you in irons."

"I wish you would—irons don't bite, if they hold fast. I'll run away—I don't mind being hung—that I don't—starved to death, bitten to death in this here way——"

"Silence, sir. It's over-feeding that makes you saucy."

"The Lord forgive you!" cried Smallbones, with surprise; "I've not had a full meal——"

"A full meal, you rascal! there's no filling a thing like you—hollow from top to bottom, like a bamboo."

"And what I does get," continued Smallbones, with energy, "I pays dear for; that ere dog flies at me, if I takes a bit o' biscuit. I never has a bite without getting a bite, and it's all my own allowance."

"A proof of his fidelity, and an example to you, you wretch," replied the lieutenant, fondly patting the dog on the head.

"Well, I wish you'd discharge me—or hang me, I don't care which. You eats so hearty, and the dog eats so hearty, that I gets nothing. We are only victualled for two."

"You insolent fellow! recollect the thief's cat."

"It's very hard," continued Smallbones, unmindful of the threat, "that that ere beast is to eat my allowance, and be allowed to half eat me too."

"You forget the keel-hauling, you scarecrow."

"Well, I hope I may never come up again, that's all."

"Leave the cabin, sir."

This order Smallbones obeyed.

"Snarleyyow," said the lieutenant, "you are hungry, my poor beast." Snarleyyow put his forepaw up on his master's knee. "You shall have your breakfast soon," continued his master, eating the burgoo between his addresses to the animal. "Yes, Snarleyyow, you have done wrong this morning—you ought to have no breakfast." Snarleyyow growled. "We are only four years acquainted, and how many scrapes you have got me into, Snarleyyow!" Snarleyyow here put both his paws upon his master's knee. "Well, you are sorry, my poor dog, and you shall have some breakfast;" and Mr Vanslyperken put the basin of burgoo on the floor, which the dog tumbled down his throat most rapidly. "Nay, my dog, not so fast; you must leave some for Smallbones, he will require some breakfast before his punishment. There, that will do;" and Mr Vanslyperken wished to remove the basin with a little of the burgoo remaining in it. Snarleyyow growled, would have snapped at his master, but Mr Vanslyperken shoved him away with the bell mouth of his speaking-trumpet, and recovering a portion of the mess, put it on the table for the use of poor Smallbones. "Now then, my dog, we will go on deck." Mr Vanslyperken left the cabin, followed by Snarleyyow; but as soon as his master was half way up the ladder, Snarleyyow turned back, leaped on the chair, from the chair to the table, and then finished the whole of the breakfast appropriated for Smallbones. Having effected this, the dog followed his master.

Chapter III

A retrospect, and short description of a new character.

BUT we must leave poor Smallbones to lament his hard fate in the fore peak of the vessel, and Mr Vanslyperken and his dog to walk the quarter-deck, while we make our readers a little better acquainted with the times in which the scenes passed which we are now describing, as well as with the history of Mr Vanslyperken.

The date in our first chapter, that of the year 1699, will, if they refer back to history, show them that William of Nassau had been a few years on the English throne, and that peace had just been concluded between England with its allies and France. The king occasionally passed his time in Holland, among his Dutch countrymen, and the English and Dutch fleets, which but a few years before were engaging with such an obstinacy of courage, had lately sailed together, and turned their guns against the French. William, like all those continental princes who have been called to the English throne, showed much favour to his own countrymen, and England was overrun with Dutch favourites, Dutch courtiers, and peers of Dutch extraction. He would not even part with his Dutch guards, and was at issue with the Commons of England on that very account. But the war was now over, and most of the English and Dutch navy lay dismantled in port, a few small vessels only being in commission to intercept the smuggling from France that was carrying on, much to the detriment of English manufacture, of certain articles then denominated alamodes and lutestrings. The cutter we have described was on this service, and was named the *Yungfrau*, although built in England, and forming a part of the English naval force.

It may readily be supposed that Dutch interest, during this period, was in the ascendant. Such was the case: and the Dutch officers and seamen who could not be employed in their own marine were appointed in the English vessels, to the prejudice of our own countrymen. Mr Vanslyperken was of Dutch extraction, but born in England long before the Prince of Orange had ever dreamt of being called to the English throne. He was a near relation of King William's own nurse, and even in these days, that would cause powerful interest. Previous to the revolution he had been laid on the shelf for cowardice in one of the engagements between the Dutch and the English, he being then a lieutenant on board of a two-decked ship, and of long standing in the service; but before he had been appointed to this vessel, he had served invariably in small craft, and his want of this necessary qualification had never been discovered. The interest used for him on the accession of the Dutch king was sufficient for his again obtaining the command of a small vessel. In those days, the service was very different from what it is now. The commanders of vessels were also the pursers, and could save a great deal of money by defrauding the crew: and further, the discipline of the service was such as would astonish the modern philanthropist; there was no appeal for subordinates, and tyranny and oppression, even amounting to the destruction of life, were practised with impunity. Smollett has given his readers some idea of the state of the service a few years after the time of which we are now writing, when it was infinitely worse, for the system of the Dutch, notorious for their cruelty, had been grafted upon that of the English: the consequence was, a combination of all that was revolting to humanity was practised without any notice being taken of it by the superior powers, provided that the commanders of the vessels did their duty when called upon, and showed the necessary talent and courage.

Lieutenant Vanslyperken's character may be summed up in the three vices of avarice, cowardice, and cruelty. A miser in the extreme, he had saved up much money by his having had the command of a vessel for so many years, during which he had defrauded and pilfered both from the men and the goverment. Friends and connections he had none on this side of the water, and, when on shore, he had lived in a state of abject misery, although he had the means of comfortable support. He was now fifty-five years of age. Since he had been appointed to the *Yungfrau*, he had been employed in carrying despatches to the States-General from King William, and had, during his repeated visits to the Hague, made acquaintance with the widow Vandersloosh, who kept a Lust Haus,* a place of resort for sailors, where they drank and danced. Discovering that the comfortably fat landlady was also very comfortably rich, Mr Vanslyperken had made advances, with the hope of obtaining her hand and handling her money. The widow had, however, no idea of accepting the offer, but was too wise to give him a decided refusal, as she knew it would be attended with his preventing the crew of the cutter from frequenting her house, and, thereby, losing much custom. Thus did she, at every return, receive him kindly and give him hopes, but nothing more. Since the peace, as we before observed, the cutter had been ordered for the prevention of smuggling.

When and how Mr Vanslyperken had picked up his favourite Snarleyyow cannot be discovered, and must remain a secret. The men said that the dog had appeared on the deck of the cutter in a supernatural way, and most of them looked upon him with as much awe as ill-will.

This is certain, that the cutter had been a little while before in a state of mutiny, and a forcible entry attempted at night into the lieutenant's cabin. It is therefore not unreasonable to suppose that Vanslyperken felt that a good watch-dog might be a very useful appendage to his establishment, and had procured one accordingly. All the affection he ever showed to anything living was certainly concentrated on this one animal, and, next to his money, Snarleyyow had possession of his master's heart.

Poor Smallbones, cast on the world without father or mother, had become starved before he was on board the

* Pleasure House.

cutter, and had been starved ever since. As the reader will perceive, his allowance was mostly eaten up by the dog, and he was left to beg a precarious support from the goodwill and charity of his shipmates, all of whom were equally disgusted with the commander's cruelty and the ungainly temper of his brute companion.

Having entered into this retrospect for the benefit of the reader, we will now proceed.

Mr Vanslyperken walked the deck for nearly a quarter of an hour without speaking: the men had finished their breakfasts, and were lounging about the deck, for there was nothing for them to do, except to look out for the return of the two boats which had been sent away the night before. The lieutenant's thoughts were, at one minute, upon Mrs Vandersloosh, thinking how he could persuade her, and, at another, upon Smallbones, thinking how he could render the punishment adequate, in his opinion, to the magnitude of the offence. While discussing these two important matters, one of the men reported the boats ahead, and broke up the commander's reverie.

"How far off?" demanded Mr Vanslyperken.

"About two miles."

"Pulling or sailing?"

"Pulling, sir; we stand right for them."

But Mr Vanslyperken was in no pleasant humour, and ordered the cutter to be hove-to.

"I tink de men have pull enough all night," said Jansen, who had just been relieved at the wheel, to Obadiah Coble, who was standing by him on the forecastle.

"I think so too: but there'll be a breeze, depend upon it—never mind, the devil will have his own all in good time."

"Got for dam," said Jansen, looking at Beachy Head, and shaking his own.

"Why, what's the matter now, old Schnapps?" said Coble.

"Schnapps—yes—the tyfel—Schnapps, I think how the French schnapped us Dutchmen here when you Englishmen wouldn't fight."

"Mind what you say, old twenty breeches—wouldn't fight—when wouldn't we fight?"

"Here, where we were now, by Got, you leave us all in the lurch, and not come down."

"Why, we couldn't come down."

"Bah!" replied Jansen, who referred to the defeat of the combined Dutch and English fleet by the French off Beachy Head in 1690.

"We wouldn't fight, heh?" exclaimed Obadiah in scorn, "what do you say to the Hogue?"

"Yes, den you fought well—dat was good."

"And shall I tell you why we fought well at the Hogue—you Dutch porpoise—just because we had no Dutchmen to help us."

"And shall I tell you why the Dutch were beat off this Head?—because the English wouldn't come down to help us."

Here Obadiah put his tongue into his right cheek. Jansen in return threw his into his left, and thus the argument was finished. These disputes were constant at the time, but seldom proceeded further than words—certainly not between Coble and Jansen, who were great friends.

The boats were soon on board; from the time that the cutter had been hove-to, every stroke of their oars having been accompanied with a nautical anathema from the crews upon the head of their commander. The steersman and first officer, who had charge of the boats, came over the gangway and went up to Vanslyperken. He was a thickset, stout man, about five feet four inches high, and, wrapped up in Flushing garments, looked very much like a bear in shape as well as in skin. His name was Dick Short, and in every respect he answered to his name, for he was short in stature, short in speech, and short in decision and action.

Now when Short came up to the lieutenant, he did not consider it at all necessary to say as usual, "Come on board, sir," for it was self-evident that he had come on board. He therefore said nothing. So abrupt was he in his speech, that he never even said "Sir," when he spoke to his superior, which it may be imagined was very offensive to Mr Vanslyperken: so it was, but Mr Vanslyperken was afraid of Short, and Short was not the least afraid of Vanslyperken.

"Well, what have you done, Short?"

"Nothing."

"Did you see anything of the boat?"

"No."

"Did you gain any information?"

"No."

"What have you been doing all night?"

"Pulling."

"Did you land to obtain information?"

"Yes."

"And you got none?"

"No."

Here Short hitched up the waistband of his second pair of trousers, turned short round, and was going below, when Snarleyyow smelt at his heels. The man gave him a back kick with the heel of his heavy boot, which sent the dog off yelping and barking, and put Mr Vanslyperken in a great rage. Not venturing to resent this affront upon his first officer, he was reminded of Smallbones, and immediately sent for Corporal Van Spitter to appear on deck.

Chapter IV

In which there is a desperate combat.

EVEN at this period of the English history, it was the custom to put a few soldiers on board of the vessels of war, and the *Yungfrau* cutter had been supplied with a corporal and six men, all of whom were belonging to the Dutch marine. To a person who was so unpopular as

Mr Vanslyperken, this little force was a great protection, and both Corporal Van Spitter and his corps were well treated by him. The corporal was his purser and purveyor, and had a very good berth of it, for he could cheat as well as his commandant. He was, moreover, his prime minister, and an obedient executor of all his tyranny, for Corporal Van Spitter was without a shadow of feeling— on the contrary, he had pleasure in administering punishment; and if Vanslyperken had told him to blow any man's brains out belonging to the vessel, Van Spitter would have immediately obeyed the order without the change of a muscle in his fat, florid countenance. The corporal was an enormous man, tall, and so corpulent, that he weighed nearly twenty stone. Jansen was the only one who could rival him; he was quite as tall as the corporal, and as powerful, but he had not the extra weight of his carcass.

About five minutes after the summons, the huge form of Corporal Van Spitter was seen to emerge slowly from the hatchway, which appeared barely wide enough to admit the egress of his broad shoulders. He had a flat foraging cap on his head, which was as large as a buffalo's, and his person was clothed in blue pantaloons, tight at the ankle, rapidly increasing in width as they ascended, until they diverged at the hips to an expanse which was something between the sublime and the ridiculous. The upper part of his body was cased in a blue jacket, with leaden buttons, stamped with the rampant lion, with a little tail behind, which was shoved up in the air by the protuberance of the parts. Having gained the deck, he walked to Vanslyperken, and raised the back of his right hand to his forehead.

"Corporal Van Spitter, get your cats up for punishment, and when you are ready fetch up Smallbones."

Whereupon, without reply, Corporal Van Spitter put his left foot behind the heel of his right, and by this manœuvre turned his body round like a capstern, so as to bring his face forward, and then walked off in that direction. He soon re-appeared with all the necessary implements of torture, laid them down on one of the lee guns, and again departed to seek out his victim.

After a short time, a scuffle was heard below, but it was soon over, and once more appeared the corporal with the spare, tall body of Smallbones under his arm. He held him, grasped by the middle part, about where Smallbones' stomach ought to have been, and the head and heels of the poor wretch both hung down perpendicularly, and knocked together as the corporal proceeded aft.

As soon as Van Spitter had arrived at the gun he laid down his charge, who neither moved nor spoke. He appeared to have resigned himself to the fate which awaited him, and made no resistance when he was stripped by one of the marines, and stretched over the gun. The men, who were on deck, said nothing; they looked at each other expressively as the preparations were made. Flogging a lad like Smallbones was too usual an occurrence to excite surprise, and to show their disgust would have been dangerous. Smallbones' back was now bared, and miserable was the spectacle; the shoulder-blades protruded, so that you might put your hand sideways under the scapula, and every bone of the vertebræ, and every process was clearly defined through the skin of the poor skeleton. The punishment commenced, and the lad received his three dozen without a murmur, the measured sound of the lash only being broken in upon by the baying of Snarleyyow, who occasionally would have flown at the victim, had he not been kept off by one of the marines. During the punishment, Mr Vanslyperken walked the deck, and turned and turned again as before.

Smallbones was then cast loose by the corporal, who was twirling up his cat, when Snarleyyow, whom the marine had not watched, ran up to the lad, and inflicted a severe bite. Smallbones, who appeared, at the moment, to be faint and lifeless—not having risen from his knees after the marine had thrown his shirt over him, roused by this new attack, appeared to spring into life and energy; he jumped up, uttered a savage yell, and to the astonishment of everybody, threw himself upon the dog as he retreated, and holding him fast with his naked arms, met the animal with his own weapons, attacking him with a frenzied resolution with his teeth. Everybody started back at this unusual conflict, and no one interfered.

Long was the struggle, and such was the savage energy of the lad, that he bit and held on with the tenacity of a bull-dog, tearing the lips of the animal, his ears, and burying his face in the dog's throat, as his teeth were firmly fixed on his windpipe. The dog could not escape, for Smallbones held him like a vice. At last, the dog appeared to have the advantage, for as they rolled over and over, he caught the lad by the side of the neck; but Smallbones recovered himself, and getting the foot of Snarleyyow between his teeth, the dog threw up his head and howled for succour. Mr Vanslyperken rushed to his assistance, and struck Smallbones a heavy blow on the head with his speaking-trumpet, which stunned him, and he let go his hold.

Short, who had come on deck, perceiving this, and that the dog was about to resume the attack, saluted Snarleyyow with a kick on his side, which threw him down the hatchway, which was about three yards off from where the dog was at the time.

"How dare you strike my dog, Mr Short?" cried Vanslyperken.

Short did not condescend to answer, but went to Smallbones and raised his head. The lad revived. He was terribly bitten about the face and neck, and what with the wounds in front, and the lashing from the cat, presented a melancholy spectacle.

Short called some of the men to take Smallbones below, in which act they readily assisted; they washed him all over with salt water, and the smarting from his various wounds brought him to his senses. He was then put in his hammock.

Vanslyperken and the corporal looked at each other during the time that Short was giving his directions—neither interfered. The lieutenant was afraid, and the corporal waited for orders. So soon as the men had carried the lad below, Corporal Van Spitter put his hand up to his foraging cap, and with his cat and seizings under his arm, went down below. As for Vanslyperken, his wrath was even greater than before, and with hands thrust even further down in his pockets than ever, and the speaking-trumpet now battered flat with the blow which he had administered to Smallbones, he walked up and down, muttering every two minutes, "I'll keel-haul the scoundrel, by heavens! I'll teach him to bite my dog."

Snarleyyow did not re-appear on deck; he had received such punishment as he did not expect. He licked the wounds where he could get at them, and then remained in the cabin in a sort of perturbed slumber, growling every minute as if he were fighting the battle over again in his sleep.

Chapter V

A consultation in which there is much mutiny.

THIS consultation was held upon the forecastle of his Majesty's cutter *Yungfrau*, on the evening after the punishment of Smallbones. The major part of the crew attended; all but the Corporal Van Spitter, who, on these points, was known to split with the crew, and his six marines, who formed the corporal's tail, at which they were always to be found. The principal personage was not the most eloquent speaker, for it was Dick Short, who was supported by Obadiah Coble, Yack Jansen, and another personage, whom we must introduce, the boatswain or boatswain's mate of the cutter; for although he received the title of the former, he only received the pay of the latter. This person's real name was James Salisbury, but for reasons which will be explained he was invariably addressed or spoken of as Jemmy Ducks. He was indeed a very singular variety of human discrepancy as to form: he was handsome in face, with a manly countenance, fierce whiskers and long pigtail, which on him appeared more than unusually long, as it descended to within a foot of the deck. His shoulders were square, chest expanded, and, as far as half-way down, that is, to where the legs are inserted into the human frame, he was a fine, well-made, handsome, well-proportioned man. But what a falling off was there!—for some reason, some accident, it is supposed, in his infancy, his legs had never grown in length since he was three years old: they were stout as well as his body, but not more than eighteen inches from the hip to the heel; and he consequently waddled about a very ridiculous figure, for he was like a man *razeed* or cut down. Put him on an eminence of a couple of feet, and not see his legs, and you would say at a distance, "What a fine looking sailor!" but let him get down and walk up to you, and you would find that nature had not finished what she had so well begun, and that you are exactly half mistaken. This malconformation below did not, however, affect his strength, it rather added to it; and there were but few men in the ship who would venture a wrestle with the boatswain, who was very appropriately distinguished by the cognomen of Jemmy Ducks. Jemmy was a sensible, merry fellow, and a good seaman: you could not affront him by any jokes on his figure, for he would joke with you. He was indeed the fiddle of the ship's company, and he always played the fiddle to them when they danced, on which instrument he was no mean performer; and, moreover, accompanied his voice with his instrument when he sang to them after they were tired of dancing. We shall only observe that Jemmy was a married man, and he had selected one of the tallest of the other sex: of her beauty the less that is said the better—Jemmy did not look to that, or perhaps, at such a height, her face did not appear so plain to him as it did who were to those more on a level with it. The effect of perspective is well known, and even children now have as playthings, castles, &c., laid down on card, which, when looked at in a proper direction, appear just as correct as they do preposterous when lying flat before you.

Now it happened that from the level that Jemmy looked up from to his wife's face, her inharmonious features were all in harmony, and thus did she appear—what is very advantageous in the marriage state—perfection to her husband, without sufficient charms in the eyes of others to induce them to seduce her from her liege lord. Moreover, let it be recollected, that what Jemmy *wanted* was *height*, and he had gained what he required in his wife, if not in his own person: his wife was passionately fond of him, and very jealous, which was not to be wondered at, for, as she said, "there never was such a husband before or since."

We must now return to the conference, observing, that all these parties were sitting down on the deck, and that Jemmy Ducks had his fiddle in his hand, holding it with the body downwards like a bass viol, for he always played it in that way, and that he occasionally fingered the strings, pinching them as you do a guitar, so as to send the sound of it aft, that Mr Vanslyperken might suppose that they were all met for mirth. Two or three had their eyes directed aft, that the appearance of Corporal Van Spitter or the marines might be immediately perceived; for, although the corporal was not a figure to slide into a conference unperceived, it was well known that he was an eavesdropper.

"One thing's sartain," observed Coble, "that a dog's not an officer."

"No," replied Dick Short.

"He's not on the ship's books, so I can't see how it can be mutiny."

"No," rejoined Short.

"Mein Got—he is not a tog, he is te tyfel," observed Jansen.

"Who knows how he came into the cutter?"

"There's a queer story about that," said one of the men.

Tum tum, tumty tum—said the fiddle of Jemmy Ducks, as if it took part in the conference.

"That poor boy will be killed if things go on this way: the skipper will never be content till he has driven his soul out of his body—poor creature; only look at him as he lies in his hammock."

"I never seed a Christian such an object," said one of the sailors.

"If the dog ain't killed, Bones will be, that's sartain," observed Coble, "and I don't see why the preference should be given to a human individual, although the dog is the skipper's dog—now then, what d'ye say, my lads?"

Tum tum, tum tum, tumty tumty tum, replied the fiddle.

"Let's hang him at once."

"No," replied Short.

Jansen took out his snickerree, looked at Short, and made a motion with the knife, as if passing it across the dog's throat.

"No," replied Short.

"Let's launch him overboard at night," said one of the men.

"But how is one to get the brute out of the cabin?" said Coble; "if it's done at all it must be done by day."

Short nodded his head.

"I will give him a launch the first opportunity," observed Jemmy Ducks, "only—" (continued he in a measured and lower tone) "I should first like to know whether he really *is* a dog or *not*."

"A tog is a tog," observed Jansen.

"Yes," replied one of the forecastle men, "we all know a dog is a dog, but the question is—is *this* dog a dog?"

Here there was a pause, which Jemmy Ducks filled up by again touching the strings of his fiddle.

The fact was, that, although every one of the sailors

wished the dog was overboard, there was not one who wished to commit the deed, not on account of the fear of its being discovered who was the party by Mr Vanslyperken, but because there was a great deal of superstition among them. It was considered unlucky to throw any dog or animal overboard; but the strange stories told about the way in which Snarleyyow first made his appearance in the vessel, added to the peculiarly diabolical temper of the animal, had often been the theme of midnight conversation, and many of them were convinced that it was an imp of Satan lent to Vanslyperken, and that, to injure or to attempt to destroy it would infallibly be followed up with terrible consequences to the party, if not to the vessel and all the crew. Even Short, Coble, and Jansen, who were the boldest and leading men, although when their sympathies were roused by the sufferings of poor Smallbones they were anxious to revenge him, had their own misgivings, and, on consideration, did not like to have anything to do with the business. But each of them kept their reflections to themselves, for, if they could not combat, they were too proud to acknowledge them.

The reader will observe that all their plans were immediately put an end to until this important question, and not a little difficult one, was decided—Was the dog a dog?

Now, although the story had often been told, yet, as the crew of the cutter had been paid off since the animal had been brought on board, there was no man in the ship who could positively detail, from his own knowledge, the facts connected with his first appearance—there was only tradition, and, to solve this question, to tradition they were obliged to repair.

"Now, Bill Spurey," said Coble, "you know more about this matter than any one, so just spin us the yarn, and then we shall be able to talk the matter over soberly."

"Well," replied Bill Spurey, "you shall have it just as I got it word for word, as near as I can recollect. You know I wasn't in the craft when the thing came on board, but Joe Geary was, and it was one night when we were boozing over a stiff glass at the new shop there, the Orange Boven, as they call it, at the Pint at Portsmouth—and so you see, falling in with him, I wished to learn something about my new skipper, and what sort of a chap I should have to deal with. When I learnt all about *him*, I'd half-a-dozen minds to shove off again, but then I was adrift, and so I thought better of it. It won't do to be nice in peace times you know, my lads, when all the big ships are rotting in Southampton and Cinque Port muds. Well, then, what he told me I recollect as well—ay, every word of it—as if he had whispered it into my ear but this minute. It was a blustering night, with a dirty south-wester, and the chafing of the harbour waves was thrown up in foams, which the winds swept up the street, they chasing one another as if they were boys at play. It was about two bells in the middle watch, and after our fifth glass, that Joe Geary said as this:

"It was one dark winter's night when we were off the Texel, blowing terribly, with the coast under our lee, clawing off under storm canvas, and fighting with the elements for every inch of ground, a hand in the chains, for we had nothing but the lead to trust to, and the vessel so flogged by the waves, that he was lashed to the rigging, that he might not be washed away; all of a sudden the wind came with a blast loud enough for the last trump, and the waves roared till they were hoarser than ever; away went the vessel's mast, although there was no more canvas on it than a jib pocket-handkerchief, and the craft rolled and tossed in the deep troughs for all the world like a wicked man dying in despair; and then she was a wreck, with nothing to help us but God Almighty, fast borne down upon the sands which the waters had disturbed, and were dashing about until they themselves were weary of the load; and all the seamen cried unto the Lord, as well they might.

"Now, they say, that *he* did not cry as they did, like men and Christians, to Him who made them and the waters which surrounded and threatened them; for Death was then in all his glory, and the foaming crests of the waves were as plumes of feathers to his skeleton head beneath them; but he cried like a child—and swore terribly as well as cried—talking about his money, his dear money, and not caring about his more precious soul.

"And the cutter was borne down, every wave pushing her with giant force nearer and nearer to destruction, when the man at the chains shrieked out—'Mark three, and the Lord have mercy on our souls!' and all the crew, when they heard this, cried out—'Lord, save us, or we perish.' But still they thought that their time was come, for the breaking waves were under their lee, and the yellow waters told them that, in a few minutes, the vessel, and all who were on board, would be shivered in fragments; and some wept and some prayed as they clung to the bulwarks of the unguided vessel, and others in a few minutes thought over their whole life, and waited for death in silence. But *he*, he did all; he cried, and he prayed, and he swore, and he was silent, and at last he became furious and frantic; and when the men said again and again, 'The Lord save us!' he roared out at last, "Will the *devil* help us, for——' In a moment, before these first words were out of his mouth, there was a flash of lightning, that appeared to strike the vessel, but it harmed her not, neither did any thunder follow the flash; but a ball of blue flame pitched upon the knight heads, and then came bounding and dancing aft to the taffrail, where *he* stood alone, for the men had left him to blaspheme by himself. Some say he was heard to speak, as if in conversation, but no one knows what passed. Be it as it may, on a sudden he walked forward as brave as could be, and was followed by this creature, who carried his head and tail slouching, as he does now.

"And the dog looked up and gave one deep bark, and as soon as he had barked the wind appeared to lull—he barked again twice, and there was a dead calm—he barked again thrice, and the seas went down—and *he* patted the dog on the head, and the animal then bayed loud for a minute or two, and then, to the astonishment and fear of all, instead of the vessel being within a cable's length of the Texel sands in a heavy gale, and without hope, the Foreland lights were but two miles on our beam with a clear sky and smooth water."

The seaman finished his legend, and there was a dead silence for a minute or two, broken first by Jansen, who in a low voice said, "Then te tog is not a tog."

"No," replied Coble, "an imp sent by the devil to his follower in distress."

"Yes," said Short.

"Well, but," said Jemmy Ducks, who for some time had left off touching the strings of his fiddle, "it would be the work of a good Christian to kill the brute."

"It's not a mortal animal, Jemmy."

"True, I forgot that."

"Gifen by de tyfel," observed Jansen.

"Ay, and christened by him too," continued Coble. "Who ever heard any Christian brute with such a damnable name?"

"Well, what's to be done?"

"Why," replied Jemmy Ducks, "at all events, imp o' Satan or not, that ere Smallbones fought him to-day with his own weapons."

"And beat him too," said Coble.

"Yes," said Short.

"Now, it's my opinion, that Smallbones ar'n't afraid of him," continued Jemmy Ducks, "and devil or no devil, he'll kill him if he can."

"He's the proper person to do it," replied Coble; "the more so, as you may say that he's his *natural* enemy."

"Yes, mein Got, de poy is de man," said Jansen.

"We'll put him up to it at all events, as soon as he is out of his hammock," rejoined Jemmy Ducks.

A little more conversation took place, and then it was carried unanimously that Smallbones should destroy the animal, if it was possible to destroy it.

The only party who was not consulted was Smallbones himself, who lay fast asleep in his hammock. The consultation then broke up, and they all went below.

Chapter VI

In which, as often happens at sea when signals are not made out, friends exchange broadsides.

NOTWITHSTANDING all the precautions of the party on the forecastle, this consultation had been heard by no less a person than the huge Corporal Van Spitter, who had an idea that there was some mystery going on forward, and had contrived to crawl up under the bulwark, and throw himself down on the forestaysail, which lay between two of the guns. Having so done without being perceived, for it was at the very moment that the party were all listening to Bill Spurey's legend of the dog's first appearance on board, he threw a part of the sail over his fat carcass, and thus remained undiscovered during the remainder of the colloquy. He heard them all descending below, and remained still quiet, till he imagined that the forecastle was clear. In the meantime Mr Vanslyperken, who had been walking the deck abaft, unaccompanied by his faithful attendant (for Snarleyyow remained coiled up on his master's bed), was meditating deeply how to gratify the two most powerful passions in our nature, love and revenge: at one moment thinking of the fat fair Vandersloosh, and of hauling in her guilders, at another reverting to the starved Smallbones and the comfort of a keel-hauling. The long conference on the forecastle had not been unperceived by the hawk's eye of the lieutenant, and as they descended, he walked forward to ascertain if he could not pick up some straggler who, unsupported by his comrades, might be induced by fear to acquaint him with the subject of the discussion. Now, just as Mr Vanslyperken came forward Corporal Van Spitter had removed the canvas from his body, and was about to rise from his bed, when he perceived somebody coming forward. Not making it out to be the lieutenant, he immediately dropped down again and drew the canvas over him. Mr Vanslyperken perceived this manœuvre, and thought he had now caught one of the conspirators, and, moreover, one who showed such fear as to warrant the supposition that he should be able to extract from him the results of the night's unusually long conference.

Mr Vanslyperken walked up to where the corporal lay as quiet, but not quite so small, as a mouse. It occurred to Mr Vanslyperken that a little taste of punishment *in esse* would very much assist the threats of what might be received *in posse;* so he laid aside his speaking-trumpet, looked round, picked up a handspike, and raising it above his head, down it came, with all the force of the lieutenant's arm, upon Corporal Van Spitter, whose carcass resounded like a huge kettle-drum.

"Tunder and flame," roared the corporal under the canvas, thinking that one of the seamen, having discovered him eavesdropping, had thus wreaked his revenge, taking advantage of his being covered up, and pretending not to know him. "Tunder and flame!" roared the corporal, muffled up in the canvas, and trying to extricate himself; but his voice was not recognised by the lieutenant, and, before he could get clear of his envelope, the handspike had again descended; when up rose the corporal, like a buffalo out of his muddy lair, half-blinded by the last blow, which had fallen on his head, ran full butt at the lieutenant, and precipitated his senior officer and commander headlong down the fore-hatchway.

Vanslyperken fell with great force, was stunned, and lay without motion at the foot of the ladder, while the corporal, whose wrath was always excessive when his blood was up, but whose phlegmatic blood could not be raised without some such decided stimulus as a handspike, now turned round and round the forecastle, like a bull looking for his assailants; but the corporal had the forecastle all to himself, and, as he gradually cooled down, he saw lying close to him the speaking-trumpet of his senior officer.

"Tousand tyfels," murmured Corporal Van Spitter, "but it must have been the skipper. Got for damn, dis is hanging matter!" Corporal Van Spitter was as cool as a cucumber as soon as he observed what a mistake he had made; in fact, he quivered and trembled in his fat. "But then," thought he, "perhaps he did not know me—no, he could not, or he never would have handspiked *me*." So Corporal Van Spitter walked down the hatchway, where he ascertained that his commandant lay insensible. "Dat is good," thought he, and he went aft, lighted his lanthorn, and, as a *ruse*, knocked at the cabin-door. Receiving no answer but the growl of Snarleyyow, he went in, and then ascended to the quarter-deck, looked round him, and inquired of the man at the wheel where Mr Vanslyperken might be. The man replied that he had gone forward a few minutes before, and thither the corporal proceeded. Of course, not finding him, he returned, telling the man that the skipper was not in the cabin or the forecastle, and wondering where he could be. He then descended to the next officer in command, Dick Short, and called him.

"Well," said Short.

"Can't find Mr Vanslyperken anywhere," said the corporal.

"Look," replied Dick, turning round in his hammock.

"Mein Got, I have looked de forecastle, de quarter-deck, and de cabin,—he not anywhere."

"Overboard," replied Dick.

"I come to you, sir, to make inquiry," said the corporal.

"Turn out," said Dick, suiting the action to the words, and lighting with his feet on the deck in his shirt.

While Short was dressing himself, the corporal summoned up all his marines; and the noise occasioned by this turn out, and the conversation overheard by those who were awake, soon gave the crew of the cutter to understand that some accident had happened to their commander. Even Smallbones had it whispered in his ear that Mr Vanslyperken had fallen overboard, and he smiled as he lay in the dark, smarting with his wounds, muttering to himself that Snarleyyow should soon follow his master. By the time that Short was on the quarter-deck, Corporal Van Spitter, who knew very well where to look for it, had, very much to the disappointment of the crew, found the body of Mr Vanslyperken, and the marines had brought it aft to the cabin, and would have laid it on the bed, had not Snarleyyow, who had no feeling in his composition, positively denied its being put there.

Short came down and examined his superior officer.

"Is he dead?" inquired the corporal with alarm.

"No," replied Short.

"Vat can it be then?" said the corporal.

"Stunned," replied Short.

"Mein Got! how could it happen?"

"Tumbled," replied Short.

"What shall we do, sir?" rejoined the corporal.

"Bed," replied Short, turning on his heel, and a minute after turning into his hammock.

"Mein Got, the dog will not let him go to bed," exclaimed the corporal.

"Let's put him in," said one of the marines, "the dog won't bite his master."

So the marines lifted up the still insensible Mr Vanslyperken, and almost tossed him into his standing bed-place, right on the body of the snarling dog, who, as soon as he could disengage himself from the weight, revenged himself by making his teeth meet more than once through the lanthorn cheek of his master, and then leaping off the bed, retreated growling under the table.

"Well, you *are* a nice dog," exclaimed one of the marines, looking after Snarleyyow in his retreat.

Now, there was no medical assistance on board so small a vessel. Mr Vanslyperken, was allowed a small quantity of medicine, unguents, &c., but these he always sold to an apothecary, as soon as he had procured them from the authorities. The teeth of the dog had, however, their effect, and Mr Vanslyperken opened his eyes, and in a faint voice cried "Snarleyyow." Oh, if the dog had any spark of feeling, how must he then have been stung with remorse at his ingratitude to so kind a master! But he apparently showed none, at least, report does not say that any symptoms were manifest.

After a little burnt oakum had excoriated his nose, and a certain quantity of the cold salt-water from alongside had wetted through his bed-clothes, Mr Vanslyperken was completely recovered, and was able to speak and look about him. Corporal Van Spitter trembled a little as his commandant fixed his eyes upon him, and he redoubled his attention.

"Mein Got, Mynheer Vanslyperken, how was this happen?" exclaimed the corporal in a pathetic tone. Whereupon Mr Vanslyperken ordered every one to leave the cabin but Corporal Van Spitter.

Mr Vanslyperken then communicated to the corporal that he had been knocked down the hatchway by one of the men when he went forward; that he could not distinguish who it was, but thought that it must have been Jansen from his size. Corporal Van Spitter, delighted to find that his skipper was on a wrong scent, expressed his opinion in corroboration of the lieutenant's: after which a long consultation took place relative to mutiny, disaffection, and the proper measures to be taken. Vanslyperken mentioned the consultation of the men during the first watch, and the corporal, to win his favour, was very glad to be able to communicate the particulars of what he had overheard, stating that he had concealed himself for that purpose.

"And where did you conceal yourself?" said Vanslyperken with a keen inquiring look: for it immediately occurred to him that, unless it was under the sail, there could be no concealment for such a huge body as that of the corporal; and he had his misgivings. But the corporal very adroitly observed, that he stood at the lower step of the fore-ladder, with his head level with the coamings; and had, by this means, overheard the conversation unperceived, and had only walked away when the party broke up. This restored the confidence of Mr Vanslyperken, and a long discussion took place, in which it was agreed between them, that the only way to prevent Snarleyyow from being destroyed, was to try some means to make away quietly with poor Smallbones. But this part of the conversation was not carried to any length: for Mr Vanslyperken, indignant at having received such injury in his face from his ungrateful cur, did not, at that moment, feel the current of his affection run so strong as usual in that direction. After this, the corporal touched his hat, swung round to the right about in military style, and left the cabin.

Chapter VII

In which Mr Vanslyperken goes on shore to woo the Widow Vandersloosh.

THREE weeks of comparative calm now passed away, during which Mr Vanslyperken recovered of his wounds and accident, and meditated how he should make away with Smallbones. The latter also recovered of his bites, and meditated how he should make away with Snarleyyow. Smallbones had returned to his avocations, and Vanslyperken, intending mischief, treated him more kindly, as a blind. Snarleyyow also, not forgetting his defeat on the quarter-deck, did not renew his attacks, even when the poor lad helped himself to biscuit.

The *Yungfrau* anchored in the Downs, and Mr Vanslyperken received despatches for the Hague; King William having written some letters to his friends, and sent over to them a little English money, which he knew would be acceptable; for continental kings on the English throne have never appeared to have a clear sense of the honour conferred upon them. England, in their ideas, has always been a *parvenue* kingdom; her nobles not able to trace farther back than the Conquest; while, in their country, the lowest baron will prove his sixteen quarters, and his descent from the darkest ages. But, nevertheless, upon the same principle that the poor aristocracy will condescend to unite themselves occasionally to city wealth, so have these potentates condescended to reign over us.

Mr Vanslyperken received his despatches, and made the best of his way to Amsterdam, where he anchored, delivered his credentials, and there waited for the letters of thanks from his Majesty's cousins.

But what a hurry and bustle there appears to be on board of the *Yungfrau*—Smallbones here, Smallbones there—Corporal Van Spitter pushing to and fro with the dog-trot of an elephant; and even Snarleyyow appears to be unusually often up and down the hatchway. What can it all be about? Oh! Mr Vanslyperken is going on shore to pay his respects, and continue his addresses, to the widow Vandersloosh. His boat is manned alongside, and he now appears on the cutter's quarter-deck.

Is it possible that this can be Mr Vanslyperken? Heavens, how gay! An uniform certainly does wonders with some people: that is to say, those who do not look well in plain clothes are invariably improved by it; while those, who look most like gentlemen in plain clothes, lose in the same proportion. At all events Mr Vanslyperken is wonderfully improved.

He has a loose pair of blue pantaloons, with boots rising above his knees pulled over them: his lower parts remind you of Charles the Twelfth. He has a long scarlet waiscoat, with large gilt buttons and flap pockets, and his uniform coat over all, of blue turned up with red, has a very commanding appearance. To a broad black belt over his shoulder hangs his cutlass, the sheath of which is mounted with silver, and the hilt of ivory and gold threads; and, above all, his small head is almost dignified by being surmounted with a three-cornered turned-up and gold-banded cocked hat, with one corner of the triangle in front parallel with his sharp nose. Surely the widow must strike her colours to scarlet, and blue, and gold. But although women are said, like mackerel, to take such baits, still widows are not fond of a man who is as thin as a herring: they are too knowing, they prefer stamina, and will not be persuaded to take the shadow for the substance.

Mr Vanslyperken was, nevertheless, very well pleased with himself, which was something, but still not quite enough on the present occasion; and he strutted the deck with great complacency, gave his final orders to Dick Short, who, as usual, gave a short answer; also to Corporal Van Spitter, who, as usual, received them with all military honour; and, lastly, to Smallbones, who received them with all humility. The lieutenant was about to step into the boat, when a doubt arose, and he stopped in his advance, perplexed. It was one of no small importance—was Snarleyyow to accompany him or not? That was the knotty question, and it really was a case which required some deliberation. If he left him on board after the conspiracy which had been formed against him, the dog would probably be overboard before he returned; that is, if Smallbones were also left on board; for Mr Vanslyperken knew that it had been decided that Smallbones alone could and should destroy the dog. He could not, therefore, leave the dog on board with safety; and, as for taking him on shore with him, in that there was much danger, for the widow Vandersloosh had set her face against the dog. No wonder: he had behaved in her parlour as bad as the dog Crab in the Two Gentlemen of Verona; and the Frau was a very clean person, and had no fancy for dogs comparing their legs with those of her polished mahogany chairs and tables. If Mr Vanslyperken's suit was to be decided according to the old adage, "love me, love my dog," he certainly had but a poor chance; for the widow detested the cur, and had insisted that it should never be brought into her house. Take the dog on shore, therefore, he could not; but, thought Mr Vanslyperken, I can take Smallbones on shore, that will do as well. I have some biscuit to dispose of, and he shall go with it and wait till I come off again. Smallbones was, therefore, ordered to put on his hat and step into the boat with two half bags of biscuit to carry up to the widow's house, for she did a little business with Mr Vanslyperken, as well as allowing him to make love to her; and was never so sweet or so gracious, as when closing a bargain. So Mr Vanslyperken waited for Smallbones, who was soon ready, for his best consisted only in a pair of shoes to his usually naked feet, and a hat for his generally uncovered head. And Mr Vanslyperken, and Smallbones, and the biscuit, were in the boat, when Snarleyyow intimated his intention to join the party; but this was refused, and the boat shoved off without him.

As soon as Mr Vanslyperken had shoved off, Dick Short, being in command, thought he might as well give himself leave, and go on shore also. So he went down, put on his best, and ordered the other boat to be manned, and leaving Obadiah Coble on board as the next officer, he took with him Jansen, Jemmy Ducks, and four or five others, to have a cruise. Now, as Snarleyyow had this time made up his mind that he would go on shore, and Short was willing to indulge him, for he knew that Smallbones, if he fell in with him, would do his best to launch him into one of the canals, so convenient in every street, the cur was permitted to get into the boat, and was landed with the rest of the party, who, as usual, repaired to the Lust Haus of the widow Vandersloosh; where we must leave them for the present, and return to our friend, Mr Vanslyperken.

Chapter VIII

In which the Widow lays a trap for Mr Vanslyperken, and Smallbones lays a trap for Snarleyyow, and both bag their game.

THE widow Vandersloosh, as we have informed the reader, was the owner of a Lust Haus, or pleasure-house for sailors: we will describe that portion of her tenements more particularly by-and-bye: at present, we must advert to her own private house, which stood adjoining, and had a communication with the Lust Haus by a private door through the party wall. This was a very small, snug little habitation, with one window in each front, and two stories high; containing a front parlour and kitchen on the basement, two small rooms on the first, and two on the second floor. Nothing could be better arranged for a widow's residence. Moreover, she had a back-yard running the whole length of the wall of the Lust Haus in the rear, with convenient offices, and a back-door into the street behind.

Mr Vanslyperken had arrived, paid his humble devoirs to the widow, more humble, because he was evidently pleased with his own person, and had been followed by Smallbones, who laid the biscuit by the scraper at the door, watching it as in duty bound. The lieutenant imagined that he was more graciously received than usual. Perhaps he was, for the widow had not had so much custom lately, and was glad the crew of the cutter were arrived to spend their money. Already had Vanslyperken removed his sword and belt, and laid them with his three-cornered laced hat on the side-table; he was already cosily, as of wont, seated upon the widow's little fubsy sofa, with the lady by his side, and he had just taken her hand and was about to renew his suit, to pour forth the impromptu effusions of his heart, concocted on the quarter-deck of the *Yungfrau*, when who should bolt into the parlour but the unwelcome Snarleyyow.

"O that nasty brute! Mynheer Vanslyperken, how dare you bring him into my house?" cried the widow, jumping up from the sofa, with her full-moon-face red with anger.

"Indeed, widow," replied Vanslyperken, "I left him on board, knowing that you were not fond of animals; but some one has brought him on shore. However, I'll find out who it was, and keel-haul him in honour of your charms."

"I am fond of animals, Mr Vanslyperken, but I am not fond of such animals as that—such a filthy, ugly, disagreeable, snarling brute; nor can I think how you can keep him after what I have said about it. It don't prove much regard, Mr Vanslyperken, when such a dog as that is kept on purpose to annoy me."

"I assure you, widow——"

"Don't assure me, Mr Vanslyperken, there's no occasion—your dog is your own—but I'll thank you to take him out of this house; and, perhaps, as he won't go without you, you had better go with him."

Now the widow had never spoken so indignantly before: if the reader wishes to know why she did so now, we will acquaint him; the widow Vandersloosh had perceived Smallbones, who sat like Patience on a monument, upon the two half bags of biscuit before her porch. It was a query to the widow whether they were to be a present, or an article to be bargained for: it was therefore very advisable to pick a quarrel, that the matter might be cleared up. The widow's ruse met with all the success which it deserved. In the first place, Mr Vanslyperken did what he never would have believed himself capable of, but the wrath of the widow had worked him also up to wrath, and he saluted Snarleyyow with such a kick on the side, as to send him howling into the back-yard, followed him out, and, notwithstanding an attempt at defence on the part of the dog, which the lieutenant's high boots rendered harmless, Snarleyyow was fairly or unfairly, as you may please to think it, kicked into an outhouse, the door shut, and the key turned upon him. After which Mr Vanslyperken returned to the parlour, where he found the widow, erect, with her back turned to the stove, blowing and bristling, her bosom heaving, reminding you of seas mountains high, as if she were still under the effect of a just resentment for the affront offered to her. There she stood waiting in all dignity for Mr Vanslyperken to repair the injury done, whether unintentional or not. In few words, there she waited, for the *biscuit* to be presented to her. And it was presented, for Vanslyperken knew no other way of appeasing her wrath. Gradually the storm was allayed—the flush of anger disappeared, the corners of the scornfully-turned-down mouth, were turned up again—Cupid's bow was no longer bent in anger, and the widow's bosom slept as when the ocean sleeps, like " an unweaned child." The biscuit bags were brought in by Smallbones, their contents stored, and harmony restored. Once more was Mr Vanslyperken upon the little sofa by the side of the fat widow, and once more did he take her melting hand. Alas! that her heart was not made of the same soft materials.

But we must not only leave Short and his companions in the Lust Haus, but the widow and the lieutenant in their soft dalliance, and now occupy ourselves with the two principal personages of this our drama, Smallbones and Snarleyyow.

When Smallbones had retired, with the empty bread-bags under his arm, he remained some time reflecting at the porch, and then having apparently made up his mind, he walked to a chandler's shop just over the bridge of the canal opposite, and purchased a needle, some strong twine, and a red-herring. He also procured, "without purchase," as they say in our War Office Gazettes, a few pieces of stick. Having obtained all these, he went round to the door of the yard behind the widow's house, and let himself in. Little did Mr Vanslyperken imagine what mischief was brewing, while he was praising and drinking the beer of the widow's own brewing.

Smallbones had no difficulty in finding out where Snarleyyow was confined, for the dog was very busy gnawing his way through the door, which, however, was a work of time, and not yet a quarter accomplished. The place had been a fowl-house, and, at the bottom of the door, there was a small hatch for the ingress and egress of these bipeds, the original invention of some thrifty spinster, to prevent the maids from stealing eggs. But this hatch was closed, or Snarleyyow would have escaped through it. Smallbones took up his quarters in another outhouse, that he might not be observed, and commenced his operations.

He first took out the bottom of one bread-bag, and then sewed that on the other to make it longer; he then ran a string through the mouth, so as to draw it close when necessary, and cut his sticks so as to support it and keep it open. All this being arranged, he went to where Snarleyyow was busy gnawing wood with great pertinacity, and allowed him not only to smell, but to tear off the tail of the red-herring, under the door; and then gradually drew the herring along until he had brought it right under the hatch in the middle, which left it at the precise distance that the dog could snuff it but not reach it, which Snarleyyow now did, in preference to gnawing wood. When you lay a trap, much depends upon the bait; Smallbones knew his enemy's partiality for savoury comestibles. He then brought out his bag, set up his supporters, fixed it close to the hatch, and put the red-herring inside of it. With the string in one hand, he lifted up the hatch with the other. Snarleyyow rushed out and rushed in, and in a moment the strings were drawn, and as soon as drawn were tied tight round the mouth of the bag. Snarleyyow was caught; he tumbled over and over, rolling now to the right and now to the left, while Smallbones grinned with delight. After amusing himself a short time with the evolutions of his prisoner, he dragged him in his bag into the outhouse where he had made his trap, shut the door, and left him. The next object was to remove any suspicion on the part of Mr Vanslyperken; and to effect this, Smallbones tore off the hatch, and broke it in two or three pieces, bit parts of it with his own teeth, and laid them down before the door, making it appear as if the dog had gnawed his own way out. The reason for allowing the dog still to remain in prison, was that Smallbones dared not attempt anything further until it was dark, and there was yet an hour or more to wait for the close of the day.

Smallbones had but just finished his work in time; for the widow having been summoned to her guests in the Lust Haus, had left Vanslyperken alone, and the lieutenant thought this a good opportunity to look after his four-footed favourite. He came out into the yard, where he found Smallbones, and he had his misgivings.

"What are you doing here, sir?"

"Waiting for you, sir," replied Smallbones, humbly.

"And the dog?" said Vanslyperken, observing the strewed fragments of the door hatch.

"He's a-bitten himself out, sir, I believe."

"And where is he, then?"

"I don't know, sir; I suppose he's gone down to the boat."

Snarleyyow hearing his master's voice, had commenced a whine, and Smallbones trembled: fortunately, at that moment, the widow's ample form appeared at the back-door of the house, and she called to Mr Vanslyperken. The widow's voice drowned the whine of the dog, and his master did not hear it. At the summons, Vanslyperken but half convinced, but not daring to show any interest about the animal in the presence of his mistress, returned to the parlour, and very soon the dog was forgotten.

But as the orgies in the Lust Haus increased, so did it become more necessary for the widow to make frequent visits there; not only to supply her customers, but to restrain them by her presence; and as the evening wore away, so did the absences of the widow become more frequent. This Vanslyperken well knew, and he therefore always pressed his suit in the afternoon, and as soon as it was dark returned on board. Smallbones, who watched at the back-door the movements of his master, perceived that he was refixing his sword-belt over his shoulder, and he knew this to be the signal for departure. It was now quite dark, he therefore hastened to the outhouse, and dragged out Snarleyyow in the bag, swung him over his shoulder, and walked out of the yard-door, proceeded to the canal in front of the widow's house, looked round him, could perceive nobody, and then dragged the bag with its contents into the stagnant water below, just as Mr Vanslyperken, who had bidden adieu to the widow, came out of the house. There was a heavy splash—and silence. Had such been heard on the shores of the Bosphorus on such a night, it would have told some tale of unhappy love and a husband's vengeance; but, at Amsterdam, it was nothing more than the drowning of a cur.

"Who's there—is it Smallbones?" said Mr Vanslyperken.

"Yes, sir," said Smallbones, with alarm.

"What was that noise I heard?"

"Noise, sir? Oh, I kicked a paving-stone into the canal."

"And don't you know there is heavy fine for that, you scoundrel? And pray where are the bread-bags?"

"The bread-bags, sir? Oh, Mr Short took them to tie up some vegetables in them."

"Mr Short! O, very well. Come along, sir, and no more throwing stones into the canal; why you might have killed somebody—there is a boat down there now, I hear the people talking." And Mr Vanslyperken hastened to his boat, which was waiting for him; anxious to ascertain if Snarleyyow, as he fully expected, was in it. But to his grief and disappointment he was not there, and Mr Vanslyperken sat in the stern sheets, in no pleasant humour, thinking whether it was or was not a paving-stone which Smallbones had thrown into the canal, and resolving that if the dog did not appear, Smallbones should be keel-hauled. There was, however, one more chance, the dog might have been taken on board.

Chapter IX

A long chapter, in which there is lamentation, singing, bibbing, and dancing.

IT may readily be supposed, that the first question asked by Mr Vanslyperken, on his gaining the quarter-deck, was, if Snarleyyow were on board. He was received with the military salute of Corporal Van Spitter, for Obadiah Coble, having been left commanding officer, had given himself leave, and, with a few men, had joined Dick Short and the first party at the Lust Haus, leaving the corporal as the next senior officer in charge. The answer in the negative was a great mortification to Mr Vanslyperken, and he descended to his cabin in no very good humour, and summoned Smallbones. But before Smallbones was summoned, he had time to whisper to one or two of the conspirators—"*He's gone.*" It was enough; in less than a minute the whisper was passed throughout the cutter. "He's gone," was sibilated above and below, until it met the ears of even Corporal Van Spitter, who had it from a marine, who had it from another marine, who had it from a seaman, who—but it was, however, soon traced up to Smallbones by the indefatigable corporal—who considered it his duty to report the report to Mr Vanslyperken. Accordingly he descended to the cabin and knocked for admission.

In the meantime Vanslyperken had been venting his ill-humour upon Smallbones, having, as he took off from his person, and replaced in his drawers, his unusual finery, administered an unusual quantity of kicks, as well as a severe blow on the head with his sheathed cutlass to the unfortunate lad, who repeated to himself, by way of consolation, the magic words—" *He's gone.*"

"If you please, sir," said Corporal Van Spitter, "I've discovered from the ship's company that the dog *is gone.*"

"I know that, corporal," replied Vanslyperken.

"And, sir, the report has been traced to Smallbones."

"Indeed!—then it was you that said that the dog is gone—now, you villain, where is he?"

"If you please, I did say that the dog was gone, and so he is; but I didn't say that I knew where he was—no more I don't. He's runned away, and he'll be back to-morrow—I'm sure he will."

"Corporal Van Spitter, if the dog is not on board again by eight o'clock to-morrow morning, you will get all ready for keel-hauling this scoundrel."

"Yes, mynheer," replied the corporal, delighted at having something to do in the way of punishment.

Smallbones made up a lachrymal face.

"It's very hard," said he; "suppose the dog has fallen into the canal, is that my fault? If he's a-gone to the bottom of the canal, that's no reason why I'm to be dragged under the bottom of the cutter."

"Yes, yes," replied Vanslyperken, "I'll teach you to throw paving-stones off the wharf. Leave the cabin, sir."

Smallbones, whose guilty conscience flew into his pallid face at the mention of the paving-stones, immediately made a hasty retreat; and Vanslyperken turned into his bed and dreamt of vengeance.

We must now return to the Lust Haus, and the party on shore; and our first task must be, to give the reader an idea of what a Lust Haus may be. It is, as its name imports, a resort for pleasure and amusement; and in this respect the Dutch are certainly very much in advance of the English, who have, in the pot-houses and low inns resorted to by seamen, no accommodation of the kind. There is barely room for Jack to foot it in a reel, the tap-room is so small; and as Jack is soon reeling after he is once on shore, it is a very great defect. Now, the Lust Haus is a room as large as an assembly-room in a country-town, well lighted up with lamps and chandeliers, well warmed with stoves, where you have room to dance fifty reels at once, and still have plenty of accommodation at the chairs and tables ranged round on each side. At the end of the room is a raised chair, with a protecting railing, on which the musicians, to the number of seven or eight, are posted, and they continue during the evening to play when requested. The people of the Lust Haus furnish wine and spirits of every description, while cakes, nuts, walnuts, oranges, &c., are supplied from the baskets of numerous young women who hand them round, and press their customers to purchase. Police officers superintend these resorts to remove those who are violent, and interfere with the amusements of others. On the whole, it is a very gay scene, and is resorted to by seamen of all nations, with a sprinkling of those who are not sailors, but who like amusement, and there are plenty of females who are ready to dance with them, and to share their beer or grog. Be it further known, that there is a great deal of decorum in a Lust Haus, particularly among the latter sex; and altogether it is infinitely more rational and less debasing, than the low pot-houses of Portsmouth or Plymouth.

Such was the place of amusement kept by the Frau Vandersloosh, and in this large room had been seated, for some hours, Dick Short, Coble, Jansen, Jemmy Ducks, and some others of the crew of his Majesty's cutter *Yungfrau*.

The room was now full, but not crowded, it was too spacious well to be so. Some sixteen couples were dancing a quadrille to a lively tune played by the band, and among the dancers were to be seen old women, and children of ten or twelve: for it was not considered improper to be seen dancing at this humble assembly, and the neighbours frequently came in. The small tables and numerous chairs round the room were nearly all filled, beer was foaming from the mouths of the opened bottles, and there was the ringing of the glasses as they pledged each other. At several tables were assemblages of Dutch seamen, who smoked with all the phlegm of their nation, as they gravely looked upon the dancers. At another were to be seen some American seamen, scrupulously neat in their attire, and with an air *distinguée*, from the superiority of their education, and all of them quiet and sober. The basket-women flitted about displaying their stores, and invited every one to purchase fruit, and particularly hard-boiled eggs, which they had brought in at this hour, when those who dined at one might be expected to be hungry. Sailors' wives were also there, and perhaps some who could not produce the marriage certificates; but as these were not asked for at the door, it was of no consequence. About the centre of the room, at two small tables joined together, were to be seen the party from the *Yungfrau*: some were drinking beer, some grog, and Jemmy Ducks was perched on the table, with his fiddle as usual held like a bass viol. He was known by those who frequented the house by the name of the Manikin, and was a universal object of admiration and good-will. The quadrille was ended, and the music stopped playing.

"Come now," said Coble, tossing off his glass, "spell oh!—let's have a song while they take their breath. Jemmy, strike up."

"Hurrah for a song!" cries Jemmy. "Here goes."

Jemmy then tuned one string of his fiddle, which was a little out, and accompanying his voice, sang as follows: all those who were present immediately keeping silence, for they were used to Jemmy's melody.

> Twas on the twenty-fourth of June, I sailed away to sea,
> I turned my pockets in the lap of Susan on my knee;
> Says I, my dear, 'tis all I have, I wish that it was more,
> It can't be helped, says Susan then, you know we've spent galore.
>
>> You know we've spent galore, my Bill,
>> And merry have been we,
>> Again you must your pockets fill,
>> For Susan on your knee.

"Chorus, my boys—"

> For Susan on my knee, my boys,
> With Susan on my knee.

The gale came on in thunder, lads, in lightning, and in foam,
Before that we had sail'd away three hundred miles from home ;
And on the Sunday morning, lads, the coast was on our lee,
Oh, then I thought of Portsmouth, and of Susan on my knee.

> For howling winds and waves to boot,
> With black rocks on the lee,
> Did not so well my fancy suit,
> As Susan on my knee.
>
> *Chorus.*—With Susan on my knee, my boys,
> With Susan on my knee.

Next morning we were cast away upon the Frenchman's shore,
We saved our lives, but not our all, for we could save no more ;
They marched us to a prison, so we lost our liberty,
I peeped between the bars, and sighed for Susan on my knee.

> For bread so black, and wine so sour,
> And a sou a-day to me,
> Made me long ten times an hour,
> For Susan on my knee.
>
> *Chorus.*—For Susan on my knee, my boys,
> For Susan on my knee.

One night we smashed our jailer's skull, and off our boat did steer,
And in the offing were picked up by a jolly privateer ;
We sailed in her the cruise, my boys, and prizes did take we,
I'll be at Portsmouth soon, thinks I, with Susan on my knee.

> We shared three hundred pounds a man,
> I made all sail with glee,
> Again I danced and tossed my can,
> With Susan on my knee.
>
> *Chorus.*—With Susan on my knee, my boys,
> With Susan on my knee.

"That's prime, Jemmy. Now, my boys, all together," cried Obadiah Coble.

Chorus.—Very good song, and very well sung,
 Jolly companions every one;
 We are all here for mirth and glee,
 We are all here for jollity.
 Very good song, and very well sung,
 Jolly companions every one;
 Put your hats on to keep your heads warm,
 A little more grog will do us no harm.

"Hurrah! now, Bill Spurey, suppose you tip us a stave. But I say, Babette, you Dutch-built galliot, tell old Frank Slush to send us another dose of the stuff; and d'ye hear, a short pipe for me, and a paper o' baccy."

The short, fat Babette, whose proportions all the exercise of waiting upon the customers could not reduce, knew quite enough English to require no further explanation.

"Come, Jemmy, my hearty, take your fingers off your fiddle, and hand in your pot," continued Coble; "and then if they are not going to dance, we'll have another song. Bill Spurey, wet your whistle, and just clear the cobwebs out of your throat. Here's more 'baccy, Short."

Short made no reply, but he shook out the ashes and filled his pipe. The music did not strike up again, so Bill Spurey sang as follows:—

 Says the parson one day, as I cursed a Jew,
  Do you know, my lad, that we call it a sin?
 I fear of you sailors there are but few,
  St Peter, to heaven, will ever let in.
 Says I, Mr Parson, to tell you my mind,
  No sailors to knock were ever yet seen,
 Those who travel by land may steer 'gainst wind,
  But we shape a course for Fidler's Green.

  For Fidler's Green, where seamen true,
   When here they've done their duty,
  The bowl of grog shall still renew
   And pledge to love and beauty.

 Says the parson, I hear you've married three wives,
  Now do you not know, that that is a sin?
 You sailors, you lead such very bad lives,
  St Peter, to heaven, will ne'er let you in.

>   Parson, says I, in each port I've but *one*,
>   And never had more, wherever I've been;
>   Below I'm obliged to be chaste as a nun,
>   But I'm promised a dozen at Fidler's Green.
>
>   At Fidler's Green, where seamen true,
>   When here they've done their duty,
>   The bowl of grog shall still renew,
>   And pledge to love and beauty.
>
>   Says the parson, says he, you're drunk, my man,
>   And do you not know that that is a sin?
>   If you sailors will ever be swigging your can,
>   To heaven you surely will never get in.
>   (*Hiccup.*) Parson, you may as well be mum,
>   'Tis only on shore I'm this way seen;
>   But oceans of punch, and rivers of rum,
>   Await the sailor at Fidler's Green.
>
>   At Fidler's Green, where seamen true,
>   When here they've done their duty,
>   The bowl of grog shall still renew,
>   And pledge to love and beauty.

"Well reeled off, Billy," cried Jemmy Ducks, finishing with a flourish on his fiddle, and a refrain of the air. I don't think we shall meet *him* and his dog at Fidler's Green —heh!"

"No," replied Short, taking his pipe from his lip.

"No, no, Jemmy, a seaman true means one true in heart as well as in knowledge; but, like a blind fiddler, he'll be led by his dog somewhere else."

"From vere de dog did come from," observed Jansen.

The band now struck up again, and played a waltz—a dance new to our country, but older than the heptarchy. Jansen, with his pipe in his mouth, took one of the women by the waist, and steered round the room about as leisurely as a capstern heaving up. Dick Short also took another, made four turns, reeled up against a Dutchman who was doing it with *sang froid*, and then suddenly left his partner and dropped into his chair.

"I say, Jemmy," said Obadiah Coble, "why don't you give a girl a twist round?"

"Because I can't, Oby; my compasses arn't long enough to describe a circle. You and I are better here, old boy. I, because I've very little legs, and you, because you havn't a leg to stand upon."

"Very true—not quite so young as I was forty years ago. Howsomever I mean this to be my last vessel. I shall bear up for one of the London dock-yards as a rigger."

"Yes, that'll do; only keep clear of the girt-lines, you're too stiff for that."

"No, that would not exactly tell; I shall pick my own work, and that's where I can bring my tarry trousers to an anchor—mousing the mainstay, or puddening the anchor, with the best of any. Dick, lend us a bit of 'baccy."

Short pulled out his box without saying a word. Coble took a quid, and Short thrust the box again into his pocket.

In the meantime the waltz continued, and being a favourite dance, there were about fifty couples going round and round the room. Such was the variety in the dress, country, language, and appearance of the parties collected, that you might have imagined it a masquerade. It was, however, getting late, and Frau Vandersloosh had received the intimation of the people of the police who superintend these resorts, that it was the time for shutting up; so that, although the widow was sorry on her own account to disperse so merry and so thirsty a party as they were now becoming, so soon as the waltz was ended the musicians packed up their instruments and departed.

This was a signal for many, but by no means for all, to depart; for music being over, and the house doors closed, a few who remained, provided they made no disturbance, were not interfered with by the police. Among those who stayed were the party from the *Yungfrau*, one or two American, and some Prussian sailors. Having closed up together,

"Come," cried Jemmy, "now that we are quiet again, let's have another song; and who is it to be—Dick Short?"

"Short, my boy, come, you must sing."
"No," replied Short.
"Yes, yes—one verse," said Spurey.
"He never sings more," replied Jemmy Ducks, "so he must give us that. Come, Short."
"Yes," replied Short, taking the pipe out of his mouth, and wetting his lips with the grog.

> *Short* stay apeak was the anchor,
>   We had but a *short* minute more,
> In *short*, I no longer could hanker,
>   For *short* was the cash in my store.
> I gave one *short* look,
>   As Poll heaved a *short* sigh
> One *short* hug I took,
>   *Short* the matter cut I,
> And off I went to sea.

"Go on, Dick."
"No," replied Short, resuming his pipe.
"Well, then, chorus, my boys."

> Very good song, and very well sung,
> Jolly companions every one;
> We all are here for mirth and glee,
> We all are here for jollity.
> Very good song, and very well sung,
> Jolly companions every one;
> Put your hats on, and keep your heads warm,
> A little more liquor will do us no harm.

"Now then, Jemmy Ducks, it's round to you again. Strike up, fiddle and all."
"Well, here goes," said Jemmy Ducks.

> The captain stood on the carronade—first lieutenant, says he,
> Send all my merry men aft here, for they must list to me:
> I havn't the gift of the gab, my sons—because I'm bred to the sea,
> That ship there is a Frenchman, who means to fight with we.
>   Odds blood, hammer and tongs, long as I've been to sea,
>   I've fought 'gainst every odds—but I've gained the victory.
>
> That ship there is a Frenchman, and if we don't take *she*,
> 'Tis a thousand bullets to one, that she will capture *we*;

I havn't the gift of the gab, my boys, so each man to his gun,
If she's not mine in half an hour, I'll flog each mother's son.
    Odds bobs, hammer and tongs, long as I've been to sea,
    I've fought 'gainst every odds—and I've gained the victory.

We fought for twenty minutes, when the Frenchman had enough,
I little thought, said he, that your men were of such stuff;
The captain took the Frenchman's sword, a low bow made to he,
I havn't the gift of the gab, Mounsieur, but polite I wish to be.
    Odds bobs, hammer and tongs, long as I've been to sea,
    I've fought 'gainst every odds—and I've gained the victory.

Our captain sent for all of us; my merry men, said he,
I havn't the gift of the gab, my lads, but yet I thankful be;
You've done your duty handsomely, each man stood to his gun,
If you hadn't, you villains, as sure as day, I'd have flogged each mother's son.
    Odds bobs, hammer and tongs, as long as I'm at sea,
    I'll fight 'gainst every odds—and I'll gain the victory.

      Chorus.—Very good song, and very well sung,
           Jolly companions every one;
           We all are here for mirth and glee,
           We all are here for jollity.
           Very good song, and very well sung,
           Jolly companions every one;
           Put your hats on to keep your heads warm,
           A little more grog will do us no harm.

"Now, Coble, we must have yours," said Jemmy Ducks.

"Mine! well, if you please: but half my notes are stranded. You'll think that Snarleyyow is baying the moon: howsomever, take it as it is."

Oh, what's the use of piping, boys, I never yet could larn,
The good of water from the eyes I never could disarn;
Salt water we have sure enough without our pumping more,
So let us leave all crying to the girls we leave on shore.

           They may pump,
           As in we jump
      To the boat, and say, "Good-bye;"
           But as for men,
           Why, I say again,
      That crying's all my eye.

I went to school when quite a boy, and never larnt to read,
The master tried both head and tail—at last it was agreed
No larning he could force in me, so they sent me off to sea,
My mother wept and wrung her hands, and cried most bitterly.

> So she did pump,
> As I did jump
> In the boat, and said, "Good-bye;"
> But as for me,
> Who was sent to sea,
> To cry was all my eye.

I courted Poll, a buxom lass; when I returned A B,
I bought her ear-rings, hat, and shawl, a sixpence did break we;
At last 'twas time to be on board, so, Poll, says I, farewell;
She roared and said, that leaving her was like a funeral knell.

> So she did pump,
> As I did jump
> In the boat, and said, "Good-bye;"
> But as for me
> With the rate A B,
> To cry was all my eye.

I soon went back, I shoved on shore, and Polly I did meet,
For she was watching on the shore, her sweetheart for to greet,
She threw her arms around me then, and much to my surprise,
She vowed she was so happy that she pumped with both her eyes.

> So she did pump,
> As I did jump
> To kiss her lovingly,
> But, I say again,
> That as for men,
> Crying is all my eye.

Then push the can around, my boys, and let us merry be;
We'll rig the pumps if a leak we spring, and work most merrily:
Salt water we have sure enough, we'll add not to its store,
But drink, and laugh, and sing and chat, and call again for more.

> The girls may pump,
> As in we jump
> To the boat, and say, "Good-bye;"
> But as for we,
> Who sailors be,
> Crying is all my eye.

"Bravo, Obadiah! now one more song, and then we'll aboard. It won't do to bowse your jib up too tight here," said Jemmy; "for it's rather dangerous navigation among all these canals—no room for yawing."

"No," replied Dick Short.

"Then," said Jemmy, jumping off the table with his

fiddle in his hand, " let's have the roarer by way of a finish—what d'ye say, my hearties?"

Up they all rose, and gathered together in the centre of the room, save Jemmy Ducks, who, flourishing with his fiddle, commenced.

> Jack's alive and a merry dog,
>   When he gets on shore,
> He calls for his glass of grog,
>   He drinks, and he calls for more.
> So drink, and call for what you please,
>   Until you've had your whack, boys;
> We think no more of raging seas,
>   Now that we've come back, boys.

"Chorus, now—"

> With a *whip*, *snip*, high cum diddledy,
>   The cog-wheels of life have need of much oiling;
> *Smack*, *crack*—this is our jubilee:
>   Huzza, my lads! we'll keep the pot boiling.

All the seamen joined in the chorus, which they accompanied both with their hands and feet, snapping their fingers at *whip* and *snip*, and smacking their hands at *smack* and *crack*, while they danced round in the most grotesque manner, to Jemmy's fiddle and voice; the chorus ended in loud laughter, for they had now proved the words of the song to be true, and were all alive and merry. According to the rules of the song, Jemmy now called out for the next singer, Coble.

> Jack's alive and merry, my boys,
>   When he's on blue water,
> In the battle's rage and noise,
>   And the main-deck slaughter.
> So drink and call for what you please,
>   Until you've had your whack, boys;
> We'll think no more of angry seas,
>   Until that we go back, boys.

Chorus.—With a *whip*, *snip*, high cum diddledy,
  The cog-wheels of life have need of much oiling;
Smack, *crack*—this is our jubilee;
  Huzza my lads! we'll keep the pot boiling.

Jansen and Jemmy Ducks, after the dancing chorus had finished,

>Yack alive and merry, my boys,
>   Ven he get him *frau*,
>And he vid her ringlet toys,
>   As he take her paw.
>So drink, and call for vat you please.
>   Until you hab your vack, boys;
>Ve'll think no more of angry seas,
>   Till ve standen back, boys.

Chorus and laughter.

>With a *whip*, *snip*, high cum diddledy,
>   The cog-wheels of life have need of much oiling;
>*Smack*, *crack*—this is our jubilee;
>   Huzza, my lads, we'll keep the pot boiling.

Bill Spurey—

>Jack's alive and merry, boys,
>   When he's got the shiners;
>Heh! for rattle, fun, and noise,
>   Hang all grumbling whiners.
>Then drink, and call for what you please,
>   Until you've had your whack, boys;
>We think no more of raging seas,
>   Now that we've come back, boys.

Chorus.—With a *whip*, *snip*, high cum diddledy,
>   The cog-wheels of life have need of much oiling;
>*Smack*, *crack*—this is our jubilee;
>   Huzza, my lads! we'll keep the pot boiling.

"Dick Short must sing."
"Yes," replied Dick.

>Jack's alive and full of fun,
>   When his hulk is crazy,
>As he basks in Greenwich sun,
>   Jolly still though lazy.
>So drink, and call for what you please,
>   Until you've had your whack, boys;
>We'll think no more of raging seas,
>   Now that we've come back, boys.

Chorus.—With a *whip*, *snip*, high cum diddledy,
>   The cog-wheels of life have need of much oiling;
>*Smack*, *crack*—this is our jubilee;
>   Huzza, my lads! we'll keep the pot boiling.

As this was the last chorus, it was repeated three or four times, and with hallooing, screaming, and dancing in mad gesticulation.

"Hurrah, my lads," cried Jemmy, "three cheers and a bravo."

It was high time that they went on board; so thought Frau Vandersloosh, who trembled for her chandeliers; so thought Babette, who had begun to yawn before the last song, and who had tired herself more with laughing at it; so thought they all, and they sallied forth out of the Lust Haus, with Jemmy Ducks having the advance, and fiddling to them the whole way down to the boat. Fortunately, not one of them fell into the canal, and in ten minutes they were all on board; they were not, however, permitted to turn into their hammocks without the important information being imparted to them, that Snarleyyow had disappeared.

Chapter X

In which is explained the sublime mystery of keel-hauling—Snarleyyow saves Smallbones from being drowned, although Smallbones would have drowned him.

IT is a dark morning; the wind is fresh from the northwest; flakes of snow are seen wafting here and there by the wind, the avant-couriers of a heavy fall; the whole sky is of one murky grey, and the sun is hidden behind a dense bank. The deck of the cutter is wet and slippery, and Dick Short has the morning watch. He is wrapt up in a Flushing pea-jacket, with thick mittens on his hands; he looks about him, and now and then a fragment of snow whirls into his eye; he winks it out, it melts and runs like a tear down his cheek. If it were not that it is contrary to man-of-war custom he would warm himself with the *double-shuffle*, but such a step would be unheard of on the quarter-deck of even the cutter *Yungfrau*.

The trapaulin over the hatchway is pushed on one side, and the space between the coamings is filled with the bull head and broad shoulders of Corporal Van Spitter, who, at last, gains the deck; he looks round him and apparently is not much pleased with the weather. Before he proceeds to business, he examines the sleeves and front of his jacket, and having brushed off with the palm of his hand a variety of blanket-hairs, adhering to the cloth, he is satisfied, and now turns to the right and to the left, and forward and aft—in less than a minute he goes right round the compass. What can Corporal Van Spitter want at so early an hour? He has not come up on deck for nothing, and yet he appears to be strangely puzzled: the fact is, by the arrangements of last night, it was decided, that this morning, if Snarleyyow did not make his appearance in the boat sent on shore for fresh beef for the ship's company, the unfortunate Smallbones was to be *keel-hauled.*

What a delightful morning for a keel-hauling!

This ingenious process, which, however, like many other good old customs, has fallen into disuse, must be explained to the non-nautical reader. It is nothing more nor less than sending a poor navigator on a voyage of discovery under the bottom of the vessel, lowering him* down over the bows, and with ropes detaining him exactly in his position under the kelson, while he is drawn aft by a hauling line until he makes his appearance at the rudder-chains, generally speaking quite out of breath, not at the rapidity of his motion, but because, when so long under the water, he has expended all the breath in his body, and is induced to take in salt water *en lieu.* There is much merit in this invention; people are very apt to be content with walking the deck of a man-of-war,

---

* The author has here explained keel-hauling as practised in those times in small *fore and aft* vessels. In large and square-rigged vessels, the man was hauled up to one main-yard arm, and dropped into the sea, and hauled under the bottom of the vessel to the other; but this in small fore and aft vessels was not so easily effected, nor was it considered sufficient punishment.

and complain of it as a hardship, but when once they have learnt, by experience, the difference between being comfortable above board, and the number of deprivations which they have to submit to when under board and overboard at the same time, they find that there are worse situations than being on the deck of a vessel—we say privations when under board, for they really are very important:—you are deprived of the air to breathe, which is not borne with patience even by a philosopher, and you are obliged to drink salt water instead of fresh. In the days of keel-hauling, the bottoms of vessels were not coppered, and in consequence were well studded with a species of shell-fish which attached themselves, called barnacles, and as these shells were all open-mouthed and with sharp cutting points, those who underwent this punishment (for they were made by the ropes at each side, fastened to their arms, to hug the kelson of the vessel) were cut and scored all over their body, as if with so many lancets, generally coming up bleeding in every part, and with their faces, especially their noses, as if they had been gnawed by the rats; but this was considered rather advantageous than otherwise, as the loss of blood restored the patient if he was not quite drowned, and the consequence was, that one out of three, it is said, have been known to recover after their submarine excursion. The Dutch have the credit, and we will not attempt to take from them their undoubted right, of having invented this very agreeable description of punishment. They are considered a heavy, phlegmatic sort of people, but on every point in which the art of ingeniously tormenting is in request, it must be admitted that they have taken the lead of much more vivacious and otherwise more inventive nations.

And now the reader will perceive why Corporal Van Spitter was in a dilemma. With all the good-will in the world, with every anxiety to fulfil his duty, and to obey his superior officer, he was not a seaman, and did not know how to commence operations. He knew nothing about foddering a vessel's bottom, much less how to fodder it with the carcass of one of his fellow-creatures. The corporal, as we said before, turned round and round the compass to ascertain if he could compass his wishes; at last, he commenced by dragging one-rope's end from one side and another from the other; those would do for the side ropes, but he wanted a long one from forward and another from aft, and how to get the one from aft under the cutter's bottom was a puzzle; and then there was the mast and the rigging in his way;—the corporal reflected—the more he considered the matter, the more his brain became confused; he was at a nonplus, and he gave it up in despair: he stood still, took out a blue cotton handkerchief from the breast of his jacket and wiped his forehead, for the intensity of thought had made him perspire—anything like reflection was very hard work for Corporal Van Spitter.

"Tousand tyfels!" at last exclaimed the corporal, and he paused and knocked his big head with his fist.

"Hundred thousand tyfels!" repeated the corporal after five minutes' more thought.

"Twenty hundred tousand tyfels!" muttered the corporal, once more knocking his head: but he knocked in vain; like an empty house, there was no one within to answer the appeal. The corporal could no more: so he returned his pocket-handkerchief to the breast of his jacket, and a heavy sigh escaped from his own breast. All the devils in hell were mentally conjured and summoned to his aid, but they were, it is to be presumed, better employed, for although the work in hand was diabolical enough, still, Smallbones was such a poor devil, that probably he might have been considered as remotely allied to the fraternity.

It may be inquired why, as this was *on service*, Corporal Van Spitter did not apply for the assistance of the seamen belonging to the vessel, particularly to the officer in charge of the deck; but the fact was, that he was unwilling to do this, knowing that his application would be in vain, for he was aware that the whole crew sided with Smallbones; it was only as a last resource that he intended to do this, and being now at his *wit's* end, he walked up to Dick Short, who had been watching the corporal's motions in silence, and accosted him.

"If you please, Mynheer Short, Mynheer Vanslyperken give orders dat de boy be keel-hauled dis morning:—I want haben de rope and de way."

Short looked at the corporal, and made no reply.

"Mynheer Short, I haben tell de order of Mynheer Vanslyperken."

Dick Short made no reply, but leaning over the hatchway, called out, "Jemmy."

"Ay, ay," replied Jemmy Ducks, turning out of his hammock and dropping on the lower deck.

Corporal Van Spitter, who imagined that Mr Short was about to comply with his request after his own Harpocratic fashion, remained quietly on the deck until Jemmy Ducks made his appearance.

"Hands," quoth Short.

Jemmy piped the hands up.

"Boat," quoth Short, turning his head to the small boat hoisted up astern.

Now as all this was apparently preparatory to the work required, the corporal was satisfied. The men soon came up with their hammocks on their shoulders, which they put into the nettings, and then Jemmy proceeded to lower down the boat. As soon as it was down and hauled up alongside, Short turned round to Coble, and waving his hand towards the shore, said,

"Beef."

Coble, who perfectly understood him, put a new quid into his cheek, went down the side, and pulled on shore to bring off the fresh beef and vegetables for the ship's company; after which Dick Short walked the deck and gave no further orders.

Corporal Van Spitter perceiving this, went up to him again.

"Mynheer Short, you please get ready."

"No!" thundered Short, turning away.

"Got for dam, dat is mutiny," muttered the corporal, who immediately backed stern foremost down the hatchway, to report to his commandant the state of affairs on deck. Mr Vanslyperken had already risen; he had slept but one hour during the whole night, and that one hour was so occupied with wild and fearful dreams that he awoke from his sleep unrefreshed. He had dreamed that he was making every attempt to drown Smallbones, but without effect, for, so soon as the lad was dead he came to life again; he thought that Smallbones' soul was incorporated in a small animal something like a mouse, and that he had to dislodge it from its tenement of clay; but as soon as he drove it from one part of the body it would force its way back again into another; if he forced it out by the mouth after incredible exertions, which made him perspire at every pore, it would run back again into the ear; if forced from thence, through the nostril, then in at the toe, or any other part; in short, he laboured apparently in his dream for years, but without success. And then the "change came o'er the spirit of his dream;" but still there was analogy, for he was now trying to press his suit, which was now a liquid in a vial, into the widow Vandersloosh, but in vain. He administered it again and again, but it acted as an emetic, and she could not stomach it, and then he found himself rejected by all—the widow kicked him, Smallbones stamped upon him, even Snarleyyow flew at him and bit him; at last, he fell with an enormous paving-stone round his neck, descending into a horrible abyss head foremost, and, as he increased his velocity, he awoke trembling and confused, and could sleep no more. This dream was not one to put Mr Vanslyperken into good humour, and two severe cuts on his cheek with the razor as he attempted to shave, for his hand still trembled, had added to his discontent, when it was raised to its climax by the entrance of Corporal Van Spitter, who made his report of the

mutinous conduct of the first officer. Never was Mr
Vanslyperken in such a tumult of rage; he pulled off
some beaver from his hat to staunch the blood, and wiping
off the remainder of the lather, for he put aside the
operation of shaving till his hand was more steady, he
threw on his coat and followed the corporal on deck,
looked round with a savage air, spied out the diminutive
form of Jemmy Ducks, and desired him to pipe "all
hands to keel-haul."

Whereupon Jemmy put his pipe to his mouth, and after
a long flourish, bawled out what appeared to Mr Vanslyperken to be—all hands to *be keel-hauled;* but Jemmy
slurred over quickly the little change made in the order,
and, although the men tittered, Mr Vanslyperken thought
it better to say nothing. But there is an old saying, that
you may bring a horse to the pond, but you cannot make
him drink. Mr Vanslyperken had given the order, but
no one attempted to commence the arrangements. The
only person who showed any activity was Smallbones
himself, who, not aware that he was to be punished, and
hearing all hands piped for something or another, came
shambling, all legs and wings, up the hatchway, and
looked around to ascertain what was to be done. He was
met by the bulky form of Corporal Van Spitter, who,
thinking that Smallbones' making his appearance in such
haste was with the intention of jumping overboard to
avoid his punishment, immediately seized him by the
collar with the left hand, turned round on a pivot towards
Mr Vanslyperken, and raising his right hand to his
foraging cap, reported, "The prisoner on deck, Mynheer
Vanslyperken." This roused the lieutenant to action, for
he had been walking the deck for a half minute in deep
thought.

"Is all ready there, forward?" cried Mr Vanslyperken.
No one replied.

"I say, boatswain, is all ready?"

"No, sir," replied Jemmy; "nobody knows how to set
about it. I don't, anyhow—I never seed anything of the

like since I've been in the service—the whole of the ship's company say the same." But even the flakes of snow, which now fell thick, and whitened the blue jacket of Mr Vanslyperken, could not assuage his wrath — he perceived that the men were refractory, so he summoned the six marines—who were completely under the control of their corporal.

Poor Smallbones had, in the meantime, discovered what was going on, and thought that he might as well urge something in his own defence.

"If you please, what are you going for to do with me?" said the lad, with a terrified look.

"Lead him forward," said Mr Vanslyperken; "follow me, marines;" and the whole party, headed by the lieutenant, went before the mast.

"Strip him," cried Mr Vanslyperken.

"Strip me, with the snow flying like this! An't I cold enough already?"

"You'll be colder when you're under the bottom of the cutter," replied his master.

"O Lord! then it is keel-hauling a'ter all; why what have I done?" cried Smallbones, as the marines divested him of his shirt, and exposed his emaciated body to the pitiless storm.

"Where's Snarleyyow, sir?—confess."

"Snarleyyow—how should I know, sir? it's very hard, because your dog is not to be found, that I'm to be dragged under the bottom of a vessel."

"I'll teach you to throw paving-stones in the canal."

"Paving-stones, sir!" and Smallbones' guilty conscience flew in his face. "Well, sir, do as you please, I'm sure I don't care; if I am to be killed, be quick about it—I'm sure I sha'n't come up alive."

Here Mr Vanslyperken remembered his dream, and the difficulty which he had in driving Smallbones' soul out of his body, and he was fearful that even keel-hauling would not settle Smallbones.

By the directions of Mr Vanslyperken, the hauling

ropes and other tackle were collected by the marines, for the seamen stood by, and appeared resolved, to a man, to do nothing, and, in about half an hour, all was ready. Four marines manned the hauling line, one was placed at each side-rope fastened to the lad's arms, and the corporal, as soon as he had lifted the body of Smallbones over the larboard gunnel, had directions to attend the bow-line, and not allow him to be dragged on too fast: a better selection for this purpose could not have been made than Corporal Van Spitter. Smallbones had been laid without his clothes on the deck, now covered with snow, during the time that the lines were making fast to him; he remained silent, and as usual, when punished, with his eyes shut, and as Vanslyperken watched him with feelings of hatred, he perceived an occasional smile to cross the lad's haggard features. He knows where the dog is, thought Vanslyperken, and his desire to know what had become of Snarleyyow overcame his vengeance—he addressed the shivering Smallbones.

"Now, sir, if you wish to escape the punishment, tell me what has become of the dog, for I perceive that you know."

Smallbones grinned as his teeth chattered—he would have undergone a dozen keel-haulings rather than have satisfied Vanslyperken.

"I give you ten minutes to think of it," continued the lieutenant; "hold all fast at present."

The snow storm now came on so thick that it was difficult to distinguish the length of the vessel. Smallbones' naked limbs were gradually covered, and, before the ten minutes were expired, he was wrapped up in snow as in a garment—he shook his head occasionally to clear his face, but remained silent.

"Now, sir," cried Vanslyperken, "will you tell me, or overboard you go at once? Will you tell me?"

"No," replied Smallbones.

"Do you know, you scoundrel?"

"Yes," replied Smallbones, whose indignation was roused.

" And you won't tell ? "

" No," shrieked the lad—" no, never, never, never ! "

" Corporal Van Spitter, over with him," cried Vanslyperken in a rage, when a sudden stir was heard amongst the men aft, and as the corporal raised up the light frame of the culprit, to carry it to the gunnel, to the astonishment of Vanslyperken, of the corporal, and of Smallbones, Snarleyyow appeared on the forecastle, and made a rush at Smallbones, as he lay in the corporal's arms, snapped at his leg, and then set up his usual deep baying, " bow, bow, bow ! "

The re-appearance of the dog created no small sensation —Vanslyperken felt that he had now no reason for keelhauling Smallbones, which annoyed him as much as the sight of the dog gave him pleasure. The corporal, who had dropped Smallbones on the snow, was also disappointed. As for Smallbones, at the baying of the dog, he started up on his knees, and looked at it as if it were an apparition, with every demonstration of terror in his countenance ; his eyes glared upon the animal with horror and astonishment, and he fell down in a swoon. The whole of the ship's company were taken aback—they looked at one another and shook their heads—one only remark was made by Jansen, who muttered, " De tog is no tog a'ter all."

Mr Vanslyperken ordered Smallbones to be taken below, and then walked aft; perceiving Obadiah Coble, he inquired whence the dog had come, and was answered that he had come off in the boat which he had taken on shore for fresh beef and vegetables. Mr Vanslyperken made no reply, but, with Snarleyyow at his heels, went down into the cabin.

Chapter XI

In which Snarleyyow does not at all assist his master's cause with the Widow Vandersloosh.

IT will be necessary to explain to the reader by what means the life of our celebrated cur was preserved. When Smallbones had thrown him into the canal, tied up, as he supposed, in his winding-sheet, what Mr Vanslyperken observed was true, that there were people below, and the supposed paving-stone might have fallen upon them: the voices which he heard were those of father and son, who were in a small boat going from a galliot to the steps where they intended to land; for this canal was not like most others, with the water in it sufficiently high to enable people to step from the vessel's gunnel to the jetty. Snarleyyow fell in his bag a few yards ahead of the boat, and the splash naturally attracted their attention; he did not sink immediately, but floundered and struggled so as to keep himself partly above water.

"What is that?" exclaimed the father to his son, in Dutch.

"Mein Gott! who is to know?—but we will see;" and the son took the boat-hook, and with it dragged the bread-bags towards the boat, just as they were sinking, for Snarleyyow was exhausted with his efforts. The two together dragged the bags with their contents into the boat.

"It is a dog or something," observed the son.

"Very well, but the bread-bags will be useful," replied the father, and they pulled on to the landing-stairs. When they arrived there they lifted out the bags, laid them on the stone steps, and proceeded to unrip them, when they found Snarleyyow, who was just giving signs of returning animation. They took the bags with them, after having rolled his carcass out, and left it on the steps, for there was a fine for throwing anything into the canal. The cur soon after recovered, and was able to stand on his legs; so soon as he could walk he made his way to the door of the widow Vandersloosh, and howled for admittance. The widow had retired: she had been reading her book of *prières*, as every one should do, who has been cheating people all day long. She was about to extinguish her light, when this serenade saluted her ears; it became intolerable as the dog gained strength.

Babette had long been fast asleep, and was with difficulty roused up and directed to beat the cur away. She attempted to perform the duty, arming herself with the broom; but the moment she opened the door Snarleyyow dashed in between her legs, upsetting her on the brick pavement. Babette screamed, and her mistress came out in the passage to ascertain the cause; the dog not being able to run into the parlour, bolted up the stairs, and snapping at the widow as he passed, secured a berth underneath her bed.

"Oh, mein Gott! it is the dog of the lieutenant," exclaimed Babette, coming up the stairs in greater dishabille than her mistress, and with the broom in her hand. "What shall we do—how shall we get rid of him?"

"A thousand devils may take the lieutenant, and his nasty dog, too," exclaimed the widow, in great wrath; "this is the last time that either of them enter my house; try, Babette, with your broom—shove at him hard."

"Yes, ma'am," replied Babette, pushing with all her strength at the dog beneath the bed, who seized the broom with his teeth, and pulled it away from Babette. It was a struggle of strength between the girl and Snarleyyow— pull, Babette—pull, dog—one moment the broom, with two-thirds of the handle, disappeared under the bed, the next the maid recovered her lost ground. Snarleyyow was first tired of this contention, and to prove that he had no thoughts of abandoning his position, he let go the broom, flew at Babette's naked legs, and having inserted his teeth half through her ankle, he returned growling to his former retreat. "O dear, mein Gott!" exclaimed

Babette, dropping her broom, and holding her ankle with both hands.

"What shall we do?" cried the widow, wringing her hands.

It was indeed a case of difficulty. Mynheer Vandersloosh, before he had quitted this transitory scene, had become a personage as bulky as the widow herself, and the bed had been made unusually wide; the widow still retained the bed for her own use, for there was no knowing whether she might not again be induced to enter the hymeneal state. It occupied more than one half of the room, and the dog had gained a position from which it was not easy for two women to dislodge him; and, as the dog snarled and growled under the bed, so did the widow's wrath rise as she stood shivering—and it was directed against the master. She vowed mentally, that so sure as the dog was under the bed, so sure should his master never get into it.

And Babette's wrath was also kindled, now that the first pain of the bite had worn off; she seized the broom again, and made some furious lunges at Snarleyyow, so furious, that he could not regain possession with his teeth. The door of the room had been left open that the dog might escape—so had the street-door; and the widow stood at the foot of the bed, waiting for some such effect being produced by Babette's vigorous attacks; but the effects were not such as she anticipated; the dog became more enraged, and at last sprang out at the foot of the bed, flew at the widow, tore her only garment, and bit her in the leg. Frau Vandersloosh screamed and reeled—reeled against the door left half open, and falling against it, slammed it to with her weight, and fell down shrieking. Snarleyyow, who probably had intended to make off, seeing that his escape was prevented, again retreated under the bed, and as soon as he was there he recommenced an attack upon Babette's legs.

Now, it appears, that what the united courage of the two females could not accomplish, was at last effected by their united fears. The widow Vandersloosh gained her legs as soon as she could, and at first opened the door to run out, but her night dress was torn to ribbons in front. She looked at her situation—modesty conquered every other feeling—she burst into tears, and exclaiming, "Mr Vanslyperken! Mr Vanslyperken!" she threw herself in an ecstasy of grief and rage on the centre of the bed. At the same moment the teeth of the dog were again fixed upon the ankles of Babette, who also shrieked, and threw herself on the bed, and upon her mistress. The bed was a good bed, and had for years done its duty; but you may even overload a bed, and so it proved in this instance. The united weights of the mistress and the maid coming down upon it with such emphasis, was more than the bed could bear—the sacking gave way altogether, and the mattress which they lay upon was now supported by the floor.

But this misfortune was their preservation—for when the mattress came down, it came down upon Snarleyyow. The animal contrived to clear his loins, or he would have perished; but he could not clear his long mangy tail, which was now caught and firmly fixed in a new species of trap, the widow's broadest proportions having firmly secured him by it. Snarleyyow pulled, and pulled, but he pulled in vain—he was fixed—he could not bite, for the mattress was between them—he pulled, and he howled, and barked, and turned himself every way, and yelped; and had not his tail been of coarse and thick dimensions, he might have left it behind him, so great were his exertions; but, no, it was impossible. The widow was a widow of substance, as Vanslyperken had imagined, and as she now proved to the dog—the only difference was, that the master wished to be in the very situation which the dog was now so anxious to escape from—to wit, tailed on to the widow. Babette, who soon perceived that the dog was so, now got out of the bed, and begging her mistress not to move an inch, and seizing the broom, she hammered Snarleyyow most unmercifully, without any fear of retaliation. The dog redoubled his exertions, and the extra weight of Babette being now removed, he was at last able to withdraw his appendage, and probably feeling that there was now no chance of a quiet night's rest in his present quarters, he made a bolt out of the room, down the stairs, and into the street. Babette chased him down, threw the broom at his head as he cleared the threshold, and then bolted the door.

"O the beast!" exclaimed Babette, going up stairs again, out of breath; "he's gone at last, ma'am."

"Yes," replied the widow, rising up with difficulty from the hole made with her own centre of gravity; "and —and his master shall go too. Make love indeed—the atomy—the shrimp—the dried-up stock-fish. Love, quotha —and refuse to hang a cur like that. O dear! O dear! get me something to put on. One of my best chemises all in rags—and his nasty teeth in my leg in two places, Babette. Well, well, Mr Vanslyperken, we shall see—I don't care for their custom. Mr Vanslyperken, you'll not sit on my sofa again, I can tell you;—hug your nasty cur —quite good enough for you. Yes, yes, Mr Vanslyperken."

By this time the widow had received a fresh supply of linen from Babette; and as soon as she had put it on she rose from the bed, the fractured state of which again called forth her indignation.

"Thirty-two years have I had this bed, wedded and single, Babette!" exclaimed the widow. "For sixteen years did I sleep on that bed with the lamented Mr Vandersloosh—for sixteen years have I slept in it, a lone widow—but never till now did it break down. How am I to sleep to-night? What am I to do, Babette?"

"'Twas well it did break down, ma'am," replied Babette, who was smoothing down the jagged skin at her ankles; "or we should never have got the nasty biting brute out of the house."

"Very well—very well. Yes, yes, Mr Vanslyperken —marriage, indeed, I'd as soon marry his cur."

"Mein Gott!" exclaimed Babette. "I think madame, if you did marry, you would soon find the master as cross as the dog; but I must make this bed."

Babette proceeded to examine the mischief, and found that it was only the cords which tied the sacking which had given way, and considering that they had done their office for thirty-two years, and the strain which had been put upon them after so long a period, there was not much to complain of. A new cord was procured, and, in a quarter of an hour, all was right again; and the widow, who had sat in the chair fuming and blowing off her steam, as soon as Babette had turned down the bed, turned in again, muttering, "Yes, yes, Mr Vanslyperken —marriage indeed. Well, well, we shall see. Stop till to-morrow, Mr Vanslyperken;" and as Babette has closed the curtains, so will we close this chapter.

Chapter XII

In which resolutions are entered into in all quarters, and Jemmy Ducks is accused of mutiny for singing a song in a snow-storm.

WHAT were the adventures of Snarleyyow after this awkward interfence with his master's speculations upon the widow, until he jumped into the beef boat to go on board of the cutter, are lost for ever; but it is to be supposed that he could not have remained the whole night without making himself disagreeable in some quarter or another. But, as we before observed, we know nothing about it; and, therefore, may be excused if we do not tell.

The widow Vandersloosh slept but little that night: her soul was full of vengeance; but although smarting with the imprints of the cur's teeth, still she had an eye to business; the custom of the crew of the cutter was not to be despised, and, as she thought of this, she gradually cooled down. It was not till four o'clock in the morning that she came to her decision; and it was a very prudent one, which was to demand the dead body of the dog to be laid at her door before Mr Vanslyperken should be allowed admittance. This was her right, and if he was sincere, he would not refuse; if he did refuse, it was not at all clear that she should lose the custom of the seamen, over the major part of whom Vanslyperken then appeared to have very little control; and all of whom, she knew, detested him most cordially, as well as his dog. After which resolution the widow Vandersloosh fell fast asleep.

But we must return on board, where there was almost as much confusion as there had been on shore. The reappearance of Snarleyyow was considered supernatural, for Smallbones had distinctly told in what manner he had tied him up in the bread-bags, and thrown him into the canal. Whisperings and murmurings were heard all round the cutter's decks. Obadiah Coble shrugged up his shoulders, as he took an extra quid—Dick Short walked about with lips compressed, more taciturn than ever—Jansen shook his head, muttering, "Te tog is no tog"—Bill Spurey had to repeat to the ship's company the legend of his coming on board over and over again. The only persons who appeared not to have lost their courage were Jemmy Ducks and poor Smallbones, who had been put in his hammock to recover him from his refrigeration. The former said, "that if they were to sail with the devil, it could not be helped, pay and prize-money would still go on;" and the latter, who had quite recovered his self-possession, "vowed that dog or devil, he would never cease his attempts to destroy him—if he was the devil, or one of his imps, it was his duty as a Christian to oppose him, and he had no chance of better treatment if he were to remain quiet." The snow-storm continued, and the men remained below, all but Jemmy Ducks, who leaned against the lee side of the cutter's mast, and, as the snow fell, sang, to a slow air, the following ditty, it probably being called to his recollection by the state of the weather.

'Twas at the landing-place that's just below Mount Wyse,
Poll leaned against the sentry's box, a tear in both her eyes,
Her apron twisted round her arms, all for to keep them warm,
Being a windy Christmas-day, and also a snow-storm.

      And Bet and Sue
      Both stood there too,
         A-shivering by her side,
      They both were dumb,
      And both looked glum,
         As they watched the ebbing tide.
      Poll put her arms a-kimbo,
         At the admiral's house looked she,
      To thoughts before in limbo,
         She now a vent gave free.
      You have sent the ship in a gale to work,
         On a lee shore to be jammed,
      I'll give you a piece of my mind, old Turk,
         Port Admiral, you be d——d.

Chorus.—We'll give you a piece of our mind, old Turk,
         Port Admiral, you be d——d.

Who ever heard in the sarvice of a frigate made to sail
On Christmas-day, it blowing hard, with sleet, and snow, and hail?
I wish I had the fishing of your back that is so bent,
I'd use the galley poker hot unto your heart's content.

      Here Bet and Sue
      Are with me too,
         A shivering by my side,
      They both are dumb,
      And both look glum,
         And watch the ebbing tide.
      Poll put her arms a-kimbo,
         At the admiral's house looked she,
      To thoughts that were in limbo,
         She now a vent gave free.
      You've got a roaring fire I'll bet,
         In it your toes are jammed,
      Let's give him a piece of our mind, my Bet,
         Port Admiral, you be d——d.

Chorus.—Let's give him a piece of our mind, my Bet,
         Port Admiral, you be d——d.

I had the flour and plums all picked, and suet all chopped fine,
To mix into a pudding rich for all the mess to dine;
I pawned my ear-rings for the beef, it weighed at least a stone,
Now my fancy man is sent to sea, and I am left alone.

Here's Bet and Sue
Who stand here too,
   A shivering by my side,
They both are dumb,
They both look glum,
   And watch the ebbing tide.
Poll put her arms a-kimbo,
   At the admiral's house looked she,
To thoughts that were in limbo,
   She now a vent gave free.
You've got a turkey I'll be bound,
   With which you will be crammed,
I'll give you a bit of my mind, old hound,
   Port Admiral, you be d——d.

Chorus.—I'll give you a bit of my mind, old hound,
   Port Admiral, you be d——d.

I'm sure that in this weather they cannot cook their meat,
To eat it raw on Christmas-day will be a pleasant treat;
But let us all go home, girls, it's no use waiting here,
We'll hope that Christmas-day to come, they will have better cheer.

So Bet and Sue
Don't stand here too,
   A shivering by my side,
Don't keep so dumb,
Don't look so glum,
   Nor watch the ebbing tide.
Poll put her arms a-kimbo,
   At the admiral's house looked she,
To thoughts that were in limbo,
   She now a vent gave free.
So while they cut their raw salt junks,
   With dainties you'll be crammed,
Here's once for all my mind, old hunks,
   Port Admiral, you be d——d.

Chorus.—So once for all our mind, old hunks,
   Port Admiral you be d——d.

"Mein Gott! but dat is rank mutiny, Mynheer Shemmy Tucks," observed Corporal Van Spitter, who had come upon the deck unperceived by Jemmy, and had listened to the song.

"Mutiny, is it?" replied Jemmy, "and report this also.

"I'll give you a bit of my mind, fat thief,
   You, corporal, may be d——d."

"Dat is better and better—I mean to say, worser and worser," replied the corporal.

"Take care I don't pitch you overboard," replied Jemmy, in wrath.

"Dat is most worse still," said the corporal, stalking aft, and leaving Jemmy Ducks to follow up the train of his own thoughts.

Jemmy, who had been roused by the corporal, and felt the snow insinuating itself into the nape of the neck, thought he might as well go down below.

The corporal made his report, and Mr Vanslyperken made his comments, but he did no more, for he was aware that a mere trifle would cause a general mutiny. The recovery of Snarleyyow consoled him, and little thinking what had been the events of the preceding night, he thought he might as well prove his devotion to the widow, by paying his respects in a snow-storm—but not in the attire of the day before—Mr Vanslyperken was too economical for that; so he remained in his long threadbare great-coat and foul-weather hat. Having first locked up his dog in the cabin, and entrusted the key to the corporal, he went on shore, and presented himself at the widow's door, which was opened by Babette, who with her person barred entrance: she did not wait for Vanslyperken to speak first.

"Mynheer Vanslyperken, you can't come in. Frau Vandersloosh is very ill in bed—the doctor says it's a bad case—she cannot be seen."

"Ill!" exclaimed Vanslyperken; "your dear, charming mistress ill! Good heavens! what is the matter, my dear Babette?" replied Vanslyperken, with all the pretended interest of a devoted lover.

"All through you, Mr Vanslyperken," replied Babette.

"Me!" exclaimed Vanslyperken.

"Well, all through your nasty cur, which is the same thing."

"My dog! I little thought that he was left here,"

replied the lieutenant; "but, Babette, let me in, if you please, for the snow falls fast, and——"

"And you must not come in, Mr Vanslyperken," replied Babette, pushing him back.

"Good heavens! what is the matter?"

Babette then narrated what had passed, and as she was very prolix, Mr Vanslyperken was a mass of snow on the windward side of him before she had finished, which she did, by pulling down her worsted stockings, and showing the wounds which she had received as her portion in the last night's affray. Having thus given ocular evidence of the truth of what she had asserted, Babette then delivered the message of her mistress; to wit, "that until the dead body of Snarleyyow was laid at the porch where they now stood, he, Mr Vanslyperken, would never gain re-admission." So saying, and not feeling it very pleasant to continue a conversation in a snow-storm, Babette very unceremoniously slammed the door in Mr Vanslyperken's face, and left him to digest the communication with what appetite he might. Mr Vanslyperken, notwithstanding the cold weather, hastened from the door in a towering passion. The perspiration actually ran down his face, and mingled with the melting snow. "To be or not to be"—give up the widow or give up his darling Snarleyyow—a dog whom he loved the more, the more he was, through him, entangled in scrapes and vexations—a dog whom every one hated, and therefore he loved—a dog which had not a single recommendation, and therefore was highly prized—a dog assailed by all, and especially by that scarecrow Smallbones, to whom his death would be a victory—it was impossible. But then the widow—with such lots of guilders in the bank, and such a good income from the Lust Haus, he had long made up his mind to settle in possession. It was the haven which, in the vista of his mind, he had been so long accustomed to dwell upon, and he could not give up the hope.

Yet one must be sacrificed. No, he could part with neither. "I have it," thought he; "I will make the widow believe that I have sacrificed the dog, and then, when I am once in possession, the dog shall come back again, and let her say a word if she dares; I'll tame her, and pay her off for old scores."

Such was the determination of Mr Vanslyperken, as he walked back to the boat. His reverie was, however, broken by his breaking his nose against a lamp-post, which did not contribute to his good-humour. "Yes, yes, Frau Vandersloosh, we will see," muttered Vanslyperken; "you would kill my dog, would you? It's a dog's life I'll lead you when I'm once secure of you, Madame Vandersloosh. You cheated me out of my biscuit—we shall see;" and Mr Vanslyperken stepped into his boat and pulled on board.

On his arrival he found that a messenger had come on board during his absence, with the letters of thanks from the king's loving cousins, and with directions that he should return with them forthwith. This suited the views of Vanslyperken; he wrote a long letter to the widow, in which he expressed his willingness to sacrifice everything for her—not only to hang his dog, but to hang himself if she wished it—lamented his immediate orders for sailing, and hinted that, on his return, he ought to find her more favourable. The widow read the letter, and tossed it into the grate with a Pish! "I was not born yesterday, as the saying is," cried the widow Vandersloosh.

Chapter XIII

In which the ship's company join in a chorus, and the corporal goes on a cruise.

Mr Vanslyperken is in his cabin, with Snarleyyow at his side, sitting upon his haunches, and looking in his master's face, which wears an air of anxiety and discomfiture; the fact is, that Mr Vanslyperken is anything but content; he is angry with the widow, with the ship's company, with the dog, and with himself; but his anger towards the dog is softened, for he feels that, if anything in this world loves him, it is the dog—not that his affection is great, but as much as the dog's nature will permit; and, at all events, if the animal's attachment to him is not very strong, still he is certain that Snarleyyow hates everybody else. It is astonishing how powerful is the feeling that is derived from habit and association. Now that the life of his cur was demanded by one, and, as he was aware, was sought for by many, Vanslyperken put a value upon him that was extraordinary. Snarleyyow had become a precious jewel in the eyes of his master, and what he suffered in anxiety and disappointment from the perverse disposition of the animal, only endeared him the more. "Yes, my poor dog," apostrophised the lieutenant, "they would seek your life—nay, that hard-hearted woman demands that you should be laid—dead at her porch. All conspire against you, but be not afraid, my dog, your master will protect you against all."

Vanslyperken patted the animal on the head, which was not a little swelled from the blows received from the broom of Babette, and Snarleyyow rubbed his nose against his master's trousers, and then raised himself up, by putting his paw upon his master's knee. This brought the dog's head more to the light, and Vanslyperken observed that one eye was swelled and closed. He examined it, and, to his horror, found that it had been beaten out by the broom of Babette. There was no doubt of it, and Mr Vanslyperken's choler was extreme. "Now, may all the curses of ophthalmia seize the fagot," cried the lieutenant; "I wish I had her here. My poor, poor dog!" and Vanslyperken kissed the *os frontis* of the cur, and what perhaps had never occurred since childhood, and what nothing else could have brought about, Mr Vanslyperken *wept*—actually wept over an animal, which was not, from any qualification he possessed, worth the charges of the cord which would have hanged him. Surely the affections have sometimes a bent towards insanity.

After a short time the lieutenant rang his bell, and ordered some warm water, to bathe the dog's eye. Corporal Van Spitter, as Smallbones was in his hammock, answered the summons, and when he returned aft with the water, he made known to Mr Vanslyperken the mutinous expressions of Jemmy Ducks. The lieutenant's small eye twinkled with satisfaction. "Damned the Admiral, did he!—which one was it—Portsmouth or Plymouth?"

This, Corporal Van Spitter could not tell; but it was certain that Jemmy had damned his superior officer; "And moreover," continued the corporal, "he damned me." Now Mr Vanslyperken had a great hatred against Jemmy Ducks, because he amused the ship's company, and he never could forgive any one who made people happy; moreover, he wanted some object to visit his wrath upon: so he asked a few more questions, and then dismissed the corporal, put on his tarpaulin hat, put his speaking-trumpet under his arm, and went on deck, directing the corporal to appoint one of the marines to continue to bathe the eye of his favourite.

Mr Vanslyperken looked at the dog-vane, and perceived that the wind was foul for sailing, and moreover, it would be dark in two hours, so he determined upon not starting till the next morning, and then he thought that he would punish Jemmy Ducks; but the question occurred to him whether he could do so or not. Was James Salisbury a boatswain by right or not? He received only the pay of a boatswain's mate, but he was styled boatswain on the books. It was a nice point, and the balance was even. Mr Vanslyperken's own wishes turned the scale, and he resolved to flog Jemmy Ducks if he could. We say, if he could, for as, at that time, tyrannical oppression on the part of the superiors was winked at, and no complaints were listened to by the Admiralty, insubordination, which was the natural result, was equally difficult to get over; and although on board of the larger vessels, the strong arm of power was certain to conquer, it was not always the case in the smaller, where the superiors were not in sufficient force, or backed by a numerous party of soldiers or marines, for there was then little difference between the two services. Mr Vanslyperken had had more than one mutiny on board of the vessels which he had commanded, and, in one instance, his whole ship's company had taken the boats and gone on shore, leaving him by himself in the vessel, preferring to lose the pay due to them, than to remain longer on board. They joined other ships in the service, and no notice was taken of their conduct by the authorities. Such was the state of half discipline at the period we speak of in the service of the king. The ships were, in every other point, equally badly fitted out and manned; peculation of every kind was carried to excess, and those who were in command thought more of their own interest than of anything else. Ship's stores and provisions were constantly sold, and the want of the former was frequently the occasion of the loss of the vessel, and the sacrifice of the whole crew. Such maladministration is said to be the case even now in some of the continental navies. It is not until a long series of years have elapsed, that such regulations and arrangements as are at present so economically and beneficially administered to our navy, can be fully established.

Having settled the point so far, Mr Vanslyperken then proceeded to debate in his own mind, whether he should flog Jemmy in harbour, or after he had sailed; and feeling that if there was any serious disturbance on part of the men, they might quit the vessel if in harbour, he decided that he would wait until he had them in blue water. His thoughts then reverted to the widow, and, as he turned and turned again, he clenched his fists in his great-coat pockets, and was heard by those near him to grind his teeth.

In the meantime, the news had been imparted by the

marine, who came up into the galley for more warm water, that the dog had had one of his eyes put out, and it was strange the satisfaction which this intelligence appeared to give to the ship's company. It was passed round like wildfire, and, when communicated, a beam of pleasure was soon apparent throughout the whole cutter, and for this simple reason, that the accident removed the fear arising from the supposition of the dog being supernatural, for the men argued, and with some reason, that if you could put out his eye, you could kill him altogether; for if you could destroy a part, you could destroy the whole. No one ever heard of the devil's eye being put out—*ergo*, the dog could not be a devil, or one of his imps: so argued a knot of the men in conclave, and Jansen wound up by observing, "Dat de tog was only a tog after all."

Vanslyperken returned to his cabin and stated his intentions to his factotum and confidant, Corporal Van Spitter. Now, in this instance, the corporal did not adhere to that secrecy to which he was bound, and the only reason we can give is, that he had as great a dislike to Jemmy Ducks as his lieutenant—for the corporal obeyed orders so exactly, that he considered it his duty not to have even an opinion or a feeling contrary to those of his superior officer. He was delighted at the idea of flogging Jemmy, and communicated the lieutenant's intention to the most favoured of his marines, who also told the secret to another, and thus in five minutes, it was known throughout the cutter, that as soon as they were in blue water, the little boatswain was to be tied up for having damned the admiral in a snow-storm. The consequence was, as the evening was clear, that there was a very numerous assemblage upon the forecastle of the cutter *Yungfrau*.

"Flog Jemmy," said Bill Spurey. "Why, Jemmy's a hofficer."

"To be sure he is," observed another; "and quite as good a one as Vanslyperken himself, though he don't wear brass on his hat."

"D—n it—what next—heh, Coble?"

Coble hitched up his trousers. "It's my opinion he'll be for flogging *us* next, Short," said the old man.

"Yes," replied Short.

"Shall we allow Jemmy to be flogged?"

"No," replied Short.

"If it warn't for them 'ere marines, and the lumpy beggar of a corporal," observed one of the seamen.

"Pish," quoth Jemmy, who was standing among them.

"Won't he make it out mutiny?" observed Spurey.

"Mein Gott! it was mutiny to flog de officer," said Jansen.

"That's very true," observed another.

"But Jemmy can't stand against the fat corporal and the six marines," observed Bill Spurey.

"One up and t'other down, I'll take them all," observed Jemmy, expanding his chest.

"Yes, but they'll all be down upon you at once, Jemmy."

"If they lays their hands upon an officer," observed Coble, "it will be mutiny; and then Jemmy calls in the ship's company to protect him."

"Exactly," observed Jemmy.

"And den, mein Gott, I zettle for de corporal," observed Jansen.

"I'll play him a trick yet."

"But now, it's no use palavering," observed Spurey; "let's come to some settlement. Obadiah, give us your opinion as to what's best to be done."

Hereupon Coble squirted out a modicum of 'baccy juice, wiped his mouth with the back of his hand, and said, "It's my opinion, that the best way of getting one man out of a scrape, is to get all the rest in it. Jemmy, d'ye see, is to be hauled up for singing an old song, in which a wench very properly damns the admiral for sending a ship out on a Christmas-day, which, let alone the unchristian-like act, as you may know, my lads, always turns up on a Friday, a day on which nothing but being blown out from your anchors can warrant any vessel sailing on.

Now, d'ye see, it may be mutiny to damn a live admiral, with his flag hoisted—I won't say but what it is—but this here admiral as Jemmy damned, is no more alive than a stock fish; and, moreover, it is not Jemmy as damns him, but Poll; therefore it can be no mutiny. Now, what I consider best is this, if so be it be against the articles—well, then, let's all be in for it together, and then Vanslyperken will be puzzled, and, moreover, it will give him a hint how matters stand, and he may think better of it; for although we must not have Jemmy touched, still it's quite as well not to have a regular breeze with the jollies; for if so be that the *Scarborough*, or any other king's ship, be in port when we arrive, Vanslyperken may run under the guns, and then whip the whole boiling of us off to the Ingies, and glad to get us, too, and that's no joke. Now, that's my idea of the matter."

"Well, but you've not told us how we are all to get into it, Coble."

"More I have—well, that's funny; left out the whole burden of my song. Why, I consider that we had better now directly sing the song over again, all in chorus, and then we shall have damned the admiral a dozen times over; and Vanslyperken will hear us, and say to himself, 'They don't sing that song for nothing.' What do you say, Dick Short, you're first hofficer?"

"Yes," replied Short.

"Hurrah! my lads, then," cried Bill Spurey; "now then, strike up, Jemmy, and let us give it lots of mouth."

The song which our readers have already heard from the lips of Jemmy Ducks, was then sung by the whole of the men, *con animo e strepito*, and two verses had been roared out, when Corporal Van Spitter, in great agitation, presented himself at the cabin door, where he found Mr Vanslyperken very busy summing up his accounts.

"Mein Gott, sar! dere is de mutiny in de *Yungfrau*," cried the corporal.

"Mutiny!" cried Vanslyperken, catching at his sword, which hung up on the bulk-head.

"Yaw, mynheer — de mutiny — hear now de ship's company."

Vanslyperken lent his ears, when the astounding chorus came rolling aft through the door of the cabin,

> "I'll give you a bit of my mind, old hunks,
> Port Admiral—you be d———d."

"Bow, wow, wow," barked Snarleyyow.

"Why, it's the whole ship's company!" cried Vanslyperken.

"All but de Corporal Van Spitter, and de six marines," replied the corporal, raising his hand up to his head *à la militaire*.

"Shut the door, corporal. This is indeed mutiny and defiance," cried Vanslyperken, jumping up from his chair.

"It is von tyfel of a song," replied the corporal.

"I must find out the ringleaders, corporal; do you think that you could contrive to overhear what they say after the song is over? they will be consulting together, and we might find out something."

"Mynheer, I'm not very small for to creep in and listen," replied the corporal, casting his eyes down upon his huge carcass.

"Are they all forward?" inquired the lieutenant.

"Yes, mynheer—not one soul baft."

"There is the small boat astern; do you think you could get softly into it, haul it up to the bows, and lie there quite still? You would then hear what they said, without their thinking of it, now that it is dark."

"I will try, mynheer," replied the corporal, who quitted the cabin.

But there were others who condescended to listen as well as the corporal, and in this instance, every word which had passed, had been overheard by Smallbones, who had been for some hours out of his hammock. When the corporal's hand touched the lock of the door, Smallbones made a hasty retreat.

Corporal Van Spitter went on the quarter-deck, which he found vacant; he hauled up the boat to the counter, and by degrees lowered into it his unwieldy carcass, which almost swamped the little conveyance. He then waited a little, and with difficulty forced the boat up against the strong flood-tide that was running, till at last he gained the chesstree of the cutter, when he shortened in the painter (or rope that held the boat), made it fast to a ring-bolt without being perceived, and there he lay concealed, not daring to move, for fear of making a noise.

Smallbones had, however, watched him carefully, and as the corporal sat in the middle thwart, with his face turned aft, catching but imperfectly the conversation of the men, the lad separated the painter with a sharp knife, and at the same time dropping his foot down, gave the bow of the boat a shove off, which made it round with the stream. The tide was then running five or six miles an hour, and before the corporal, in the utter darkness, could make out what had occurred, or raise his heavy carcass to assist himself, he was whirled away by the current clear of the vessel, and soon disappeared from the sight of Smallbones, who was watching his progress.

It is true that the corporal shouted for assistance when he found himself astern, and also that he was heard by the men, but Smallbones had leaped among them, and in a few words told them what he had done; so of course they took no notice, but rubbed their hands with delight at the idea of the corporal being adrift like a bear in a washing-tub, and they all prayed for a gale of wind to come on that he might be swamped, and most of them remained on deck to hear what Mr Vanslyperken would say and do when the corporal's absence was discovered. Mr Vanslyperken remained nearly two hours without sending for the corporal; at last, surprised at not seeing him return, he went on deck. The men on the forecastle perceiving this, immediately disappeared gently down the fore-hatchway.

Mr Vanslyperken walked forward and found that every one was, as he supposed, either in bed or below; for in harbour the corporal kept one of the watches, and this night it was his first watch. Vanslyperken looked over the side all round the cutter, and could see no boat and no Corporal Van Spitter, and it immediately occurred to him that the corporal must have gone adrift, and he was very much puzzled how to act. It would be flood-tide for two hours more, and then the whole ebb would run before it was daylight. Corporal Van Spitter would traverse the whole Zuyder Zee before they might find him. Unless he had the fortune to be picked up by some small craft, he might perish with cold and hunger. He could not sail without him; for what could he do without Corporal Van Spitter, his protection, his factotum, his distributer of provisions, &c. The loss was irreparable, and Mr Vanslyperken, when he thought of the loss of the widow's favour and the loss of his favourite, acknowledged with bitterness that his star was not in the ascendant. After some reflection, Mr Vanslyperken thought that as nothing could be gained by making the fact known, the wisest thing that he could do was to go to bed and say nothing about it, leaving the whole of the ulterior proceedings until the loss of the boat should be reported to him in the morning. Having arranged this in his mind, Mr Vanslyperken took two or three turns more, and then went down and turned in.

Chapter XIV

In which some new characters appear on the stage, although the corporal is not to be heard of.

THE loss of the boat was reported by Obadiah Coble at daylight, and Mr Vanslyperken immediately went on deck with his spy-glass to ascertain if he could distinguish the corporal coming down with the last of the ebb-tide but he was nowhere to be seen. Mr Vanslyperken went to the mast-head and surveyed in every direction, but he could neither see anything like the boat or Corporal Van Spitter. His anxiety betrayed to the men that he was a party to the corporal's proceedings, and they whispered among themselves. At last Mr Vanslyperken came down on deck, and desired Corporal Van Spitter to be sent to him. Of course, it was soon reported to him that Corporal Van Spitter was nowhere to be found, and Mr Vanslyperken pretended to be much astonished. As the lieutenant took it for granted that the boat had been swept out with the ebb, he determined to get under weigh in pursuance of his orders, pick up the corporal, if he could find him, and then proceed to Portsmouth, which was the port of his destination. Smallbones attended his master, and was so unusually active that the suspicious Mr Vanslyperken immediately decided that he had had a finger in the business; but he took no notice, resolving in his own mind that Smallbones should some day or another be adrift himself as the corporal was, but with this difference, that there should be no search made after him. As soon as the men had finished their breakfasts, the cutter was got under weigh and proceeded to sea. During the whole day Vanslyperken cruised in the Zuyder Zee looking for the boat, but without success, and at last he unwillingly shaped his course for England, much puzzled and perplexed, as now he had no one to act as his steward to whom he could confide, or by whose arrangements he could continue to defraud the ship's company; and, farther, he was obliged to put off for the present all idea of punishing Jemmy Ducks, for, without the corporal, the marines were afraid to move a step in defiance of the ship's company. The consequence was, that the three days that they were at sea, Mr Vanslyperken confined himself altogether to his cabin, for he was not without some fears for his own safety. On his arrival at Portsmouth, he delivered his letters to the admiral, and received orders to return to his cruising ground after the smugglers as soon as he had replaced his lost boat.

We have observed that Mr Vanslyperken had no relations on this side of the water; but in saying that, we referred to the epoch that he was in the service previous to the accession of King William. Since that, and about a year from the time we are now writing about, he had brought over his mother, whom he had not, till the peace, seen for years, and had established her in a small apartment in that part of the town now known by the name of the Halfway Houses. The old woman lived upon a small pension allowed by the Dutch court, having been employed for many years in a subordinate capacity in the king's household. She was said to have once been handsome, and when young, prodigal of her favours; at present she was a palsied old woman, bent double with age and infirmity, but with all her faculties as complete as if she was in her prime. Nothing could escape her little twinkling bloodshot eyes, or her acute ear; she could scarcely hobble fifty yards, but she kept no servant to assist her, for, like her son, she was avaricious in the extreme. What crime she had committed was not known, but that something lay heavy on her conscience was certain; but if there was guilt, there was no repentance, only fear of future punishment. Cornelius Vanslyperken was her only living child: she had been twice married. The old woman did not appear to be very fond of him, although she treated him still as a child, and executed her parental authority as if he were still in petticoats. Her coming over was a sort of mutual convenience. She had saved money, and Vanslyperken wished to secure that, and also have a home and a person to whom he could trust; and she was so abhorred, and the reports against her so shocking where she resided, that she was glad to leave a place where every one, as she passed, would get out of her way, as if to avoid contamination. Yet these reports were vague, although hinting at some horrid and appalling crimes. No one knew what they exactly were, for the old woman had outlived her contemporaries, and the tradition was imperfect, but she had been handed down to the next generation as one to be avoided as a basilisk.

It was to his mother's abode, one room on the second floor, to which Mr Vanslyperken proceeded as soon as he had taken the necessary steps for the replacing of the boat. As he ascended the stairs, the quick ear of the old woman heard his footstep, and recognised it. It must be observed, that all the conversation between Vanslyperken and his mother was carried on in Dutch, of which we, of course, give the translation.

"There you come, Cornelius Vanslyperken; I hear you, and by your hurried tread you are vexed. Well, why should you not be vexed as well as your mother, in this world of devils?"

This was a soliloquy of the old woman's before that Vanslyperken had entered the room, where he found his mother sitting over a few cinders half ignited in a very small grate. Parsimony would not allow her to use more fuel, although her limbs trembled as much from cold as palsy; her nose and chin nearly met; her lips were like old scars, and of an ashy white; and her sunken hollow mouth reminded you of a small, deep, dark sepulchre; teeth she had none.

"How fare you, mother?" said Vanslyperken on entering the room.

"I'm alive."

"And long may you live, dear mother."

"Ah," replied the woman, as if doubting.

"I am here but for a short time," continued Vanslyperken.

"Well, child, so much the better; when on board you save money, on shore you must spend some. Have you brought any with you?"

"I have, mother, which I must leave to your care."

"Give it me then."

Vanslyperken pulled out a bag and laid it on the lap of his mother, whose trembling hands counted it over.

"Gold, and good gold—while you live, my child, part not with gold. I'll not die yet—no, no, the devils may pull at me, and grin at me, but I'm not theirs yet."

Here the old woman paused, and rocked herself in her chair.

"Cornelius, lock this money up and give me the key:—there, now that is safe, you may talk, if you please, child: I can hear well enough."

Vanslyperken obeyed; he mentioned all the events of the last cruise, and his feelings against the widow, Smallbones, and Jemmy Ducks. The old woman never interrupted him, but sat with her arms folded up in her apron.

"Just so, just so," said she, at last, when he had done speaking; "I felt the same, but then you have not the soul to act as I did. I could do it, but you—you are a coward; no one dared cross my path, or if they did—ah, well, that's years ago, and I'm not dead yet."

All this was muttered by the old woman in a sort of half soliloquy: she paused and continued, "Better leave the boy alone,—get nothing by it;—the woman—there's work there, for there's money."

"But she refuses, mother, if I do not destroy the dog."

"Refuses—ah, well—let me see:—can't you ruin her character, blast her reputation; she is yours and her money too;—then, then—there will be money and revenge—both good;—but money—no—yes, money's best. The dog must live, to gnaw the Jezebel—gnaw her bones—but you, you are a coward—you dare do nothing."

"What do I fear, mother?"

"Man—the gallows, and death. I fear the last, but I shall not die yet:—no, no, I *will* live—I will *not* die. Ay, the corporal—lost in Zuyder Zee—dead men tell no tales; and he could tell many of you, my child. Let the fish fatten on him."

"I cannot do without him, mother."

"A hundred thousand devils!" exclaimed the old mother, "that I should have suffered such throes for a craven. Cornelius Vanslyperken, you are not like your mother:—your father, indeed——"

"Who was my father?"

"Silence, child,—there, go away—I wish to be alone with memory."

Vanslyperken, who knew that resistance or remonstrance would be useless, and only lead to bitter cursing and imprecation on the part of the old woman, rose and walked back to the sallyport, where he slipped into his boat and pulled on board of the *Yungfrau*, which lay at anchor in the harbour, about a cable's length from the shore.

"Here he comes," cried a tall bony woman, with nothing on her head but a cap with green faded ribbons, who was standing on the forecastle of the cutter. "Here he comes; —he, the willain, as would have flogged my Jemmy." This was the wife of Jemmy Ducks, who lived at Portsmouth, and who, having heard what had taken place, vowed revenge.

"Silence, Moggy," said Jemmy, who was standing by her.

"Yes, I'll hold my tongue till the time comes, and then I'll sarve him out, the cheating wagabond."

"Silence, Moggy."

"And as for that 'peaching old Corporal Blubber, I'll *Wan Spitter* him if ever he turns up again to blow the gaff against my own dear Jemmy."

"Silence, Moggy—there's rowed of all, and a marine at your elbow."

"Let him take that for his trouble," cried Moggy, turning round, and delivering a swinging box of the ear upon the astonished marine, who not liking to encounter such an Amazon, made a hasty retreat down the fore-hatchway.

"So there you are, are you?" continued Moggy, as Vanslyperken stepped on the deck.

"Silence, Moggy."

"You, that would flog my own dear darling duck—my own Jemmy."

"Silence! Moggy, will you?" said Jemmy Ducks, in an angry tone, "or I'll smash your peepers."

"You must climb on the gun to reach them, my little man," replied his wife. "Well, the more I holds my tongue now, the more for him when I gets hold on him. Oh! he's gone to his cabin, has he, to kiss his Snarleyyow:—I'll make *smallbones* of that beast afore I'm done with him. Flog my Jemmy—my own, dear, darling Jemmy—a nasty lean——"

"Go down below, Moggy," said Jemmy Ducks, pushing her towards the hatchway.

"Snivelling, great-coated——"

"Go below," continued Jemmy, shoving her.

"Ferret-eyed, razor-nosed——"

"Go down below, will you?" cried Jemmy, pushing her near to the hatchway.

"Herring-gutted, bare-poled——"

"Confound it! go below."

"Cheating rip of a wagabond! Lord, Jemmy, if you a'n't a shoved me down the hatchway! Well, never mind, my darling, let's go to supper;" and Moggy caught hold of her husband as she was going down, and with surprising strength lifted him off his legs and carried him down in her arms as she would have done a child, much to the amusement of the men who were standing on the forecastle.

When it was dusk, a boat dropped alongside of the cutter, and a man stepped out of it on the deck, when he was met by Obadiah Coble, who asked him, "What's your pleasure?"

"I must speak with the commander of this vessel directly."

"Wait a moment, and I'll tell him what you say," replied Coble, who reported the message to Mr Vanslyperken.

"What sort of a person is he?" demanded the lieutenant.

"Oh, I don't know,—sort of half-bred, long-shore chap—looks something between a bumbailey and a bumboatman."

"Well, you may show him down."

The man, who shortly after entered the cabin, was a short, punchy little fellow, with a red waistcoat, knee-breeches, and a round jacket of green cloth. His face was covered with carbuncles, some of them so large that his small pug-nose was nothing more in appearance than a larger blotch than the others. His eyes were small and keen, and his whiskers of a deep red. As soon as he entered the cabin, he very deliberately locked the door after him.

"Nothing like making sure," observed he.

"Why, what the devil do you want?" exclaimed Vanslyperken, rather alarmed; while Snarleyyow walked round and round the thick calves of the man's legs, growling, and in more than two minds to have a bite through his blue worsted stockings; and the peculiar obliquity with which he carried his head, now that he surveyed with only one eye, was by no means satisfactory.

"Take your cur away, and let us proceed to business, for there is no time to lose," said the man coolly, taking a chair. "Now there can be no eavesdropping, I trust, for my life may be forfeited, if I'm discovered."

"I cannot understand a word of all this," replied Vanslyperken, much surprised.

"In a few words, do you want to put some five thousand pounds in your pocket?"

At this question Vanslyperken became attentive. He beat off the dog, and took a chair by the side of the stranger.

"Ah! interest will always bring civility; so now to the point. You command this cutter, do you not?"

"I do," replied Vanslyperken.

"Well, you are about to cruise after the smugglers?"

"Yes."

"I can give information of a cargo to be landed on a certain night worth ten thousand pounds or more."

"Indeed!" replied Vanslyperken.

"Yes, and put your boats in such a position that they must seize the whole."

"I'm very much obliged to you. Will you take something, sir, any scheedam?" said Vanslyperken, unlocking one of his cupboards, and producing a large stone bottle, and a couple of glasses, which he filled.

"This is very good stuff," observed the man; "I'll trouble you for another glass."

This was one more than Mr Vanslyperken intended; but on second thoughts, it would make his new acquaintance more communicative, so another was filled, and as soon as it was filled, it was emptied.

"Capital stuff!" said he of the rubicund face, shoving his glass towards Vanslyperken, by way of hint; but the lieutenant would not take the hint, as his new guest had already swallowed as much as lasted himself for a week.

"But now," observed Vanslyperken, "where is this cargo to be seen, and when?"

"That's tellings," replied the man.

"I know that; but you have come to tell, or what the devil else?" replied Vanslyperken, who was getting angry.

"That's according," replied the man.

"According to what?"

"The snacks," replied the man. "What will you give up?"

"Give up! How do you mean?"

"What is my share to be?"

"Share! you can't share—you're not a king's officer."

"No, but I'm an informer, and that's the same thing."

"Well, depend upon it, I'll behave very liberally."

"How much, I ask?"

"We'll see to that afterwards; something handsome, depend upon it."

"That won't do. Wish you good-evening, sir. Many thanks for the scheedam—capital stuff!" and the man rose from his chair.

But Mr Vanslyperken had no intention to let him go;

his avarice induced him at first to try if the man would be satisfied with his promise to reward him—a promise which would certainly never have been adhered to.

"Stop! my dear sir, do not be in such a hurry. Take another glass."

"With pleasure," replied the man, re-seating himself, and drinking off the scheedam. "That's really prime; I like it better every time I taste it. Now, then, shall we go to business again? I'll be plain with you. Half is my conditions, or I don't inform."

"Half!" exclaimed Vanslyperken; "half of ten thousand pounds? What, five thousands pounds?"

"Exactly so; half of ten is five, as you say."

"What, give you five thousand pounds?"

"I rather think it is I who offer you five thousand, for the devil a penny will you get without me. And that I will have, and this bond you must sign to that effect, or I'm off. You're not the only vessel in the harbour."

Vanslyperken tried for some time to reduce the terms, but the man was positive. Vanslyperken then tried if he could not make the man intoxicated, and thus obtain better terms; but fifteen glasses of his prime scheedam had no effect further than extorting unqualified praise as it was poured down, and at last Mr Vanslyperken unwillingly consented to the terms, and the bond was signed.

"We must weigh at the ebb," said the man, as he put the bond in his pocket. "I shall stay on board; we have a moonlight night, and if we had not, I could find my way out in a yellow fog. Please to get your boats all ready, manned and armed, for there may be a sharp tussle."

"But when do they run, and where?" demanded Vanslyperken.

"To-morrow night at the back of the Isle. Let me see," continued the man, taking out his watch; "mercy on me! how time has flown—that's the scheedam. In a couple of hours we must weigh. I'll go up and see if the wind holds in the same quarter. If you please, lieutenant, we'll just drink success to the expedition. Well, that's prime stuff, I do declare."

Chapter XV

In which the crew of the *Yungfrau* lose a good prize, and Snarleyyow loses his character.

THE next morning the *Yungfrau* was clear of St Helens, and sounding the eastern part of the Isle of Wight, after which she made sail into the offing, that she might not be suspected by those on shore waiting to receive the cargo. The weather was fine, and the water smooth, and as soon as she was well out, the cutter was hove-to. In the hurry of weighing, Mr Vanslyperken had not thought, or had not known perhaps, that the wife of Jemmy Ducks was still on board, and as he was turning up and down on the quarter-deck, he perceived her on the forecastle, laughing and talking with the men.

"What woman is that?" said he to Jansen, who was at the wheel.

"De frau, mynheer. Dat is de frau of Shimmy Duk."

"How dare she come on board? Send her aft here, marine."

The marine went forward and gave the order; and Jemmy, who expected a breeze, told his wife to behave herself quietly. His advice did not, however, appear to be listened to, as will be shown in the sequel.

"How came you on board, woman?" cried Vanslyperken, looking at her from top to toe several times, as usual, with his hands in his great-coat pockets, and his battered speaking-trumpet under his arm.

"How did I come on board! why, in a boat to be sure," replied Moggy, determined to have a breeze.

"Why did you not go on shore before the cutter sailed?" replied Vanslyperken, in an angry tone.

"Why, just for the contrary reason, because there was no boat."

"Well, I'll just tell you this, if ever I see you on board again, you'll take the consequences," retorted Vanslyperken,

"And I'll just tell you this," replied Moggy; "if ever you come on shore again you shall take the consequences. I'll have you—I give you warning. Flog my Jemmy, heh! my own dear darling Jemmy." Hereupon Moggy held out one arm bent, and with the palm of her other hand slapped her elbow—"*There!*" cried she.

What Jemmy's wife meant by this sign, it is impossible for us to say; but that it was a very significant one was certain, for Mr Vanslyperken foamed with rage, and all the cutter's crew were tittering and laughing. It was a species of free-masonry known only to the initiated at the Sallyport.

"Send the marines aft here. Take this woman below," cried Vanslyperken. "I shall put all this down to your husband's account, and give him a receipt in full, depend upon it."

"So you may. Marines, keep off, if you don't wish your heads broken; and I'll put all this down to your account; and as you say that you'll pay off on my pet, mark my words, if I don't pay off on yours—on your nasty cur there. I'll send him to cruise after Corporal Van Spitter. As sure as I stand here, if you dare to lay a finger on my Jemmy, I'll kill the brute wherever I find him, and make him into *saussingers*, just for the pleasure of eating him. I'll send you a pound as a present. You marine, don't be a fool—I can walk forward without your hoffering your arm, and be d——d to you." So saying, Moggy stalked forward and joined the men on the forecastle.

"D'ye know much of that strapping lass?" said Mr Vanslyperken's new acquaintance.

"Not I," replied Vanslyperken, not much pleased at the observation.

"Well, look out for squalls, she'll be as good as her

word. We'll draw the foresheet, and stand in now, if you please."

It was about dusk, for the days were now short, and the cutter was eight miles off the land. By the directions of the informer, for we have no other name to give him, they now bore up and ran along the island until they were, by his calculations, for it then was dark, abreast of a certain point close to the Black Gang Chyne. Here they hove-to, hoisted out their boats, three in number, and the men were sent in, well armed with pistols and cutlasses. Short had the charge of one, Coble of the second, the stern-sheets of the third was occupied by Vanslyperken and the informer. As soon as all was ready, Jemmy Ducks, who, much against Vanslyperken's wish, was left in charge of the cutter, received his orders to lie-to where he was, and when the tide made flood, to stand close in-shore; and all was prepared for a start, when it occurred to Vanslyperken that to leave Snarleyyow, after the threat of Jemmy's wife, and the known animosity of Smallbones, would be his death-warrant. He determined, therefore, to take him in the boat. The informer protested against it, but Vanslyperken would not listen to his protestations. The dog was handed into the boat, and they shoved off. After they had pulled a quarter of an hour in-shore, they altered their course, and continued along the coast until the informer had made out exactly where he was. He then desired the other two boats to come alongside, told the crews that they must keep the greatest silence, as where they were about to proceed was directly under where the smugglers would have a party to receive the goods, and that the least alarm would prevent them from making the capture. The boats then pulled in to some large rocks, against which the waves hoarsely murmured, although the sea was still smooth, and passing between them, found themselves in a very small cove, where the water was still, and in which there was deep water.

The cove was not defended so much by the rocks above water, for the mouth of it was wide; but there appeared to be a ridge below, which broke off the swell of the ocean. Neither was it deep, the beach not being more than perhaps fifty feet from the entrance. The boats, which had pulled in with muffled oars, here lay quietly for nearly an hour, when a fog came on and obscured the view of the offing, which otherwise was extensive, as the moon was at her full, and had shone bright.

"This is all the better," whispered the informer, "they will fall into the trap at once. Hark! hist! I hear oars."

They all listened; it was true, the sound of oars was heard, and the men prepared their arms.

The splash of the oars was now more plain. "Be silent and ready," whispered the informer, and the whisper was passed round. In another minute a large lugger-built boat, evidently intended for sailing as well as pulling, was seen through the fog looming still larger from the mist, pulling into the cove.

"Silence, and not a word. Let her pass us," whispered the informer.

The boat approached rapidly—she was within ten fathoms of the entrance, when Snarleyyow, hearing the sound, darted forward under the thwarts, and jumping on the bow of the boat, commenced a most unusual and prolonged baying of Bow wow, bow wow wow wow!

At the barking of the dog the smugglers backed water to stop their way. They knew that there was no dog with those they expected to meet, it was therefore clear that the Philistines were at hand. The dog barked in spite of all attempts to prevent him, and acting upon this timely warning, the lugger-boat pulled short round, just as lights were shown from the cliffs to notify an enemy at hand, for the barking of the dog had not escaped the vigilance of those on shore, and in a few seconds she disappeared in the mist.

"Blast your cur! Five thousand pounds out of my pocket;" exclaimed the informer. "I told you so. Chuck him overboard, my men, for your pockets would have been lined."

Vanslyperken was as savage, and exclaimed, "Give way, my men, give way; we'll have them yet."

"Send a cow to chase a hare," replied the informer, throwing himself back in the stern-sheets of the boat. "I know better; you may save yourself the trouble, and the men the fatigue. May the devil take you, and your cursed dog with you! Who but a fool would have brought a dog upon such an occasion? Well, I've lost five thousand pounds; but there's one comfort, you've lost too. That will be a valuable beast, if you put all down to his account."

At this moment Vanslyperken was so much annoyed at the loss of what would have been a fortune to him, that he felt as angry as the informer. The boats' crew were equally enraged, the dog was pommelled, and kicked, and passed along from one to the other, until he at last gained the stern-sheets, and crouched between the legs of his master, who kicked him away in a rage, and he saved himself under the legs of the informer, who, seizing a pistol, struck him with the butt-end of it such a blow, that nothing but the very thick skull of the dog could have saved him. Snarleyyow was at a sad discount just then, but he very wisely again sought protection with his master, and this time he was not noticed.

"What are we to do now?" observed Vanslyperken.

"Go back again, like dogs with their tails between their legs; but observe, Mr Lieutenant, you have made me your enemy, and that is more serious than you think for."

"Silence, sir, you are in a king's boat."

"The king be d——d," replied the informer, falling back sulkily against the gunnel of the boat.

"Give way, men, and pull on board," said Vanslyperken, in equally bad humour.

In equally bad humour the men did give way, and in about an hour were on board of the cutter.

Every one was in a bad humour when the affair was made known; but Smallbones observed, "that the dog could be no such great friend, as supposed, of Vanslyperken's, to thwart his interests in that way; and certainly no imp sent by the devil to his assistance." The ship's company were consoled with this idea, and Jansen again repeated, "that the *tog* was but a tog, after all."

Chapter XVI

In which we change the scene, and the sex of our performers.

WE must now leave the cutter to return to Portsmouth, while we introduce to our readers a new and strange association. We stated that the boats had been ensconced in a very small cove at the back of the Isle of Wight. Above these hung the terrific cliff of the Black Gang Chyne, which, to all appearance, was inaccessible. But this was not the case, or the smugglers would not have resorted there to disembark their cargo. At that time, for since that period much of the cliff has fallen down, and the aspect is much changed, the rocks rose up from the water nearly perpendicularly, to the height of fifty or sixty feet. At that height there was a flat of about one hundred feet square in front of a cave of very great depth. The flat, so called in contradistinction to the perpendicular cliff, descended from the seaward to the cave, so that the latter was not to be seen either by vessels passing by, or by those who might be adventurous enough to peep over the ridge above; and fragments of rocks, dispersed here and there on this flat, or platform, induced people to imagine that the upper cliff was a continuation of the lower. The lower cliff, on which this platform in front of the cave was situated, was on the eastern side as abrupt as on that fronting the sea to the southward; but on the western side, its height was decreased to about fifteen feet, which was surmounted by a ladder removed at pleasure. To this means of access to the cave there was a zigzag path, used only by the smugglers, leading from the small cove, and another much more tedious, by which they could transport their goods to the summit of this apparently inaccessible mass of rocks. The cave itself was large, and with several diverging galleries, most of which were dry; but in one or two there was a continual filtering of clear pure water through the limestone rock, which was collected in pits dug for that purpose on the floor below; these pits were always full of water, the excess being carried off by small open drains which trickled over the eastern side of the platform. Some attention to comfort had been paid by the inhabitants of these caverns, which were portioned off here and there by sail-cloth and boards, so as to form separate rooms and storehouses. The cookery was carried on outside at the edge of the platform nearest the sea, under an immense fragment of rock, which lay at the very edge; and by an ingenious arrangement of smaller portions of the rock neither the flame was to be distinguished, nor was the smoke, which was divided and made to find its passage through a variety of fissures, never in such a volume as to be supposed to be anything more than the vapours drawn up by the heat of the sun.

In this abode there were at least thirty people residing, and generally speaking, it might be called a convent, for it was tenanted by women. Their husbands, who brought over the cargoes, returning immediately in their boat to the opposite shore, for two reasons; one, that their boats could only land in particular seasons, and could never remain in the cove without risk of being dashed to pieces; and the other, that the absence of all men prevented suspicion; the whole of the interior smuggling being carried on by the other sex, who fearlessly showed themselves on every part of the island, and purchased their necessary supplies of provisions here and there, without exciting any misgivings as to the nature of their employment. A few isolated cottages, not far from the beetling brow of the cliff above, were their supposed abodes; but no one ever troubled them with a visit, and if they did, and found that they could gain no admittance, they imagined that the occupants had locked their doors for security, while they were busied with their labours in the field. Accustomed to climb up the tortuous path from the cave to the summit, the women would, on the darkest night, carry up their burdens and deposit them in the cottages above, until they had an opportunity of delivering their contraband articles into the hands of their agents; and this traffic had been carried on for many years, without the government or excise having the slightest suspicion by what means the smuggling was accomplished. As we before observed, the great articles in request, and which were now smuggled from France, were alamodes and lute-strings. The attention of government had been called to check the admission of these goods, but hitherto their attempts had not been attended with much success.

At the grey of the morning after the attempt to seize the smugglers had been defeated by the instrumentality of Snarleyyow, upon the top of the immense fragment of the rock which we have described as lying upon the sea-edge of the platform, was perched a fair, slight-made little girl, of about twelve years of age. She was simply clad in a short worsted petticoat and bodice of a dark colour; her head was bare, and her hair fluttered with the breeze; her small feet, notwithstanding the severity of the weather, were also naked, and her short petticoat discovered her legs half way up to the knee. She stood there, within a few inches of the precipice below, carelessly surveying the waves as they dashed over the rocks, for she was waiting until the light would enable her to see further on the horizon. By those who might have leaned over the ridge above, as well as by those who sailed below, she might have been taken, had she been seen to move, for some sea bird reposing after a flight, so small was her frame in juxtaposition with the wildness and majesty of nature which surrounded her on every side. Accustomed from infancy to her mode of life, and this unusual domicile, her eye quailed not, nor did her heart beat quicker, as she looked down into the abyss below, or turned her eyes up to the beetling mass of rock which appeared, each moment, ready to fall down and overwhelm her. She passed her hand across her temples to throw back the hair which the wind had blown over her eyes, and again scanned the distance as the sun's light increased, and the fog gradually cleared away.

"A sharp look out, Lilly, dear; you've the best eyes among us, and we must have a clue from whence last night's surprise proceeded."

"I can see nothing yet, mother; but the fog is driving back fast."

"It's but a cheerless night your poor father had, to pull twice across the channel, and find himself just where he was. God speed them, and may they be safe in port again by this time."

"I say so too, mother, and amen."

"D'ye see nothing, child?"

"Nothing, dear mother; but it clears up fast to the eastward, and the sun is bursting out of the bank, and I think I see something under the sun."

"Watch well, Lilly," replied the woman, who was throwing more wood on the fire.

"I see a vessel, mother. It is a sloop beating to the eastward."

"A coaster, child?"

"No, mother, I think not. No, it is no coaster—it is that king's vessel, I think, but the glare of the sun is too great. When he rises higher I shall make it out better."

"Which do you mean, the king's cutter on the station, the *Yungfrau?*"

"Yes, mother," replied Lilly, "it is. I'm sure it is the *Yungfrau.*"

"Then it is from her that the boats came last night. She must have received some information. There must be treachery somewhere; but we'll soon find that out."

It may appear singular that Lilly could speak so positively

as to a vessel at a great distance; but it must be remembered that she had been brought up to it, nearly all her life. It was her profession, and she had lived wholly with seamen and seamen's wives, which will account for her technical language being so correct. What Lilly said was true; it was the *Yungfrau*, which was beating up to regain her port, and having to stem a strong ebb-tide during the night, had not made very great progress.

"There are three other vessels in the offing," said Lilly, looking round, "a ship and two brigs, both going down channel:" and as she said this, the little thing dropped lightly from rock to rock till she stood by her mother, and commenced rubbing her hands before the now blazing fire.

"Nancy must go over to Portsmouth," observed the mother, "and find out all about this. I hardly know whom to suspect; but let Nancy alone, she'll ferret out the truth—she has many gossips at the Point. Whoever informed against the landing, must know of this cave."

But we must introduce the mother of Lilly to the reader. She was a tall, finely-featured woman, her arms beautifully moulded, and bare. She was rather inclined to be stout, but her figure was magnificent. She was dressed in the same costume as her daughter, with the exception of a net worsted shawl of many colours over her shoulders. Her appearance gave you the idea that she was never intended for the situation which she was now in; but of that hereafter. As the reader may have observed, her language was correct, as was that of the child, and proved that she had not only been educated herself, but had paid attention to the bringing up of Lilly. The most perfect confidence appeared to subsist between the mother and daughter: the former treated her child as her equal, and confided everything to her; and Lilly was far advanced beyond her age in knowledge and reflection; her countenance beamed with intelligence; perhaps a more beautiful and more promising creature never existed.

A third party now appeared from the cave; although not in canonicals, his dress indicated his profession of a priest. He approached the mother and daughter with, "Peace be with you, ladies."

"You forget, good father," replied the elder of the females, "my name is Alice—nothing more."

"I crave pardon for my forgetting who you were. I will be more mindful. Well, then, Alice—yet that familiar term sounds strangely, and my tongue will not accustom itself, even were I to remain here weeks, instead of but two days—I was about to say, that the affair of last night was most untoward. My presence is much wished for, and much required, at St Germains. It was unfortunate, because it proves that we have traitors among us somewhere; but of that, and of the whole affair, I will have cognizance in a few days."

"And should you discover the party?"

"His doom is sealed."

"You are right."

"In so important and so righteous a cause, we must not stop at aught necessary to secure our purpose. But, tell me, think you that your husband will soon be here again?"

"I should think not to-night, but to-morrow or the next he will be off; and if we can show the signals of surety he will land, if the weather will permit."

"'Tis indeed time that I were over. Something might now be done."

"I would so too, father; it is a tedious time that I have spent here."

"And most unfitting for you, were it not that you laboured in a great cause; but it must soon be decided, and then that fair lily shall be transplanted, like a wild flower from the rock, and be nurtured in a conservatory."

"Nay, for that, the time is hardly come. She is better here, as you see her, father, than in the chambers of a court. For her sake I would still remain; but for my husband's sake, and the perils he encounters, I wish that one way or the other it were decided."

"Had there been faith in that Italian, it had been so

before now," replied the priest, grinding his teeth, and turning away.

But the conversation was closed at the appearance of some women who came out of the cave. They were variously clothed, some coarsely, and others with greater pretensions to finery: they brought with them the implements for cooking, and appeared surprised at the fire being already lighted. Among them was one about twenty-five years of age, and although more faded than she ought to have been at that early age, still with pretensions to almost extreme beauty. She was more gaily dressed than the others, and had a careless, easy air about her, which suited to her handsome, slight figure. It was impossible to see her without being interested, and desiring to know who she was.

This person was the Nancy mentioned by Alice in her conversation with Lilly. Her original name had been Nancy Dawson, but she had married one of the smugglers, of the name of Corbett. Her original profession, previous to her marriage, we will not dwell upon; suffice it to say, that she was the most celebrated person of that class in Portsmouth, both for her talent and extreme beauty. Had she lived in the days of King Charles II., and had he seen her, she would have been more renowned than ever was Eleanor Gwynne; even as it was, she had been celebrated in a song, which has not been lost to posterity. After a few years of dissipated life, Nancy reformed, and became an honest woman, and an honest wife. By her marriage with the smuggler, she had become one of the fraternity, and had taken up her abode in the cave, which she was not sorry to do, as she had become too famous at Portsmouth to remain there as a married woman. Still she occasionally made her appearance, and to a certain degree kept up her old acquaintances, that she might discover what was going on—very necessary information for the smugglers. She would laugh, and joke, and have her repartee as usual, but in other points she was truly reformed. Her acquaintance was so general, and she was such a favourite, that she was of the greatest use to the band, and was always sent over to Portsmouth when her services were required. It was supposed there, for she had reported it, that she had retired to the Isle of Wight, and lived there with her husband, who was a pilot, and that she came over to Portsmouth occasionally, to inquire after her old friends, and upon business.

"Nancy Corbett, I must speak to you," said Alice. "Come aside: I wish you, Nancy, to go over immediately. Can you go up, do you think, without being perceived?"

"Yes, Mistress Alice, provided there is no one to see me."

"The case is so important, that we must run the risk."

"We've run cargoes of more value than that."

"But still you must use discretion, Nancy."

"That's a commodity that I've not been very well provided with through life; but I have my wits in its stead."

"Then you must use your wit, Nancy."

"It's like an old knife, well worn, but all the sharper."

Alice then entered into a detail of what she would find out, and gave her instructions to Nancy. The first point was, to ascertain whether it was the cutter which had received the information; the second, who the informer was.

Nancy, having received her orders, tied the strings of her bonnet, caught up a handful of the victuals which were at the fire, and bidding the others a laughing good-bye, with her mouth full, and one hand also occupied, descended the ladder, previously to mounting the cliff.

"Nancy," said Lilly, who stood by the ladder, "bring me some pens."

"Yes, dear; will you have them alive, or dead?"

"Nonsense, I mean some quills."

"So do I, Miss Lilly; but if you want them dead, I shall bring them in my pocket—if alive, I shall bring the goose under my arm."

"I only want the quills, Nancy," replied Lilly, laughing.

"And I think I shall want the feathers of them before

I'm at the top," replied Nancy, looking up at the majestic cliff above her. "Good-bye, Miss Lilly."

Nancy Corbett again filled her handsome mouth with bread, and commenced her ascent. In less than a quarter of an hour she had disappeared over the ridge.

Chapter XVII

In which there is a great deal of plotting, and a little execution.

WE will follow Nancy Corbett for the present. Nancy gained the summit of the cliff, and panting for breath, looked round to ascertain if there was any one in sight, but the coast was clear: she waited a minute to recover herself a little, and then set off at a brisk pace in the direction of the hamlet of Ryde, which then consisted of a few fishermen's huts. It was an hour and a-half before she gained this place, from whence she took a boat, and was safely landed at the Point. The fisherman who brought her over was an old acquaintance of Nancy's, and knew that he would have to remain to take her back, but he was well paid for his trouble, and it was a lucky day for him when Nancy required his services. The *Yungfrau* had rounded St Helen's, and was standing into Spithead, when Nancy landed, and the first door at which she knocked was at the lodgings of Moggy Salisbury, with whom she was well acquainted, and from whom she expected to be able to gain information. On inquiry, she found that Moggy had not come on shore from the cutter, which had sailed during the night very unexpectedly.

This information pleased Nancy, as Moggy would in all probability be able to give her important information, and she took up her quarters in Moggy's apartments, anxiously awaiting her arrival, for Nancy was not at all desirous to be seen. In due time the cutter was again anchored in the harbour, and the first order of Mr

Vanslyperken's was, that Moggy Salisbury should be sent on shore, which order was complied with, and she left the vessel, vowing vengeance upon the lieutenant and his dog. The informer also hastened into a boat, and pulled on shore on the Gosport side, with a very significant farewell look at Mr Vanslyperken. Moggy landed, and hastened, full of wrath, to her own lodgings, where she found Nancy Corbett waiting for her. At first she was too full of her own injuries, and the attempt to flog her dear darling Jemmy, to allow Nancy to put in a word. Nancy perceived this, and allowed her to run herself down like a clock; and then proposed that they should send for some purl and have a cosy chat, to which Moggy agreed, and as soon as they were fairly settled, and Moggy had again delivered herself of her grievances, Nancy put the requisite questions, and discovered what the reader is already acquainted with. She requested, and obtained a full description of the informer, and his person was too remarkable, for Nancy not to recognise immediately who it was.

"The villain!" cried she; "why, if there was any man in whom we thought we could trust, it was—him;" for Nancy had, in her indignation, nearly pronounced his name.

"Nancy," said Moggy, "you have to do with the smugglers, I know, for your husband is one of them, if report says true. Now, I've been thinking, that the cutter is no place for my Jemmy, and that with this peak-nosed villain, he will always be in trouble. Tell me, will they let him in, if he volunteers."

"I can't exactly say, Moggy; but this I can tell you, that you may be very useful to them in giving us information, which you may gain through your husband."

"Ay, and not only through my husband, but from everybody on board the cutter. I'm yours, Nancy—and here's my hand on it—you'll see what I can do. The wagabond, to attempt to flog my own dear, darling duck—my own Jemmy. Only tell me what you want to know, and if I don't ferret it out, my name's not Moggy. But hear me, Nancy; I join you now hand and heart, though I gain nothing by it; and when you choose to have him, I'll bring you my little duck of a husband, and he will be worth his weight in gold, though I say it that shouldn't say it."

"Thanky, Moggy; but you shall not work for nothing;" and Nancy laid a gold Jacobus on the table. "This for your present information. Be secret and cautious, and no gossiping, and you'll find that you shall have all you wish, and be no loser in the bargain. And now, good-night—I must be away. You shall see me soon, Moggy; and remember what I have told you."

Moggy was astonished at the sight of the gold Jacobus, which she took up and examined as Nancy departed. "Well," thought she, "but this smuggling must be a pretty consarn; and as sure as gold is gold, my Jemmy shall be a smuggler."

Nancy turned down the street, and passed rapidly on, until she was clear of the fortifications, in the direction of South Sea Beach. A few scattered cottages were at that time built upon the spot. It was quite dark as she passed the lines, and held her way over the shingle. A man was standing alone, whose figure she recognised. It was the very person that she wished to find. Nancy watched him for awhile, and observed him pull out a paper, tear it in two, and throw it down with gesticulations of anger and indignation. She then approached.

"What's o'clock?" said Nancy.

"Do you want the right time?" replied the man.

"To a minute," replied Nancy, who, finding that the password was given correctly, now stopped, and faced the other party. "Is that you, Cornbury?"

"Yes, Nancy," replied the man, who, was the same person who went on board of the cutter to give the information.

"I have been seeking you," replied Nancy. "There has been some information laid, and the boats were nearly surprised. Alice desires that you will find out what boats entered the cove, whom they belonged to, and, if possible, how they obtained the information."

"Boats nearly surprised!—you don't say so," replied Cornbury, with affected astonishment. "This must indeed be looked to. Have you no idea——"

"None," replied Nancy. "There was no vessel to be seen the next morning—the fog was too thick. Have you seen Wahop?"

"No; I thought he was on the Isle."

"He ought to have been, but has not come; I have been at the oak-tree for three nights running. It's very strange. Do you think that he can have played false?"

"I never much liked the man," replied Cornbury.

"Nor I either," replied Nancy; "but I must go now, for I must be back at the crags before daylight. Find out what you can, and let us know as soon as possible. I shall be over again as soon as the cargo is run; if you find out anything, you had better come to-morrow night."

"I will," replied Cornbury; and the parties separated.

"Traitor," muttered Nancy, when she was once more alone. "If he comes, it shall be to his death;" and Nancy stooped down, picked up the pieces of paper which Cornbury had torn up, and put them in the basket she carried on her arm.

It will be observed that Nancy had purposely thrown out hints against Wahop, to induce Cornbury to believe that he was not suspected. Her assertion that Wahop was not on the island was false. He had been three days at Ryde, according to the arrangement. The bait took. Cornbury perceiving that the suspicion was against Wahop, thought that he could not do better than to boldly make his appearance at the cave, which would remove any doubts as to his own fidelity.

Nancy hastened down to the Point, and returned that night to Ryde, from whence she walked over to the cave, and was there before daylight. She communicated to Alice the intelligence which she had received from Moggy

Salisbury, and the arrangements she had proposed to her, by which the motions of the cutter could be known.

"Is that woman to be trusted, think you, Nancy?" inquired Alice.

"Yes, I believe sincerely she may be. I have known her long; and she wishes her husband to join us."

"We must reflect upon it. She may be most useful. What is the character of the officer who commands the vessel?"

"A miser, and a coward. He is well known—neither honour nor conscience in him."

"The first is well, as we may act upon it, but the second renders him doubtful. You are tired, Nancy, and had better lie down a little."

Nancy Corbett delivered the pens to Lilly, and then took the advice of her superior. The day was remarkably fine, and the water smooth, so that the boats were expected that night. At dusk two small lights, at even distances, were suspended from the cliff, to point out to the boats that the coast was free, and that they might land. Alice, however, took the precaution to have a watch on the beach, in case of any second surprise being attempted; but of this there was little fear, as she knew from Nancy, that all the cutter's boats were on board when she entered the harbour. Lilly, who thought it a delight to be one moment sooner in her father's arms, had taken the watch on the beach, and there the little girl remained perched upon a rock, at the foot of which the waves now only sullenly washed, for the night was beautifully calm and clear. To a passer on the ocean she might have been mistaken for a mermaid who had left her watery bower to look upon the world above.

What were the thoughts of the little maiden as she remained there fixed as a statue? Did she revert to the period at which her infant memory could retrace silken hangings and marble halls, visions of splendour, dreamings of courtly state, or was she thinking of her father, as her quick ear caught the least swell of the increasing breeze? Was she, as her eye was fixed as if attempting to pierce the depths of the ocean, wondering at what might be its hidden secrets, or as they were turned towards the heavens, bespangled with ten thousand stars, was she meditating on the God who placed them there? Who can say?—but that that intellectual face bespoke the mind at work is certain, and from one so pure and lovely could emanate nothing but what was innocent and good.

But a distant sound falls upon her ear; she listens, and by its measured cadence knows that it is the rowers in a boat: nearer it comes and more distinct, and now her keen eye detects the black mass approaching in the gloom of night. She starts from the rock ready to fly up to the cave to give notice of an enemy, or, if their anticipated friends, to fly into the arms of her father. But her alarm is over, she perceives that it is the lugger, the boat dashes into the cove, and the first who lands strains her to his bosom.

"My dearest Lilly, is all well?"

"Yes, all is well, father; but you are well come."

"Run up, dearest, and let the women be ready to assist. We have that here which must soon be out of sight. Is the Father Innis here?"

"Since Thursday last."

"'Tis well, dear; you may go. Quick, my lads, and beach the cargo:—see to it, Ramsay; I must at once unto the cave." Having given these directions, the father of Lilly commenced his ascent over the rough and steep rocks which led up to the cavern, anxious to obtain what information could be imparted relative to the treachery which had led to their narrow escape two nights preceding.

He was met by Alice, who cordially embraced him; but he appeared anxious to release himself from her endearments, that he might at once enter upon matters to him of more serious importance. "Where is the Father Innis, my dear?" said he, disengaging himself from her arms.

"He sleeps, Robert, or, at least, he did just now, but probably he will rise now that you are come. But in the meantime, I have discovered who the traitor is."

"By all the saints, he shall not escape my vengeance!"

Alice then entered into the particulars related by Nancy Corbett, and already known to the reader. She had just concluded when Father Innis made his appearance from the cave.

"Welcome, thrice welcome, holy father."

"Welcome, too, my son. Say, do we start to-night?"

"Not till to-morrow night," replied the husband of Alice, who having ascertained that in all probability Cornbury would come that night, determined, at all risks, to get possession of him: "we could well be over before daylight, and with your precious person, I must not risk too much. You are anxiously expected."

"And I have important news," replied the priest; "but I will not detain you now; I perceive that your presence is wanted by your men."

During this colloquy the women had descended the ladder, and had been assisting the men to carry up the various packages of which the boat's cargo consisted, and they now awaited directions as to the stowing away.

"Ramsay," said the leader, "we do not return to-night; take the men, and contrive to lift the boat up on the rocks, so that she may not be injured."

An hour elapsed before this was effected, and then the leader, as well as the rest of the smugglers, retired to the cave to refresh themselves with sleep after their night of fatigue. As usual, one woman kept watch, and that woman was Nancy Corbett. The ladder had been hauled up, and she was walking up and down, with her arms under a shawl, to a sort of stamping trot, for the weather was frosty, when she heard a low whistle at the west side of the flat.

"Oh, ho! have I lured you, you traitorous villain?" muttered Nancy, "you come in good time:" and Nancy walked to the spot where the ladder was usually lowered down, and looked over. Although the moon had risen, it was too dark on that side of the platform to distinguish more than that there was a human form, who repeated the whistle.

"What's o'clock?" said Nancy, in a low tone.

"Do you want the right time to a minute?" replied a voice, which was recognised as Cornbury's. Nancy lowered down the ladder, and Cornbury ascended the platform.

"I am glad you are come, Cornbury. Have you heard anything of Wahop?"

"No one has seen or heard of him," replied the man, "but I have found out what boats they were. Did the lugger come over to-night?"

"Yes," replied Nancy, "but I must go in and let Mistress Alice know that you are here."

Nancy's abrupt departure was to prevent Cornbury from asking if the boat had remained, or returned to the French coast; for she thought it not impossible that the unusual circumstance of the boat remaining, might induce him to suppose that his treachery had been discovered, and to make his immediate escape, which he, of course, could have done, and given full information of the cave and the parties who frequented it.

Nancy soon re-appeared, and familiarly taking the arm of Cornbury, led him to the eastern side of the platform, asking him many questions. As soon as he was there, the leader of the gang, followed by half a dozen of his men, rushed out and secured him. Cornbury now felt assured that all was discovered, and that his life was forfeited. "Bind him fast," said the leader, "and keep watch over him;—his case shall soon be disposed of. Nancy, you will call me at daylight."

When Cornbury had been secured, the men returned into the cave, leaving one with a loaded pistol to guard him. Nancy still remained on the watch.

"Nancy Corbett," said Cornbury, "why am I treated thus?"

"Why?" replied Nancy, with scorn; "ask yourself why. Do you think that I did not know when I sought you at the beach that you had sailed in the cutter, had brought the boats here, and that if it had not been for the lieutenant taking his dog in the boat, and its barking, you would have delivered us all into the hands of the Philistines?—wretched traitor."

"D—n!" muttered Cornbury; "then it is to you, you devil, that I am indebted for being entrapped this way."

"Yes, to me," replied Nancy, with scorn. "And, depend upon it, you will have your deserts before the sun is one hour in the heavens."

"Mistress Nancy, I must beg you to walk your watch like a lady, and not to be corresponding with my prisoner anyhow, whether you talk raison or traison, as may happen to suit your convanience," observed the man who was guard over Cornbury.

"Be aisy, my jewel," replied Nancy, mimicking the Irishman, "and I'll be as silent as a magpie, anyhow. And, Mr Fitzpatrick, you'll just be plased to keep your two eyes upon your prisoner, and not be staring at me, following me up and down, as you do, with those twinklers of yours."

"A cat may look at a king, Mistress Nancy, and no harm done either."

"You forget, Mr Fitzpatrick," replied Nancy, "that I am now a modest woman."

"More's the pity, Mrs Nancy, I wish you'd forget it too, and I dying of love for you."

Nancy walked away to the end of the platform to avoid further conversation. The day was now dawning, and as, by degrees, the light was thrown upon the face of Cornbury, it was strange to witness how his agitation and his fear had changed all the ruby carbuncles on his face to a deadly white. He called to Nancy Corbett in a humble tone once or twice as she passed by in her walk, but received no reply further than a look of scorn. As soon as it was broad daylight, Nancy went into the cave to call up the leader.

In a few minutes he appeared, with the rest of the smugglers.

"Philip Cornbury," said he, with a stern and unrelenting countenance, "you would have betrayed us for the sake of money."

"It is false," replied Cornbury.

"False, is it?—you shall have a fair trial. Nancy Corbett, give your evidence before us all."

Nancy recapitulated all that had passed.

"I say again, that it is false," replied Cornbury. "Where is the woman whom she states to have told her this? This is nothing more than assertion, and I say again, it is false. Am I to be condemned without proofs? Is my life to be sacrificed to the animosity of this woman, who wishes to get rid of me, because——"

"Because what?" interrupted Nancy.

"Because I was too well acquainted with you before your marriage, and can tell too much."

"Now, curses on you, for a liar as well as a traitor!" exclaimed Nancy. "What I was before I was married is well known; but it is well known, also, that I pleased my fancy, and could always choose. I must, indeed, have had a sorry taste to be intimate with a blotched wretch like you. Sir," continued Nancy, turning to the leader, "it is false; and whatever may be said against me on other points, Nancy Dawson, or Nancy Corbett, was never yet so vile as to assert a lie. I put it to you, sir, and to all of you, is not my word sufficient in this case?"

The smugglers nodded their heads in assent.

"And, now that is admitted, I will prove his villany and falsehood. Philip Cornbury, do you know this paper?" cried Nancy, taking out of her bosom the agreement signed by Vanslyperken, which she had picked up on the night when Cornbury had torn it up and thrown it away. "Do you know this paper, I ask you? Read it, sir," continued Nancy, handing it over to the leader of the smugglers.

The paper was read, and the inflexible countenance of the leader turned towards Cornbury,—who saw his doom.

" Go in, Nancy Corbett, and let no women appear till all is over."

" Liar ! " said Nancy, spitting on the ground as she passed by Cornbury.

" Bind his eyes, and lead him to the western edge," said the leader.

" Philip Cornbury, you have but a few minutes to live. In mercy, you may see the holy father, if you wish it."

" I'm no d——d papist," replied Cornbury, in a sulky tone.

" Lead him on then."

Cornbury was led to the western edge of the flat, where the cliff was most high and precipitous, and then made to kneel down.

" Fitzpatrick," said the leader, pointing to the condemned.

Fitzpatrick walked up to the kneeling man with his loaded pistol, and then the others, who had led Cornbury to the edge of the cliff, retired.

Fitzpatrick cocked the lock.

" Would you like to say, ' God have mercy on my treacherous sinful sowl,' or anything short and sweet like that ? " said Fitzpatrick; " if so, I'll wait a couple of seconds more for your convanience, Philip Cornbury."

Cornbury made no reply. Fitzpatrick put the pistol to his ear, the ball whizzed through his brain, the body half raised itself from its knees with a strong muscular action, and then toppled over and disappeared down the side of the precipice.

" It's to be hoped that the next time you lave this world, Master Cornbury, it will be in a purliter sort of manner. A civil question demands a civil answer anyhow," said Fitzpatrick, coolly rejoining the other men.

Chapter XVIII

The whole of which has been fudged out of the History of England, and will therefore be quite new to the majority of our readers.

WERE we in want of materials for this eventful history, we have now a good opportunity for spinning out our volumes; but, so far from this being the case, we hardly know how to find space for what it is now absolutely necessary that the reader should be acquainted with. Our friends may probably recollect, when we remind them of the fact, that there was a certain king, James II., who sat upon our throne, and who was a very good Catholic—that he married his daughter, Mary, to one William of Orange, who, in return for James's kindness in giving him his daughter, took away from him his kingdom, on the plea, that if he was a bad son-in-law, at all events, he was a sound Protestant. They may also recollect, that the exiled king was received most hospitably by the grand monarque, Louis XIV., who gave him palaces, money, and all that he required, and, moreover, gave him a fine army and fleet to go to Ireland and recover his kingdom, bidding him farewell with this equivocal sentence, "That the best thing he, Louis, could wish to him was, never to see his face again." They may further recollect, that King James and King William met at the battle of the Boyne, in which the former was defeated, and then went back to St Germains and spent the rest of his life in acts of devotion and plotting against the life of King William. Now, among other plots real and pretended, there was one laid in 1695, to assassinate King William on his way to Richmond; this plot was revealed, many of the conspirators were tried and executed, but the person who was at the head of it, a Scotchman, of the name of Sir George Barclay, escaped. In the year 1696, a bill was passed, by which Sir George Barclay and nine others who had escaped from justice, were attainted of high treason, if they did not choose to surrender themselves on or before the 25th day of March ensuing. Strange to say, these parties did not think it advisable to surrender themselves; perhaps it was because they knew that they were certain to be hung; but it is impossible to account for the actions of men: we can only lay the facts before our readers.

Sir George Barclay was by birth a Scotchman, of high family, and well connected. He had been an officer in the army of King James, to whom he was strongly attached. Moreover, he was a very bigoted Catholic. Whether he ever received a commission from King James, authorising him to assassinate King William, has never been proved; but, as King James is well known to have been admitted into the order of the Jesuits, it is not at all unlikely. Certain it is, that the baronet went over to St Germains, landed again in England, and would have made the attempt, had not the plot been discovered through some of the inferior accomplices; and it is equally sure that he escaped, although many others were hung—and few people knew what had become of him. The fact was, that when Barclay had fled to the sea-side, he was assisted over the water by a band of smugglers, who first concealed him in the cave we have described, which was their retreat. This led to a communication and arrangement with them. Sir George Barclay, who, although foiled in his attempt at assassination, never abandoned the cause, immediately perceived what advantages might be derived in keeping up a communication by means of these outlaws. For some time the smugglers were employed in carrying secret despatches to the friends of James in England and Scotland; and, as the importance of the correspondence increased, and it became necessary to have personal interviews instead of written communications, Sir George frequently passed over to the cave as a rendezvous, at which he might meet the adherents of the exiled king. In the course of time he saw the prudence of having the entire control of the band, and found little difficulty in being appointed their leader. From the means he obtained from St

Germains, the smuggling was now carried on to a great and very profitable extent; and by the regulations which he enacted, the chance of discovery was diminished. Only one point more was requisite for safety and secrecy, which was, a person to whom he could confide the charge of the cave. Lady Barclay, who was equally warm in the cause, offered her services, and they were accepted; and at the latter end of the year 1696, about one year after the plot had failed, Lady Barclay, with her only child, took up her abode in this isolated domicile; Sir George then first making the arrangement that the men should always remain on the other side of the water, which would be an additional cause of security. For upwards of four years, Lady Barclay had remained an inmate, attending to the instruction of her little Lilly, and carrying on all the correspondence, and making all the necessary arrangements with vigour and address, satisfied with serving the good cause, and proving her devoted allegiance to her sovereign. Unfortunate and unwise as were the Stuart family, there must have been some charm about them, for they had instances of attachment and fidelity shown to them, of which no other line of kings could boast.

Shortly after the tragical event recorded in the last chapter, the Jesuit came out of the cave and went up to Sir George, who coolly observed, "We have just been sending a traitor to his account, good father."

"So may they all perish," replied the priest. "We start this evening?"

"Certainly. What news have you for St Germains?"

"Much that is important. Discontent prevails throughout the country. The affair of Bishop Watson hath brought much odium on the usurper. He himself writhes under the tyrannical commands of the Commons, and is at issue with them."

"And in Scotland, father?"

"All is there ripe and ready—and an army once landed, would be joined by thousands. The injustice of the usurper in wishing to sacrifice the Scotch Settlement, has worked deep upon the minds of those who advanced their money upon that speculation—in the total, a larger sum than ever yet was raised in Scotland. Our emissaries have fanned the flame up to the highest pitch."

"To my thoughts, good father, there needed not further discontent. Have we not our king dethroned, and our holy religion persecuted?"

"True, my son—true; but still we must lose no means by which we may increase the number of our adherents. Some are swayed by one feeling, and some by another. We have contrived to throw no small odium upon the usurper and betrayer of his wife's father, by exposing and magnifying, indeed, the sums of money which he has lavished upon his courtesan, Mistress Villiers, now, by his heretic and unsanctified breath, raised into the peerage by the title of Countess of Orkney. All these items added together, form a vast sum of discontent; and could we persuade his Catholic majesty to rouse himself to assert once more his rights by force of arms, I should not fear for the result."

"Had I not been betrayed," observed Sir George, musing, "before this the king would have had his own again."

"And thrice blessed would have been the arm that had laid the usurper low," rejoined the Jesuit; "but more of this hereafter. Your lady hath had much converse with me. She thinks that the character of the man who commands that cutter, is such as to warrant his services for gold—and wishes to essay him."

"The woman Corbett is of that opinion, and she is subtle. At all events, it can be tried; for he would be of much utility, and there would be no suspicion. The whole had better be left to her arrangement. We may employ, and pay, yet not trust him."

"That is exactly what Lady Alice had proposed," replied the Jesuit. Here Lilly came out to tell her father that the morning meal was ready, and they all returned to the cave.

That evening the boat was launched, and the Jesuit went over with Sir George, and landed at Cherbourg, from whence they both proceeded with all expedition to the court of King James.

We have entered into this short detail, that the reader may just know the why and the wherefore these parties in the cave were introduced, and now we shall continue our most faithful and veracious history.

Chapter XIX

In which Smallbones is sent to look after a pot of black paint.

WE must now return to the cutter, which still remains at anchor off the Point in Portsmouth harbour. It is a dark, murky, blowing day, with gusts of rain and thick fog. Mr Vanslyperken is more than usually displeased, for, as he had to wait for the new boat which he had demanded, he thought this a good opportunity of enlivening the bends of the *Yungfrau* with a little black paint—not before it was required, most certainly, for she was as rusty in appearance as if she had been built of old iron. But paint fetched money, and as Mr Vanslyperken always sold his, it was like parting with so much of his own property, when he ordered up the paint-pots and brushes. Now the operation of beautifying the *Yungfrau* had been commenced the day before, and the unexpected change in the weather during the night, had washed off the greater portion of the paint, and there was not only all the trouble, but all the expense, to be incurred again. No wonder that Mr Vanslyperken was in a bad humour—not only in a bad humour, but in the very worst of humours. He had made up his mind to go on shore to see his mother, and was pacing the quarter-deck in his great-coat, with his umbrella under his arm, all ready to be unfurled as soon as he was on shore. He was just about to order his boat to be manned: Mr Vanslyperken looked up at the weather—the fog was still thick, and the rain fell. You could not even make out the houses on the point. The wind had gone down considerably. Mr Vanslyperken looked over the gunnel—the damage was even greater than he thought. He looked over the stern, there was the stage still hanging where the painters had been standing or sitting, and, what was too bad, there was a pot of paint, with the brush in it, half full of rain water, which some negligent person had left there. Mr Vanslyperken turned forward to call somebody to take the paint below, but the decks were empty, and it was growing dark. A sudden thought, instigated no doubt by the devil, filled the brain of Mr Vanslyperken. It was a glorious, golden opportunity, not to be lost. He walked forward, and went down into his cabin again, where he found Smallbones helping himself to biscuit, for the lad was hungry, as well he might be; but on this occasion Mr Vanslyperken took no notice.

"Smallbones," said he, "one of the men has left his paint-pot on the stage, under the stern, go and bring it in immediately."

"Yes, sir," replied Smallbones, surprised at the unusually quiet style of his master's address to him.

Smallbones ran up the ladder, went aft, and slid down by the rope which held the plank used as a stage by the painters. Mr Vanslyperken seized his carving-knife, and following softly on deck, went aft. He took a hurried look forward—there was no one on deck. For a moment, he hesitated at the crime; he observed the starboard rope shake, for Smallbones was just about to shin up again. The devil prevailed. Mr Vanslyperken sawed through the rope, heard the splash of the lad in the water, and, frightened at his own guilt, ran down below, and gained his cabin. There he seated himself, trembling like an aspen leaf. It was the first time that he had been a *murderer*. He was pale as ashes. He felt sick, and he staggered to his cupboard, poured out a tumbler of scheedam, and drank it off at a draught. This recovered him, and he again felt brave. He returned on deck, and ordered his boat to be manned, which was presently done. Mr Vanslyperken would have given the world to have gone aft, and to have looked over the stern, but he dared not; so, pushing the men into the boat, he slipped in, and was pulled on shore. Without giving any directions to the men he stepped out, and felt a relief when he found himself on terra firma. He walked away as fast as he could—he felt that he could not walk fast enough—he was anxious to arrive at his mother's. The rain fell fast, but he thought not of his umbrella, it remained under his arm, and Mr Vanslyperken, as if he were chased by a fiend, pushed on through the fog and rain; he wanted to meet a congenial soul, one who would encourage, console him, ridicule his fears, and applaud the deed which he would just then have given the world to have recalled.

Where could he seek one more fitted to the purpose than his mother? The door of the house where she lodged was common to many, and therefore opened with a latch. He went in, and up-stairs, tried the door of his mother's room, and found it fastened within. He knocked, heard the grumbling of the old woman at her being obliged to rise from her chair: she opened the door, and Vanslyperken, as soon as he was in, slammed it to, and exhausted with his emotions, fell back in a chair.

"Hey day! and what's the matter now?" cried the old woman, in Dutch; "one would think that you had been waylaid, robbed, and almost murdered."

"Murdered!" stammered Vanslyperken; "yes—it was murder."

"What was murder, my child?" replied the old woman, reseating herself.

"Did I say murder, mother?" said Vanslyperken, wiping the blended rain and perspiration from his brow with a cotton handkerchief.

"Yes, you did, Cornelius Vanslyperken; not that I believe a craven like you would ever attempt such a thing."

"But I have, mother. I have done the deed," replied Vanslyperken.

"You have!" cried his mother; "then at last you have done something, and I shall respect you. Come, come, child, cheer up, and tell me all about it. There is a slight twinge the first time—but the second is nothing. Did you get gold? Hey, my son, plenty of gold?"

"Gold! no, no—I got nothing—indeed I lost by it—lost a pot full of black paint—but never mind that. He's gone," replied Vanslyperken, recovering himself fast.

"Who is gone?"

"The lad, Smallbones."

"Pish," replied the old woman, rocking her chair. "Ay, well, never mind—it was for revenge, then—that's sweet—very sweet. Now, Cornelius, tell me all about it."

Vanslyperken, encouraged by the sympathy, if we may use the term, shown by his mother, narrated what he had done.

"Well, well, child, 'tis a beginning," replied the old woman, "and I'll not call you craven again."

"I must go back," said Vanslyperken, starting up from his chair.

"Go, child, it is late—and dream it over. Vengeance is sweet, even in sleep. I have had mine—and for years have I dwelt on it—and shall for years to come. I shall not die yet—no, no."

Vanslyperken quitted the house; the weather had cleared up, the breeze was fresh and piercing, and the stars twinkled every now and then, as the wild scud which flew across the heavens admitted them to view. Vanslyperken walked fast—he started at the least sound—he hurried by everyone whom he met, as if fearful to be recognised—he felt relieved when he had gained the streets of Portsmouth, and he at last arrived at the Point; but there was no cutter's boat, for he had given no orders. He was therefore obliged to hire one to go on board. The old man whom he engaged shoved into the stream; the tide was running in rapidly.

"A cold night, sir," observed the man.

"Yes," replied Vanslyperken, mechanically.

"And a strong tide, with the wind to back it. He'd have but a poor chance, who fell overboard such a night as this. The strongest swimmer, without help, would be soon in eternity."

Vanslyperken shuddered. Where was Smallbones at this moment? and then, the mention of eternity!

"Silence, man, silence," said Vanslyperken.

"Hope no offence, Mr Lieutenant," replied the man, who knew who his fare was.

The boat pulled alongside of the *Yungfrau*, and Vanslyperken paid his unusual fare, and stepped on the deck. He went down below, and had the precaution to summon Smallbones to bring lights aft. The word was passed along the lower deck, and Vanslyperken sat down in the dark, awaiting the report that Smallbones could not be found.

Snarleyyow went up to his master, and rubbed his cold nose against his hand, and then, for the first time, it occurred to Vanslyperken, that in his hurry to leave the vessel, he had left the dog to the mercy of his enemies. During the time that Vanslyperken waited for the report of the lights, he passed over in his mind the untoward events which had taken place—the loss of the widow's good-will, the loss of Corporal Van Spitter, who was adrift in the Zuyder Zee, the loss of five thousand pounds through the dog, and, strange to say, what vexed him more, the loss of the dog's eye; and when he thought of all these things his heart was elated, and he rejoiced in the death of Smallbones, and no longer felt any compunction. But a light is coming aft, and Vanslyperken is waiting the anticipated report. It is a solitary purser's dip, as they are termed at sea, emitting but feeble rays, and Vanslyperken's eyes are directed to the door of the cabin to see who carries it. To his horror, his dismay, it is brought in by the drowned Smallbones, who, with a cadaverous, and as he supposes, unearthly face and vacant look, drawls out, "It's a-blowed out twice, sir, with the wind."

Vanslyperken started up, with his eyes glaring and fixed. There could be no mistake. It was the apparition of the murdered lad, and he fell back in a state of unconsciousness.

"You've a-got it this time," said Smallbones, chuckling as he bent over the body of the lieutenant with his purser's dip, and perceived that he was in a state of insensibility.

Had Mr Vanslyperken had the courage to look over the stern of the cutter when he re-ascended on the deck, he would have discovered Smallbones hanging on by the rudder chains; for had the fog not been so thick, Mr Vanslyperken would have perceived that at the time that he cut Smallbones adrift it was slack water, and the cutter was lying across the harbour. Smallbones was not, therefore, carried away by the tide, but being a very fair swimmer, had gained the rudder chains without difficulty; but at the time that Smallbones was climbing up again by the rope, he had perceived the blade of the carving-knife working at the rope, and was assured that Vanslyperken was attempting his life. When he gained the rudder chains, he held on. At first he thought of calling for assistance; but hearing Vanslyperken order his boat to be manned, the lad then resolved to wait a little longer, and allow his master to think that he was drowned. The result was as Smallbones intended. As soon as the lad saw the boat was out of hearing he called out most lustily, and was heard by those on board, and rescued from his cold immersion. He answered no questions which were put to him till he had changed his clothing and recovered himself, and then with great prudence summoned a council, composed of Short, Coble, and Jemmy Ducks, to whom he narrated what had taken place. A long consultation succeeded, and at last it was agreed that Smallbones should make his appearance as he did, and future arrangements to be taken according to circumstances.

As soon as Smallbones had ascertained the situation of

his master, he went forward and reported it to Dick Short, who with Coble came aft in the cabin. Short looked at Vanslyperken.

"Conscience," said Short.

"And a d———d bad un, too," replied Coble, hitching up his trousers. "What's to be done, Short?"

"Nothing," replied Short.

"Just my idea," replied Coble; "let him come to if he pleases, or die and be d———d. Who cares?"

"Nobody," replied Short.

"My eyes, but he must have been frightened," said Smallbones; "for he has left the key in the cupboard. I'll see what's in it for once and away."

Snarleyyow, when Smallbones opened the cupboard, appeared to have an intuitive idea that he was trespassing, so he walked out growling from under the table; Short saluted him with a kick in the ribs, which tossed him under the feet of Coble, who gave him a second with his fisherman's boots, and the dog howled, and ran out of the cabin. O Mr Vanslyperken! see what your favourite was brought to, because you did not come to.

At this time Smallbones had his nose in the stone jar of scheedam—the olfactory examination was favourable, so he put his mouth to it—the labial essay still more so, so he took down a wine glass, and, without any ceremony, filled a bumper, and handed it to Coble.

"We'll drink to his recovery," said Obadiah, tossing off the contents.

"Yes," replied Short, who waited till the glass was refilled, and did the same.

"Here's bad luck to him in his own good stuff," said Smallbones, tossing off a third glass, and, filling it again, he handed it to Coble.

"Here's reformation to him," said Coble, draining the glass again.

"Yes," replied Short, taking the replenished vessel.

"Here's d———n to him and his dog for ever and ever, Amen," cried Smallbones, tippling off his second allowance.

"Who's there?" said Vanslyperken in a faint voice, opening his eyes with a vacant look.

Smallbones replaced the bottle in the cupboard, and replied, "It's only Smallbones, sir, and the mates, come to help you."

"Smallbones!" said Vanslyperken, still wandering. "Smallbones is drowned—and the whole pot of black paint."

"Conscience," said Short.

"Carving-knife," rejoined Coble.

"Carving-knife!" said Vanslyperken, raising himself up; "I never said a word about a carving-knife, did I? Who is it that I see? Short—and Coble—help me up. I've had a sad fall. Where's Smallbones? Is he alive—really alive?"

"I believe as how I bees," replied Smallbones.

Mr Vanslyperken had now recovered his perfect senses. He had been raised on a chair, and was anxious to be rid of intruders, so he told Short and Coble that he would now do very well, and they might go; upon which, without saying a word, they both quitted the cabin.

Mr Vanslyperken collected himself—he wished to know how Smallbones had been saved, but still dared not broach the subject, as it would be admitting his own guilt.

"What has happened, Smallbones?" said Vanslyperken. "I still feel very faint."

"Take a glass of this," replied Smallbones, opening the cupboard, and bringing out the scheedam. He poured out a glass, which Vanslyperken drank, and then observed, "How did you know what was in that cupboard, sirrah?"

"Because you called for it when you were in your fits," replied Smallbones.

"Called for scheedam?"

"Yes, sir, and said you had lost the carving-knife."

"Did I?" replied Vanslyperken, afraid that he had committed himself. "I have been ill, very ill," continued he, putting his hand up to his forehead. "By-the-bye,

Smallbones, did you bring in that pot of paint?" said Vanslyperken, adroitly.

"No, sir, I didn't, because I tumbled overboard, pot and all," replied Smallbones.

"Tumbled overboard! why, I did not leave the ship till afterwards, and I heard nothing about it."

"No, sir, how could you?" replied Smallbones, who was all prepared for this explanation, "when the tide swept me past the saluting battery in a moment."

"Past the saluting battery?" exclaimed Vanslyperken, "why, how were you saved?"

"Because, thanks to somebody, I be too light to sink. I went out to the Nab buoy, and a mile ayond it."

"The Nab buoy!" exclaimed Vanslyperken.

"Yes, and ayond it, afore the tide turned, and then I were swept back again, and came into harbour again, just half-an-hour afore you come aboard."

Mr Vanslyperken looked aghast; the lad must have had a charmed life. Nine miles at least out to sea, and nine miles back again.

"It's as true as I stand here, sir," continued Smallbones; "I never were so cold in all my life, a-floating about like a bit of duck-weed with the tide, this way and that way."

"As true as you stand here!" repeated Vanslyperken; "but do you stand here?" and he made a desperate grasp at the lad's arm to ascertain whether he held substance or shadow.

"Can I do anything more, sir?" continued Smallbones; "for I should like to turn in—I'm as cold as ice, even now."

"You may go," replied Vanslyperken, whose mind was again becoming confused at what had passed. For some time, the lieutenant sat in his chair, trying to recollect and reason; but it was in vain—the shocks of the day had been too great. He threw himself, dressed as he was, upon his bed—never perceived the absence of his favourite—the candle was allowed to burn itself to the socket, and Vanslyperken fell off into a trance-like sleep.

Chapter XX

In which Mr Vanslyperken proves false to the Widow Vandersloosh, and many strange things take place.

Mr Vanslyperken was awakened, the next morning, by the yelping of his dog, who, having been shut out of the cabin, had ventured up the ladder in the morning when the men were washing the deck, and had a bucket shied at him by Jemmy Ducks, with such excellent precision, that it knocked him over, and nearly broke his hind leg, which he now carried high up in the air as he howled upon the other three at the cabin door. Mr Vanslyperken rose, and tried to recollect what had passed; but it was more than a minute before he could recall the circumstances of the day before. He then tried to call to mind how he had gone to bed, and by what means Snarleyyow was left outside, but he could make nothing of it. He opened the cabin door, and let in the dog, whose lame leg instantly excited his indignation, and he then rang his bell for Smallbones, who soon made his appearance.

" How came the dog out of the cabin, sir ? "

" I'm sure I don't know, sir ; I never put him out."

" Who is it that has hurt him ? "

" I'm sure I don't know, sir ; I never touched him."

Vanslyperken was about to vent his anger, when Smallbones said, "If you please, I don't know what's a-going on. Why here, sir, the men washing the decks have found your carving-knife abaft, by the traffrail. Somebody must have taken it there, that's sartain."

Vanslyperken turned pale.

" Who could have taken it ? "

" That's what I said, sir. Who dare come in the cabin to take the knife ? and what could they have taken it for, but unless it was to cut summut ? " And Smallbones looked his master full in the face. And the lieutenant quailed before his boy. He could not meet his gaze, but turned away.

"Very odd," continued Smallbones, perceiving the advantage he had gained.

"Leave the cabin, sir," cried Vanslyperken.

"Sha'n't I make no inquiries how this ere knife came there, sir?" replied Smallbones.

"No, sir, mind your own business. I've a great mind to flog you for its being found there—all your carelessness."

"That would be a pretty go," murmured Smallbones, as he shut the cabin door.

The feeling of vengeance against Smallbones, was now redoubled in the breast of his master; and the only regret he felt at the transactions of the day before was, that the boy had not been drowned.

"I'll have him yet," muttered the lieutenant; but he forgot that he was shaving himself, and the involuntary movements of his lips caused him to cut a large gash on his right cheek, from which the blood trickled fast.

"Curses on the "—(razor he was going to say, but he changed it to) " —scoundrel!"

A slice with a razor is certainly a very annoying thing. After a certain time, Mr Vanslyperken finished his toilet, called for his breakfast, went on deck, and as the day was fine, ordered the paint to be renewed, and then went on shore to ascertain if there were any commands for him at the admiral's office.

As he walked up the street in a brown study, he at last observed that a very pretty woman dogged him, sometimes walking a-head and looking back, at others dropping astern, and then again ranging up alongside. He looked her in the face, and she smiled sweetly, and then turned her head coquettishly, and then looked again with eyes full of meaning. Now, although Mr Vanslyperken had always avoided amours on account of the expense entailed upon them, yet he was, like a dry chip, very inflammable, and the extreme beauty of the party made him feel unusual emotions. Her perseverance too—and her whole appearance so very respectable—so superior to the class of people who generally accosted him. He thought of the widow and her money-bags, and thought, also, how infinitely more desirable the widow would be, if she possessed but the beauty of the present party.

"I do believe I've lost my way," exclaimed the young person. "Pray, sir, can you tell me the way to Castle Street, for I'm almost a stranger? And" (added she, laughing) "I really don't know my way back to my own house."

Castle Street was, at that time, one of the best streets in Portsmouth, as Mr Vanslyperken well knew. This assured him of her respectability. He very gallantly offered his arm which, after a little demur, was accepted, and Mr Vanslyperken conveyed her to her house. Of course she could do no less than ask him to walk up, and Mr Vanslyperken, who had never been in anything approaching to good society, was in astonishment at the furniture. All appeared to denote wealth. He was soon in an interesting conversation, and by degrees found out that the lady was a young widow of the name of Malcolm, whose husband had been factor to the new company, called the East India Company; that she had come down to Portsmouth expecting him home, and that she had learnt that he had died on shore a few days before his intended embarkation for England. Since which, as she liked the place and the society, she had thoughts of remaining here.

"They say that gold in India is to be had for nothing."

"It must be very plentiful," replied the widow, "if I am to judge by the quantity my poor husband sent me home, and he was not out more than three years. He left me a week after our marriage."

Here the lovely widow put her handkerchief up to her eyes, and Mr Vanslyperken attempted to console her.

"It's so very unpleasant to be left without any one to advise you, and exposed to be cheated so dreadfully."

What can a poor lone woman do? Did you ever see me before, sir?"

"I never did," replied our lieutenant. "May I ask the same question, for I thought you appeared to know me?"

"O yes! I've seen you very often, and wished to know who you were, but I was ashamed to ask. One cannot be too particular in my situation."

Mr Vanslyperken was much pleased, but he had remained some time, and he thought it right to depart, so he rose and made his adieus.

"I hope I shall see you again," cried the widow, earnestly. "You will call again, sir, won't you?"

"Most certainly, and with the greatest pleasure," replied Vanslyperken.

The lady extended her gloved hand, and as it was closed in that of Vanslyperken, he thought he felt a slight, a very slight pressure, which made his heart leap. And then, as he shut the door, she gave him such a look—O those eyes!—they pierced right through the heart of Vanslyperken.

The reader may not, perhaps, be aware who this gay widow might be. It was Nancy Corbett, who had, by the advice of Lady Alice, taken this step to entrap Mr Vanslyperken. Nancy had obtained from Moggy all the particulars of the lieutenant's wooing of the widow Vandersloosh, and his character as a miser and a coward. Had he been a miser only, she would have attacked by gold alone, but being a coward, it was decided that he should have some further stimulus to betray his country, and enlist himself among the partisans of King James.

Beauty, joined with wealth, the chance of possessing both, with the attractive arts of Nancy, were considered necessary to sway him. Indeed they were so far right, that had any one made the bold proposal to Vanslyperken of joining the other party, and offered him at the same time ample remuneration, he would have been too suspicious or too timorous to run the risk. It was necessary to win him over by means which appeared accidental rather than otherwise. The difficulty of correspondence was very great; and as the cutter constantly was despatched to the Hague, and the French had agents there, not only letters, but even messengers, might be sent over without risk and without suspicion; for open boats being then the only means of communication, during the wintry part of the year, the correspondence was very precarious, and at long intervals.

Thus was Nancy Corbett changed into a buxom widow, all for the good cause, and well did she perform her part; for there was no lack of money when such services were required. Vanslyperken left the house quite enchanted. "This will do," thought he, "and if I succeed, Frau Vandersloosh may go to the devil." He returned on board, unlocked his cabin, where Snarleyyow had been secured from the machinations of Smallbones and other malcontents, and sat down to enjoy the castle-building which he had commenced after he left the house. He patted his dog, and apostrophised it. "Yes, my poor brute," said Vanslyperken, "your master will get a rich widow, without it being necessary that you should be laid dead at her porch. D—n Frau Vandersloosh."

The widow was more enchanting when Vanslyperken called on the ensuing day, than she was on the first. Her advances to the lieutenant were no longer doubtful to him. She entered freely into the state of her affairs, asked his advice upon money matters, and fully proved to his satisfaction that, independent of her beauty, she would be a much greater catch than Frau Vandersloosh. She spoke about her family; said that she expected her brother over, but that he must come *incog.*, as he was attached to the court of the exiled king, lamented the difficulty of receiving letters from him, and openly expressed her adherence to the Stuart family. Vanslyperken appeared to make very little objection to her political creed; in fact, he was so fascinated that he fell blindly into the snare; he accepted an invitation to dine with her on that very day, and went on board to dress himself as fine for her as he had for the widow Vandersloosh. The lovely widow admired his uniform, and gave him many gentle hints upon which he might speak: but this did not take place until a *tête-à-tête* after dinner, when he was sitting on a sofa with her (not on such a fubsy sofa as that of Frau Vandersloosh, but one worked in tapestry); much in the same position as we once introduced him in to the reader, to wit, with the lady's hand in his. Vanslyperken was flushed with wine, for Nancy had pushed the bottle, and, at last, he spoke out clearly what his aspirations were. The widow blushed, laughed, wiped her eyes as if to brush away a falling tear, and eventually, with a slight pressure of the hand, stammered that she did not know what to say, the acquaintance was so short—it was so unexpected—she must reflect a little: at the same time, she could not but acknowledge, that she had been taken with him when she first saw him; and then she laughed and said, that she did really begin to believe that there was such a thing as love at first sight, and then—he had better go now, she wished to b   alone—she really had a headache. Oh! Nancy Corbett! you were, indeed, an adept in the art of seduction—no wonder that your name has been handed down to posterity. Mr Vanslyperken perceived his advantage, and pressed still more, until the blushing widow declared that she would really think seriously about the matter, if on further acquaintance she found that her good opinion of him was not overrated.

Vanslyperken returned on board intoxicated with his success. On his arrival, he was informed that a messenger had been sent for him, but no one knew where to find him, and that he must be at the admiral's early the next morning, and have all ready for immediate sailing. This was rather annoying, but there was no help for it. The next day Vanslyperken went to the admiral's, and received orders to sail immediately to the Hague with despatches of consequence, being no less than an answer from King William to the States General.

Mr Vanslyperken proceeded from the admiral's to the charming widow, to whom he imparted this unwelcome intelligence. She, of course, was grave, and listened to his protestations with her little finger in her mouth, and a pensive, down-cast eye.

"How long will you be away?" inquired she.

"But a week or ten days at the farthest. I shall fly back to see you again."

"But, tell me the truth, have you no acquaintances there?—now, tell me the truth. I don't mean men."

"Upon my honour, fair widow, I don't know a single woman there," replied Vanslyperken, pleased with this little appearance of jealousy; "but I'm afraid that I must leave you, for the admiral is very severe."

"Will you do me one favour, Mr Vanslyperken?"

"Anything :—ask what you will."

"I want this letter forwarded to my brother—I am very anxious about it. The French agent there will send it on;—it is enclosed to him. Will you do me that favour, my dear sir? —I'm sure you will if——"

"If what?"

"If you love me," replied the widow, laying her hand upon Vanslyperken.

"I will, most certainly," said Vanslyperken, taking the letter and putting it in his pocket.

"Then I shall ask you another," said the widow. "You will think me very foolish, but there may be an opportunity—will you write to me—just a few lines—only to tell me that you have given the letter, that's all—and to say how you are—don't you think me very foolish?"

"I will write, dearest, since you wish it—and now, good-bye."

Vanslyperken took the widow round the waist, and after a little murmuring and reluctance, was permitted to snatch a kiss. Her eyes followed him mournfully till he shut the door and disappeared, and then Nancy Corbett gave way to unbounded mirth.

"So the fool has bit already," thought she; "now if

he only writes to me, and I get his acknowledgment of having delivered the letter, the beast is in my power, and I can hang him any day I please. Upon his honour, he did not know a single woman there:—Lord have mercy!—what liars men are—but we can sometimes beat them with their own weapons." And Nancy's thoughts reverted to her former life, which she now dwelt upon with pain and sorrow.

Mr Vanslyperken returned on board; the anchor was weighed immediately that the boats had been hoisted up, and the *Yungfrau* ran out with a fair wind, which lasted until the evening, when it fell almost calm, and the cutter made but little way through the water. Many of the men were conversing on the forecastle as usual, and the subject of their discourse was the surmising what had become of Corporal Van Spitter. In one point they all appeared to agree, which was, that they hoped he would never return to the cutter.

"If he does I owe him one," observed Jemmy Ducks. "It's all through him that my wife was turned out of the vessel."

"And a little bit from her tongue, Jemmy," observed Coble.

"Why, perhaps so," replied Jemmy; "but what was it set her tongue loose but the threat of *him* to flog me, and what made him threaten that but the 'peaching of that fat marine?"

"Very good arguments, Jemmy. Well, I will say that for your wife, Jemmy, she does love you, and there's no sham about it."

"Never mind Jemmy's wife, let's have Jemmy's song," said Spurey; "he hasn't piped since he was pulled up by the corporal."

"No: he put my pipe out, the hippopotamus. Well, I'll give it you—it shall be about what we are talking of, Obadiah." Jemmy perched himself on the fore-end of the booms, and sang as follows:

"I suppose that you think 'cause my trousers are tarry,
   And because that I ties my long hair in a tail,
While landsmen are figged out as fine as Lord Harry,
   With breast-pins and cravats as white as old sail;
That I'm a strange creature, a know-nothing ninny,
   But fit for the planks for to walk in foul weather;
That I ha'n't e'er a notion of the worth of a guinea,
   And that you, Poll, can twist me about as a feather,—
      Lord love you!!

"I know that this life is but short at the best on't,
   That Time it flies fast, and that work must be done;
That when danger comes 'tis as well for to jest on't,
   'Twill be but the lighter felt when it do come:
If you think, then, from this that I an't got a notion
   Of a heaven above, with its mercy in store,
And the devil below, for us lads of the ocean,
   Just the same as it be for the landsmen on shore,-
      Lord love you!!

"If because I don't splice with some true-hearted woman,
   Who'd doat on my presence, and sob when I sail,
But put up with you, Poll, though faithful to no man,
   With a fist that can strike, and a tongue that can rail;
'Tis because I'm not selfish, and know 'tis my duty
   If I marry to moor by my wife, and not leave her,
To dandle the young ones,—watch over her beauty,
   D'ye think that I'd promise and vow, then deceive her?—
      Lord love you!!

"I suppose that you think 'cause I'm free with my money,
   Which others would hoard and lock up in their chest,
All your billing and cooing, and words sweet as honey,
   Are as gospel to me while you hang on my breast;
But no, Polly, no;—you may take every guinea,
   They'd burn in my pocket, if I took them to sea;
But as for your love, Poll, I indeed were a ninny,—
   D'ye think I don't know you cheat others than me?
      Lord love you!!"

"Well, that's a good song, Jemmy, and he can't pull you up for that, anyhow."

Mr Vanslyperken appeared to think otherwise, for he sent a marine forward to say, that no singing would be permitted in future, and that they were immediately to desist.

"I suppose we shall have a song considered as mutiny

soon," observed Coble. "Ah, well, it's a long lane that has no turning."

"Yes," replied Jemmy, in an under tone, "and for every rogue there's a rope laid up. Never mind, let us go below."

Mr Vanslyperken's dreaming thoughts of the fair widow were nevertheless occasionally interrupted by others not quite so agreeable. Strange to say, he fully believed what Smallbones had asserted about his being carried out by the tide to the Nab buoy and he canvassed the question in his mind, whether there was not something supernatural in the affair, a sort of interposition of Providence in behalf of the lad, which was to be considered as a warning to himself not to attempt anything further. He was frightened, although his feeling for revenge was still in all its force. As for any one suspecting him of having attempted the boy's life, he had recovered from that feeling; even if they did, who dare say a word? There was another point which also engrossed the moody Vanslyperken, which was how he should behave relative to the widow Vandersloosh. Should he call or should he not? he cared nothing for her, and provided he could succeed with the Portsmouth lady, he would pitch her to the devil; but still he remembered the old proverb, "You should never throw away dirty water before you are sure of clean." After some cogitation he determined upon still pressing his suit, and hoped at the same time that the widow would not admit him into her presence. Such were the different resolves and decisions which occupied the mind of Mr Vanslyperken until he dropped his anchor at Amsterdam, when he ordered his boat to go on shore, and gave positive directions to Dick Short that no one was to leave the cutter on any pretence, for he was determined that as the widow would not have his company, she should not have the profits arising from his men spending their money at her house.

"So," cried Coble, after the boat shoved off, "liberty's stopped as well as singing. What next, I wonder? I sha'n't stand this long."

"No," replied Short.

"Stop till he makes friends with the widow," observed Bill Spurey; "she'll get us all leave."

"Mein Gott, he nebber say anyting before," observed Jansen.

"No; we might almost go and come as we wished. We must not stand this."

"We won't," replied Jemmy Ducks.

"No," replied Short.

While the crew of the cutter were in this incipient state of mutiny, Vanslyperken bent his steps to deliver up to the authorities the despatches with which he was charged; and having so done, he then took out the letter intrusted to him by Nancy Corbett and read the address. It was the same street in which lived the Frau Vandersloosh. This was awkward, as Vanslyperken did not want to be seen by her; but there was no help for it. He trusted to her not seeing him, and he proceeded thither: he ran down the numbers on the doors until he came to the right one, which was exactly opposite to the widow's house:—this was more unfortunate. He rang the bell; it was some time before the door was opened, and while he was standing there he could not help looking round to see if any one saw him. To his annoyance, there stood the widow filling up her door with her broad frame, and Babette peeping over her shoulder. Mr Vanslyperken, as there was only the canal and two narrow roads between them, could do no less than salute her, but she took no notice of him farther than by continuing her stare. At last, upon a second pulling of the bell, the door opened, and on Mr Vanslyperken saying that he had a letter for such an address, he was admitted, and the door immediately closed. He was ushered into a room, the window-panes of which were painted green, so that no one outside could look in, and found himself in the presence of a tall man, in a clerical dress, who motioned to him to sit down.

Vanslyperken delivered the letter, and then took a seat.

The gentleman made a graceful bow, as if to ask permission to break the seal, and then opened the letter.

"Sir, I am obliged to you for charging yourself with these packets — infinitely obliged to you. You are in command of a sloop here, I believe."

"A king's cutter, sir," replied Vanslyperken, with importance; "I am Lieutenant Vanslyperken."

"I thank you, sir. I will take down your name. You expect, I presume, to be rewarded for this small service," continued the gentleman, with a bland smile.

"Why, she must have told him," thought Vanslyperken; who replied with another smile, "that he certainly trusted that he should be."

Upon which reply, the other went to an escritoire, and taking out a bag, opened it and poured out a mass of gold, which made Vanslyperken's mouth water, but why he did so Vanslyperken did not give a thought, until having counted out fifty pieces, the gentleman very gracefully put them into his hand, observing,

"A lieutenant's pay is not great, and we can afford to be generous. Will you oblige me by calling here before you sail for England, and I will beg you to take charge of a letter."

Vanslyperken was all amazement: he began to suspect what was the fact, but he had the gold in his hand, and for the life of him, he could not have laid it down again on the table. It was too great a sacrifice, for it was his idol—his god. He therefore dropped it into his pocket, and promising to call before he sailed, bowed and took his leave. As he went out, there were the Frau Vandersloosh and Babette still watching him at the door, but Vanslyperken was in a state of agitation, and he hurried off as fast as he could. Had he known why they watched so earnestly, and what had occurred, his agitation would have been greater still. As soon as Mr Vanslyperken had arrived on board, he hastened down into his cabin, and throwing the money down on the table, feasted his eyes with it, and remained for nearly half-an-hour in a state of deep cogitation, during which he often asked himself the question, whether he had not been a traitor to the king and country in whose pay he was employed. The answer that he gave to himself was anything but satisfactory: but the prospect of possessing the fair Portsmouth widow, and the gold displayed upon the table, were very satisfactory, and the balance was on the latter side: so Vanslyperken gradually recovered himself, and had risen from his chair to collect the gold and deposit it in a place of safety, when he was interrupted by a tap at the door. Hastily sweeping off the gold pieces, he cried, "Come in;" when who, to his surprise, should appear, in excellent condition and fresh as a peony, but the lost and almost forgotten Corporal Van Spitter, who, raising his hand to his forehead as usual, reported himself man-of-war fashion, "Vas come on board, Mynheer Vanslyperken." But as the corporal did not tell all the facts connected with his cruise in the jolly-boat to Mr Vanslyperken, for reasons which will hereafter appear, we shall reserve the narrative of what really did take place for another chapter.

Chapter XXI

In which are narrated the adventures which took place in the corporal's cruise in the jolly-boat.

CORPORAL VAN SPITTER, so soon as he had expended all his breath in shouting for help, sat down with such a flop of despair on the thwart of the boat, as very nearly to swamp it. As it was, the water poured in over the starboard-gunnel, until the boat was filled up to his ankles. This alarmed him still more, and he remained mute as a stockfish for a quarter of an hour, during which he was swept away by the tide until he was unable to discover the lights on shore. The wind freshened, and the water became more rough; the night was dark as pitch, and the corporal skimmed along before the wind and tide. " A tousand tyfels ! " at last muttered the corporal, as the searching blast crept round his fat sides, and made him shiver. Gust succeeded gust, and, at last, the corporal's teeth chattered with the cold : he raised his feet out of the water at the bottom of the boat, for his feet were like ice, but in so doing, the weight of his body being above the centre of gravity, the boat careened over, and with a " Mein Gott ! " he hastily replaced them in the cold water. And now a shower of rain and sleet came down upon the unprotected body of the corporal, which added to his misery, to his fear, and to his despair.

"Where am I ? " muttered he ; " what will become of me ? Ah, mein Gott ! twenty tousand tyfels—what had I to do in a boat—I, Corporal Van Spitter ? " and then he was again silent for nearly half an hour. The wind shifted to the northward, and the rain cleared up, but it was only to make the corporal suffer more, for the freezing blast poured upon his wet clothes, and he felt chilled to the very centre of his vitals. His whole body trembled convulsively, he was frozen to the thwart, yet there was no appearance of daylight coming, and the corporal now abandoned himself to utter hopelessness and desperation, and commenced praying. He attempted the Lord's Prayer in Dutch, but could get no further than "art in heaven," for the rest, from disuse, had quite escaped the corporal's memory. He tried to recollect something else, but was equally unsuccessful ; at last, he made up a sad mixture of swearing and praying.

" Mein Gott—a hundred tousand tyfels—gut Gott— twenty hundred tousand tyfels ! Ah, Gott of mercy— million of tyfels ! holy Gott Jesus ! twenty millions of tyfels—Gott for dam, I die of cold ! " Such were the ejaculations of the corporal, allowing about ten minutes to intervene between each, during which the wind blew more freshly, the waves rose, and the boat was whirled away.

But the corporal's miseries were to be prolonged ; the flood-time of water was now spent, and the ebb commenced flowing against the wind and sea. This created what is called boiling water, that is, a contest between the wind forcing the waves one way, and the tide checking them the other, which makes the waves to lose their run, and they rise, and dance, and bubble into points. The consequence was, that the boat, as she was borne down by the tide against them, shipped a sea every moment, which the wind threw against the carcass of the corporal, who was now quite exhausted with more than four hours' exposure to a wintry night, the temperature being nearly down to zero. All the corporal's stoicism was gone; he talked wildly, crouched and gibbered in his fear, when he was suddenly roused by a heavy shock. He raised his head, which had sunk upon his chest, and beheld something close to him, and to the gunnel of the boat. It was a thin, tall figure, holding out his two arms at right angles, and apparently stooping over him. It was just in the position that Smallbones lay on the forecastle of the cutter on that day morning, when he was about to keel-haul him, and the corporal, in his state of mental and bodily depression, was certain that it was the ghost of the poor lad whom he had so often tortured. Terror raised his hair erect—his mouth was wide open—he could not speak—he tried to analyse it, but a wave dashed in his face—his eyes and mouth were filled with salt water, and the corporal threw himself down on the thwarts of the boat, quite regardless whether it went to the bottom or not; there he lay, half groaning, half praying, with his hands to his eyes, and his huge nether proportion raised in the air, every limb trembling with blended cold and fright. One hour more, and there would have been nothing but corporal parts of Corporal Spitter.

The reason why the last movement of the corporal did not swamp the boat, was simply that it was aground on one of the flats; and the figure which had alarmed the conscience-stricken corporal, was nothing more than the outside beacon of a weir for catching fish, being a thin post with a cross bar to it, certainly not unlike Smallbones in figure, supposing him to have put his arms in that position.

For upwards of an hour did the corporal lie reversed, when the day dawned, and the boat had been left high and dry upon the flat. The fishermen came down to examine their weir, and see what was their success, when they discovered the boat with its contents. At first they could not imagine what it was, for they could perceive nothing but the capacious round of the corporal, which rose up in the air, but, by degrees, they made out that there was a head and feet attached to it, and they contrived, with the united efforts of four men, to raise him up, and discovered that life was not yet extinct. They poured a little schnappes into his mouth, and he recovered so far as to open his eyes, and they having brought down with them two little carts drawn by dogs, they put the corporal into one, covered him up, and yoking all the dogs to the one cart, for the usual train could not move so heavy a weight, two of them escorted him up to their huts, while the others threw the fish caught into the cart which remained, and took possession of the boat. The fishermen's wives, perceiving the cart so heavily laden, imagined, as it approached the huts, that there had been unusual success, and were not a little disappointed when they found that instead of several bushels of fine fish, they had only caught a corporal of marines; but they were kind-hearted, for they had known misery, and Van Spitter was put into a bed, and covered up with all the blankets they could collect, and very soon was able to drink some warm soup offered to him. It was not, however, till long past noon, that the corporal was able to narrate what had taken place.

"Will your lieutenant pay us for saving you and bringing him his boat?" demanded the men.

Now, it must be observed, that a great revolution had taken place in the corporal's feelings since the horror and sufferings of the night. He felt hatred towards Vanslyperken, and good-will towards those whom he had treated unkindly. The supernatural appearance of Smallbones, in which he still believed, and which appeared to him as a warning—what he had suffered from cold and exhaustion, which by him was considered as a punishment for his treatment of the poor lad but the morning before, had changed the heart of Corporal Van Spitter, so he replied in Dutch,

"He will give you nothing, good people, not even a glass of schnappes, I tell you candidly—so keep the boat if you wish—I will not say a word about it, except that it is lost. He is not likely to see it again. Besides, you can alter it, and paint it."

This very generous present of his Majesty's property by the corporal, was very agreeable to the fishermen, as it amply repaid them for all their trouble. The corporal put on his clothes, and ate a hearty meal, was freely supplied with spirits, and went to bed quite recovered. The next morning, the fishermen took him down to Amsterdam in their own boat, when Van Spitter discovered that the *Yungfrau* had sailed; this was very puzzling, and Corporal Van Spitter did not know what to do. After some cogitation, it occurred to him that, for Vanslyperken's sake, he might be well received at the Lust Haus by widow Vandersloosh, little imagining how much at a discount was his lieutenant in that quarter.

To the Frau Vandersloosh accordingly he repaired, and the first person he met was Babette, who finding that the corporal was a Dutchman, and belonging to the *Yungfrau*, and who presumed that he had always felt the same ill-will towards Vanslyperken and Snarleyyow, as did the rest of the ship's company, immediately entered into a narrative of the conduct of Snarleyyow on the preceding night, the anger of her mistress, and every other circumstance with which the reader is already acquainted. Corporal Van Spitter thus fortunately found out how matters stood previous to his introduction to the widow. He expatiated upon his sufferings, upon the indifference of his lieutenant in sailing as to what had become of him, and fully persuaded Babette not only that he was inimical, which now certainly he was, but that he always had been so, to Mr Vanslyperken. Babette, who was always ready to retail news, went up to the widow, and amused her, as she dressed her, with the corporal's adventures, and the widow felt an interest in, before she had seen, Corporal Van Spitter, from the account of his "moving accidents by flood and field."

But if prepossessed in his favour before she saw him, what did she feel when she first beheld the substantial proportions of Corporal Van Spitter! There she beheld the beau ideal of her imagination—the very object of her widow's dreams—the antipodes of Vanslyperken, and as superior as "Hyperion to a Satyr." He had all the personal advantages, with none of the defects of her late husband; he was quite as fleshy, but had at least six inches more in height, and, in the eyes of the widow, the Corporal Van Spitter was the finest man she ever had beheld, and she mentally exclaimed, "There is the man for my money;" and, at the same time, resolved that she would win him. Alas! how short-sighted are mortals; little did the corporal imagine that the most untoward event in his life would be the cause of his being possessed of ease and competence. The widow received him most graciously, spoke in no measured terms against Vanslyperken, at which the corporal raised his huge shoulders, as much as to say, "He is even worse than you think him," was very violent against Snarleyyow, whom the corporal, aware that it was no mutiny, made no ceremony in "damning in heaps," as the saying is.

The widow begged that he would feel no uneasiness, as he should remain with her till the cutter returned; and an hour after the first introduction, Corporal Van Spitter had breakfasted with, and was actually sitting, by her request, on the little fubsy sofa, in the very place of Vanslyperken, with Frau Vandersloosh by his side.

We must pass over the few days during which the cutter was away. Widows have not that maiden modesty to thwart their wishes, which so often prevents a true love tale from being told. And all that the widow could not tell, Babette, duly instructed, told for her, and it was understood, before the cutter's arrival, that Corporal Van Spitter was the accepted lover of the Frau Vandersloosh. But still it was necessary that there should be secrecy, not only on account of the corporal's being under the command of the lieutenant, who, of course, would not allow himself to be crossed in his love without resenting it, but also, because it was not advisable that the crew of the *Yungfrau* should not be permitted to spend their money at the Lust Haus. It was therefore agreed that the lieutenant should be blinded, as to the real nature of the intimacy, and that nothing should take place until the cutter was paid off, and Corporal Van Spitter should be a gentleman at large.

Independent of the wisdom of the above proceedings, there was a secret pleasure to all parties in deceiving the deceiver Vanslyperken. But something else occurred which we must now refer to. The corporal's residence at the widow's house had not been unobserved by the Jesuit, who was the French agent in the house opposite, and it appeared to him, after the inquiries he had made, that Corporal Van Spitter might be made serviceable. He had been sent for and sounded, and it was canvassed with the widow whether he should accept the offers or not, and finally it was agreed that he should, as there would be little or no risk. Now, it so happened, that the corporal had gone over to the Jesuit's house to agree to the proposals, and was actually in the house conversing with him, when Vanslyperken arrived and knocked at the door. The corporal ascertaining who it was by a small clear spot left in the painted window for scrutiny, begged that he might be concealed, and was immediately shown into the next room by a door, which was hid behind a screen. The Jesuit did not exactly shut the door, as he supposed he did, and the corporal, who wondered what could have brought Vanslyperken there, kept it ajar during the whole of the interview and the counting out of the money. Vanslyperken left, and as he shut the other door the corporal did the same with the one he held ajar, and took a seat at the other end of the room, that the Jesuit might not suspect his having overheard all that had passed.

Now the Jesuit had made up his mind that it was better to treat with the principal than with a second, and therefore did not further require the services of Corporal Van Spitter. He told him that the lieutenant having received private information that one of the people of the cutter had been seen at his house, and knowing that he was the French agent, had come to inform him that if he attempted to employ any of his men in carrying letters, that he would inform against him to the authorities. That he was very sorry, but that after such a notice he was afraid that the arrangements could not proceed. The corporal appeared to be satisfied, and took his final leave. No wonder, therefore, that the widow and Babette were on the watch, when they saw Vanslyperken enter the house, at the very time the corporal was there also.

The corporal went over to the widow's, and narrated all that he had heard and seen.

"Why, the traitor!" exclaimed the widow.

"Yes, mein Gott!" repeated the corporal.

"The villain to sell his country for gold."

"Yes, mein Gott!" repeated the corporal.

"Fifty guineas, did you say, Mynheer Van Spitter?"

"Yes, mein Gott!" repeated the corporal.

"Oh, the wretch!—well," continued the widow, "at all events he is in your power."

"Yes, mein Gott!"

"You can hang him any day in the week."

"Yes, mein Gott!"

"Ho, ho! Mr Vanslyperken:—well, well, Mr Vanslyperken, we will see," continued the widow, indignant at the lieutenant receiving so large a sum, which would otherwise have been, in all probability, made over to Corporal Van Spitter, with whom she now felt that their interests were in common.

"Tousand tyfels!" roared the corporal, dashing his foot upon one of the flaps of the little table before them with so much force, that it was broken short off and fell down on the floor.

"Hundred tousand tyfels!" continued the corporal, when he witnessed the effects of his violence.

Although the widow lamented her table, she forgave the corporal with a smile; she liked such proofs of strength in her intended, and she, moreover, knew that the accident was occasioned by indignation at Vanslyperken.

"Yes, yes, Mr Vanslyperken, you'll pay me for that," exclaimed she; "I prophesy that before long you and your nasty cur will both swing together."

The corporal now walked across the little parlour and back again, then turned to the widow Vandersloosh, and with a most expressive look slowly muttered,

"Yes, mein Gott!"

After which he sat down again by the side of the widow, and they had a short consultation; before it was over, Corporal Van Spitter declared himself the deadly enemy of Lieutenant Vanslyperken; swore that he would be his ruin, and ratified the oath upon the widow's lips. Alas! what changes there are in this world!

After which solemn compact the corporal rose, took his leave, went on board, and reported himself, as we have stated in the preceding chapter.

Chapter XXII

In which Snarleyyow proves to be the devil, and no mistake.

THAT the corporal mystified his lieutenant, may easily be supposed; but the corporal had other work to do, and he did it immediately. He went up to Jemmy Ducks, who looked daggers at him, and said to him quietly, "That he had something to say to him as soon as it was dusk, and they would not be seen together." Vanslyperken ordered the corporal to resume his office, and serve out the provisions that afternoon: and to the astonishment of the men, he gave them not only full, but overweight; and instead of abusing them, and being cross, he was good-humoured, and joked with them; and all the crew stared at each other, and wondered what could be the matter with Corporal Van Spitter. But what was their amazement, upon Snarleyyow's coming up to him as he was serving out provisions, instead of receiving something from the hand of the corporal as usual, he, on the contrary, received a sound kick on the ribs from his foot which sent him yelping back into the cabin. Their astonishment could only be equalled by that of Snarleyyow himself. But that was not all; it appeared as if wonders would never cease, for when Smallbones came up to receive his master's provisions, after the others had been served and gone away, the corporal not only kindly received him, but actually presented him with a stiff glass of grog mixed with the corporal's own hand. When he offered it, the lad could not believe his eyes, and even when he had poured it down his throat, he would not believe his own mouth; and he ran away, leaving his provisions, chuckling along the lower deck till he could gain the forecastle, and add this astonishing piece of intelligence to the other facts, which were already the theme of admiration.

"There be odd chops and changes in this here world, for sartin," observed Coble. (Exactly the same remark as we made at the end of the previous chapter.)

"Mayn't it all be gammon?" said Bill Spurey.

"Gammon, for why?" replied Jemmy Ducks.

"That's the question," rejoined Spurey.

"It appears to me that he must have had a touch of conscience," said Coble.

"Or else he must have seen a ghost," replied Smallbones.

"I've heard of ghosts ashore, and sometimes on board of a ship, but I never heard of a ghost in a jolly-boat," said Coble, spitting under the gun.

"'Specially when there were hardly room for the corporal," added Spurey.

"Yes," observed Short.

"Well, we shall know something about it to-night, for the corporal and I am to have a palaver."

"Mind he don't circumwent you, Jimmy," said Spurey.

"It's my opinion," said Smallbones, "that he must be in real arnest, otherwise he would not ha' come for to go for to give me a glass of grog—there's no gammon in that;—and such a real stiff 'un too," continued Smallbones, who licked his lips at the bare remembrance of the unusual luxury.

"True," said Short.

"It beats my comprehension altogether out of nothing," observed Spurey. "There's something very queer in the wind. I wonder where the corporal has been all this while."

"Wait till this evening," observed Jemmy Ducks; and, as this was very excellent advice, it was taken, and the parties separated.

In the despatches it had been requested, as important negotiations were going on, that the cutter might return immediately, as there were other communications to make to the States General on the part of the King of England; and a messenger now informed Vanslyperken that he might sail as soon as he pleased, as there was no reply to the despatches he had conveyed. This was very agreeable to Vanslyperken, who was anxious to return to the fair widow at Portsmouth, and also to avoid the Frau Vandersloosh. At dusk, he manned his boat and went on shore to the French agent, who had also found out that the cutter was ordered to return, and had his despatches nearly ready. Vanslyperken waited about an hour; when all was complete he received them, and then returned on board.

As soon as he had quitted the vessel, Corporal Van Spitter went to Jemmy Ducks, and without letting him know how matters stood on shore, told him that he was convinced that Vanslyperken had sent him into the boat on purpose to lose him, and that the reason was, that he, Van Spitter, knew secrets which would at any time hang the lieutenant. That in consequence he had determined upon revenge, and in future would be heart and hand with the ship's company; but that to secure their mutual object, it would be better that he should appear devoted to Vanslyperken as before, and at variance with the ship's company.

Now Jemmy, who was with all his wits at work, knew that it was Smallbones who cut the corporal adrift; but that did not alter the case, as the corporal did not know it. It was therefore advisable to leave him in that error. But he required proofs of the corporal's sincerity, and he told him so.

"Mein Gott! what proof will you have? De proof of de pudding is in de eating."

"Well, then," replied Jemmy, "will you shy the dog overboard?"

"Te tog?—in one minute—and de master after him."

Whereupon Corporal Van Spitter went down into the cabin, which Vanslyperken, trusting to his surveillance, had left unlocked, and seizing the cur by the neck, carried him on deck, and hurled him several yards over the cutter's quarter.

"Mein Gott! but dat is well done," observed Jansen.

"And he'll not come back wid de tide. I know de tide, Mein Gott!" observed the corporal, panting with the exertion.

But here the corporal was mistaken. Snarleyyow did not make for the vessel, but for the shore, and they could not in the dark ascertain what became of him, neither was the tide strong, for the flood was nearly over; the consequence was, that the dog gained the shore, and landed at the same stairs where the boats land. The men were not in the boat, but waiting at a beer-shop a little above, which Vanslyperken must pass when he came down again. Recognising the boat, the cur leapt into it, and after a good shaking under the thwarts, crept forward to where the men had thrown their pea-jackets under the bow-sheets, curled himself up, and went to sleep.

Shortly afterwards the lieutenant came down with the men, and rowed on board; but the dog, which, exhausted with his exertion, was very comfortable where he was, did not come out, but remained in his snug berth.

The lieutenant and men left the boat when they arrived on board, without discovering that the dog was a passenger. About ten minutes after the lieutenant had come on board, Snarleyyow jumped on deck, but, as all the men were forward in close consultation, and in anticipation of Mr Vanslyperken's discovery of his loss, the dog gained the cabin, unperceived not only by the ship's company, but by Vanslyperken, who was busy locking up the letters entrusted to him by the French agent. Snarleyyow took his station under the table, and lay down to finish his nap, where we must leave him for the present in a sound sleep, and his snoring very soon reminded Vanslyperken of what he had, for a short time unheeded, that his favourite was present.

"Well, it's very odd," observed Spurey, "that he has been on board nearly half-an-hour, and not discovered that his dog is absent without leave."

"Yes," said Short.

"I know for why, mein Gott!" exclaimed the corporal, who shook his head very knowingly.

"The corporal knows why," observed Jemmy Ducks.

"Then why don't he say why?" retorted Bill Spurey, who was still a little suspicious of the corporal's fidelity.

"Because Mynheer Vanslyperken count his money—de guineas," replied the corporal, writhing at the idea of what he had lost by his superior's interference.

"Ho, ho! his money; well, that's a good reason, for

he would skin a flint if he could," observed Coble; "but that can't last for ever."

"That depends how often he may count it over," observed Jemmy Ducks—"but there's his bell;" and soon after Corporal Van Spitter's name was passed along the decks, to summon him into the presence of his commanding officer.

"Now for a breeze," said Coble, hitching up his trousers.

"Yes," replied Short.

"For a regular *shindy*," observed Spurey.

"Hell to pay and no pitch hot," added Jemmy, laughing; and they all remained in anxious expectation of the corporal's return.

Corporal Van Spitter had entered the cabin with the air of the profoundest devotion and respect—had raised his hand up as usual, but before the hand had arrived to its destination, he beheld Vanslyperken seated on the locker, patting the head of Snarleyyow, as if nothing had happened. At this unexpected resuscitation, the corporal uttered a tremendous "Mein Gott!" and burst like a mad bull out of the cabin, sweeping down all who obstructed his passage on the lower deck, till he arrived to the fore-ladder, which he climbed up with tottering knees, and then sank down on the forecastle at the feet of Jemmy Ducks.

"Mein Gott, mein Gott, mein Gott!" exclaimed the corporal, putting his hands to his eyes as if to shut out the horrid vision.

"What the devil is the matter?" exclaimed Coble.

"Ah! mein Gott, mein Gott!"

As it was evident that something uncommon had happened, they all now crowded round the corporal, who, by degrees, recovered himself.

"What is it, corporal?" inquired Jemmy Ducks.

Before the corporal could reply, Smallbones, who had been summoned to the cabin on account of the corporal's unaccountable exit, sprang up the ladder with one bound, his hair flying in every direction, his eyes goggling, and his mouth wide open: lifting his hands over his head, and pausing as if for breath, the lad exclaimed with a solemn sepulchral voice, "By all the devils in hell he's come again!"

"Who?" exclaimed several voices at once.

"Snarleyyow," replied Smallbones, mournfully.

"Yes—mein Gott!" exclaimed Corporal Van Spitter, attempting to rise on his legs.

"Whew!" whistled Jemmy Ducks—but nobody else uttered a sound; they all looked at one another, some with compressed lips, others with mouths open. At last one shook his head—then another. The corporal rose on his feet and shook himself like an elephant.

"Dat tog is de tyfel's imp, and dat's de end on it," said he, with alarm still painted on his countenance.

"And is he really on board again?" inquired Coble, doubtingly.

"As sartin as I stands on this here forecastle—a-kissing and slobbering the lieutenant for all the world like a Christian," replied Smallbones, despondingly.

"Then he flare fire on me wid his one eye," said the corporal.

"Warn't even wet," continued Smallbones.

Here there was another summons for Corporal Van Spitter.

"Mein Gott, I will not go," exclaimed the corporal.

"Yes, yes, go, corporal," replied Smallbones; "it's the best way to face the devil."

"Damn the devil!—and that's not swearing," exclaimed Short—such a long sentence out of his mouth was added to the marvels of the night—some even shrugged up their shoulders at that, as if it also were supernatural.

"I always say so," said Jansen, "I always say so—no tog, no tog, after all."

"No, no," replied Coble, shaking his head.

Corporal Van Spitter was again summoned, but the corporal was restive as a rhinoceros.

"Corporal," said Smallbones, who, since the glass of grog, was his sincere ally, and had quite forgotten and forgiven his treatment, "go down and see if you can't worm the truth out of him."

"Ay, do, do!" exclaimed the rest.

"Smallbones—Smallbones—wanted aft," was the next summons.

"And here I go," exclaimed Smallbones. "I defy the devil and all his works—as we said on Sunday at the workhouse."

"That lad's a prime bit of stuff," observed Spurey, "I will say that."

"Yes," replied Short.

In a few seconds Smallbones came hastily up the ladder.

"Corporal, you must go to the cabin directly. He is in a devil of a rage—asked me why you wouldn't come—told him that you had seen something dreadful—didn't know what. Tell him you saw the devil at his elbow—see if it frightens him."

"Yes, do," exclaimed the others.

Corporal Van Spitter made up his mind; he pulled down the skirts of his jacket, descended the ladder, and walked aft into the cabin. At the sight of Snarleyyow the corporal turned pale—at the sight of the corporal, Mr Vanslyperken turned red.

"What's the meaning of all this?" exclaimed Vanslyperken, in a rage. "What is all this about, corporal? Explain your conduct, sir. What made you rush out of the cabin in that strange manner?"

"Mein Gott, Mynheer Vanslyperken, I came for orders; but I no come keep company wid de tyfel."

"With the devil!—what do you mean?" exclaimed Vanslyperken, alarmed. The corporal, perceiving that the lieutenant was frightened, then entered into a detail, that when he had entered the cabin he had seen the devil sitting behind Mr Vanslyperken, looking over his shoulder, and grinning with his great eyes, while he patted him over the back with his left hand and fondled the dog with his right.

This invention of the corporal's, whom Mr Vanslyperken considered as a stanch friend and incapable of treachery, had a great effect upon Mr Vanslyperken. It immediately rushed into his mind that he had attempted murder but a few days before, and that, that very day he had been a traitor to his country—quite sufficient for the devil to claim him as his own.

"Corporal Van Spitter," exclaimed Vanslyperken with a look of horror, "are you really in earnest, or are you not in your senses—you really saw him?"

"As true as I stand here," replied the corporal, who perceived his advantage.

"Then the Lord be merciful to me a sinner!" exclaimed Vanslyperken, falling on his knees, at the moment forgetting the presence of the corporal, and then recollecting himself, he jumped up—"It is false, Corporal Van Spitter; false as you are yourself—confess," continued the lieutenant, seizing the corporal by the collar, "confess, that it is all a lie."

"A lie," exclaimed the corporal, who now lost his courage, "a lie, Mynheer Vanslyperken! If it was not the tyfel himself it was one of his imps, I take my Bible oath."

"One of his imps," exclaimed Vanslyperken; "it's a lie—an infamous lie. confess," continued he, shaking the corporal by the collar—"confess the truth."

At this moment Snarleyyow considered that he had a right to be a party in the fray, so he bounded forward at the corporal, who, terrified at the supernatural beast, broke from Vanslyperken's grasp, and rushed out of the cabin, followed, however, the whole length of the lower deck by the dog, who snapped and bayed at him till he had gained the fore ladder.

Once more did the corporal make his appearance on the forecastle, frightened and out of breath.

"Mein Gott! de man is mad," exclaimed he, "and de

tog is de tyfel himself." The corporal then narrated in broken English what had passed. For some time there was a confused whispering among the men; they considered the dog's reappearance on this occasion even more wonderful than on the former, for the men declared positively that he never came off in the boat, which, had he done, would have unravelled the whole mystery; and that a dog thrown overboard, and swept away by the tide should be discovered shortly after perfectly dry and comfortable, not only on board of the cutter, which he could not have got on board of, but also in his master's cabin, which he could not get into without being seen, proved at once that the animal was supernatural. No one was now hardy enough to deny it, and no one appeared to have the least idea of how to proceed except Smallbones, who, as we have shown, was as full of energy as he was deficient in fat. On all occasions of this kind the bravest becomes the best man and takes the lead, and Smallbones, who appeared more collected and less alarmed than the others, was now listened to with attention, and the crowd collected round him.

"I don't care for him or for his dog either," exclaimed Smallbones, with a drawling intrepid tone; "that dog I'll settle the hash of some way or the other, if it be the devil's own cousin. I'll not come for to go to leave off now, that's sartain, as I am Peter Smallbones—I'se got a plan."

"Let's hear Smallbones,—let's hear Smallbones!" exclaimed some of the men. Whereupon they all collected round the lad, who addressed the crew as follows. His audience, at first, crowded up close to him, but Smallbones, who could not talk without his arms, which were about as long and thin as a Pongo's are in proportion to his body, flapped and flapped as he discoursed, until he had cleared a little ring, and when in the height of his energy he threw them about like the arms of a windmill, every one kept at a respectable distance.

"Well, now, I considers this, if so be as how the dog be a devil, and not a dog, I sees no reason for to come for to go for to be afraid; for ar'n't we all true Christians, and don't we all fear God and honour the king? I sartainly myself does consider that that ere dog could not a have cummed into this here vessel by any manner of means natural not by no means, 'cause it's very clear, that a dog if he be as he be a dog, can't do no more than other dogs can; and if he can do more than heither dog or man can, then he must be the devil, and not a dog —and so he is—that's sartain. But if so be as he is the devil, I say again, I don't care, 'cause I sees exactly how it is,—he be a devil, but he be only a sea-devil and not a shore-devil, and I'll tell you for why. Didn't he come on board some how no how in a gale of wind when he was called for? Didn't I sew him up in a bread-bag, and didn't he come back just as nothing had happened; and didn't the corporal launch him into a surge over the taffrail, and he comes back just as if nothing had happened? Well, then, one thing is clear; that his power be on the water, and no water will drown that ere imp, so it's no use trying no more in that way, for he be a sea-devil. But I thinks this: he goes on shore and he comes back with one of his impish eyes knocked out clean by somebody or another somehow or another, and, therefore, I argues that he have no power on shore not by no means; for if you can knock his eye out, you can knock his soul out of his body, by only knocking a little more to the purpose. Who ever heard of any one knocking out the devil's eye, or injuring him in any way?—No; because he have power by sea and by land: but this here be only a water-devil, and he may be killed on dry land. Now, that's just my opinion, and as soon as I gets him on shore, I means to try what I can do. I don't fear him, nor his master, nor anything else, 'cause I'm a Christian, and was baptised Peter; and I tells you all, that be he a dog, or be he a devil, I'll have a shy at him as soon as I can, and if I don't, I hope I may be d—d, that's all."

Such was the oration of Smallbones, which was remarkably well received. Everyone agreed with the soundness of his arguments, and admired his resolution, and as he had comprised in his speech all that could be said upon the subject, they broke up the conference, and everyone went down to his hammock.

Chapter XXIII

In which Mr Vanslyperken finds great cause of vexation and satisfaction.

In the meanwhile Mr Vanslyperken was anything but comfortable in his mind. That Corporal Van Spitter should assert that he saw the devil at his shoulder, was a matter of no small annoyance any way; for either the devil was at his shoulder or he was not. If he was, why then it was evident that in consequence of his having attempted murder, and having betrayed his country for money, the devil considered him as his own, and this Mr Vanslyperken did not approve of; for, like many others in this world, he wished to commit every crime, and go to heaven after all. Mr Vanslyperken was superstitious and cowardly, and he did believe that such a thing was possible; and when he canvassed it in his mind, he trembled, and looked over his shoulder.

But Corporal Van Spitter might have asserted it only to frighten him. It was possible—but here again was a difficulty: the corporal had been his faithful confidant for so long a while, and to suppose this, would be to suppose that the corporal was a traitor to him, and that, upon no grounds which Vanslyperken could conjecture, he had turned false: this was impossible—Mr Vanslyperken would not credit it; so there he stuck, like a man between the horns of a dilemma, not knowing what to do; for Mr Vanslyperken resolved, had the devil really been there, to have repented immediately, and have led a new life; but if the devil had not been there, Mr Vanslyperken did not perceive any cause for such an immediate hurry.

At last, an idea presented itself to Mr Vanslyperken's mind, which afforded him great comfort, which was, that the corporal had suffered so much from his boat adventures—for the corporal had made the most of his sufferings—that he was a little affected in his mind, and had thought that he had seen something. "It must have been so," said Mr Vanslyperken, who fortified the idea with a glass of scheedam, and then went to bed.

Now, it so happened, that at the very time that Mr Vanslyperken was arguing all this in his brain, Corporal Van Spitter was also cogitating how he should get out of his scrape; for the Corporal, although not very bright, had much of the cnnning of little minds, and he felt the necessity of lulling the suspicions of the lieutenant. To conceal his astonishment and fear at the appearance of the dog, he had libelled Mr Vanslyperken, who would not easily forgive, and it was the corporal's interest to continue on the best terms with, and enjoy the confidence of his superior. How was this to be got over? It took the whole of the first watch, and two-thirds of the middle, before the corporal, who lay in his hammock, could hit upon any plan. At last he thought he had succeeded. At daybreak, Corporal Van Spitter entered the cabin of Mr Vanslyperken, who very coolly desired him to tell Short to get all ready for weighing at six o'clock.

"If you please, Mynheer Vanslyperken, you think me mad last night 'cause I see de tyfel at your shoulder. Mynheer Vanslyperken, I see him twice again this night on lower deck. Mein Gott! Mynheer Vanslyperken, I say twice."

"Saw him again twice!" replied the lieutenant.

"Yes, Mynheer Vanslyperken, I see twice again—I see him very often since I drift in de boat. First, I see him when in de boat—since that I see him one time, two times, in de night."

"It's just as I thought," said Mr Vanslyperken, "he

has never got over his alarm of that night.—Very well, Corporal Van Spitter, it's of no consequence. I was very angry with you last night, because I thought you were taking great liberties; but I see now how it is, you must keep yourself quiet, and as soon as we arrive at Portsmouth, you had better lose a little blood."

"How much, Mynheer Vanslyperken, do you wish I should lose?" replied the corporal, with his military salute.

"About eight ounces, corporal."

"Yes, sir," replied the corporal, turning on his pivot, and marching out of the cabin.

This was a peculiarly satisfactory interview to both parties. Mr Vanslyperken was overjoyed at the corporal's explanation, and the corporal was equally delighted at having so easily gulled his superior.

The cutter weighed that morning, and sailed for Portsmouth. We shall pass over the passage without any further remarks than that the corporal was reinstated into Mr Vanslyperken's good graces—that he appeared as usual to be harsh with the ship's company, and to oppress Smallbones more than ever; but this was at the particular request of the lad, who played his own part to admiration —that Mr Vanslyperken again brought up the question of flogging Jemmy Ducks, but was prevented by the corporal's expressing his fears of a mutiny—and had also some secret conference with the corporal as to his desire of vengeance upon Smallbones, to which Van Spitter gave a ready ear, and appeared to be equally willing with the lieutenant to bring it about. Things were in this state when the cutter arrived at Portsmouth, and, as usual, ran into the harbour. It may be supposed that Mr Vanslyperken was in all haste to go on shore to pay his visit to his charming widow, but still there was one thing to be done first, which was to report himself to the admiral.

On his arrival at the admiral's, much to his dissatisfaction, he was informed that he must hold himself ready for sailing immediately, as despatches for the Hague were expected down on the next morning. This would give but a short time to pay his addresses, and he therefore made all haste to the widow's presence, and was most graciously received. She almost flew into his arms, upbraided him for being so long away, for not having written to her, and showed such marks of strong attachment, that Vanslyperken was in ecstasies. When he told her that he expected to sail again immediately, she put her handkerchief up to her eyes, and appeared, to Vanslyperken at least, to shed a few bitter tears. As soon as she was a little more composed, Vanslyperken produced the packet with which he was entrusted, which she opened, and took out two letters, one for herself, and the other addressed to a certain person in a house in another street.

"This," said the widow, "you must deliver yourself—it is of consequence. I would deliver it, but if I do, I shall not be able to look after my little arrangements for dinner, for you dine with me of course. Besides, you must be acquainted with this person one time or another, as it will be for OUR advantage."

"OUR advantage!" how delightful to Mr Vanslyperken was that word! He jumped up immediately, and took his hat to execute the commission, the injunction of the widow to be soon back hastening his departure. Vanslyperken soon arrived at the door, knocked, and was admitted.

"Vat vash you vant, sare?" said a venerable looking old Jew, who opened the door to him.

"Is your name Lazarus?" inquired the lieutenant.

"Dat vash my name."

"I have a letter for you."

"A letter for me!—and from vare?"

"Amsterdam."

"Shee! silence," said the Jew, leading the way into a small room, and shutting the door.

Vanslyperken delivered the letter, which the Jew did not open, but laid on the table. "It vas from my worthy friend in Billen Shaaten. He ist vell?"

"Quite well," replied Vanslyperken.

"Ven do you sail again, mynheer?"

"To-morrow morning."

"Dat is good. I have the letters all ready; dey come down yesterday—vil you vait and take them now?"

"Yes," replied Vanslyperken, who anticipated another rouleau of gold on his arrival at Amsterdam.

"An den I will give you your monish at de same time."

More money, thought Vanslyperken, who replied then, "With all my heart," and took a chair.

The Jew left the room, and soon returned with a small yellow bag, which he put into Vanslyperken's hand, and a large packet carefully sealed. "Dis vas of de hutmost importance," said the old man, giving him the packet. "You will find you monish all right, and now vas please just put your name here, for I vas responsible for all de account;" and the Jew laid down a receipt for Vanslyperken to sign. Vanslyperken read it over. It was an acknowledgment for the sum of fifty guineas, but not specifying for what service. He did not much like to sign it, but how could he refuse? Besides, as the Jew said, it was only to prove that the money was paid; nevertheless he objected.

"Vy vill you not sign? I must not lose my monish, and I shall lose it if you do not sign. Vat you fear—you not fear that we peach; ven peoples pay so high, they not pay for noting. We all sall hang togeder if de affair be found."

Hang together! thought Vanslyperken, whose fears were roused, and he turned pale.

"You are vell paid for your shervices—you vas vell paid at doder side of de vater, and you are now von of us. You cannot go back, or your life vill be forfeit, I can assure you—you vill sign if you please—and you vill not leave dis house, until you do sign," continued the Jew. "You vill not take our monish and den give de information, and hang us all. You vill sign, if you please, sare."

There was a steadiness of countenance and a firmness in the tone of the old man, which told Vanslyperken that he was not to be trifled with, and assured him that he must have help at hand if requisite. If left to himself, the Jew would have been easily mastered by the lieutenant, but that such was not the case, was soon proved, by the old man ringing a small silver bell on the table, and shortly afterwards there was a rustling and noise, as if of several persons, heard in the passage. Vanslyperken now perceived that he was entrapped, and he also felt that it was too late to retreat. Actuated by his fear of violence on the one hand, and his love of gold on the other, he consented to sign the voucher required. As soon as this was done, the old Jew was all civility. He took the paper, and locked it up in a large cabinet, and then observed,

"It is for your own shafety, sare lieutenant, dat we are obliged to do dis. You have noting to fear—we are too much in want of good friends like you, to lose them, but we must be safe and shure; now you are von of us—you cannot tell but we can tell too—we profit togeder, and I vill hope dat we do run no risk to be hang togeder. Fader Abraham! we must not think of that, but of de good cause, and of de monish. I am a Jew, and I care not whether de Papist or de Protestant have de best of it —but I call it all de good cause, because every cause is good which brings de monish."

So thought Vanslyperken, who was in heart a Jew.

"And now, sare, you vill please to take great care of de packet, and deliver it to our friend at Amsterdam, and you vill of course come to me ven you return here."

Vanslyperken took his leave, with the packet in his pocket, not very well pleased; but as he put the packet in, he felt the yellow bag, and that to a certain degree consoled him. The old Jew escorted him to the door, with his little keen gray eyes fixed upon him, and Vanslyperken quailed before it, and was glad when he was once more in the street. He hastened back to the widow's house, full of thought—he certainly had never intended to have so committed himself as he had done, or to have positively enrolled himself among the partisans of the exiled king; but the money had entrapped him—he had twice taken their wages, and he had now been obliged to give them security for his fidelity, by enabling them to prove his guilt whenever they pleased. All this made Mr Vanslyperken rather melancholy—but his meditations were put an end to by his arrival in the presence of the charming widow. She asked him what had passed, and he narrated it, but with a little variation, for he would not tell that he had signed through a fear of violence, but, at the same time, he observed, that he did not much like signing a receipt.

"But that is necessary," replied she; "and besides, why not? I know you are on our side, and you will prove most valuable to us. Indeed, I believe it was your readiness to meet my wishes that made me so fond of you, for I am devotedly attached to the rightful king, and I never would marry any man who would not risk life and soul for him, as you have done now."

The expression "life and soul," made Vanslyperken shudder, and his flesh crept all over his body.

"Besides," continued the widow, "it will be no small help to us, for the remuneration is very great."

"To us!" thought Vanslyperken, who now thought it right to press his suit. He was listened to attentively, and at last he proposed an early day for the union. The widow blushed, and turned her head away, and at last replied, with a sweet smile, "Well, Mr Vanslyperken, I will neither tease you nor myself—when you come back from your next trip, I consent to be yours."

What was Vanslyperken's delight and exultation! He threw himself on his knees, promised, and vowed, and thanked, kissed hands, and was in such ecstasies! He could hardly imagine that his good fortune was real. A beautiful widow with a handsome fortune—how could he ever have thought of throwing himself away upon such a bunch of deformity as the Frau Vandersloosh? Poor Mr Vanslyperken! Dinner put an end to his protestations. He fared sumptuously, and drank freely to please the widow. He drank death to the usurper, and restoration to the King James. What a delightful evening! The widow was so amiable, so gentle, so yielding, so, so, so—what with wine and love, and fifty guineas in his pocket, Mr Vanslyperken was so overcome with his feelings, that at last he felt but so so. After a hundred times returning to kiss her dear, dear hand, and at last sealing the contract on her lips, Mr Vanslyperken departed, full of wine and hope—two very good things to lay in a stock of.

But there was something doing on board during Mr Vanslyperken's absence. Notwithstanding Mr Vanslyperken having ordered Moggy out of the cutter, she had taken the opportunity of his being away to go on board to her dear, darling Jemmy. Dick Short did not prevent her coming on board, and he was commanding officer, so Moggy once more had her husband in her arms; but the fond pair soon retired to a quiet corner, where they had a long and serious conversation; so long, and so important, it would appear, that they did not break off until Mr Vanslyperken came on board, just before dark. His quick eye soon perceived that there was a petticoat at the taffrail, where they retired that they might not be overheard, and he angrily inquired who it was, his wrath was not appeased when he heard that it was Salisbury's wife, and he ordered her immediately to be put on shore, and sent for Corporal Van Spitter in his cabin, to know why she was on board. The corporal replied, " That Mr Short had let her in; that he had wished to speak on the subject, but that Mr Short would not speak," and then entertained his superior with a long account of mutinous expressions on the lower deck, and threats of doing him (Mr Vanslyperken) a mischief. This conversation was interrupted by a messenger coming on board with the despatches, and an order to sail at daylight, and return immediately without waiting for any answers.

The reader may wish to know the subject of the long conversation between Jemmy Ducks and his wife. It involved the following question. Moggy had become very useful to Nancy Corbett, and Nancy, whose services were required at the cave, and could not well be dispensed with, had long been anxious to find some one, who, with the same general knowledge of parties, and the same discrimination, could be employed in her stead. In Moggy she had found the person required, but Moggy would not consent without her husband was of the same party, and here lay the difficulty. Nancy had had a reply, which was satisfactory, from Sir Robert Barclay, so far as this. He required one or two more men, and they must be trustworthy, and able to perform the duty in the boats. Jemmy was not very great at pulling, for his arms were too short as well as his legs, but he was a capital steersman. All this had been explained to Nancy, who at last consented to Jemmy being added to the crew of the smuggler, and Moggy had gone off to the cutter to persuade Jemmy to desert, and to join the smugglers.

Now, as to joining the smugglers, Jemmy had not the least objection: he was tired of the cutter, and being separated from his wife had been to him a source of great discontent; but, as Jemmy very truly observed, "If I desert from the vessel, and am ever seen again, I am certain to be known, and taken up; therefore I will not desert, I will wait till I am paid off, unless you can procure my discharge by means of your friends." Such had been the result of the colloquy, when interrupted by the arrival of Vanslyperken, and the case thus stood, when, on the next morning, at daylight, the cutter weighed, and steered her course for the Texel.

Chapter XXIV

In which Mr Vanslyperken has nothing but trouble from the beginning to the end.

So soon as the cutter had sailed, Moggy hastened to the pretended widow to report the answer of her husband.

Nancy considered that there was much sound judgment in what Jemmy had said, and immediately repaired to the house of the Jew, Lazarus, to whom she communicated her wishes. At that time, there were many people high in office who secretly favoured King James, and the links of communication between such humble individuals as we are treating of, with those in power, although distant, were perfect.

In a few days, an order came down for the discharge of James Salisbury from the cutter *Yungfrau*, and the letter the same day was put into the hands of the delighted Moggy.

Mr Vanslyperken made his short passage to the Zuyder Zee, and anchored as usual; and when he had anchored, he proceeded to go on shore. Previously, however, to his stepping into the boat, the ship's company came aft, with Jemmy at their head, to know whether they might have leave on shore, as they were not very well pleased at their liberty having been stopped at Portsmouth.

Mr Vanslyperken very politely told them that he would see them all at the devil first, and then stepped into his boat; he at once proceeded to the house of the Jesuit, and this time, much to his satisfaction, without having been perceived, as he thought, by the widow Vandersloosh and Babette, who did not appear at the door. Having delivered his despatches, and received his customary fee, Mr Vanslyperken mentioned the difficulty of his coming to the house, as he was watched by some people opposite, and inquired if he could have the letters sent under cover to himself by some trusty hand, mentioning the ill-will of the parties in question. To this the Jesuit consented, and Vanslyperken took his leave; but on leaving the house he was again annoyed by the broad form of the widow, with Babette, as usual, at her shoulder, with their eyes fixed upon him. Without attempting a recognition, for Vanslyperken cared little for the opinion of the Frau Vandersloosh, now that he was accepted by the fair widow of Portsmouth, Mr Vanslyperken walked quietly away.

"Ah, very well, Mr Vanslyperken — very well," exclaimed the Frau Vandersloosh, as he pursued his way at a rapid rate; "very well, Mr Vanslyperken—we shall see—three times have you entered those doors, and with a fifty guineas in your pocket, I'll be bound, every time that you have walked out of them. Treason is paid high, but the traitor sometimes hangs higher still. Yes, yes, Mr Vanslyperken, we shall see—we are evidence, Mr Vanslyperken—and I'll not be married before I see you well hanged, Mr Vanslyperken. Deary me, Babette," exclaimed the widow, altering her tone, "I wonder how the corporal is: poor dear man, to be ruled by such a traitorous atomy as he."

"Perhaps he will come ashore, madam," replied Babette.

"No, no, he will never let him; but, as you say, perhaps he may. Put half a dozen bottles of the best beer to the stove—not too near, Babette—he is fond of my beer, and it does one's heart good to see him drink it, Babette. And, Babette, I'll just go up and put on something a little tidier. I think he will come—I know he will if he can."

We must leave the widow to decorate her person, and follow Vanslyperken down to the boat, and on board. On his arrival, he went down into the cabin to lock up his money. When Corporal Van Spitter went to the cabin-door, the corporal heard the clanking of the pieces as Vanslyperken counted them, and his bile was raised at the idea of Vanslyperken possessing that which should have been his own. The corporal waited a little, and then knocked. Vanslyperken put away the rest of his money, shut the drawer, and told him to come in.

The corporal saluted, and made a request to be allowed to go on shore for an hour or two.

"Go on shore! *you* go on shore, corporal? why you never asked to go on shore before," replied the suspicious Vanslyperken.

"If you please, sir," replied the corporal, "I wish to

pay de people who gave me de board and de lodging ven I vas last on shore."

"Ah, very true, I forgot that, corporal. Well, then, you may go on shore; but do not stop long, for the people are much inclined to mutiny, and I cannot do without you."

The corporal quitted the cabin and was put on shore by two of the men in the small boat. He hastened up to the widow's house, and was received with open arms. Seated on the squab sofa, with a bottle of beer on the table, and five others all ready at the stove, the widow's smiles beaming on him, who could be more happy than the Corporal Van Spitter? The blinds were up at the windows, the front door fast to prevent intrusion, and then the widow and he entered into a long colloquy, interrupted occasionally by little amorous dallyings, which reminded you of the wooings of a male and female elephant.

We shall give the substance of the conversation. The widow expressed her indignation against Vanslyperken, and her resolution not to be married until he was hanged. The corporal immediately became an interested party, and vowed that he would assist all in his power. He narrated all that had passed since he had left the widow's, and the supernatural appearance of the dog after he had thrown it overboard. He then pointed out that it was necessary that Vanslyperken should not only be blinded as to the state of matters between them, but that, to entrap him still more, the widow should, if possible, make friends with him. To this the widow unwillingly consented; but as the corporal pointed out that that was the only chance of her occasionally seeing him, and that by his pretending to be in love with Babette, Vanslyperken might be deceived completely, she did consent; the more so, that the greater would be his disappointment at the end, the more complete would be her vengeance. Their plans being arranged, it was then debated whether it would not be better to send some message on board to Vanslyperken, and it was agreed that it should be taken by the corporal. At last all was arranged, the six bottles of beer were finished, and the corporal having been permitted to imprint as many hearty smacks upon the widow's thick and juicy lips, he returned on board.

"Come on board, Mynheer Vanslyperken," said the corporal, entering the cabin.

"Very well, corporal; did you do all you wanted? for we sail again at daylight."

"Yes, mynheer, and I see somebody I never see before."

"Who was that, corporal?" replied Vanslyperken, for he had been feasting upon the recollections of the fair Portsmouth widow, and was in a very good humour.

"One fine Frau, Mynheer Vanslyperken—very fine Frau. Babette came up to me in the street."

"Oh, Babette—well, what did she say?"

Hereupon the corporal, as agreed with the widow, entered into a long explanation, stating his Babette had told him that her mistress was very much surprised that Mr Vanslyperken had passed close to the door, and had never come in to call upon her; that her mistress had been quite satisfied with Mr Vanslyperken's letter, and would wish to see him again; and that he, the corporal, had told Babette the dog had been destroyed by him, Mr Vanslyperken, and he hoped he had done right in saying so.

"No," replied Vanslyperken, "you have done wrong; and if you go on shore again, you may just give this answer, that Mr Vanslyperken don't care a d--n for the old woman; that she may carry her carcass to some other market, for Mr Vanslyperken would not touch her with a pair of tongs. Will you recollect that, corporal?"

"Yes," replied the corporal, grinding his teeth at this insult to his betrothed, "yes, mynheer, I will recollect that. Mein Gott! I shall not forget it."

"Kill my dog, heh!" continued Vanslyperken, talking to himself aloud. "Yes, yes, Frau Vandersloosh, you shall fret to some purpose. I'll worry down your fat for you. Yes, yes, Madam Vandersloosh, you shall bite your nails to the quick yet. Nothing would please you but Snarleyyow dead at your porch. My dog, indeed!—you may go now, corporal."

"Mein Gott! but ve vill see as well as you, Mynheer Vanslyperken," muttered the corporal, as he walked forward.

After dark, a man came alongside in a small boat, and desired to see Mr Vanslyperken. As soon as he was in the cabin and the door shut, he laid some letters on the table, and without saying a word went on deck and on shore again. At daybreak the cutter weighed, and ran with a fair wind to Portsmouth.

With what a bounding heart did Mr Vanslyperken step into the boat attired in his best! He hardly could prevail upon himself to report his arrival to the admiral, so impatient was he to throw himself at the fair widow's feet, and claim her promise upon his return. He did so, however, and then proceeded to the house in Castle Street.

His heart beat rapidly as he knocked at the door, and he awaited the opening with impatience. At last it was opened, but not by the widow's servant. "Is Mrs Malcolm at home?" inquired Vanslyperken.

"Malcolm, sir!" replied the woman; "do you mean the lady who was living here, and left yesterday?"

"Left yesterday!" exclaimed Vanslyperken, hardly able to stand on his feet.

"Yes, only yesterday afternoon. Went away with a gentleman."

"A gentleman!" exclaimed Vanslyperken, all amazement.

"Yes, sir; pray, sir, be you the officer of the king's cutter?"

"I am!" exclaimed Vanslyperken, leaning against the door-jamb for support.

"Then, sir, here be a letter for you." So saying, the woman pulled up her dirty apron, then her gown, and at last arrived at a queer fustian pocket, out of which she produced the missive, which had been jumbled in company with a bit of wax, a ball of blue worsted, some halfpence, a copper thimble, and a lump of Turkey rhubarb, from all of which companions it had received a variety of hues and colours. Vanslyperken seized the letter as soon as it was produced, and passing by the woman, went into the dining-parlour, where, with feelings of anxiety, he sat down, brushed the perspiration from his forehead, and read as follows:

"*My dear, dear, ever dear Mr Vanslyperken,*

"Pity me, pity me, O pity me! Alas! how soon is the cup of bliss dashed from the lips of us poor mortals. I can hardly write, hardly hold my pen, or hold my head up. I cannot bear that, from my hand, you should be informed of the utter blight of all our hopes which blossomed so fully. Alas! alas! but it must be. O my head, my poor, poor head—how it swims! I was sitting at the fireside, thinking when you would return, and trying to find out if the wind was fair, when I heard a knock at the door. It was so like yours, that my heart beat, and I ran to the window, but I could not see who it was, so I sat down again. Imagine my surprise, my horror, my vexation, my distress, my agony, when who should come in but my supposed dead husband! I thought I should have died when I saw him. I dropped as it was, down into a swoon, and when I came to my senses, there he was hanging over me; thinking, poor fool, that I had swooned for joy, and kissing me—pah! yes, kissing me. O dear! O dear! My dear Mr Vanslyperken, I thought of you, and what your feelings would be, when you know all this; but there he was alive, and in good health, and now I have nothing more to do but to lie down and die.

"It appears that in my ravings I called upon you over and over again, and discovered the real state of my poor bleeding heart, and he was very angry: he packed up everything, and he insisted upon my leaving Portsmouth.

Alas! I shall be buried in the north, and never see you again. But why should I, my dear Mr Vanslyperken? what good will come of it? I am a virtuous woman, and will be so: but, O dear! I can write no more.

"Farewell, then, farewell! Farewell for ever! Dear Mr Vanslyperken, think no more of your disconsolate, unhappy, heart-broken, miserable

"ANN MALCOLM.

"*P.S.*—For my sake you will adhere to the good cause; I know you will, my dearest."

Mr Vanslyperken perused this heart-rending epistle, and fell back on his chair almost suffocated. The woman, who had stood in the passage while he read the letter, came to his assistance, and pouring some water into his mouth, and throwing a portion of it over his face, partially revived him. Vanslyperken's head fell on the table upon his hands, and for some minutes remained in that position. He then rose, folded the letter, put it in his pocket, and staggered out of the house without saying a word.

O Nancy Corbett! Nancy Corbett! this was all your doing.

You had gained your point in winning over the poor man to commit treason—you had waited till he was so entangled that he could not escape, or in future refuse to obey the orders of the Jacobite party—you had seduced him, Nancy Corbett—you had intoxicated him—in short, Nancy, you had ruined him, and then you threw him over by this insidious and perfidious letter.

Vanslyperken walked away, he hardly knew whither —his mind was a chaos. It did so happen, that he took the direction of his mother's house, and, as he gradually recovered himself, he hastened there to give vent to his feelings. The old woman seldom or ever went out; if she did, it was in the dusk, to purchase in one half-hour enough to support existence for a fortnight.

She was at home with her door locked, as usual, when he demanded admittance.

"Come in, child, come in," said the old beldame, as with palsied hands she undid the fastenings. "I dreamt of you, last night, Cornelius, and when I dream of others it bodes them no good."

Vanslyperken sat down on a chest, without giving any answer. He put his hand up to his forehead, and groaned in the bitterness of his spirit.

"Ah! ah!" said his mother "I have put my hand up in that way in my time. Yes, yes—when my brain burned—when I had done the deed. What have you done, my child? Pour out your feelings into your mother's bosom. Tell me all—tell me why—and tell me, did you get any money?"

"I have lost everything," replied Vanslyperken, in a melancholy tone.

"Lost everything! then you must begin over again, and take from others till you have recovered all. That's the way—I'll have more yet, before I die. I shall not die yet—no, no."

Vanslyperken remained silent for some time. He then, as usual, imparted to his mother all that had occurred.

"Well, well, my child; but there is the other one. Gold is gold, one wife is as good—to neglect—as another. My child, never marry a woman for love—she will make a fool of you. You have had a lucky escape—I see you have, Cornelius. But where is the gold you said you took for turning traitor—where is it?"

"I shall bring it on shore to-morrow, mother."

"Do, child, do. They may find you out—they may hang you—but they shall never wrest the gold from me. It will be safe—quite safe, with me, as long as I live. I shall not die yet—no, no."

Vanslyperken rose to depart; he was anxious to be aboard.

"Go, child, go. I have hopes of you—you have murdered, have you not?"

"No, no," replied Vanslyperken, "he lives yet."

"Then try again. At all events, you have wished to

murder, and you have sold your country for gold. Cornelius Vanslyperken, by the hatred I bear the whole world, I feel that I almost love you now;—I see you are my own child. Now go, and mind to-morrow you bring the gold."

Vanslyperken quitted the house, and walked down to go on board again; the loss of the fair widow, all his hopes dashed at once to the ground, his having neglected the widow Vandersloosh and sent her an insulting message, had only the effect of raising his bile. He vowed vengeance against everybody and everything, especially against Smallbones, whom he was determined he would sacrifice: murder now was no longer horrible to his ideas; on the contrary, there was a pleasure in meditating upon it, and the loss of the expected fortune of the fair Mrs Malcolm only made him more eager to obtain gold, and he contemplated treason as the means of so doing without any feelings of compunction.

On his arrival on board, he found an order from the Admiralty to discharge James Salisbury. This added to his choler and his meditations of revenge. Jemmy Ducks had not been forgotten; and he determined not to make known the order until he had punished him for his mutinous expressions; but Moggy had come on board during his absence, and delivered to her husband the letter from the Admiralty notifying his discharge. Vanslyperken sent for Corporal Van Spitter to consult, but the corporal informed him that Jemmy Ducks knew of his discharge. Vanslyperken's anger was now without bounds. He hastened on deck, and ordered the hands to be turned up for punishment, but Corporal Van Spitter hastened to give warning to Jemmy, who did not pipe the hands when ordered.

"Where is that scoundrel, James Salisbury?" cried Vanslyperken.

"Here is James Salisbury," replied Jemmy, coming aft.

"Turn the hands up for punishment, sir."

"I don't belong to the vessel," replied Jemmy, going forward.

"Corporal Van Spitter — where is Corporal Van Spitter?"

"Here, sir," said the corporal, coming up the hatchway in a pretended bustle.

"Bring that man, Salisbury, aft."

"Yes, sir," replied the corporal, going forward with assumed eagerness.

But all the ship's company had resolved that this act of injustice should not be done. Salisbury was no longer in the service, and although they knew the corporal to be on their side, they surrounded Jemmy on the forecastle, and the corporal came aft, declaring that he could not get near the prisoner. As he made this report a loud female voice was heard alongside.

"So, you'd flog my Jemmy, would you, you varmint? But you won't though; he's not in the service, and you sha'n't touch him; but I'll tell you what, keep yourself on board, Mr Leeftenant, for if I cotches you on shore, I'll make you sing in a way you don't think on. Yes, flog my Jemmy, my dear darling duck of a Jemmy—stop a minute—I'm coming aboard."

Suiting the action to the word, for the sailors had beckoned to Moggy to come on board, she boldly pulled alongside, and skipping over, she went up direct to Mr Vanslyperken. "I'll just trouble you for my husband, and no mistake," cried Moggy.

"Corporal Van Spitter, turn that woman out of the ship."

"Turn me, a lawful married woman, who comes arter my own husband with the orders of your masters, Mr Leeftenant!—I'd like to see the man. I axes you for my Jemmy, and I'll trouble you just to hand him here—if not, look out for squalls, that's all. I demand my husband in the king's name, so just hand him over," continued Moggy, putting her nose so close to that of Mr Vanslyperken that they nearly touched, and then after a few seconds' pause, for Vanslyperken could not speak for rage, she added, "Well, you're a nice leeftenant, I don't think."

"Send for your marines, Corporal Van Spitter."

"I have, Mynheer Vanslyperken," replied the corporal, standing erect and saluting; "and if you please, sir, they have joined the ship's company. You and I, mynheer, are left to ourselves."

"I'll just trouble you for my little duck of a husband," repeated Moggy. Vanslyperken was at a nonplus. The crew were in a state of mutiny, the marines had joined them—what could he do? To appeal to the higher authorities would be committing himself, for he knew that he could not flog a man who no longer belonged to the vessel.

"I wants my husband," repeated Moggy, putting her arms a-kimbo.

Mr Vanslyperken made no reply. The corporal waited for orders, and Moggy waited for her husband.

Just at this moment, Snarleyyow, who had followed his master on deck, had climbed up the small ladder, and was looking over the gunnel on the side where the boat lay in which Moggy came on board. Perceiving this, with the quickness of thought she ran at the dog and pushed him over the side into the boat, in which he fell with a heavy bound; she then descended the side, ordered the man to shove off, and kept at a short distance from the cutter with the dog in her possession.

"Now, now," cried Moggy, slapping her elbow, "hav'n't I got the dog, and won't I cut him up into sassingers and eat him in the bargain, if you won't give me my dear darling Jemmy and all his papers in the bargain?"

"Man the boat," cried Vanslyperken. But no one would obey the order.

"Look here," cried Moggy, flourishing a knife which she had borrowed from the man in the boat. "This is for the cur; and unless you let my Jemmy go, ay and directly too——"

"Mercy, woman!" exclaimed Vanslyperken, "Do not harm the poor dog, and your husband shall go on shore."

"With his papers all ready to receive his pay?" inquired Moggy.

"Yes, with his papers and everything, if you'll not harm the poor beast."

"Be quick about them, for my fingers are itching, I can tell you," replied Moggy. "Recollect, I will have my Jemmy, and cut the dog's throat in the bargain if you don't look sharp."

"Directly, good woman, directly," cried Vanslyperken, "be patient."

"Good woman! no more a good woman than yourself," replied Moggy.

Vanslyperken desired the corporal to see Jemmy Ducks in the boat, and went down into the cabin to sign his pay order. He then returned, for he was dreadfully alarmed lest Moggy should put her threats in execution.

Jemmy's chest and hammocks were in the boat. He shook hands with his shipmates, and receiving the papers and his discharge from Corporal Van Spitter, and exchanging an intelligent glance with him, he went down the side. The boat pulled round the stern to take in Moggy, who then ordered the waterman to put the dog on board again.

"My word's as good as my bond," observed Moggy, as she stepped into the other boat, "and so there's your cur again, Mr Leeftenant; but mark my words: I owe you one, and I'll pay you with interest before I have done with you."

Jemmy then raised his pipe to his lips, and sounded its loudest note: the men gave him three cheers, and Mr Vanslyperken in a paroxysm of fury, ran down into his cabin.

Chapter XXV

In which Mr Vanslyperken proves that he has a great aversion to cold steel.

MR VANSLYPERKEN had been so much upset by the events of the day, that he had quite forgotten to deliver the letters entrusted to him to the care of the Jew Lazarus; weighty indeed must have been the events which could have prevented him from going to receive money.

He threw himself on his bed with combined feelings of rage and mortification, and slept a feverish sleep in his clothes.

His dreams were terrifying, and he awoke in the morning unrefreshed. The mutiny and defection of the ship's company, he ascribed entirely to the machinations of Smallbones, whom he now hated with a feeling so intense, that he felt he could have murdered him in the open day. Such were the first impulses that his mind resorted to upon his awaking, and after some little demur, he sent for Corporal Van Spitter, to consult with him. The corporal made his appearance, all humility and respect, and was again sounded as to what could be done with Smallbones, Vanslyperken hinting very clearly what his wishes tended to.

Corporal Van Spitter, who had made up his mind how to act after their previous conference, hummed and ha'ed, and appeared unwilling to enter upon the subject, until he was pushed by his commandant, when the corporal observed there was something very strange about the lad, and hinted at his being sent in the cutter on purpose to annoy his superior.

"That on that night upon which he had stated that he had seen the devil three times, once it was sitting on the head-clue of Smallbones' hammock, and at another time that he was evidently in converse with the lad, and that there were strange stories among the ship's company, who considered that both Smallbones and the dog were supernatural agents."

"My dog — Snarleyyow — a — what do you mean, corporal?"

The corporal then told Mr Vanslyperken that he had discovered that several attempts had been made to drown the dog, but without success; and that among the rest, he had been thrown by Smallbones into the canal, tied up in a bread-bag, and had miraculously made his appearance again.

"The villain!" exclaimed Vanslyperken. "That then was the paving-stone. Now I've found it out, I'll cut his very soul out of his body."

But the corporal protested against open measures, as, although it was known by his own confession to be the case, it could not be proved, as none of the men would tell.

"Besides, he did not think that any further attempts would be made, as Smallbones had been heard to laugh and say, 'that water would never hurt him or the dog,' which observation of the lad's had first made the ship's company suspect."

"Very true," exclaimed Vanslyperken; "he floated out to the Nab buoy and back again, when I——" Here Mr Vanslyperken stopped short, and he felt a dread of supernatural powers in the lad, when he thought of what had passed and what he now heard.

"So they think my dog——"

"De tyfel," replied the corporal.

Vanslyperken was not very sorry for this, as it would be the dog's protection; but at the same time he was not at all easy about Smallbones; for Mr Vanslyperken, as we have observed before, was both superstitious and cowardly.

"Water won't hurt him, did you say, corporal?"

"Yes, mynheer."

"Then I'll try what a pistol will do, by heavens!" replied Vanslyperken. "He threw my dog into the canal, and I'll be revenged, if revenge is to be had. That will do, corporal, you may go now," continued Vanslyperken, who actually foamed with rage.

The corporal left the cabin, and it having occurred to Vanslyperken that he had not delivered the letters, he dressed himself to go on shore.

After having once more read through the letter of the fair widow, which, at the same time that it crushed all his hopes, from its kind tenour, poured some balm into his wounded heart, he sighed, folded it up, put it away, and went on deck.

"Pipe the gig away," said Mr Vanslyperken.

"No pipe," replied Short.

This reminded Mr Vanslyperken that Jemmy Ducks had left the ship, and vexed him again. He ordered the word to be passed to the boat's crew, and when it was manned he went on shore. As soon as he arrived at the house of Lazarus, he knocked, but it was some time before he was admitted, and the chain was still kept on the door, which was opened two inches to allow a scrutiny previous to entrance.

"Ah! it vash you, vash it, good sar? you may come in," said the Jew.

Vanslyperken walked into the parlour, where he found seated a young man of very handsome exterior, dressed according to the fashion of the cavaliers of the time. His hat, with a plume of black feathers, lay upon the table. This personage continued in his careless and easy position without rising when Vanslyperken entered, neither did he ask him to sit down.

"You are the officer of the cutter?" inquired the young man, with an air of authority not very pleasing to the lieutenant.

"Yes," replied Vanslyperken, looking hard and indignantly in return.

"And you arrived yesterday morning? Pray, sir, why were not those letters delivered at once?"

"Because I had no time," replied Vanslyperken, sulkily.

"No time, sir; what do you mean by that? Your time is ours, sir. You are paid for it; for one shilling that you receive from the rascally government you condescend to serve and to betray, you receive from us pounds. Let not this happen again, my sir, or you may repent it."

Vanslyperken was not in the best of humours, and he angrily replied, "Then you may get others to do your work, for this is the last I'll do; pay me for them, and let me go."

"The last you'll do; you'll do as much as we please, and as long as we please. You are doubly in our power, scoundrel! You betray the government you serve, but you shall not betray us. If you had a thousand lives, you are a dead man the very moment you flinch from or neglect our work. Do your work faithfully, and you will be rewarded; but either you must do our work or die. You have but to choose."

"Indeed!" replied Vanslyperken.

"Yes, indeed! And to prove that I am in earnest, I shall punish you for your neglect, by not paying you this time. You may leave the letters and go. But mind that you give us timely notice when you are ordered back to the Hague, for we shall want you."

Vanslyperken, indignant at this language, obeyed his first impulse, which was to snatch up the letters and attempt to leave the room.

"No pay, no letters!" exclaimed he, opening the door.

"Fool!" cried the young man with a bitter sneer, not stirring from his seat.

Vanslyperken opened the door, and to his amazement there were three swords pointed to his heart. He started back.

"Will you leave the letters now?" observed the young man.

Vanslyperken threw them down on the table with every sign of perturbation, and remained silent and pale.

"And now perfectly understand me, sir," said the young

cavalier. "We make a great distinction between those who have joined the good cause, or rather, who have continued steadfast to their king from feelings of honour and loyalty, and those who are to be bought and sold. We honour the first, we despise the latter. Their services we require, and therefore we employ them. A traitor to the sovereign from whom he receives his pay, is not likely to be trusted by us. I know your character, that is sufficient. Now, although the government make no difference between one party or the other, with the exception that some may be honoured with the axe instead of the gibbet, you will observe what we do: and as our lives are already forfeited by attainder, we make no scruple of putting out of the way any one whom we may even suspect of betraying us. Nay, more; we can furnish the government with sufficient proofs against you without any risk to ourselves, for we have many partisans who are still in office. Weigh now well all you have heard, and be assured, that although we despise you, and use you only as our tool, we will have faithful and diligent service; if not, your life is forfeited."

Vanslyperken heard all this with amazement and confusion: he immediately perceived that he was in a snare, from which escape was impossible. His coward heart sank within him, and he promised implicit obedience.

"Nevertheless, before you go you will sign your adherence to King James and his successors," observed the young cavalier. "Lazarus, bring in writing materials." The Jew, who was at the door, complied with the order.

The cavalier took the pen and wrote down a certain form, in which Vanslyperken dedicated his life and means, as he valued his salvation, to the service of the exiled monarch. "Read that, and sign it, sir," said the cavalier, passing it over to Vanslyperken.

The lieutenant hesitated. "Your life depends upon it," continued the young man coolly; "do as you please."

Vanslyperken turned round; the swords were still pointed, and the eyes of those which held them were fixed upon the cavalier awaiting his orders. Vanslyperken perceived that there was no escape. With a trembling hand he affixed his signature.

"'Tis well:—now, observe, that at the first suspicion, or want of zeal, even, on your part, this will be forwarded through the proper channel, and even if you should escape the government, you will not escape us:—our name is Legion. You may go, sir;—do your work well, and you shall be well rewarded."

Vanslyperken hastened away, passing the swords, the points of which were now lowered for his passage. Perhaps he never till then felt how contemptible was a traitor. Indignant, mortified, and confused, still trembling with fear, and, at the same time, burning with rage, he hastened to his mother's house, for he had brought on shore with him the money which he had received at Amsterdam.

"What, more vexation, child?" said the old woman, looking Vanslyperken in the face as he entered.

"Yes," retorted Vanslyperken, folding his arms as he sat down.

It was some time before he would communicate to his mother all that happened. At last the truth, which even he felt ashamed of, was drawn out of him.

"Now may all the curses that ever befell a man fall on his head!" exclaimed Vanslyperken as he finished. "I would give soul and body to be revenged on him."

"That's my own child—that is what I have done, Cornelius, but I shall not die yet awhile. I like to hear you say that; but it must not be yet. Let them plot and plot, and when they think that all is ripe, and all is ready, and all will succeed—then—then is the time to revenge yourself—not yet—but for that revenge, death on the gallows would be sweet."

Vanslyperken shuddered:—he did not feel how death could in any way be sweet;—for some time he was wrapped up in his own thoughts.

"Have you brought the gold at last?" inquired the old woman.

"I have," replied Vanslyperken, who raised himself

and produced it. "I ought to have had more,—but I'll be revenged."

"Yes, yes, but get more gold first. Never kill the goose that lays the golden egg, my child," replied the old woman, as she turned the key.

So many sudden and mortifying occurrences had taken place in forty-eight hours that Vanslyperken's brain was in a whirl. He felt goaded to do something, but he did not know what. Perhaps it would have been suicide had he not been a coward. He left his mother without speaking another word, and walked down to the boat, revolving first one and then another incident in his mind. At last, his ideas appeared to concentrate themselves into one point, which was a firm and raging animosity against Smallbones; and with the darkest intentions he hastened on board and went down into his cabin.

What was the result of these feelings will be seen in the ensuing chapter.

Chapter XXVI

In which Mr Vanslyperken sees a ghost.

BEFORE we acquaint the reader with the movements of Mr Vanslyperken, we must again revert to the history of the period in which we are writing. The Jacobite faction had assumed a formidable consistency, and every exertion was being made by them for an invasion of England. They knew that their friends were numerous, and that many who held office under the ruling government were attached to their cause, and only required such a demonstration to fly to arms with their numerous partisans.

Up to the present, all the machinations of the Jacobites had been carried on with secrecy and dexterity, but now was the time for action and decision. To aid the cause, it was considered expedient that some one of known fidelity should be sent to Amsterdam, where the projects of William might be discovered more easily than in England: for, as he communicated with the States General, and the States General were composed of many, secrets would come out, for that which is known to many soon becomes no longer a secret.

To effect this, letters of recommendation to one or two of those high in office in Holland, and who were supposed to be able to give information, and inclined to be confiding and garrulous, had been procured from the firm allies of King William, by those who pretended to be so only, for the agent who was about to be sent over, and this agent was the young cavalier who had treated Vanslyperken in so uncourteous a manner. He has already been mentioned to the reader by the name of Ramsay, and second in authority among the smugglers. He was a young man of high family, and a brother to Lady Alice, of course trusted by Sir Robert and his second in command. He had been attainted for non-appearance, and condemned for high treason at the same time as had been his brother-in-law, Sir Robert Barclay, and had ever since been with him doing his duty in the boat and in command of the men, when Sir Robert's services or attendance were required at St Germains.

No one could be better adapted for the service he was to be employed upon. He was brave, cool, intelligent, and prepossessing. Of course, by his letters of introduction, he was represented as a firm ally of King William, and strongly recommended as such. The letters which Vanslyperken had neglected to deliver were of the utmost importance, and the character of the lieutenant being well known to Ramsay, through the medium of Nancy Corbett and others, he had treated him in the way which he considered as most likely to enforce a rigid compliance with their wishes.

Ramsay was right; for Vanslyperken was too much of a coward to venture upon resistance, although he might threaten it. It was the intention of Ramsay, moreover, to take a passage over with him in the *Yungfrau*, as his arrival in a king's vessel would add still more to the success of the enterprise which he had in contemplation.

We will now return to Mr Vanslyperken, whom we left boiling with indignation. He is not in a better humour at this moment. He requires a victim to expend his wrath upon, and that victim he is resolved shall be Smallbones, upon whom his hate is concentrated.

He has sent for the corporal, and next ordered him to bring him a pistol and cartridge, which the corporal has complied with. Vanslyperken has not made the corporal a further confidant, but he has his suspicions, and he is on the watch. Vanslyperken is alone, his hand trembling as he loads the pistol which he has taken down from the bulkhead where it hung, but he is nevertheless determined upon the act. He has laid it down on the table, and goes on deck, waiting till it is dusk for the completion of his project. He has now arranged his plan and descends; the pistol is still on the table, and he puts it under the blanket on his bed, and rings for Smallbones.

"Did you want me, sir?" said Smallbones.

"Yes, I am going on shore to sleep a little way in the country, and I want you to carry my clothes; let everything be put up in the blue bag, and hold yourself ready to come with me."

"Yes, sir," replied Smallbones; "am I to come on board again to-night?"

"To be sure you are."

Smallbones put up as desired by his master, whose eyes followed the lad's motions as he moved from one part of the cabin to the other, his thoughts wandering from the recollection of Smallbones having attempted to drown his dog, to the more pleasing one of revenge.

At dusk, Mr Vanslyperken ordered his boat to be manned, and so soon as Smallbones had gone into it with the bag, he took the pistol from where he had hid it, and concealing it under his great-coat, followed the lad into the boat.

They landed, and Vanslyperken walked fast; it was

now dark, and he was followed by Smallbones, who found difficulty in keeping pace with his master, so rapid were his strides.

They passed the half-way houses, and went clear of the fortifications, until they had gained five or six miles on the road to London.

Smallbones was tired out with the rapidity of the walk, and now lagged behind. The master desired him to come on. "I does come on as fast as I can, sir, but this here walking don't suit at all, with carrying a bag full of clothes," replied Smallbones.

"Make haste, and keep up with me," cried Vanslyperken, setting off again at a more rapid pace.

They were now past all the buildings, and but occasionally fell in with some solitary farmhouse, or cottage, on the road side; the night was cloudy, and the scud flew fast; Vanslyperken walked on faster, for in his state of mind he could feel no bodily fatigue, and the lad dropped astern.

At last the lieutenant found a spot which afforded him an opportunity of executing his fell purpose. A square wall, round a homestead for cattle, was built on the side of the footpath. Vanslyperken turned round, and looked for Smallbones, who was too far behind to be seen in the obscurity. Satisfied by this that the lad could not see his motions, Vanslyperken secreted himself behind the angle of the wall so as to allow Smallbones to pass. He cocked his pistol, and crouched down, waiting for the arrival of his victim.

In a minute or two he heard the panting of the lad, who was quite weary with his load. Vanslyperken compressed his lips, and held his breath. The lad passed him; Vanslyperken now rose from behind, levelled the pistol at the lad's head, and fired. Smallbones uttered a yell, fell down on his face, and then rolled on his back without life or motion.

Vanslyperken looked at him for one second, then turned back, and fled with the wings of the wind. Conscience now appeared to pursue him, and he ran on until he was so exhausted, that he fell; the pistol was still in his hand, and as he put out his arm mechanically to save himself, the lock of the pistol came in violent contact with his temple.

After a time he rose again, faint and bleeding, and continued his course at a more moderate pace, but as the wind blew, and whistled among the boughs of the trees, he thought every moment that he beheld the form of the murdered lad. He quickened his pace, arrived at last within the fortifications, and putting the pistol in his coat-pocket, he somewhat recovered himself. He bound his silk handkerchief round his head, and proceeded to the boat, which he had ordered to wait till Smallbones' return. He had then a part to act, and told the men that he had been assailed by robbers, and ordered them to pull on board immediately. As soon as he came on board he desired the men to assist him down into his cabin, and then he sent for Corporal Van Spitter to dress his wounds. He communicated to the corporal, that as he was going out in the country as he had proposed, he had been attacked by robbers, that he had been severely wounded, and had, he thought, killed one of them, as the others ran away; what had become of Smallbones he knew not, but he had heard him crying out in the hands of the robbers.

The corporal, who had felt certain that the pistol had been intended for Smallbones, hardly knew what to make of the matter; the wound of Mr Vanslyperken was severe, and it was hardly to be supposed that it had been self-inflicted. The corporal therefore held his tongue, heard all that Mr Vanslyperken had to say, and was very considerably puzzled.

"It was a fortunate thing that I thought of taking a pistol with me, corporal, I might have been murdered outright."

"Yes, mynheer," replied the corporal, and binding the handkerchief round Vanslyperken's head, he then assisted him into bed. "Mein Gott! I make no head or tail of de business," said the corporal, as he walked forward; "but I must know de truth soon; I not go to bed for two or three hours, and den I hear others."

It is needless to say that Mr Vanslyperken passed a restless night, not only from the pain of his wound, but from the torments of conscience; for it is but by degrees that the greatest villain can drive away its stings, and then it is but for a short time, and when it does force itself back upon him, it is with redoubled power. His occasional slumbers were broken by fitful starts, in which he again and again heard the yell of the poor lad, and saw the corpse rolling at his feet. It was about an hour before daylight that Mr Vanslyperken again woke, and found that the light had burnt out. He could not remain in the dark, it was too dreadful; he raised himself, and pulled the bell over his head. Some one entered. "Bring a light immediately," cried Vanslyperken.

In a minute or two the gleams of a light were seen burning at a distance by the lieutenant. He watched its progress aft, and its entrance, and he felt relieved; but he had now a devouring thirst upon him, and his lips were glued together, and he turned over on his bed to ask the corporal, whom he supposed it was, for water. He fixed his eyes upon the party with the candle, and by the feeble light of the dip, he beheld the pale, haggard face of Smallbones, who stared at him, but uttered not a word.

"Mercy, O God! mercy!" exclaimed Vanslyperken, falling back, and covering his face with the bedclothes.

Smallbones did not reply; he blew out the candle, and quitted the cabin.

Chapter XXVII

In which Mr Vanslyperken is taught a secret.

WE are anxious to proceed with our narrative, but we must first explain the unexpected appearance of Smallbones. When Corporal Van Spitter was requested by Vanslyperken to bring a pistol and cartridge, the corporal, who had not forgotten the hints thrown out by Vanslyperken during their last consultation, immediately imagined that it was for Smallbones' benefit. And he was strengthened in his opinion, when he learnt that Smallbones was to go on shore with his master after it was dusk. Now Corporal Van Spitter had no notion of the poor lad's brains being blown out, and when Mr Vanslyperken went on deck and left the pistol, he went into the cabin, searched for it, and drew the bullet, which Vanslyperken, of course, was not aware of. It then occurred to the corporal, that if the pistol were aimed at Smallbones, and he was uninjured, it would greatly add to the idea, already half entertained by the superstitious lieutenant, of there being something supernatural about Smallbones, if he were left to suppose that he had been killed, and had reappeared. He, therefore, communicated his suspicions to the lad, told him what he had done, and advised him, if the pistol were fired, to pretend to be killed, and when left by his master, to come on board quietly in the night. Smallbones, who perceived the drift of all this, promised to act accordingly, and in the last chapter it will be observed how he contrived to deceive his master. As soon as the lieutenant was out of hearing, Smallbones rose, and leaving the bag where it lay, hastened back to Portsmouth, and came on board about two hours before Vanslyperken rang his bell. He narrated what had passed, but, of course, could not exactly swear that it was Vanslyperken who fired the pistol, as it was fired from behind, but even if he could have so sworn, at that time he would have obtained but little redress.

It was considered much more advisable that Smallbones should pretend to believe that he had been attacked by robbers, and that the ball had missed him, after he had frightened his master by his unexpected appearance, for Vanslyperken would still be of the opinion that the lad possessed a charmed life.

The state of Mr Vanslyperken during the remainder of that night was pitiable, but we must leave the reader to suppose, rather than attempt to describe it.

In the morning the corporal came in, and after asking after his superior's health, informed him that Smallbones had come on board, that the lad said that the robbers had fired a pistol at him, and then knocked him down with the butt end of it, and that he had escaped but with the loss of the bag.

This was a great relief to the mind of Mr Vanslyperken, who had imagined that he had been visited by the ghost of Smallbones during the night: he expressed himself glad at his return, and a wish to be left alone, upon which the corporal retired. As soon as Vanslyperken found out that Smallbones was still alive, his desire to kill him returned; although, when he supposed him dead, he would, to escape from his own feelings, have resuscitated him. One chief idea now whirled in his brain, which was, that the lad must have a charmed life; he had floated out to the Nab buoy and back again, and now he had had a pistol-bullet passed through his skull without injury. He felt too much fear to attempt anything against him for the future, but his desire to do so was stronger than ever.

Excitement and vexation brought on a slow fever, and Mr Vanslyperken lay for three or four days in bed; at the end of which period he received a message from the admiral, directing him to come or send on shore (for his state had been made known) for his despatches, and to sail as soon as possible.

Upon receiving the message, Mr Vanslyperken recollected his engagement at the house of the Jew Lazarus, and weak as he was, felt too much afraid of the results, should he fail, not to get out of bed and go on shore. It was with difficulty he could walk so far. When he arrived he found Ramsay ready to receive him.

"To sail as soon as possible:—'tis well, sir. Have you your despatches?"

"I sent to the admiral's for them," replied Vanslyperken.

"Well, then, be all ready to start at midnight. I shall come on board about a quarter of an hour before; you may go, sir."

Vanslyperken quailed under the keen eye and stern look of Ramsay, and obeyed the uncourteous order in silence; still he thought of revenge as he walked back to the boat and re-embarked in the cutter.

"What's this, Short?" observed Coble: "here is a new freak; we start at midnight, I hear."

"Yes," replied Short.

"Something quite new, anyhow:—don't understand it: do you?"

"No," replied Dick.

"Well, now Jemmy's gone, I don't care how soon I follow, Dick."

"Nor I," replied Short.

"I've a notion there's some mystery in all this. For," continued Coble, "the admiral would never have ordered us out till to-morrow morning, if he did not make us sail this evening. It's not a man-of-war fashion, is it, Dick?"

"No," replied Short.

"Well, we shall see," replied Coble. "I shall turn in now. You've heard all about Smallbones, heh! Dick?"

Short nodded his head.

"Well, we shall see: but I'll back the boy 'gainst master and dog too, in the long run. D—n his Dutch carcass, he seems to make but small count of English subjects, heh!"

Short leant over the gunwale and whistled.

Coble, finding it impossible to extract one monosyllable more from him, walked forward, and went down below.

A little before twelve o'clock a boat came alongside, and Ramsay stepped out of it into the cutter. Vanslyperken had been walking the deck to receive him, and immediately showed him down into the cabin, where he left him to go on deck, and get the cutter under way. There was a small stove in the cabin, for the weather was still cold; they were advanced into the month of March. Ramsay threw off his coat, laid two pair of loaded pistols on the table, locked the door of the cabin, and then proceeded to warm himself, while Vanslyperken was employed on deck.

In an hour the cutter was outside and clear of all danger, and Vanslyperken had to knock to gain admittance into his own cabin. Ramsay opened the door, and Vanslyperken, who thought he must say something, observed gloomily,

"We are all clear, sir."

"Very good," replied Ramsay; "and now, sir, I believe that you have despatches on board?"

"Yes," replied Vanslyperken.

"You will oblige me by letting me look at them."

"My despatches!" said Vanslyperken with surprise.

"Yes, sir, your despatches; immediately, if you please—no trifling."

"You forget, sir," replied Vanslyperken angrily, "that I am not any longer in your power, but on board of my own vessel."

"You appear not to know, sir, that you are in my power even on board of your own vessel," replied Ramsay, starting up, and laying his hand over the pistols, which he drew towards him, and replaced in his belt. "If you trust to your ship's company you are mistaken, as you will soon discover. I demand the despatches."

"But, sir, you will ruin me and ruin yourself," replied Vanslyperken, alarmed.

"Fear not," replied Ramsay; "for my own sake, and that of the good cause, I shall not hurt you. No one will know that the despatches have been ever examined, and——"

" And what ?" replied Vanslyperken, gloomily.

" For the passage, and this service, you will receive one hundred guineas."

Vanslyperken no longer hesitated; he opened the drawer in which he had deposited the letters, and produced them.

" Now lock the door," said Ramsay, taking his seat.

He then examined the seals, pulled some out of his pocket, and compared them; sorted the letters according to the seals, and laid one corresponding at the heading of each file, for there were three different government seals upon the despatches. He then took a long Dutch earthen pipe which was hanging above, broke off the bowl, and put one end of the stem into the fire. When it was of a red heat he took it out, and applying his lips to the cool end, and the hot one close to the sealing-wax, he blew through it, and the heated blast soon dissolved the wax, and the despatches were opened one after another without the slightest difficulty or injury to the paper. He then commenced reading, taking memorandums on his tablets as he proceeded.

When he had finished, he again heated the pipe, melted the wax, which had become cold and hard again, and resealed all the letters with his counterfeit seals.

During this occupation, which lasted upwards of an hour, Vanslyperken looked on with surprise, leaning against the bulk-head of the cabin.

" There, sir, are your despatches," said Ramsay, rising from his chair: " you may now put them away; and, as you may observe, you are not compromised."

" No, indeed," replied Vanslyperken, who was struck with the ingenuity of the method; " but you have given me an idea."

" I will tell you what that is," replied Ramsay. " You are thinking, if I left you these false seals, you could give me the contents of the despatches, provided you were well paid. Is it not so?"

"It was," replied Vanslyperken, who had immediately been struck with such a new source of wealth; for he cared little what he did—all he cared for was discovery.

"Had you not proposed it yourself, I intended that you should have done it, sir," replied Ramsay; "and that you should also be paid for it. I will arrange all that before I leave the vessel. But now I shall retire to my bed. Have you one ready?"

"I have none but what you see," replied Vanslyperken. "It is my own, but at your service."

"I shall accept it," replied Ramsay, putting his pistols under his pillow, after having thrown himself on the outside of the bedclothes, pulling his roquelaure over him. "And now you will oblige me by turning that cur out of the cabin, for his smell is anything but pleasant."

Vanslyperken had no idea of his passenger so coolly taking possession of his bed, but to turn out Snarleyyow as well as himself, appeared an unwarrantable liberty. But he felt that he had but to submit, for Ramsay was despotic, and he was afraid of him.

After much resistance, Snarleyyow was kicked out by his master, who then went on deck not in the very best of humours, at finding he had so completely sold himself to those who might betray and hang him the very next day. "At all events," thought Vanslyperken, "I'm well paid for it."

It was now daylight, and the cutter was running with a favourable breeze; the hands were turned up, and Corporal Van Spitter came on deck. Vanslyperken, who had been running over in his mind all the events which had latterly taken place, had considered that, as he had lost the Portsmouth widow, he might as well pursue his suit with the widow Vandersloosh, especially as she had sent such a conciliating message by the corporal; and perceiving the corporal on deck, he beckoned to him to approach. Vanslyperken then observed, that he was angry the other day, and that the corporal need not give that message to the Frau Vandersloosh, as he intended to call upon her himself upon his arrival. Van Spitter, who did not know anything about the Portsmouth widow, and could not imagine why the angry message had been given, of course assented, although he was fully determined that the widow should be informed of the insult. The question was now, how to be able to go on shore himself; and to compass that without suspicion, he remarked that the maid Babette was a very fine maid, and he should like to see her again.

This little piece of confidence was not thrown away. Vanslyperken was too anxious to secure the corporal, and he replied, that the corporal should go ashore and see her, if he pleased; upon which Corporal Van Spitter made his best military salute, turned round on his heel, and walked away, laughing in his sleeve at having so easily gulled his superior.

On the third morning the cutter had arrived at her destined port. During the passage Ramsay had taken possession of the cabin, ordering everything as he pleased, much to the surprise of the crew. Mr Vanslyperken spoke of him as a king's messenger, but still Smallbones, who took care to hear what was going on, reported the abject submission shown to Ramsay by the lieutenant, and this was the occasion of great marvel; moreover, they doubted his being a king's messenger, for, as Smallbones very shrewdly observed, "Why, if he was a king's messenger, did he not come with the despatches?" However, they could only surmise, and no more. But the dog being turned out of the cabin in compliance with Ramsay's wish, was the most important point of all. They could have got over all the rest, but that was quite incomprehensible; and they all agreed with Coble, when he observed, hitching up his trousers, "Depend upon it, there's a screw loose somewhere."

As soon as the cutter was at anchor, Ramsay ordered his portmanteau into the boat, and Vanslyperken having accompanied him on shore, they separated, Ramsay informing Vanslyperken that he would wish to see him the next day, and giving him his address.

Vanslyperken delivered his despatches, and then hastened to the widow Vandersloosh, who received him with a well-assumed appearance of mingled pleasure and reserve.

Vanslyperken led her to the sofa, poured forth a multitudinous compound composed of regret, devotion, and apologies, which at last appeared to have melted the heart of the widow, who once more gave him her hand to salute.

Vanslyperken was all rapture at so unexpected a reconciliation; the name of the cur was not mentioned, and Vanslyperken thought to himself, "This will do,—let me only once get you, my Frau, and I'll teach you to wish my dog dead at your porch."

On the other hand the widow thought, "And so this atomy really believes that I would look upon him! Well, well, Mr Vanslyperken, we shall see how it ends. Your cur under my bed, indeed, so sure do you never———. Yes, yes, Mr Vanslyperken."

There is a great deal of humbug in this world, that is certain.

Chapter XXVIII

In which we have at last introduced a decent sort of heroine, who, however, only plays a second in our history, Snarleyyow being first fiddle.

BUT we must leave Mr Vanslyperken, and the widow, and the *Yungfrau*, and all connected with her, for the present, and follow the steps of Ramsay, in doing which we shall have to introduce new personages in our little drama.

As soon as Ramsay had taken leave of Vanslyperken, being a stranger at Amsterdam, he inquired his way to the Golden Street, in which resided Mynheer Van Krause, syndic of the town, and to whom he had obtained his principal letters of introduction. The syndic's house was too well known not to be immediately pointed out to him, and in ten minutes he found himself, with the sailors at his heels who had been ordered to carry up his baggage, at a handsomely carved door painted in bright green, and with knockers of massive brass which glittered in the sun.

Ramsay, as he waited a few seconds, looked up at the house, which was large and with a noble front to the wide street in face of it, not, as usual with most of the others, divided in the centre by a canal running the whole length of it. The door was opened, and led into a large paved yard, the sides of which were lined with evergreens in large tubs, painted of the same bright green colour; adjoining to the yard was a small garden enclosed with high walls, which was laid out with great precision, and in small beds full of tulips, ranunculuses, and other bulbs now just appearing above the ground. The sailors waited outside while the old gray-headed servitor who had opened the gate, ushered Ramsay through the court to a second door which led into the house. The hall into which he entered was paved with marble, and the staircase bold and handsome which led to the first floor, but on each side of the hall there were wooden partitions and half-glass doors, through which Ramsay could see that the rest of the basement was appropriated to warehouses, and that in the warehouse at the back of the building there were people busily employed hoisting out merchandise from the vessels in the canal, the water of which adjoined the very walls. Ramsay followed the man upstairs, who showed him into a very splendidly-furnished apartment, and then went to summon his master, who, he said, was below in the warehouse. Ramsay had but a minute or two to examine the various objects which decorated the room, particularly some very fine pictures, when Mynheer Van Krause made his appearance, with some open tablets in his hand and his pen across his mouth. He was a very short man, with a respectable paunch, a very small head, quite bald, a keen blue eye, reddish but straight nose, and a very florid complexion. There was nothing vulgar about his appearance, although his figure was against him. His countenance was one of extreme frankness, mixed with considerable intelligence, and his whole manner gave you the idea of precision and calculation.

"You would—tyfel—I forgot my pen," said the syndic, catching it as it fell out of his mouth. "You would speak with me, mynheer? To whom have I the pleasure of addressing myself?"

"These letters, sir," replied Ramsay, "will inform you."

Mynheer Van Krause laid his tablets on the table, putting his pen across to mark the leaf where he had them open, and taking the letters begged Ramsay to be seated. He then took a chair, pulled a pair of hand-glasses out of his pocket, laid them on his knees, broke the seals, and falling back so as to recline, commenced reading. As soon as he had finished the first letter, he put his glasses down from his eyes, and made a bow to Ramsay, folded the open letter the length of the sheet, took out his pencil, and on the outside wrote the date of the letter, the day of the month, name, and the name of the writer. Having done this, he laid the first letter down on the table, took up the second, raised up his glasses, and performed the same duty towards it, and thus he continued until he had read the whole six; always, as he concluded each letter, making the same low bow to Ramsay which he had after the perusal of the first. Ramsay, who was not a little tired of all this precision, at last fixed his eyes upon a Wouvermann which hung near him, and only took them off when he guessed the time of bowing to be at hand.

The last having been duly marked and numbered, Mynheer Van Krause turned to Ramsay, and said, "I am most happy, mynheer, to find under my roof a young gentleman so much recommended by many valuable friends; moreover, as these letters give me to understand, so warm a friend to our joint sovereign, and so inimical to the Jacobite party. I am informed by these letters that you intend to remain at Amsterdam. If so, I trust that you will take up your quarters in this house."

To this proposal Ramsay, who fully expected it, gave a willing consent, saying, at the same time, that he had proposed going to an hotel; but Mynheer Van Krause insisted on sending for Ramsay's luggage. He had not far to send, as it was at the door.

"How did you come over?" inquired the host.

"In a king's cutter," replied Ramsay, "which waited for me at Portsmouth."

This intimation produced another very low bow from Mynheer Van Krause, as it warranted the importance of his guest; but he then rose, and apologising for his presence being necessary below, as they were unloading a cargo of considerable value, he ordered his old porter to show Mr Ramsay into his rooms, and to take up his luggage, informing his guest that, it being now twelve o'clock, dinner would be on the table at half-past one, during which interval he begged Ramsay to amuse himself, by examining the pictures, books, &c., with which the room was well furnished. Then, resuming his tablets and pen, and taking the letters with him, Mynheer Van Krause made a very low bow, and left Ramsay to himself, little imagining that he had admitted an attainted traitor under his roof.

Ramsay could speak Dutch fluently, for he had been quartered two years at Middleburg, when he was serving in the army. As soon as the sailors had taken up his portmanteau, and he had dismissed them with a gratuity, the extent of which made the old porter open his eyes with astonishment, and gave him a favourable opinion of his master's new guest, he entered into conversation with the old man, who, like Eve upon another occasion, was tempted, nothing loth, for the old man loved to talk; and in a house so busy as the syndic's there were few who had time to chatter, and those who had, preferred other conversation to what, it must be confessed, was rather prosy.

"Mein Gott, mynheer, you must not expect to have company here all day. My master has the town business and his own business to attend to: he can't well get through it all: besides, now is a busy time, the schuyts are bringing up the cargo of a vessel from a far voyage, and Mynheer Krause always goes to the warehouse from breakfast till dinner, and then again from three or four o'clock till six. After that he will stay above, and then sees company, and hears our young lady sing."

" Young lady! has he a daughter then ? "

"He has a daughter, mynheer—only one—only one child—no son, it is a pity; and so much money too, they say. I don't know how many stivers and guilders she will have by-and-bye."

" Is not Madame Krause still alive ? "

"No, mynheer, she died when this maiden was born. She was a good lady, cured me once of the yellow jaundice."

Ramsay, like all young men, wondered what sort of a person this lady might be; but he was too discreet to put the question. He was, however, pleased to hear that there was a young female in the house, as it would make the time pass away more agreeably; not that he expected much. Judging from the father, he made up his mind, as he took his clothes out of his valise, that she was very short, very prim, and had a hooked nose.

The old man now left the room to allow Ramsay to dress, and telling him that if he wanted anything, he had only to call for Koops, which was his name, but going out, he returned to say, that Ramsay must call rather loud, as he was a little hard of hearing.

"Well," thought Ramsay, as he was busy with his toilet, " here I am safe lodged at last, and everything appears as if it would prosper. There is something in my position which my mind revolts at, but stratagem is necessary in war. I am in the enemy's camp to save my own life, and to serve the just cause. It is no more than what they attempt to do with us. It is my duty to my lawful sovereign, but still——I do not like it. Then the more merit in performing a duty so foreign to my inclinations."

Such were the thoughts of Ramsay, who like other

manly and daring dispositions, was dissatisfied with playing the part of a deceiver, although he had been selected for the service, and his selection had been approved of at the Court of St Germains.

Open warfare would have suited him better; but he would not repine at what he considered he was bound in fealty to perform, if required, although he instinctively shrank from it. His toilet was complete, and Ramsay descended into the reception-room: he had been longer than usual, but probably that was because he wished to commune with himself; or it might be, because he had been informed that there was a young lady in the house.

The room was empty when Ramsay entered it, and he took the advice of his host, and amused himself by examining the pictures, and other articles of *virtu*, with which the room was filled.

At last, having looked at everything, Ramsay examined a splendid clock on the mantelpiece, before a fine glass, which mounted to the very top of the lofty room, when, accidentally casting his eyes to the looking-glass, he perceived in it that the door of the room, to which his back was turned, was open, and that a female was standing there, apparently surprised to find a stranger, and not exactly knowing whether to advance or retreat. Ramsay remained in the same position, as if he did not perceive her, that he might look at her without her being aware of it. It was, as he presumed, the syndic's daughter; but how different from the person he had conjured up in his mind's eye, when at his toilet! Apparently about seventeen or eighteen years of age, she was rather above the height of woman, delicately formed, although not by any means thin in her person: her figure possessing all that feminine luxuriance, which can only be obtained when the bones are small, but well covered. Her face was oval, and brilliantly fair. Her hair of a dark chestnut, and her eyes of a deep blue. Her dress was simple in the extreme. She wore nothing but the white woollen petticoats of the time, so short, as to show above her ankles, and a sort of little jacket of fine green cloth, with lappets, which descended from the waist, and opened in front. Altogether, Ramsay thought that he had never in his life seen a young female so peculiarly attractive at first sight: there was a freshness in her air and appearance so uncommon, so unlike the general crowd. As she stood in a state of uncertainty, her mouth opened, and displayed small and beautifully white teeth.

Gradually she receded, supposing that she had not been discovered, and closed the door quietly after her, leaving Ramsay for a few seconds at the glass, with his eyes fixed upon the point at which she had disappeared.

Ramsay of course fell into a reverie, as most men do in a case of this kind; but he had not proceeded very far into it before he was interrupted by the appearance of the syndic, who entered by another door.

" I am sorry to have been obliged to leave you to your own company, Mynheer Ramsay, so soon after your arrival; but my arrangement of time is regular, and I cannot make any alteration. Before you have been with us long, I trust that you will find means of amusement. I shall have great pleasure in introducing you to many friends whose time is not so occupied as mine. Once again let me say how happy I am to receive so distinguished a young gentleman under my roof. Did the cutter bring despatches for the States General, may I enquire?"

"Yes," replied Ramsay, "she did; and they are of some importance."

"Indeed?" rejoined Mynheer inquisitively.

"My dear sir," said Ramsay, blushing at his own falsehood, "we are, I believe, both earnest in one point, which is to strengthen the good cause. Under such an impression, and having accepted your hospitality, I have no right to withhold what I know, but with which others are not acquainted."

"My dear sir," interrupted Krause, who was now fully convinced of the importance of his guest, " you do me justice; I am firm and steadfast in the good cause. I am known to be so, and I am also, I trust, discreet; confiding to my tried friends, indeed, but it will be generally acknowledged that Mynheer Krause has possessed, and safely guarded, the secrets of the state."

Now, in the latter part of this speech, Mynheer Krause committed a small mistake. He was known to be a babbler, one to whom a secret could not be imparted, without every risk of its being known; and it was from the knowledge of this failing in Mynheer Krause that Ramsay had received such very particular recommendations to him. As syndic of the town, it was impossible to prevent his knowledge of government secrets, and when these occasionally escaped, they were always traced to his not being able to hold his tongue.

Nothing pleased Mynheer Krause so much as a secret, because nothing gave him so much pleasure as whispering it confidentially into the ear of a dozen confidential friends. The consequence was, the government was particularly careful that he should not know what was going on, and did all they could to prevent it; but there were many others who, although they could keep a secret, had no objection to part with it for a consideration, and in the enormous commercial transactions of Mynheer Krause, it was not unfrequent for a good bargain to be struck with him by one or more of the public functionaries, the difference between the sum proposed and accepted being settled against the interests of Mynheer Krause, by the party putting him in possession of some government movement which had hitherto been kept *in petto*. Every man has his hobby, and usually pays dear for it, so did Mynheer Krause.

Now when it is remembered that Ramsay had opened and read the whole of the despatches, it may at once be supposed what a valuable acquaintance he would appear to Mynheer Krause; but we must not anticipate. Ramsay's reply was, "I feel it my bounden duty to impart all I am possessed of to my very worthy host, but allow me to observe, mynheer, that prudence is necessary—we may be overheard."

"I am pleased to find one of your age so circumspect," replied Krause ; " perhaps it would be better to defer our conversation till after supper, but in the meantime, could you not just give me a little inkling of what is going on ?"

Ramsay had difficulty in stifling a smile at this specimen of Mynheer Krause's eagerness for intelligence. He very gravely walked up to him, looked all round the room as if he was afraid that the walls would hear him, and then whispered for a few seconds into the ear of his host.

" Indeed !" exclaimed Krause, looking up into Ramsay's face.

Ramsay nodded his head authoritatively.

" Gott in himmel !" exclaimed the syndic ; but here the bell for dinner rang a loud peal. " Dinner is on the table, mynheer," continued the syndic, " allow me to show you the way. We will talk this over to-night. Gott in himmel ! Is it possible ?"

Mynheer Krause led the way to another saloon, where Ramsay found not only the table prepared, but, as he had anticipated, the daughter of his host, to whom he was introduced. " Wilhelmina," said Mynheer Krause, " our young friend will stay with us, I trust, some time, and you must do all you can to make him comfortable. You know, my dear, that business must be attended to. With me, time is money ; so much so, that I can scarcely do justice to the affairs of the state devolving upon me in virtue of my office. You must, therefore, join with me, and do your best to amuse our guest."

To this speech, Wilhelmina made no reply, but by a gracious inclination of her head towards Ramsay, which was returned with all humility. The dinner was excellent, and Ramsay amused himself very well indeed until it was over. Mynheer Krause then led the way to the saloon, called for coffee, and, so soon as he had finished it, made an apology to his guest, and left him alone with his beautiful daughter.

Wilhelmina Krause was a young person of a strong mind irregularly cultivated ; she had never known the advantage of a mother's care, and was indeed self-educated. She had a strong tinge of romance in her character, and, left so much alone, she loved to indulge in it.

In other points she was clever, well read, and accomplished; graceful in her manners, open in her disposition, to a fault; for, like her father, she could not keep a secret, not even the secrets of her own heart; for whatever she thought she gave utterance to, which is not exactly the custom in this world, and often attended with unpleasant consequences.

The seclusion in which she had been kept added to the natural timidity of her disposition—but when once intimate, it also added to her confiding character. It was impossible to see without admiring her, to know her without loving her; for she was nature herself, and, at the same time, in her person one of Nature's masterpieces.

As we observed, when they retired to the saloon, Mynheer Krause very shortly quitted them, to attend to his affairs below, desiring his daughter to exert herself for the amusement of his guest; the contrary, however, was the case, for Ramsay exerted himself to amuse her, and very soon was successful, for he could talk of courts and kings, of courtiers and of people, and of a thousand things, all interesting to a young girl who had lived secluded; and as his full-toned voice, in measured and low pitch, fell upon Wilhelmina's ear, she never perhaps was so much interested. She seldom ventured a remark, except it was to request him to proceed, and the eloquent language with which Ramsay clothed his ideas, added a charm to the novelty of his conversation. In the course of two hours Ramsay had already acquired a moral influence over Wilhelmina, who looked up to him with respect, and another feeling which we can only define by saying that it was certainly anything but ill-will.

The time passed so rapidly, that the two young people could hardly believe it possible that it was past six o'clock, when they were interrupted by the appearance of Mynheer Krause, who came from his counting-house, the labours of the day being over. In the summer-time it was his custom to take his daughter out in the carriage at this hour, but the weather was too cold, and, moreover, it was nearly dark. A conversation ensued on general topics, which lasted till supper-time ; after this repast was over Wilhelmina retired, leaving Ramsay and the syndic alone.

It was then that Ramsay made known to his host the contents of the despatches, much to Mynheer Krause's surprise and delight, who felt assured that his guest must be strong in the confidence of the English government, to be able to communicate such intelligence. Ramsay, who was aware that the syndic would sooner or later know what had been written, of course was faithful in his detail; not so, however, when they canvassed the attempts of the Jacobite party; then Mr Krause was completely mystified.

It was not till a late hour that they retired to bed. The next morning, the syndic, big with his intelligence, called upon his friends in person, and much to their surprise told them the contents of the despatches which had been received—and, much to his delight, discovered that he had been correctly informed. He also communicated what Ramsay had told him relative to the movements of the Court of St Germains, and thus, unintentionally, false intelligence was forwarded to England as from good authority. It hardly need be observed, that, in a very short time, Ramsay had gained the entire confidence of his host, and we may add also, of his host's daughter; but we must leave him for the present to follow up his plans, whatever they may be, and return to the personages more immediately connected with this narrative.

Chapter XXIX

In which Jemmy Ducks proves the truth of Moggy's assertion, that there was no one like him before or since—Nancy and Jemmy serenade the stars.

As soon as Moggy landed at the Point with her dear darling duck of a husband, as she called him, she put his chest and hammock on a barrow and had them wheeled up to her own lodgings, and then they went out to call upon Nancy Corbett to make their future arrangements; Moggy proceeding in rapid strides, and Jemmy trotting with his diminutive legs behind her, something like a stout pony by the side of a large horse. It was in pedestrianism that Jemmy most felt his inferiority, and the protecting, fond way in which Moggy would turn round every minute and say, " Come along, my duck," would have been irritating to any other but one of Jemmy's excellent temper. Many looked at Jemmy, as he waddled along, smiled and passed on; one unfortunate nymph, however, ventured to stop, and putting her arms a-kimbo, looked down upon him and exclaimed, "Vell! you are a nice little man," and then commenced singing the old refrain—

> "I had a little husband no bigger than my thumb,
> I put him in a pint pot, and there I bid him drum:"

when Moggy, who had turned back, saluted her with such a box on the ear, that she made the drum of it ring again. The young lady was not one of those who would offer the other cheek to be smitten, and she immediately flew at Moggy and returned the blow; but Jemmy, who liked quiet, caught her round the legs, and, as if she had been a feather, threw her over his head, so that she fell down in the gutter behind him with a violence which was anything but agreeable. She gained her legs again, looked at her soiled garments, scraped the mud off her cheek—we are sorry to add, made use of some very improper language, and finding herself in the minority, walked off, turning round and shaking her fist at every twenty paces.

Moggy and her husband continued their course as if nothing had happened, and arrived at the house of Nancy Corbett, who had, as may be supposed, changed her lodgings and kept out of sight of Vanslyperken. Nancy was no stranger to Jemmy Ducks; so far as his person went he was too remarkable a character not to be known by her who knew almost everybody; and, moreover, she had made sufficient inquiries about his character. The trio at once proceeded to business: Jemmy had promised his wife to join the smugglers, and it was now arranged, that both he and his wife should be regularly enlisted in the gang, she to remain at the cave with the women, unless her services were required elsewhere, he to belong to the boat. There was, however, one necessary preliminary still to be taken, that of Jemmy and his wife both taking the oath of fidelity at the house of the Jew Lazarus; but it was not advisable to go there before dusk, so they remained with Nancy till that time, during which she was fully satisfied that, in both parties, the band would have an acquisition, for Nancy was very keen and penetrating, and had a great insight into human nature.

At dusk, to the house of Lazarus they accordingly repaired, and were admitted by the cautious Jew. Nancy stated why they had come, and there being, at the time, several of the confederates, as usual, in the house, they were summoned by the Jew to be witnesses to the oath being administered. Half-a-dozen dark-looking, bold men soon made their appearance, and recognised Nancy by nods of their heads.

"Who have we here, old Father Abraham?" exclaimed a stout man, who was dressed in a buff jerkin and a pair of boots which rose above his knees.

"A good man and true," replied Nancy, taking up the answer.

"Why, you don't call that thing a man!" exclaimed the fierce-looking confederate with contempt.

"As good a man as ever stood in your boots," replied Moggy in wrath.

"Indeed: well, perhaps so, if he could only see his way when once into them," replied the man with a loud laugh, in which he was joined by his companions.

"What can you do, my little man?" said another of a slighter build than the first, coming forward and putting his hand upon Jemmy's head.

Now Jemmy was the best-tempered fellow in the world, but, at the same time, the very best-tempered people have limits to their forbearance, and do not like to be taken liberties with by strangers: so felt Jemmy, who, seizing the young man firmly by the waistband of his trousers just below the hips, lifted him from the ground, and with a strength which astonished all present, threw him clean over the table, his body sweeping away both the candles, so they were all left in darkness.

"I can douse a glim anyhow," cried Jemmy.

"That's my darling duck," cried Moggy, delighted with this proof of her husband's vigour.

Some confusion was created by this manœuvre on the part of Jemmy, but candles were reproduced, and the first man who spoke, feeling as if this victory on the part of Jemmy was a rebuke to himself, again commenced his interrogations.

"Well, my little man, you are strong in the arms, but what will you do without legs?"

"Not run away, as you have done a hundred times," replied Jemmy, scornfully.

"Now by the God of War you shall answer for this," replied the man, catching hold of Jemmy by the collar; but in a moment he was tripped up by Jemmy, and fell down with great violence on his back.

"Bravo, bravo!" exclaimed the rest, who took part with Jemmy.

"That's my own little duck," cried Moggy; "you've shown him what you can do, anyhow."

The man rose, and was apparently feeling for some

arms secreted about his person, when Nancy Corbett stepped forward.

"Do you dare?" cried she; "take what you have received, and be thankful, or——" and Nancy held up her little forefinger.

The man slunk back among the others in silence. The old Jew, who had not interfered, being in presence of Nancy, who had superior commands, now read the oath, which was of a nature not to be communicated to the reader without creating disgust. It was, however, such an oath as was taken in those times, and has since been frequently taken in Ireland. It was subscribed to by Jemmy and his wife without hesitation, and they were immediately enrolled among the members of the association. As soon as this ceremony had been gone through, Nancy and her protegés quitted the house and returned to her lodgings, when it was agreed that the next night they should go over to the island, as Jemmy's services were required in the boat in lieu of Ramsay, whose place as steersman he was admirably qualified to occupy, much better, indeed, than that of a rower, as his legs were too short to reach the stretcher, where it was usually fixed.

The next evening the weather was calm and clear, and when they embarked in the boat of the old fisherman, with but a small portion of their effects, the surface of the water was unruffled, and the stars twinkled brightly in the heavens; one article which Jemmy never parted with, was in his hand, his fiddle. They all took their seats, and the old fisherman shoved off his boat, and they were soon swept out of the harbour by the strong ebb tide.

"An't this better than being on board with Vanslyperken, and your leave stopped?" observed Moggy.

"Yes," replied the husband.

"And I not permitted to go on board to see my duck of a husband—confound his snivelling carcass?" continued Moggy.

"Yes," replied Jemmy, thoughtfully.

"And in company with that supernatual cur of his?"

Jemmy nodded his head, and then in his abstraction touched the strings of his violin.

"They say that you are clever with your instrument, Mr Salisbury," observed Nancy Corbett.

"That he is," replied Moggy; "and he sings like a darling duck. Don't you, Jemmy, my dear?"

"Quack, quack," replied Jemmy.

"Well, Mr Salisbury, there's no boat that I can see near us, or even in sight; and if there was it were little matter. I suppose you will let me hear you, for I shall have little opportunity after this?"

"With all my heart," replied Jemmy; who, taking up his fiddle, and playing upon the strings like a guitar, after a little reflection, sang as follows:

> Bless my eyes, how young Bill threw his shiners away,
>   As he drank and he danced, when he first came on shore!
> It was clear that he fancied that with his year's pay,
>   Like the Bank of Old England, he'd never be poor.
> So when the next day, with a southerly wind in
>   His pockets, he came up, my rhino to borrow;
> "You're welcome," says I, "Bill, as I forked out the tin,
>   But when larking to-day—*don't forget there's to-morrow*"
>
> When our frigate came to from a cruise in the west,
>   And her yards were all squared, her sails neatly furled,
> Young Tom clasped his Nancy, so loved, to his breast,
>   As if but themselves there was none in the world.
> Between two of the guns they were fondly at play,
>   All billing and kissing, forgetting all sorrow;
> "Love, like cash," says I, "Nan, may all go in a day,
>   While you hug him so close—*don't forget there's to-morrow.*"
>
> When a hurricane swept us smack smooth fore and aft,
>   When we dashed on the rock, and we floundered on shore,
> As we sighed for the loss of our beautiful craft,
>   Convinced that the like we should never see more,
> Says I, "My good fellows," as huddled together,
>   They shivered and shook, each phiz black with sorrow,
> "Remember, it's not to be always foul weather,
>   So with ill-luck to-day—*don't forget there's to-morrow!*"

"And not a bad hint, neither, Mr Salisbury," said

Nancy, when Jemmy ceased. "You sailors never think of to-morrow, more's the pity. You're no better than overgrown babies."

"I'm not much better, at all events," replied Jemmy, laughing: "however, I'm as God made me, and so all's right."

"That's my own darling Jemmy," said Moggy; "and if you're content, and I'm content, who is to say a word, I should like to know? You may be a rum one to look at, but I think them fellows found you but a rum customer the other night."

"Don't put so much rum in your discourse, Moggy, you make me long for a glass of grog."

"Then your mouth will find the water," rejoined Nancy; "but, however, singing is dry work, and I am provided. Pass my basket aft, old gentleman, and we will find Mr Salisbury something with which to whet his whistle." The boatman handed the basket to Nancy, who pulled out a bottle and glass, which she filled, and handed to Jemmy.

"Now, Mr Salisbury, I expect some more songs," said Nancy.

"And you shall have them, mistress; but I've heard say that you've a good pipe of your own; suppose that you give me one in return, that will be but fair play."

"Not exactly, for you'll have the grog in the bargain," replied Nancy.

"Put my fiddle against the grog, and then all's square."

"I have not sung for many a day," replied Nancy, musing, and looking up at the bright twinkling stars. "I once sang, when I was young—and happy—I then sang all the day long; that was really singing, for it came from the merriness of my heart;" and Nancy paused. "Yes, I have sung since, and often, for they made me sing; but 'twas when my heart was heavy—or when its load had been, for a time, forgotten and drowned in wine. That was not singing, at least not the singing of bygone days."

"But those times are bygone too, Mistress Nancy,"

said Moggy; "you have now your marriage lines, and are made an honest woman."

"Yes, and God keep me so, amen," replied Nancy mournfully.

Had not the night concealed it, a tear might have been seen by the others in the boat to trickle down the cheek of Nancy Corbett, as she was reminded of her former life; and as she again fixed her eyes upon the brilliant heavens, each particular star appeared to twinkle brighter, as if they rejoiced to witness tears like those.

"You must be light o' heart now, Mistress Nancy," observed Jemmy, soothingly.

"I am not unhappy," replied she, resting her cheek upon her hand.

"Mistress Nancy," said Moggy, "I should think a little of that stuff would do neither of us any harm; the night is rather bleak."

Moggy poured out a glass and handed it to Nancy; she drank it, and it saved her from a flood of tears, which otherwise she would have been unable to repress. In a minute or two, during which Moggy helped herself and the old boatman, Nancy's spirits returned.

"Do you know this air?" said Nancy to Jemmy, humming it.

"Yes, yes, I know it well, Mistress Nancy. Will you sing to it?"

Nancy Corbett who had been celebrated once for her sweet singing, as well as her beauty, immediately commenced in a soft and melodious tone, while Jemmy touched his fiddle.

> Lost, stolen, or strayed,
> The heart of a young maid;
> Whoever the same shall find,
> And prove so very kind,
> To yield it on desire,
> They shall rewarded be,
> And that most handsomely,
> With kisses one, two, three.
>   Cupid is the crier,
>   Ring-a-ding, a-ding,
>   Cupid is the crier.

O yes! O yes! O yes!
Here is a pretty mess!
A maiden's heart is gone,
And she is left forlorn,
And panting with desire;
Whoever shall bring it me,
They shall rewarded be,
With kisses one, two, three.
    Cupid is the crier,
    Ring-a-ding, a-ding,
    Cupid is the crier.

'Twas lost on Sunday eve,
Or taken without leave,
A virgin's heart so pure,
She can't the loss endure,
And surely will expire;
Pity her misery.
Rewarded you shall be,
With kisses one, two, three.
    Cupid is the crier,
    Ring-a-ding, a-ding,
    Cupid is the crier.

The maiden sought around,
It was not to be found,
She searched each nook and dell,
The haunts she loved so well,
All anxious with desire;
The wind blew ope his vest,
When, lo! the toy in quest,
She found within the breast
    Of Cupid, the false crier,
    Ring-a-ding, a-ding-a-ding,
    Cupid the false crier.

"Many thanks, Mistress Corbett, for a good song, sung in good tune, with a sweet voice," said Jemmy. "I owe you one for that, and am ready to pay you on demand. You've a pipe like a missel thrush."

"Well, I do believe that I shall begin to sing again," replied Nancy. "I'm sure if Corbett was only once settled on shore in a nice little cottage, with a garden, and a blackbird in a wicker cage, I should try who could sing most, the bird or me."

"He will be by-and-bye, when his work is done."

"Yes, when it is; but open boats, stormy seas, and the halter, are heavy odds, Mr Salisbury."

"Don't mention the halter, Mistress Nancy, you'll make me melancholy," replied Jemmy, "and I sha'n't be able to sing any more. Well, if they want to hang me, they need not rig the yard-arm, three handspikes as sheers, and I shouldn't find soundings, heh! Moggy?"

Nancy laughed at the ludicrous idea; but Moggy exclaimed with vehemence, "Hang my Jemmy! my darling duck! I should like to see them."

"At all events, we'll have another song from him, Moggy, before they spoil his windpipe, which, I must say, would be a great pity; but Moggy, there have been better men hung than your husband."

"Better men than my Jemmy, Mrs Corbett! There never was one like him afore or since;" replied Moggy, with indignation.

"I only meant of longer pedigree, Moggy," replied Nancy soothingly.

"I don't know what that is," replied Moggy, still angry.

"Longer legs, to be sure," replied Jemmy. "Never mind that, Moggy. Here goes, a song in two parts. It's a pity, Mistress Nancy, that you couldn't take one."

> "When will you give up this life of wild roving?
> When shall we be quiet and happy on shore?
> When will you to church lead your Susan, so loving,
> And sail on the treacherous billows no more?"

> "My ship is my wife, Sue, no other I covet,
> Till I draw the firm splice that's betwixt her and me;
> I'll roam on the ocean, for much do I love it—
> To wed with another were rank bigamy."

> "O William, what nonsense you talk, you are raving;
> Pray how can a ship and a man become one?
> You say so because you no longer are craving,
> As once you were truly—and I am undone."

> "You wrong me, my dearest, as sure as I stand here,
> As sure as I'll sail again on the wide sea;
> Some day I will settle, and marry with you, dear,
> But now 'twould be nothing but rank bigamy."

> "Then tell me the time, dear William, whenever
>   Your Sue may expect this divorce to be made;
> When you'll surely be mine, when no object shall sever,
>   But locked in your arms I'm no longer afraid."
>
> "The time it will be when my pockets are lined,
>   I'll then draw the splice 'tween my vessel and me,
> And lead you to church, if you're still so inclined—
>   But before, my dear Sue, 'twere rank bigamy."

"Thank you, Mr Salisbury. I like the moral of that song; a sailor never should marry till he can settle on shore."

"What's the meaning of big-a-me?" said Moggy.

"Marrying two husbands or two wives, Mrs Salisbury. Perhaps you might get off on the plea that you had only one and a half," continued Nancy, laughing.

"Well, perhaps she might," replied Jemmy, "if he were a judge of understanding."

"I should think, Mistress Nancy, you might as well leave my husband's legs alone," observed Moggy, affronted.

"Lord bless you, Moggy, if he's not angry, you surely should not be; I give a joke, and I can take one. You surely are not jealous?"

"Indeed I am though, and always shall be of anyone who plays with my Jemmy."

"Or if he plays with anything else?"

"Yes, indeed."

"Yes, indeed! then you must be downright jealous of his fiddle, Moggy," replied Nancy; "but never mind, you sha'n't be jealous now about nothing. I'll sing you a song, and then you'll forget all this." Nancy Corbett then sang as follows:

> Fond Mary sat on Henry's knee,
> "I must be home exact," said he,
>   And see, the hour is come."
> "No, Henry, you shall never go
> Until me how to count you show;
>   That task must first be done."
>
> Then Harry said, "As time is short,
> Addition you must first be taught;—
>   Sum up these kisses sweet;

> Now prove your sum by kissing me :—
> Yes, that is right, 'twas three times three ;—
> Arithmetic's a treat.
>
> "And now there is another term,
> Subtraction you have yet to learn ;
> Take four away from these."
> "Yes, that is right, you've made it out,"
> Says Mary, with a pretty pout,
> "Subtraction don't me please."
>
> Division's next upon the list ;
> Young Henry taught while Mary kissed,
> And much admired the rule ;
> "Now, Henry, don't you think me quick ?"
> "Why, yes, indeed, you've learned the trick ;
> At kissing you're no fool."
>
> To multiply was next the game,
> Which Henry by the method same,
> To Mary fain would show ;
> But here his patience was worn out,
> She multiplied too fast I doubt,
> He could no farther go.
>
> "And now we must leave off, my dear ;
> The other rules are not so clear,
> We'll try at them to-night ;"
> "I'll come at eve, my Henry sweet ;
> Behind the hawthorn hedge we'll meet,
> For learning's my delight."

"That's a very pretty song, Mistress Corbett, and you've a nice collection, I've no doubt. If you've no objection, I'll exchange another with you."

"I should be most willing, Mr Salisbury ; but we are now getting well over, and we may as well be quiet, as I do not wish people to ask where we are going."

"You're right, ma'am," observed the old fisherman, who pulled the boat. "Put up your fiddle, master ; there be plenty on the look out, without our giving them notice."

"Very true," replied Jemmy, "so we break up our concert."

The whole party were now silent. In a quarter of an hour the boat was run into a cut, which concealed it from view; and, as soon as the fisherman had looked round to see the coast clear, they landed and made haste to pass by the cottages; after that Nancy slackened her pace, and they walked during the night over to the other side of the island, and arrived at the cottages above the cave.

Here they left a portion of their burdens and then proceeded to the path down the cliff which led to the cave. On Nancy giving the signal, the ladder was lowered, and they were admitted. As soon as they were upon the flat, Moggy embraced her husband, crying, "Here I have you, my own dear Jemmy, all to myself, and safe for ever."

Chapter XXX

In which Mr Vanslyperken treats the ladies.

On the second day after his arrival, Vanslyperken, as agreed, went up to the syndic's house to call upon Ramsay. The latter paid him down one hundred pounds for his passage and services, and Vanslyperken was so pleased, that he thought seriously, as soon as he had amassed sufficient money, to withdraw himself from the service, and retire with his ill-gotten gains; but when would a miser like Vanslyperken have amassed sufficient money? Alas! never, even if the halter were half round his neck. Ramsay then gave his instructions to Vanslyperken, advising him to call for letters previously to his sailing, and telling him that he must open the government despatches in the way to which he had been witness, take full memorandums of the contents, and bring them to him, for which service he would each time receive fifty pounds as a remuneration. Vanslyperken bowed to his haughty new acquaintance, and quitted the house.

"Yes," thought Ramsay, " that fellow is a low, contemptible traitor, and how infamous does treason appear in that wretch! but—I—I am no traitor—I have forfeited my property and risked my life in fidelity to my king, and in attempting to rid the world of a usurper and a tyrant. Here, indeed, I am playing a traitor's part to my host, but still I am doing my duty. An army without spies would be incomplete, and one may descend to that office for the good of one's country without tarnish or disgrace. Am I not a traitor to her already? Have not I formed visions in my imagination already of obtaining her hand, and her heart, and her fortune? Is not this treachery? Shall I not attempt to win her affections under disguise as her father's friend and partisan? But what have women to do with politics? Or if they have, do not they set so light a value upon them, that they will exchange them for a feather? Yes, surely; when they love, their politics are the politics of those they cling to. At present, she is on her father's side; but if she leave her father and cleave to me, her politics will be transferred with her affections. But then her religion. She thinks me a Protestant. Well, love is all in all with women; not only politics but religion must yield to it; " thy people shall be my people, and thy God shall be my God," as Ruth says in the scriptures. She is wrong in politics, I will put her right. She is wrong in religion, I will restore her to the bosom of the church. Her wealth would be sacrificed to some heretic; it were far better that it belonged to one who supports the true religion and the good cause. In what way, therefore, shall I injure her? On the contrary." And Ramsay walked down stairs to find Wilhelmina. Such were the arguments used by the young cavalier, and with which he fully satisfied himself that he was doing rightly; had he argued the other side of the question, he would have been equally convinced, as most people are, when they argue without any opponent; but we must leave him to follow Vanslyperken.

Mr Vanslyperken walked away from the syndic's house with the comfortable idea that one side of him was heavier than the other by one hundred guineas. He also ruminated; he had already obtained three hundred pounds, no small sum, in those days, for a lieutenant. It is true that he had lost the chance of thousands by the barking of Snarleyyow, and he had lost the fair Portsmouth widow; but then he was again on good terms with the Frau Vandersloosh, and was in a fair way of making his fortune, and, as he considered, with small risk. His mother, too, attracted a share of his reminiscences; the old woman would soon die, and then he would have all that she had saved. Smallbones occasionally intruded himself, but that was but for a moment. And Mr Vanslyperken walked away very well satisfied, upon the whole, with his *esse* and *posse*. He wound up by flattering himself that he should wind up with the savings of his mother, his half-pay, the widow's guilders, and his own property,—altogether it would be pretty comfortable. But we leave him and return to Corporal Van Spitter.

Corporal Van Spitter had had wisdom enough to dupe Vanslyperken, and persuade him that he was very much in love with Babette; and Vanslyperken, who was not at all averse to this amour, permitted the corporal to go on shore and make love. As Vanslyperken did not like the cutter and Snarleyyow to be left without the corporal or himself, he always remained on board when the corporal went, so that the widow had enough on hand—pretending love all the morning with the lieutenant, and indemnifying herself by real love with the corporal after dusk. Her fat hand was kissed and slobbered from morning to night, but it was half for love and half for revenge.

But we must leave the corporal, and return to Jemmy Ducks. Jemmy was two days in the cave before the arrival of the boat, during which he made himself a great favourite, particularly with Lilly, who sat down and listened to his fiddle and his singing. It was a novelty in the cave, anything like amusement. On the third night, however, Sir R. Barclay came back from Cherbourg, and as he only remained one hour, Jemmy was hastened on board, taking leave of his wife, but not parting with his fiddle. He took his berth as steersman, in lieu of Ramsay, and gave perfect satisfaction. The intelligence brought over by Sir Robert rendered an immediate messenger to Portsmouth necessary; and, as it would create less suspicion, Moggy was the party now entrusted in lieu of Nancy, who had been lately seen too often, and, it was supposed, had been watched. Moggy was not sorry to receive her instructions, which were, to remain at Portsmouth until Lazarus the Jew should give her further orders; for there was one point which Moggy was most anxious to accomplish, now that she could do it without risking a retaliation upon her husband, which was, to use her own expression, to pay off that snivelling old rascal, Vanslyperken.

But we must leave Moggy and the movements of individuals, and return to our general history. The *Yungfrau* was detained a fortnight at Amsterdam, and then received the despatches of the States General and those of Ramsay, with which Vanslyperken returned to Portsmouth. On his arrival, he went through his usual routine at the admiral's and the Jew's, received his douceur, and hastened to his mother's house, when he found the old woman, as she constantly prophesied, not dead yet.

"Well, child, what have you brought—more gold?"

"Yes," replied Vanslyperken, laying down the one hundred and fifty guineas which he had received.

"Bless thee, my son—bless thee!" said the old woman, laying her palsied hand upon Vanslyperken's head. "It is not often I bless—I never did bless as I can recollect—I like cursing better. My blessing must be worth something, if it's only for its scarcity; and do you know why I bless thee, my Cornelius? Because—ha, ha, ha! because you are a murderer and a traitor, and you love gold."

Even Vanslyperken shuddered at the hag's address.

"What do you ever gain by doing good in this world? nothing but laughter and contempt. I began the world like a fool, but I shall go out of it like a wise woman, hating, despising everything but gold. And I have had my revenge in my time—yes—yes—the world, my son, is divided into only two parts, those who cheat, and those who are cheated—those who master, and those who are mastered—those who are shackled by superstitions and priests, and those who, like me, fear neither God nor devil. We must all die; yes, but I shan't die yet, no, no."

And Vanslyperken almost wished that he could gain the unbelief of the decrepit woman whom he called mother, and who, on the verge of eternity, held fast to such a creed.

"Well, mother, perhaps it may be you are right—I never gained anything by a good action yet."

Query. Had he ever done a good action?

"You're my own child, I see, after all; you have my blessing, Cornelius, my son—go and prosper. Get gold —get gold," replied the old hag, taking up the money, and locking it up in the oak chest.

Vanslyperken then narrated to his mother the unexpected interview with Smallbones, and his surmise that the lad was supernaturally gifted. "Ah, well," replied she, "those who are born to be hung will die by no other death; but still it does not follow that they will not die. You shall have your revenge, my child. The lad shall die. Try again; water, you say, rejects him? Fire will not harm him. There is that which is of the earth and of the air left. Try again, my son; revenge is sweet, next to gold."

After two hours' conversation, it grew dark, and Vanslyperken departed, revolving in his mind, as he walked away, the sublime principles of religion and piety, in the excellent advice given by his aged mother. "I wish I could only think as she does," muttered Vanslyperken at last; and as he concluded this devout wish, his arm was touched by a neatly-dressed little girl, who curtsied, and asked if he was not Lieutenant Vanslyperken, belonging to the cutter. Vanslyperken replied in the affirmative, and the little girl then said that a lady, her mistress, wished to speak to him.

"Your mistress, my little girl?" said Vanslyperken, suspiciously; "and pray who is your mistress?"

"She is a lady, sir," replied the latter; "she was married to Major Williams, but he is dead."

"Hah! a widow; well, what does she want? I don't know her."

"No, sir, and she don't know you; but she told me if you did not come at once, to give you this paper to read."

Vanslyperken took the paper, and walking to the window of a shop in which there was a light, contrived to decipher as follows:—

"Sir,

"The lady who lived in Castle Street has sent me a letter, and a parcel, to deliver up into your own hands, as the parcel is of value. The bearer of this will bring you to my house.

"Your very obedient,
"JANE WILLIAMS."

"*Two o'clock.*"

"Where does your mistress live, little girl?" enquired Vanslyperken, who immediately anticipated the portrait of the fair widow set in diamonds.

"She lives in one of the publics on the hard, sir, on the first floor, while she is furnishing her lodgings."

"One of the publics on the hard; well, my little girl, I will go with you."

"I have been looking for you everywhere, sir," said the little girl, walking, or rather trotting by the side of Vanslyperken, who strided along.

"Did your mistress know the lady who lived in Castle Street?"

"O yes, sir, my mistress then lived next door to her in Castle Street, but her lease was out, and now she has a much larger house in William Street, but she is painting and furnishing all so handsome, sir, and so now she has taken the first floor of the 'Wheatsheaf' till she can get in again."

And Mr Vanslyperken thought it would be worth his while to reconnoitre this widow before he closed with the Frau Vandersloosh. How selfish men are!

In a quarter of an hour Mr Vanslyperken and the little girl had arrived at the public-house in question. Mr Vanslyperken did not much admire the exterior of the building, but it was too dark to enable him to take an accurate survey. It was, however, evident, that it was a pot-house, and nothing more; and Mr Vanslyperken thought that lodgings must be very scarce in Portsmouth. He entered the first and inner door, and the little girl said she would go upstairs and let her mistress know that he was come. She ran up, leaving Mr Vanslyperken alone in the dark passage. He waited for some time, when his naturally suspicious temper made him think he had been deceived, and he determined to wait outside of the house, which appeared very disreputable. He therefore retreated to the inner door to open it, but found it fast. He tried it again and again, but in vain, and he became alarmed and indignant. Perceiving a light through another keyhole, he tried the door, and it was open; a screen was close to the door as he entered, and he could not see its occupants. Mr Vanslyperken walked round, and as he did so, he heard the door closed and locked. He looked on the other side of the screen, and, to his horror, found himself in company with Moggy Salisbury, and about twenty other females. Vanslyperken made a precipitate retreat to the door, but he was met by three or four women, who held him fast by the arms. Vanslyperken would have disgraced himself by drawing his cutlass; but they were prepared for this, and while two of them pinioned his arms, one of them drew his cutlass from its sheath, and walked away with it. Two of the women contrived to hold his arms, while another pushed him in the rear, until he was brought from behind the screen into the middle of the room, facing his incarnate enemy, Moggy Salisbury.

"Good evening to you, Mr Vanslyperken," cried

Moggy, not rising from her chair. "It's very kind of you to come and see me in this friendly way—come, take a chair, and give us all the news."

"Mistress Salisbury, you had better mind what you are about with a king's officer," cried Vanslyperken, turning more pale at this mockery, than if he had met with abuse. "There are constables, and stocks, and gaols, and whipping-posts on shore, as well as the cat on board."

"I know all that, Mr Vanslyperken," replied Moggy, calmly; "but that has nothing to do with the present affair: you have come of your own accord to this house to see somebody, that is plain, and you have found me. So now do as you're bid, like a polite man; sit down, and treat the ladies. Ladies, Mr Vanslyperken stands treat, and please the pigs, we'll make a night of it. What shall it be? I mean to take my share of a bottle of Oporto. What will you have, Mrs Slamkoe?"

"I'll take a bowl of burnt brandy, with your leave, Mrs Salisbury, not being very well in my inside."

"And you, my dear?"

"O, punch for me—punch to the mast," cried another. "I'll drink enough to float a jolly-boat. It's very kind of Mr Vanslyperken."

All the ladies expressed their several wishes, and Vanslyperken knew not what to do; he thought he might as well make an effort, for the demand on his purse he perceived would be excessive, and he loved his money.

"You may all call for what you please," said Vanslyperken, "but you'll pay for what you call for. If you think that I am to be swindled in this way out of my money, you're mistaken. Every soul of you shall be whipped at the cart's tail to-morrow."

"Do you mean to insinuate that I am not a respectable person, sir?" said a fierce-looking virago, rubbing her fist against Vanslyperken's nose. "Smell that!"

It was not a nosegay at all to the fancy of Mr Vanslyperken; he threw himself back, and his chair fell with him. The ladies laughed, and Mr Vanslyperken rose in great wrath.

"By all the devils in hell," he exclaimed, whirling the chair round his head, "but I'll do you a mischief!"

But he was soon pinioned from behind.

"This is very unpolite conduct," said one; "you call yourself a gentleman?"

"What shall we do, ladies?"

"Do," replied another; "let's strip him, and pawn his clothes, and then turn him adrift."

"Well, that's not a bad notion," replied the others, and they forthwith proceeded to take off Mr Vanslyperken's coat and waistcoat. How much further they would have gone it is impossible to say, for Mr Vanslyperken had made up his mind to buy himself off as cheap as he could.

Be it observed, that Moggy never interfered, nor took any part in this violence; on the contrary, she continued sitting in her chair, and said, "Indeed, ladies, I request you will not be so violent, Mr Vanslyperken is my friend. I am sorry that he will not treat you; but if he will not, I beg you will allow him to go away."

"There, you hear," cried Mr Vanslyperken; "Mrs Salisbury, am I at liberty to depart?"

"Most certainly, Mr Vanslyperken; you have my full permission. Ladies, I beg that you will let him go."

"No, by the living jingo! not till he treats us," cried one of the women; "why did he come into this shop, but for nothing else? I'll have my punch afore he starts."

"And I my burnt brandy." So cried they all, and Mr Vanslyperken, whose coat and waistcoat were already off, and finding many fingers very busy about the rest of his person, perceived that Moggy's neutrality was all a sham, so he begged to be heard.

"Ladies, I'll do anything in reason. As far as five shillings——"

"Five shillings!" exclaimed the woman; "no, no—why, a foremast man would come down with more than that. And you a lieutenant? Five guineas, now, would be saying something."

"Five guineas! why I have not so much money. Upon my soul I hav'n't."

"Let us see," said one of the party, diving like an adept into Vanslyperken's trousers-pocket, and pulling out his purse. The money was poured out on the table, and twelve guineas counted out.

"Then whose money is this?" cried the woman; "not yours on your soul; have you been taking a purse to-night? I vote we sends for a constable."

"I quite forgot that I had put more money in my purse," muttered Vanslyperken, who never expected to see it again. "I'll treat you, ladies—treat you all to whatever you please."

"Bravo! that's spoken like a man," cried the virago, giving Vanslyperken a slap on the back which knocked the breath out of his body.

"Bravo!" exclaimed another, "that's what I call handsome; let's all kiss him, ladies."

Vanslyperken was forced to go through this ordeal, and then the door was unlocked, but carefully guarded, while the several orders were given.

"Who is to pay for all this?" exclaimed the landlady.

"This gentleman treats us all," replied the woman.

"Oh! very well—is it all right, sir?"

Vanslyperken dared not say no: he was in their power, and every eye watched him as he gave his answer; so he stammered out "Yes," and, in a fit of despair at the loss of his money, he threw himself into his chair, and meditated revenge.

"Give Mr Vanslyperken his purse, Susan," said the prudent Moggy to the young woman who had taken it out of his pocket.

The purse was returned, and, in a few minutes, the various liquors and mixtures demanded made their appearance, and the jollification commenced. Every one was soon quite happy, with the exception of Mr Vanslyperken, who, like Pistol, ate his leek, swearing in his own mind he would be horribly revenged.

"Mr Vanslyperken, you must drink my health in some of this punch." Vanslyperken compressed his lips, and shook his head. "I say yes, Mr Vanslyperken," cried the virago, looking daggers; "if you don't, we quarrel—that's all."

But Vanslyperken argued in his mind that his grounds of complaint would be weakened, if he partook of the refreshment which he had been forced to pay for, so he resolutely denied.

"Von't you listen to my harguments, Mr Vanslyperken?" continued the woman. "Vell, then, I must resort to the last, which I never knew fail yet." The woman went to the fire and pulled out the poker, which was red hot, from between the bars. "Now then, my beauty, you must kiss this, or drink some punch;" and she advanced it towards his nose, while three or four others held him fast on his chair behind; the poker, throwing out a glow of heat, was within an inch of the poor lieutenant's nose: he could stand it no more, his face and eyes were scorched.

"Yes, yes," cried he at last, "if I must drink, then, I will. We will settle this matter by-and-bye," cried Vanslyperken, pouring down with indignation the proffered glass.

"Now, Susan, don't ill-treat Mr Vanslyperken: I purtest against all ill-treatment."

"Ill-treat, Mrs Salisbury! I am only giving him a lesson in purliteness."

"Now, Mr What-the-devil's-your-name, you must drink off a glass of my burnt brandy, or I shall be jealous," cried another; "and when I am jealous I always takes to red-hot pokers." Resistance was in vain, the poker was again taken from between the bars, and the burnt brandy went down.

Again and again was Mr Vanslyperken forced to pour down his throat all that was offered to him, or take the chance of having his nose burnt off.

"Is it not wrong to mix your liquors in this way, Mr Vanslyperken?" said Moggy, in bitter mockery.

The first allowance brought in was now despatched, and the bell rung, and double as much more ordered, to Vanslyperken's great annoyance; but he was in the hands of the Philistines. What made the matter worse, was, that the company grew every moment more uproarious, and there was no saying when they would stop.

"A song—a song—a song from Mr Vanslyperken," cried one of the party.

"Hurrah! yes, a song from the jolly lieutenant."

"I can't sing," replied Vanslyperken.

"You shall sing, by the piper who played before Moses," said the virago; "if not, you shall sing out to some purpose;" and the red-hot poker was again brandished in her masculine fist, and she advanced to him, saying, "suppose we hargue that point?"

"Would you murder me, woman?"

"No; singing is no murder, but we ax a song, and a song we must have."

"I don't know one—upon my honour I don't," cried Vanslyperken.

"Then, we'll larn you. And now you repeat after me."

"'Poll put her arms a-kimbo.' Sing—come, out with it." And the poker was again advanced.

"O God!" cried Vanslyperken.

"Sing, or by Heavens I'll shorten your nose! Sing, I say," repeated the woman, advancing the poker so as actually to singe the skin.

"Take it away, and I will," cried Vanslyperken, breathless.

"Well then, 'Poll put her arms a-kimbo.'"

"'Poll put her arms a-kimbo,'" repeated Vanslyperken.

"That's saying, not singing," cried the woman. "Now again. 'At the admiral's house looked she.'"

"'At the admiral's house looked she,'" replied Vanslyperken, in a whining tone.

Thus, with the poker staring him in the face, was

Vanslyperken made to repeat the very song for singing which he would have flogged Jemmy Ducks. There was, however, a desperate attempt to avoid the last stanza.

> "I'll give you a bit of my mind, old boy,
> Port Admiral, you be d——d."

Nothing but the tip of his nose actually burnt would have produced these last words; but fear overcame him, and at last they were repeated. Upon which all the women shouted and shrieked with laughter, except Moggy, who continued sipping her port wine.

"Your good health, Mr Vanslyperken," said Moggy, drinking to him.

Vanslyperken wiped the perspiration off his forehead, and made no reply.

"You call yourself a gentleman, and not drink the health of the lady of the house!" cried virago Mrs Slamkoe. "I'll hargue this point with you again."

The same never-failing argument was used, and Mr Vanslyperken drank Mrs Salisbury's health in a glass of the port wine which he was to have the pleasure of paying for.

"I must say, Mr Vanslyperken," said Moggy, "it was very hard for to wish to flog my poor Jemmy for singing a song which you have just now been singing yourself."

"Did he want to flog your Jemmy for that?"

"Yes, he did indeed, ladies."

"Then as sure as I stand here, and may this punch be my poison, if he sha'n't beg your pardon on his knees. Sha'n't he, girls?" cried Mrs Slamkoe.

"Yes, yes, that he shall, or we'll poke him with the poker."

This was a dreadful threat, but the indignity was so great, that Vanslyperken attempted to resist. It was, however, in vain; he was forced to go on his knees, and ask Mrs Salisbury's pardon.

"Indeed, ladies, I do not wish it," said Moggy; "no,

pray don't. Well, Mr Vanslyperken, pardon granted ; so now kiss and make friends."

Mr Vanslyperken, surrounded now by furies rather than Bacchanalians, kissed Mrs Salisbury.

"What in the world would you have me do, you she-devils?" cried he at last, driven to desperation.

"This is language for a gentleman," said Mrs Slamkoe.

"They shall make you do nothing more," replied Moggy. "I must retire, ladies, your freak's up. You know I never keep late hours. Ladies, I wish you all a very good-night."

"Perhaps, Mr Vanslyperken, you would wish to go. I'll send for the woman of the house that you may settle the bill; I think you offered to treat the company?"

Vanslyperken grinned ghastly. The bell was rung, and while Mr Vanslyperken was pulling out the sum demanded by the landlady, the ladies all disappeared.

Vanslyperken put up his diminished purse. "There is your sword, Mr Vanslyperken," said Moggy; who, during the whole of the scene, had kept up a *retenue* very different from her usual manners.

Vanslyperken took his sword, and appeared to feel his courage return—why not? he was armed, and in company with only one woman, and he sought revenge.

He rang the bell, and the landlady appeared.

"Landlady," cried Vanslyperken, " you'll send for a constable directly. Obey me, or I'll put you down as a party to the robbery which has been committed. I say, a constable immediately. Refuse on your peril, woman; a king's officer has been robbed and ill-treated."

"Lauk-a-mercy ! a constable, sir? I'm sure you've had a very pleasant jollification."

"Silence, woman; send for a constable immediately."

"Do you hear, Mrs Wilcox?" said Moggy, very quietly, "Mr Vanslyperken wants a constable. Send for one by all means."

"Oh! certainly, ma'am, if you wish it," said the landlady, quitting the room.

"Yes, you infamous woman, I'll teach you to rob and ill-treat people in this way."

"Mercy on me! Mr Vanslyperken, why I never interfered."

"Ay, ay, that's all very well; but you'll tell another story when you're all before the authorities."

"Perhaps I shall," replied Moggy, carelessly. "But I shall now wish you a good-evening, Mr Vanslyperken."

Thereupon Mr Vanslyperken very valorously drew his sword, and flourished it over his head.

"You don't pass here, Mrs Salisbury. No—no—it's my turn now."

"Your turn now, you beast!" retorted Moggy. "Why, if I wished to pass, this poker would soon clear the way; but I can pass without that, and I will give you the countersign. Hark! a word in your ear, you wretch. You are in my power. You have sent for a constable, and I swear by my own Jemmy's little finger, which is worth your old shrivelled carcass, that I shall give you in charge of the constable."

"Me!" exclaimed Vanslyperken.

"Yes, you—you wretch—you scum. Now I am going, stop me if you dare. Walls have ears, so I'll whisper. If you wish to send a constable after me, you'll find me at the house of the Jew Lazarus. Do you understand?"

Vanslyperken started back as if an adder had come before him, his sword dropped out of his hand, he stood transfixed.

"May I go now, Mr Vanslyperken, or am I to wait for the constable? Silence gives consent," continued Moggy, making a mock courtesy, and walking out of the room.

For a minute, Vanslyperken remained in the same position. At last, bursting with his feelings, he snatched up his sword, put it into the sheath, and was about to quit the room, when in came the landlady with the constable.

"You vants me, sir?" said the man.

"I did," stammered Vanslyperken, "but she is gone."

"I must be paid for my trouble, sir, if you please."

Vanslyperken had again to pull out his purse; but this time he hardly felt the annoyance, for in his mind's eye his neck was already in the halter. He put the money into the man's hand without speaking, and then left the room, the landlady courtesying very low, and hoping that she soon should again have the pleasure of his company at the Wheatsheaf.

Chapter XXXI

In which Snarleyyow again triumphs over his enemies.

BUT we must return to the cabin, and state what took place during this long absence of the commander, who had gone on shore about three o'clock, and had given directions for his boat to be at the Point at sunset. There had been a council of war held on the forecastle, in which Corporal Van Spitter and Smallbones were the most prominent; and the meeting was held to debate, whether they should or should not make one more attempt to destroy the dog; singular that the arguments and observations very nearly coincided with those made use of by Vanslyperken and his mother, when they debated how to get rid of Smallbones.

"Water won't touch him, I sees that," observed Smallbones.

"No. Mein Gott, dat was to trow time and de trouble away," replied the corporal.

"Hanging's just as natural a death for a cur," observed Spurey.

"Yes," observed Short.

"I'm afeard that the rope's not laid that's to hang that animal," observed Coble, shaking his head. "If water won't do, I'm persuaded nothing will, for did not they use, in former days, to lay all spirits in the Red Sea?"

"Yes," quoth Short.

"But he ban't a spirit yet," replied Smallbones; "he be flesh and blood o' some sort. If I gets fairly rid of his body, d———n his soul, I say, he may keep that and welcome."

"But then, you know, he'll haunt us just as much as ever—we shall see him here just the same."

"A spirit is only a spirit," observed Smallbones; "he may live in the cabin all day and night afore I care; but, d'ye see, there's a great difference between the ghost of a dog, and the dog himself."

"Why, if the beast ar'n't natural, I can't see much odds," observed Spurey.

"But I can feel 'em," replied Smallbones. "This here dog has a-bitten me all to bits, but a ghost of a dog can't bite anyhow."

"No," replied Short.

"And now, d'ye see, as Obadiah Coble has said as how spirits must be laid, I think if we were to come for to go for to lay this here hanimal in the cold hearth, he may perhaps not be able to get up again."

"That's only a perhaps," observed Coble.

"Well, a perhaps is better than nothing at all," said the lad.

"Yes," observed Short.

"That depends upon sarcumstances," observed Spurey. "What sort of a breakfast would you make upon a perhaps?"

"A good one, perhaps," replied Smallbones, grinning at the jingling of the words.

"Twenty dozen tyfels, Smallbones is in de right," observed Jansen, who had taken no part in the previous conversation. "Suppose you bury de dog, de dog body not get up again. Suppose he will come, his soul come, leave him body behind him."

"That's exactly my notion of the thing," observed Smallbones

"Do you mean for to bury him alive?" inquired Spurey.

"Alive! Gott in himmel—no. I knock de brains out first, perry afterwards."

"There's some sense in that, corporal."

"And the dog can't have much left anyhow, dog or devil, when his brains are all out."

"No," quoth Short.

"But who is to do it?"

"Corporal and I," replied Smallbones; "we be agreed, ban't we, corporal?"

"Mein Gott, yes!"

"And now I votes that we tries it off-hand; what's the use of shilly-shally? I made a mortal vow that that 'ere dog and I won't live together—there ban't room enough for us two."

"It's a wide world, nevertheless," observed Coble, hitching up his trousers; "howsomever, I have nothing to say, but I wish you luck; but if you kill that dog, I'm a bishop—that's all."

"And if I don't try for to do so, I am an harchbishop, that's all," replied the gallant Smallbones. "Come along, corporal."

And here was to be beheld a novel scene. Smallbones followed in obedience by his former persecutor and his superior officer; a bag of bones—a reed—a lath—a scarecrow; like a pilot cutter ahead of an Indiaman, followed in his wake by Corporal Van Spitter, weighing twenty stone. How could this be? It was human nature. Smallbones took the lead, because he was the more courageous of the two, and the corporal following, proved he tacitly admitted it.

"He be a real bit of stuff, that 'ere Peter Smallbones," said one of the men.

"I thinks he be a supernatural himself, for my part," rejoined Spurey.

"At all events, he ar'n't afeard of him," said another.

"We shall see," replied Coble, squirting out his tobacco-juice under the gun.

"Come, men, we must go to work now. Shall we, Mr Short?"

"Yes," replied the commanding officer, and the conference broke up.

In the meantime the consultation was continued between Smallbones and the corporal. The latter had received instruction to take on shore Mr Vanslyperken's dirty linen to the washerwoman, and of course, as a corporal, he was not obliged to carry it, and would take Smallbones for that purpose. Then he could easily excuse taking the dog on shore, upon the plea of taking care of it. It was therefore so arranged; the dog would follow the corporal in the absence of his master, but no one else. In a few minutes the corporal, Smallbones, Snarleyyow, and a very small bundle of linen, were in the boat, and shoved off with as many good wishes and as much anxiety for their success, as probably Jason and his followers received when they departed in search of the Golden Fleece.

The three parties kept in company, and passed through the town of Portsmouth. The washerwoman lived outside the Lines, and there they proceeded, Snarleyyow very much in spirits at being able to eat the grass, which his health very much required. They walked on until they arrived at a large elm-tree, on the side of the road, which lay between two hedges and ditches.

"This will do," observed the corporal solemnly. "Mein Gott! I wish it was over," continued he, wiping the perspiration from his bull-forehead.

"How shall we kill him, corporal?" inquired Smallbones.

"Mein Gott! knock him head against de tree, I suppose."

"Yes, and bury him in the ditch. Here, dog—Snarleyyow—here, dog," said Smallbones; "come, a poor doggy—come here."

But Snarleyyow was not to be coaxed by Smallbones; he suspected treachery.

"He won't a-come to me, corporal, or I'd soon settle his hash," observed Smallbones.

The corporal had now got over a little panic which had seized him. He called Snarleyyow, who came immediately. Oh! had he imagined what the corporal was about to do, he might have died like Cæsar, exclaiming, "Et tu Brute," which, in plain English means, "and you—you brute."

The corporal, with a sort of desperation, laid hold of the dog by the tail, drawing him back till he could swing him round. In a second or two Snarleyyow was whirling round the corporal, who turned with him, gradually approaching the trunk of the elm-tree, till at last his head came in contact with it with a resounding blow, and the dog fell senseless. "Try it again, corporal, let's finish him." The corporal again swung round the inanimate body of the dog; again, and again, and again, did the head come in contact with the hard wood; and then the corporal, quite out of breath with the exertion, dropped the body on the grass. Neither of them spoke a word for some time, but watched the body, as it lay motionless, doubled up, with the fore and hind feet meeting each other, and the one eye closed.

"Well, I've a notion that he is done for, anyhow," said Smallbones, "at last."

"Mein Gott, yes!" replied the corporal. "He never get on his legs again, be he tog or be he tyfel."

"Now for to come for to go for to bury him," said Smallbones, swinging the dog by the tail, and dragging him towards the ditch. "I wonder if we could get a spade anywhere, corporal."

"Mein Gott! if we ask for a spade they will ask what for, and Vanslyperken may find it all out."

"Then I'll bury him and cover him up, anyhow; he'll not come to life again, if he does may I be knocked on the head like him, that's all." Smallbones dragged the body into the ditch, and collecting out of the other parts of the ditch a great quantity of wet leaves, covered the body a foot deep. "There, they won't find him now, because they won't know where to look for him. I say, corporal, I've a notion we had better not be seen here too long."

"No," said the corporal, wiping his forehead, putting his handkerchief in his cap, and his cap on his head; "we must go now."

They went to the washerwoman's, delivered the bundle, and then returned on board, when the whole crew were informed of the success of the expedition, and appeared quite satisfied that there was an end of the detested cur; all but Coble, who shook his head.

"We shall see," says he; "but I'm blessed if I don't expect the cur back to-morrow morning."

We must now return to Vanslyperken, who left the public-house in a state of consternation. "How could she possibly know anything about it?" exclaimed he. "My life in the power of that she-devil!" And Vanslyperken walked on, turning over the affair in his mind. "I have gone too far to retreat now. I must either go on, or fly the country. Fly, where? What a fool have I been!" but then Vanslyperken thought of the money. "No, no, not a fool, but I am very unfortunate." Vanslyperken continued his route, until it at last occurred to him that he would go to the Jew Lazarus, and speak with him; for, thought Vanslyperken, if all is discovered, they may think that I have informed, and then my life will be sought by both parties. Vanslyperken arrived at the Jew's abode, knocked softly, but received no answer: he knocked again, louder; a bustle and confusion was heard inside, and at last the door, with the chain fixed, was opened a couple of inches, and the Jew stammered out, "Wot vash there at this late hour of the night?"

"It is me, the lieutenant of the cutter," replied Vanslyperken. "I must speak with you directly."

The door was opened, several figures, and the clatter of arms, were heard in the dark passage, and as soon as Vanslyperken had entered it was relocked, and he was left in the dark.

In a minute the Jew, in a woollen wrapper, made his appearance with a light, and led Vanslyperken into the room where he had been shown before.

"Now then, Mishter Leeftenant, vat vash de matter?"

"We are discovered, I'm afraid!" exclaimed Vanslyperken.

"Holy father Abraham!" exclaimed the Jew, starting back. "But tell me vy you shay sho."

"A woman told me this night that she knew why I came to your house—that I was in her power."

"Vat woman?"

"A hell-cat, who hates me as she does the devil."

"A hell-cat vould not hate de divil," slowly observed the Jew.

"Well, perhaps not; but she will ruin me if she can."

"Vat vash her name?" said Lazarus.

"Moggy Salisbury."

"Paah! is dat all? vy, my good friend, she is one of us. Dere, you may go vay—you may go to bed, Mr Vanslyperken."

"What do you mean?"

"I mean dat she laughed at you, and frighten you—dat she is one of us, and so is her husband, who vas in your chip. Ven you hang, she and I vill all hang together; now you comprehend?"

"Yes," replied Vanslyperken, "I do now: but how could you trust such people?"

"Trust such people, Mr Vanslyperken? If you prove as true as those peoples, vy all de bitter; now go avay—go to bed—you have vaked up all the peoples here. Good night, Mr Leeftenant;" and the Jew led the way to the door, and let Vanslyperken out.

"So then," thought Vanslyperken, as he pursued his way down to the Point, "that woman and her husband are—damnation, but I've a great mind to discover all, if it's only to hang them." But on second thoughts, Vanslyperken thought that it was not worth while to be hanged himself, just for the pleasure of hanging others. It was a great relief to his mind to know that there was no fear of discovery. The tip of his nose itched, and he rubbed it mechanically; the rubbing brought away all the skin. He remembered the hot poker—the money he had been forced to pay—his being made to sing and to beg pardon on his knees ; and he cursed Moggy in his heart, the more so, as he felt that he dare not take any steps against her.

When he came to the Point, he stood on the shingle, looking for his boat, but the men had waited till twelve o'clock, and then presuming that their commander did not intend to come at all that night, had pulled on board again. He was looking round for a waterman to pull him off, when something cold touched his hand. Vanslyperken started, and almost screamed with fear. He looked, and it was the cold nose of Snarleyyow, who now leaped upon his master.

"Snarleyyow, my poor dog! how came you on shore?"

But the dog not being able to speak, made no answer.

While Vanslyperken was wondering how the dog could possibly have come on shore, and what Corporal Van Spitter could be about to have allowed it, the small casement of a garret window near him was opened, and a head was thrust out.

"Do you want to go on board, sir?" said a tremulous voice.

"Yes," replied Vanslyperken.

"I will be down directly, sir," replied the old boatman, who in a minute or two appeared with his sculls on his shoulder.

"Not easy to find a boat at this time of the morning, sir," said the man; "but I heard you speaking, for I've had such a toothache these two nights that I can't shut my eyes."

The old man unlocked the chain which fastened his wherry, and in a few minutes Vanslyperken was on the deck of the cutter, but he found there was no one to receive him,—no watch kept.

"Very well," thought he, "we'll talk about this to-morrow morning. Short or Coble, I wonder which of the two—pretty neglect of duty, indeed—report to the admiral, by heavens!"

So saying, Mr Vanslyperken, with Snarleyyow at his heels, went down into the cabin—undressed in the dark, for he would not let anyone know that he was on board. It being about three o'clock in the morning, and Mr Vanslyperken being well tired with the events of the day, he was soon in a sound sleep. There will be no difficulty in accounting for the return of the dog, which had a skull much thicker than even the corporal's. He had been stunned with the heavy blows, but not killed. After a certain time he came to himself in his bed of leaves, first scratched with one paw, and then with another, till his senses returned: he rose, worked his way out, and lay down to sleep. After he had taken a long nap, he rose recovered, shook himself, and trotted down to the beach, but the boat had shoved off, and the cur had remained there waiting for an opportunity to get on board, when his master came down with the same object in view.

But as every soul is fast asleep, we shall now finish the chapter.

Chapter XXXII

Listeners never hear any good of themselves.

VANSLYPERKEN was awakened three hours after he had fallen asleep by the noise of the buckets washing the decks. He heard the men talking on deck, and aware that no one knew that he was on board, he rose from his bed, and opened one of the sliding sashes of the skylight, that he might overhear the conversation. The first words he heard were from Bill Spurey.

"I say, Coble, I wonder what the skipper will say when he comes on board, and finds that the dog is gone?"

"Hoh! hoh!" thought Vanslyperken.

"I arn't convinced that he is gone yet," replied Coble.

"Smallbones swears that he's settled, this time," replied Spurey.

"So he did before," replied Coble.

"Smallbones again," thought Vanslyperken. "I'll—— Smallbones him, if I hang for it."

"Why, he says he buried him two feet deep."

"Ay, ay; but what's the use of burying an animal who's not a human creature? For my part, I say this, that the imp belongs to his master, and is bound to serve him as long as his master lives. When he dies the dog may be killed, and then——"

"Then what?"

"Why, with the blessing of God, they'll both go to hell together, and I don't care how soon."

"Kill me, you old villain!" muttered Vanslyperken, grinding his teeth.

"Well, anyhow, if the dog be not made away with, no more be Smallbones. He ar'n't afeard of the devil himself."

"No, not he; I'm of opinion Smallbones wa'n't sent here for nothing."

"He's escaped him twice, at all events."

"Then they know it," thought Vanslyperken, turning pale.

"Ay, and I will take you any bet you please, that the skipper never takes that boy's life. He's charmed, or I am a gudgeon."

Vanslyperken felt that it was his own suspicion, and he trembled at the idea of the lad being supernatural.

"Out of the way, Coble, or I'll fill your shoes," cried out one of the men, slashing a bucket of water.

"That's not quite so easy, 'cause I've got boots on," replied Coble. "However, I'll take up another berth."

The men walked away, and Vanslyperken could hear no more; but he had heard quite enough. The life of the dog had been attempted by Smallbones, it was evident. Mr Vanslyperken, after a little agitation, rang the bell.

"By all that's blue, the skipper's on board!" exclaimed the men on deck.

"When the devil did he come?"

"Not in my watch, at all events," replied Coble. "Did he come in yours, Short?"

" No," replied Short.

" Then it must have been in the corporal's."

" The corporal never called me, nor was he on deck," replied Coble. "I've a notion he never kept his watch."

The ring at the bell particularly concerned two people, the two culprits, Smallbones and Corporal Van Spitter.

The latter made his appearance; but previous to his answering the bell, Mr Vanslyperken had time to reflect. "So they think my dog is supernatural," said he; "so much the better. I'll make them believe it still more." Mr Vanslyperken called the dog, and pointed to his bed. The dog, who was fond of a warm berth, and but seldom allowed to get on the bed, immediately jumped up into it when invited, and Mr Vanslyperken patted him, and covered him up with the bedclothes. He then drew the curtains of the bed, and waited to see who would answer the bell. Corporal Van Spitter made his appearance.

"Corporal, I came on board very late, where have you put the dog? Bring him into the cabin."

Here the corporal, who was prepared, shook his head, smoothed down the hair of his forehead, and made a very melancholy face.

" It was all my fault, Mynheer Vanslyperken; yet I do for the best, but de tog be lost."

" How is that, corporal?"

The corporal then stated that he had taken the precaution to take the dog on shore, as he was afraid to leave it on board when he went to the washerwoman's, and that he was not long there, but while he was, the dog disappeared. He had looked everywhere, but could not find it.

" You took Smallbones with you?" said Vanslyperken.

" Yes, mynheer, to carry de linen."

" And where was he when you were at the washerwoman's."

" He was here and dere."

"I know that it was he who killed and buried the dog, corporal."

Corporal Van Spitter started; he thought he was discovered.

"Kilt and perryed, mein Gott!" said the corporal, obliged to say something.

"Yes, I overheard the men say so on deck, corporal. He must have taken the opportunity when you were in the house counting the linen."

Now the corporal had time to recover himself, and he argued that anything was better than that he should be suspected. Smallbones was already known to have attempted the life of the dog, so he would leave the lieutenant in his error.

"Mein Gott! he is von d——d kill-dog feller," observed the corporal. "I look everywhere, I no find te tog. Den de dog is dead?"

"Yes," replied Vanslyperken, "but I'll punish the scoundrel, depend upon it. That will do, corporal; you may go."

As Snarleyyow remained perfectly quiet during this conversation, we must give Vanslyperken great credit for his manœuvre. The corporal went to Smallbones, and repeated what had passed. Smallbones snapped his fingers.

"He may keel-haul, or hang me, for all I care. The dog is dead. Never fear, corporal, I won't peach upon you. I'm game, and I'll die so—if so be I must."

Vanslyperken sent for Smallbones. Smallbones, who was worked up to the highest state of excitement, came in boldly.

"So, you villain, you've killed my dog, and buried it."

"No, I ar'n't," replied Smallbones. "I knows nothing about your dog, sir."

"Why, the men on deck said so, you scoundrel, I heard them."

"I don't care what the men say; I never killed your dog, sir."

"You rascal, I'll have your life!" exclaimed Vanslyperken.

Smallbones grinned diabolically, and Vanslyperken, who remembered all that the men had said in confirmation of his own opinion relative to Smallbones, turned pale. Smallbones, on his part, aware from Corporal Van Spitter, that the lieutenant had such an idea, immediately took advantage of the signs in the lieutenant's countenance, and drawled out,—" That's—not—so—easy!"

Vanslyperken turned away. "You may go now, sir, but depend upon it you shall feel my vengeance!" and Smallbones quitted the cabin.

Vanslyperken finished his toilet, and then turned the dog out of the bed.

He went on deck, and after he had walked a little while, sent for Corporal Van Spitter to consult as to the best method of ascertaining what had become of Snarleyyow. Having entered apparently very earnestly into the corporal's arrangements, who was to go on shore immediately, he desired the corporal to see his breakfast got ready in the cabin.

It so happened, that the corporal went into the cabin, followed by Smallbones; the first object that met his view, was Snarleyyow, sitting upon the chest, scratching his ragged ear as if nothing had happened.

" Gott in himmel!" roared the corporal, turning back, and running out of the cabin, upsetting Smallbones, whom he met in the passage, and trotting, like an elephant, right over him. Nor was Smallbones the only one who suffered; two marines and three seamen were successively floored by the corporal, who, blinded with fear, never stopped till he ran his head butt against the lining in the forepeak of the cutter, which, with the timbers of the vessel, brought him up, not all standing, in one sense of the word, for in his mad career his head was dashed so violently against them, that the poor corporal fell down, stunned to insensibility.

In the meantime Smallbones had gained his feet, and was rubbing his ribs, to ascertain if they were all whole.

"Well, I'm sure," said he, "if I ar'n't flattened for all the world like a pancake, with that 'ere corporal's weight. One may as well have a broad-wheel waggon at once go over one's body; but what could make him come for to go to run away bellowing in that ere manner? He must have seen the devil; or, perhaps," thought Smallbones, "that imp of the devil, Snarleyyow. I'll go and see what it was, anyhow."

Smallbones, rubbing his abdomen, where the corporal had trod hardest, walked into the cabin, where he beheld the dog. He stood with his mouth wide open.

"I defy the devil and all his works," exclaimed he, at last, "and you be one of his, that's sartain. I fear God, and I honour the king, and the parish taught me to read the bible. There you be resurrectioned up again. Well, it's no use, I suppose. Satan, I defy you, anyhow, but it's very hard that a good Christian should have to get the breakfast ready, of which you'll eat one half; I don't see why I'm to wait upon the devil or his imps."

Then Smallbones stopped, and thought a little. "I wonder whether he bee'd dead, as I thought. Master came on board last night without no one knowing nothing about it, and he might have brought the dog with him, if so be he came to again. I won't believe that he's haltogether not to be made away with, for how come his eye out? Well, I don't care, I'm a good Christian, and may I be swamped if I don't try what he's made of yet! First time we cuts up beef, I'll try and chop your tail, anyhow, that I will, if I am hung for it."

Smallbones regained his determination. He set about laying the things for breakfast, and when they were ready he went up to the quarter-deck, reporting the same to Mr Vanslyperken, who had expected to see him frightened out of his wits, and concluding his speech by saying, "If you please, sir, the dog be in the cabin, all right; I said as how I never kilt your dog, nor buried him neither."

"The dog in the cabin!" exclaimed Mr Vanslyperken,

with apparent astonishment. "Why, how the devil could he have come there?"

"He cummed off, I suppose, sir, same way as you did, without nobody knowing nothing about it," drawled out Smallbones, who then walked away.

In the meantime the corporal had been picked up, and the men were attempting to recover him. Smallbones went forward to see what had become of him, and learnt how it was that he was insensible.

"Well, then," thought Smallbones, "it may have been all the same with the dog, and I believe there's humbug in it, for if the dog had made his appearance, as master pretends he did, all of a sudden, he'd a been more frightened than me."

So reasoned Smallbones, and he reasoned well. In the meantime the corporal opened his eyes, and gradually returned to his senses, and then for the first time, the ship's company, who were all down at their breakfast, demanded of Smallbones the reason of the corporal's conduct.

"Why," replied Smallbones, "because that 'ere beast, Snarleyyow, be come back again, all alive, a'ter being dead and buried—he's in the cabin now—that's all."

"That's all!" exclaimed one. "All!" cried another. "The devil!" said a third.

"I said as how it would be," said Obadiah Coble—"that dog is no dog, as sure as I sit here."

The return of the dog certainly had a strong effect upon the whole of the ship's company. The corporal swore that he was not in the cabin, and that Mr Vanslyperken had arranged for his going on shore to look for him, when all of a sudden the dog made his appearance, no one knew how. Smallbones found himself so much in the minority, that he said nothing. It was perfect heresy not to believe that the dog was sent from the lower regions; and as for any further attempts to destroy it, it was considered as perfect insanity

But this renewed attempt on the part of Smallbones,

for Vanslyperken was convinced that an attempt had been made, although it had not been successful, again excited the feelings of Mr Vanslyperken against the lad, and he resolved somehow or another to retaliate. His anger overcame his awe, and he was reckless in his desire of vengeance. There was not the least suspicion of treachery on the part of Corporal Van Spitter in the heart of Mr Vanslyperken, and the corporal played his double part so well, that if possible he was now higher in favour than ever.

After a day or two, during which Mr Vanslyperken remained on board, he sent for the corporal, determining to sound him as to whether he would make any attempts upon Smallbones; for to such a height had Vanslyperken's enmity arrived, that he now resolved to part with some of his darling money, to tempt the corporal, rather than not get rid of the lad. After many hints thrown out, but not taken by the wily corporal, who was resolved that Vanslyperken should speak plainly, the deed and the reward of ten guineas were openly proclaimed, and Vanslyperken waited for the corporal's reply.

"Mein Gott, Mynheer Vanslyperken! suppose it vas possible, I not take your money, I do it wid pleasure; but, sir, it not possible."

"Not possible!" exclaimed Vanslyperken.

"No, mynheer," replied the corporal, "I not tell you all, tousand tyfel, I not tell you all;" and here the corporal put his hand to his forehead and was silent, much to Vanslyperken's amazement. But the fact was, that Corporal Van Spitter was thinking what he possibly could say. At last, a brilliant thought struck him—he narrated to the lieutenant how he had seen the ghost of Smallbones, as he thought, when he was floating about, adrift on the Zuyder Zee—described with great force his horror at the time of the appearance of the supernatural object, and tailed on to what he believed to be true, that which he knew to be false, to wit, that the apparition had cried out to him, that "*he was not to be hurt by mortal man.*"

"Gott in Himmel," finished the corporal, "I never was so frightened in my life. I see him now, as plain as I see you, mynheer. Twenty tousand tyfels, but the voice was like de tunder—and his eye like de lightning—I fell back in one swoon. Ah, mein Gott, mein Gott!"

So well did the corporal play his part, that Vanslyperken became quite terrified; the candle appeared to burn dim, and he dared not move to snuff it. He could not but credit the corporal, for there was an earnestness of description, and a vividness of colouring, which could not have been invented; besides, was not the corporal his earnest and only friend? "Corporal," said Vanslyperken, "perhaps you'll like a glass of scheedam; there's some in the cupboard."

This was very kind of Mr Vanslyperken, but he wanted one himself, much more than the corporal. The corporal produced the bottle and the glass, poured it out, made his military salute, and tossed it off.

"Give me another glass, corporal," said Vanslyperken, in a tremulous tone. The lieutenant took one, two, three glasses, one after another, to recover himself.

The corporal had really frightened him. He was convinced that Smallbones had a charmed life. Did he not float to the Nab buoy and back again?—did not a pistol ball pass through him without injury? Vanslyperken shuddered; he took a fresh glass, and then handed the bottle to the corporal, who helped himself, saluted, and the liquor again disappeared in a moment.

Dutch courage is proverbial, although a libel upon one of the bravest of nations. Vanslyperken now felt it, and again he commenced with the corporal. "What were the words?" inquired he.

"Dat he was not to be hurt by mortal man, mynheer. I can take mine piple oath of it," replied the corporal.

"Damnation!" cried Vanslyperken; "but stop—mortal man—perhaps he may be hurt by woman."

"Dat is quite anoder ting, mynheer."

"He shan't escape if I can help it," retorted Vanslyperken. "I must think about it." Vanslyperken poured out another glass of scheedam, and pushed the stone bottle to the corporal, who helped himself without ceremony. Mr Vanslyperken was now about two-thirds drunk, for he was not used to such a quantity of spirits.

"Now, if I had only been friends with that—that—hell-fire Moggy Salisbury," thought Vanslyperken, speaking aloud to himself.

"Mein Gott, yes, mynheer," replied the corporal.

Vanslyperken took another glass—spilling a great deal on the table as he poured it out; he then covered his eyes with his hand, as if in thought. Thereupon the corporal filled without being asked; and, as he perceived that his superior remained in the same position, and did not observe him, he helped himself to a second glass, and then waited till Vanslyperken should speak again; but the liquor had overpowered him, and he spoke no more.

The corporal, after a few minutes, went up to his superior; he touched him on the shoulder, saying, "Mynheer," but he obtained no reply. On the contrary, the slight touch made Mr Vanslyperken fall forward on the table. He was quite insensible.

So the corporal took him up in his arms, laid him in his bed, then taking possession of the lieutenant's chair, for he was tired of standing so long, he set to work to empty the bottle, which, being large and full at the time that it was produced from the cupboard, took some time, and before it was accomplished, the Corporal Van Spitter had fallen fast asleep in the chair. Shortly afterwards the candle burnt out, and the cabin was in darkness.

It was about three o'clock in the morning when Mr Vanslyperken began to recover his senses, and as his recollection returned, so were his ears met with a stupendous roaring and unusual noise. It was, to his imagination, unearthly, for he had been troubled with wild dreams about Smallbones, and his appearance to the corporal. It sounded like thunder, and Mr Vanslyperken thought that he could plainly make out, "*Mortal man! mortal man!*" and, at times, the other words of the supernatural intimation to the corporal. The mortal man was drawn out in lengthened cadence, and in a manner truly horrible. Vanslyperken called out, "Mor—tal—man," was the reply.

Again Vanslyperken almost shrieked in a perspiration of fear. The sound now ceased; but it was followed up by a noise like the rattling of glasses, tumbling about of the chairs and table, and Vanslyperken buried his face under the clothes. Then the door, which had been shut, was heard by him to slam like thunder; and then Snarleyyow barked loud and deep. "Oh! God forgive me!" cried the terrified lieutenant. "Our Father—which art in heaven—save me—save me!"

Shortly afterwards the corporal made his appearance with a light, and inquired if Mr Vanslyperken had called. He found him reeking with perspiration, and half dead with fear. In broken words he stated how he had been visited, and how the same intimation that no mortal man could hurt Smallbones had been rung into his ears.

"It was only one dream, Mynheer Vanslyperken," observed the corporal.

"No—it was no dream," replied Vanslyperken. "Stay in the cabin, good corporal."

"Yes, mynheer," replied the corporal, drawing the curtains of the bed; and then quietly picking up the various articles on the floor, the table and chairs which had been overturned.

Alas! Fear is the mate of guilt. All this horrid visitation was simply that Mr Vanslyperken had heard the corporal's tremendous snoring, as he slept in the chair, and which his imagination had turned into the words, "Mortal man." The first exclamation of Mr Vanslyperken had awoke the corporal, who, aware of the impropriety of his situation, had attempted to retreat; in so doing he had overturned the table and chairs, with the bottles and glasses upon them.

Fearful of discovery upon this unexpected noise, he had hastened out of the cabin, slammed the door, and waked up Snarleyyow; but he knew, from the exclamations of Vanslyperken, that the lieutenant was frightened out of his wits; so he very boldly returned with a candle to ascertain the result of the disturbance, and was delighted to find that the lieutenant was still under the delusion.

So soon as he had replaced everything, the corporal took a chair, and finding that he had fortunately put the cork into the stone bottle before he fell asleep, and that there was still one or two glasses in it, he drank them off, and waited patiently for daylight. By this time Vanslyperken was again asleep and snoring; so the corporal took away all the broken fragments, put the things in order, and left the cabin.

When Vanslyperken awoke and rang his bell, Smallbones entered. Vanslyperken got up, and finding the cabin as it was left the night before, was more than ever persuaded that he had been supernaturally visited. Fear made him quite civil to the lad, whose life he now considered, as the ship's company did that of the dog's, it was quite useless for him, at least, to attempt, and thus ends this chapter of horrors.

Chapter XXXIII

In which there is nothing very particular or very interesting.

WE must now change the scene for a short time, and introduce to our readers a company assembled in the best inn which, at that time, was to be found in the town of Cherbourg. The room in which they were assembled was large in dimensions, but with a low ceiling—the windows were diminutive, and gave but a subdued light, on account of the vicinity of the houses opposite. The window-frames were small, and cut diamond-wise; and, in the centre of each of the panes, was a round of coarsely-painted glass.

A narrow table ran nearly the length of the room, and, at each end of it, there was a large chimney, in both of which logs of wood were burning cheerfully. What are now termed *chaises longues*, were drawn to the sides of the table, or leaning against the walls of the room, which were without ornament, and neatly coloured with yellow ochre.

The company assembled might have been about thirty in number, of which half a dozen, perhaps, were in the ecclesiastical dress of the time ; while the others wore the habiliments then appropriated to cavaliers or gentlemen, with very little difference from those as worn in the times of the Charleses in England, except that the cloak had been discarded, and the more substantial roquelaure substituted in its place. Most of the party were men who had not yet arrived to middle age, if we except the clericals, who were much more advanced in life ; and any one, who had ever fallen in with the smuggling lugger and its crew, would have had no difficulty in recognising many of them, in the well-attired and evidently high-born and well-educated young men, who were seated or standing in the room. Among them Sir Robert Barclay was eminently conspicuous ; he was standing by the fire conversing with two of the ecclesiastics.

"Gentlemen," said he at last, "our worthy Father Lovell has just arrived from St Germains ; and, as the most rapid communication is now necessary, he is empowered to open here and before us, every despatch which we bring over, before it is transmitted to head-quarters, with permission to act as may seem best to the friends of his Majesty here assembled."

The fact was, that King James had lately completely given himself up to religious exercises and mortification, and any communication to him was attended with so much delay, that it had been considered advisable to act without consulting him ; and to avoid the delay consequent on the transmission of communications to Paris, the most active parties had determined that they would, for the present, take up their residence at Cherbourg, and merely transmit to their friends at St Germains, an account of their proceedings, gaining, at least, a week by this arrangement. The party assembled had many names of some note. Among the ecclesiastics were Lovell, Collier, Snatt, and Cooke; among the cavaliers were those of Musgrave, Friend, and Perkins, whose relatives had suffered in the cause; Smith, Clancey, Herbert, Cunningham, Leslie, and many others.

When Sir Robert Barclay approached the table, the others took their seats in silence.

"Gentlemen," said Sir Robert, laying down the despatches, which had been opened, "you must be aware that our affairs now wear a very prosperous appearance. Supported as we are by many in the government of England, and by more in the House of Commons, with so many adherents here to our cause, we have every rational prospect of success. During the first three months of this year, much has been done; and, at the same time, it must be confessed that the usurper and the heretics have taken every step in their power to assail and to crush us. By this despatch, now in my hand, it appears that a Bill has passed the Commons, by which it is enacted, 'that no person born after the 25th March next, being a Papist, shall be capable of inheriting any title of honour or estate, within the kingdom of England, dominion of Wales, or town of Berwick-on-the-Tweed.'"

Here, some of the ecclesiastics lifted up their eyes, others struck their clenched hands on the table, and the cavaliers, as if simultaneously, made the room ring, by seizing hold of the handles of their swords.

"And further, gentlemen, 'that no Papist shall be capable of purchasing any lands, tenements, or hereditaments, either in his own name, or in the name of any other person in trust for him.'"

The reader must be reminded, that in those days, there was no *Times* or *Morning Herald* laid upon the breakfast table with the debates of the House—that communication was anything but rapid, there being no regular post—so that what had taken place two months back, was very often news.

"It appears then, gentlemen, that our only chance is to win our properties with our own good swords."

"We will!" was the unanimous reply of the laity present.

"In Scotland, our adherents increase daily; the interests of so many have been betrayed by the usurper, that thousands of swords will start from their scabbards so soon as we can support the cause with the promised assistance of the court of Versailles: and we have here intelligence that the parliament are in a state of actual hostility to the usurper, and that the national ferment is so great as to be almost on the verge of rebellion. I have also gained from a private communication from our friend Ramsay, who is now at Amsterdam, and in a position to be most useful to us, that the usurper has intimated to his own countrymen, although it is not yet known in England, that he will return to the Hague in July. Such, gentlemen, is the intelligence I have to impart as respects our own prospects in our own country —to which I have to add, that the secret partition treaty, which is inimical to the interests of the French king, has been signed both in London and the Hague, as well as by the French envoy there. A more favourable occurrence for us, perhaps, never occurred, as it will only increase the already well-known ill-will of his Catholic Majesty against the usurper of his own father-in-law's crown. I have now, gentlemen, laid before you our present position and future prospects; and, as we are met to consult upon the propriety of further measures, I shall be most happy to hear the suggestions of others."

Sir Robert Barclay then sat down.

Lovell, the Jesuit, first rose. "I have," said he, "no opinion to offer relative to warlike arrangements, those not being suitable to my profession. I leave them to men like Sir Robert, whose swords are always ready, and whose talents are so well able to direct their swords; still, it is well known, that the sources of war must be obtained, if war is to be carried on; and I have great pleasure in announcing to those assembled, that from our friends in England, I have received advice of the two several sums of ninety-three thousand pounds and twenty-nine thousand pounds, sterling money, having been actually collected, and now held in trust for the support of the good cause; and, further, that the collections are still going on with rapidity and success. From his most Catholic Majesty we have received an order upon the minister for the sum of four thousand louis, which has been duly honoured, and from our blessed father, the Pope, an order for five hundred thousand paolis, amounting to about thirteen thousand pounds in sterling money, together with entire absolution for all sins already committed, and about to be committed, and a secure promise of paradise to those who fall in the maintenance of the true faith and the legitimate king. I have, further, great expectations from Ireland, and many promises from other quarters, in support of the cause which, with the blessing of God, I trust will yet triumph."

As soon as Lovell sat down, Collier, the ecclesiastic, rose.

"That we shall find plenty of willing swords, and a sufficient supply of money for our purposes, there can be no doubt; but I wish to propose one question to the company here assembled. It is an undoubted article of the true faith, that we are bound to uphold it by any and by every means. All human attempts are justifiable in the service of God. Many have already been made to get rid of the usurper, but they have not been crowned with success, as we too well know; and the blood of our friends, many of whom were not accessories to the act, has been lavishly spilt by the insatiate heretic.

"But they have, before this, received immortal crowns, in suffering as martyrs in the cause of religion and justice. I still hold that our attempts to cut off the usurper should be continued; some hand more fortunate may succeed. But not only is his life to be taken, if possible, but the succession must be cut off root and branch. You all know that, of the many children born to the heretic William, all but one have been taken away from him in judgment for his manifold crimes. One only remains, the present Duke of Gloucester, and I do consider that this branch of heresy should be removed, even in preference to his parent, whose conduct is such as to assist our cause, and whose death may weaken the animosity of his Catholic Majesty, whose hostility is well known to be personal. I have neither men nor money to offer to you, but I have means, I trust, soon to accomplish this point, and I dedicate my useless life to the attempt."

It would occupy too much of our pages, if we were to narrate all that was said and done at this conference, which we have been obliged to report, as intimately connected with our history. Many others addressed the meeting, proposals were made, rejected, and acceded to. Lists of adherents were produced, and of those who might be gained over. Resolutions were entered into and recorded, and questions debated. Before the breaking up, the accounts of the sums expended, and the monies still on hand, were brought forward; and in the former items, the name of Vanslyperken appeared rather prominent. As soon as the accounts were audited, the conference broke up.

We have said that, among those who were at the conference, might be observed some persons who might be recognised as part of the crew of the lugger. Such was the case; Sir Robert Barclay and many others were men of good family, and stout Jacobites. These young men served in the boat with the other men, who were no more than common seamen; but this was considered necessary in those times of treachery. The lugger pulled eighteen oars, was clinker built, and very swift, even with a full cargo. The after-oars were pulled by the adherents of Sir Robert, and the arm-chest was stowed in the stern-sheets: so that these young men being always armed, no attempt to betray them, or to rise against them, on the part of the smugglers, had they been so inclined, could have succeeded. Ramsay's trust as steersman had been appropriated to Jemmy Salisbury, but no other alteration had taken place. We have entered into this detail to prove the activity of the Jacobite party. About an hour after the conference, Sir Robert and his cavaliers had resumed their seamen's attire, for they were to go over that night; and two hours before dusk, those who had been at a conference, in which the fate of kingdoms and crowned heads was at stake, were to be seen labouring at the oar, in company with common seamen, and urging the fast boat through the yielding waters, towards her haven at the cove.

Chapter XXXIV

Besides other Matter, containing an Argument.

WE left Ramsay domiciliated in the house of the syndic Van Krause, on excellent terms with his host, who looked upon him as the mirror of information, and not a little in the good graces of the syndic's daughter, Wilhelmina. There could not be a more favourable opportunity, perhaps, for a handsome and well-informed young man to prosecute his addresses and to gain the affections of the latter, were he so inclined. Wilhelmina had been brought up in every luxury, but isolated from the world. She was now just at the age at which it was her father's intention to introduce her; but romantic in her disposition, she cared little for the formal introduction which it was intended should take place. Neither had she seen, in any of the young Dutch aristocracy, most of whom were well known to her by sight, as pointed out to her by her father when riding with him, that form and personal appearance which her mind's eye had embodied in her visions of her future lover. Her mind was naturally refined, and she looked for that elegance and grace of deportment which she sought for in vain among her countrymen, but which had suddenly been presented to her in the person of Edward Ramsay.

In the few meetings of her father's friends at their house, the conversation was uninteresting, if not disgusting; for it was about goods and merchandise, money and speculation, occasionally interrupted by politics, which were to her of as little interest. How different was the demeanour, the address, and the conversation of the young Englishman, who had been bred in courts, and, at the same time, had travelled much! There was an interest in all he said, so much information blended with novelty and amusement, so much wit and pleasantry crowning all, that Wilhelmina was fascinated without her being aware of it; and, before the terms of intimacy had warranted her receiving his hand on meeting, she had already unconsciously given her heart. The opportunities arising from her father's close attention to his commercial affairs, and the mutual attraction which brought them together during the major part of the day, she, anxious to be amused, and he attracted by her youth and beauty, were taken advantage of by them both, and the consequence was that, before ten days, they were inseparable.

The syndic either did not perceive the danger to which his child was exposed, provided that there was any objection to the intimacy, or else, equally pleased with Ramsay, he had no objection to matters taking their course.

As for Ramsay, that he had at first cultivated the intimacy with Wilhelmina more perhaps from distraction than with any definite purpose, is certain; but he soon found that her attractions were too great to permit him to continue it, if he had not serious intentions. When he had entered his own room, before he had been a week in the house, he had taxed himself severely as to the nature of his feelings, and he was then convinced that he must avoid her company, which was impossible if he remained in the house, or, as a man of honour, make a timely retreat; for Ramsay was too honourable to trifle with the feelings of an innocent girl. Having well weighed this point, he then calculated the probability of his being discovered, and the propriety of his continuing his attentions to the daughter of one whom he was deceiving, and whose political opinions were at such variance with his own—but this was a point on which he could come to no decision. His duty to the cause he supported would not allow him to quit the house—to remain in the house without falling in love was impossible.

Why should his political opinions ever be known? and why should not Wilhelmina be of the same opinion as he was?—and why——Ramsay fell asleep, putting these questions to himself, and the next morning he resolved that things should take their chance.

It was about a fortnight since the cutter had left for England. Ramsay was rather impatient for intelligence, but the cutter had not yet returned. Breakfast had been over some time, Mynheer Van Krause had descended to his warehouses, and Ramsay and Wilhelmina were sitting together upon one of the sofas in the saloon, both reclining and free from that restraint of which nothing but extreme intimacy will divest you.

"And so, my Wilhelmina," said Ramsay, taking up her hand, which lay listless at her side, and playing with her taper fingers, "you really think William of Nassau is a good man."

"And do not you, Ramsay?" replied Wilhelmina, surprised.

"However I may rejoice at his being on the throne of England, I doubt whether I can justify his conduct to the unfortunate King James; in leaguing against his own father-in-law and dispossessing him of his kingdom. Suppose now, Wilhelmina, that any fortunate man should become one day your husband: what a cruel—what a diabolical conduct it would be on his part—at least, so it appears to me—if, in return for your father putting him in possession of perhaps his greatest treasure on earth, he were to seize upon all your father's property, and leave him a beggar, because other people were to invite him so to do."

"I never heard it placed in that light before, Ramsay; that the alliance between King William and his father-in-law should have made him very scrupulous, I grant, but when the happiness of a nation depended upon it, ought not a person in William's situation to waive all minor considerations?"

"The happiness of a nation, Wilhelmina? In what way would you prove that so much was at stake?"

"Was not the Protestant religion at stake? Is not King James a bigoted Catholic?"

"I grant that, and therefore ought not to reign over a Protestant nation; but if you imagine that the happiness of any nation depends upon his religion, I am afraid you are deceived. Religion has been made the excuse for interfering with the happiness of a nation whenever no better excuse could be brought forward; but depend upon it, the mass of the people will never quarrel about religion if they are left alone, and their interests not interfered with. Had King James not committed himself in other points, he might have worshipped his Creator in any form he thought proper. That a Protestant king was all that was necessary to quiet the nation, is fully disproved by the present state of the country, now that the sceptre has been, for some years, swayed by King William, it being, at this moment, in a state very nearly approaching to rebellion."

"But is not that occasioned by the machinations of the Jacobite party, who are promoting dissension in every quarter?" replied Wilhelmina.

"I grant that they are not idle," replied Ramsay; "but observe the state of bitter variance between William and the House of Commons, which represents the people of England. What can religion have to do with that? No, Wilhelmina; although, in this country there are few who do not rejoice at their king being called to the throne of

England, there are many, and those the most wise, in that country, who lament it quite as much."

"But why so?"

"Because mankind are governed by interest, and patriotism is little more than a cloak. The benefits to this country, by the alliance with England, are very great, especially in a commercial point of view, and therefore you will find no want of patriots; but to England the case is different; it is not her interest to be involved and mixed up in continental wars and dissensions, which must now inevitably be the case. Depend upon it, that posterity will find that England will have paid very dear for a Protestant king; religion is what everyone is willing to admit the propriety and necessity of, until they are taxed to pay for it, and then it is astonishing how very indifferent, if not disgusted, they become to it."

"Why, Ramsay, one would never imagine you to be such a warm partisan of the present government, as I believe you really are, to hear you talk this morning," replied Wilhelmina.

"My public conduct, as belonging to a party, does not prevent my having my private opinions. To my party, I am, and ever will be steadfast; but knowing the world, and the secret springs of most people's actions, as I do, you must not be surprised at my being so candid with you, Wilhelmina. Our conversation, I believe, commenced upon the character of King William; and I will confess to you, that estimating the two characters in moral worth, I would infinitely prefer being the exiled and Catholic James than the unnatural and crowned King William?"

"You will say next, that you would just as soon be a Catholic as a Protestant."

"And if I had been brought up in the tenets of the one instead of the other, what difference would it have made, except that I should have adhered to the creed of my forefathers, and have worshipped the Almighty after their fashion, form, and ceremonies? And are not all religions good if they be sincere?—do not they all tend to the same object, and have the same goal in view—that of gaining heaven? Would you not prefer a good, honest, conscientious man, were he a Catholic, to a mean, intriguing, and unworthy person, who professed himself a Protestant?"

"Most certainly; but I should prefer to the just Catholic, a man who was a just Protestant."

"That is but natural; but recollect, Wilhelmina, you have seen and heard, as yet, but one side of the question; and if I speak freely to you, it is only to give you the advantage of my experience from having mixed with the world. I am true to my party, and, as a man, I must belong to a party, or I become a nonentity. But were I in a condition so unshackled that I might take up or lay down my opinions as I pleased, without loss of character—as a woman may, for instance—so little do I care for party—so well balanced do I know the right and the wrong to be on both sides—that I would, to please one I loved, at once yield up my opinions, to agree with her, if she would not yield up hers to agree with mine."

"Then you think a woman might do so? that is no compliment to the sex, Ramsay; for it is as much as to assert that we have not only no weight or influence in the world, but also that we have no character or stability."

"Far from it; I only mean to say that women do not generally enter sufficiently into politics to care much for them; they generally imbibe the politics of those they live with, without further examination, and that it is no disgrace to them if they change them. Besides, there is one feeling in women so powerful as to conquer all others, and when once that enters the breast, the remainder are absorbed or become obedient to it."

"And that feeling is——"

"Love, Wilhelmina; and if a woman happens to have been brought up in one way of thinking by her parents, when she transfers her affections to her husband, should his politics be adverse, she will soon come round to his opinion, if she really loves him."

"I am not quite so sure of that, Ramsay."

"I am quite sure she ought. Politics and party are ever a subject of dispute, and therefore should be avoided by a wife; besides, if a woman selects one as her husband, her guide and counsellor through life, one whom she swears to love, honour, cherish, and obey, she gives but a poor proof of it, if she does not yield up her judgment in all matters more peculiarly his province."

"You really put things in such a new light, Ramsay, that I hardly know how to answer you, even when I am not convinced."

"Because you have not had sufficient time for reflection, Wilhelmina; but weigh well, and dwell upon what I have said, and then you will either acknowledge that I am right, or find arguments to prove that I am wrong. But you promised me some singing. Let me lead you into the music-room."

We have introduced this conversation between Wilhelmina and Ramsay, to show not only what influence he had already gained over the artless, yet intelligent girl, but also the way by which he considerately prepared her for the acknowledgment which he resolved to make to her on some future opportunity; for, although Ramsay cared little for deceiving the father, he would not have married the daughter without her being fully aware of who he was. These conversations were constantly renewed, as if accidentally, by Ramsay; and long before he had talked in direct terms of love, he had fully prepared her for it, so that he felt she would not receive a very severe shock when he threw off the mask, even when she discovered that he was a Catholic, and opposed to her father in religion as well as in politics. The fact was, that Ramsay, at first, was as much attracted by her wealth as by her personal charms; but, like many other men, as his love increased, so did he gradually become indifferent to her wealth, and he was determined to win her for his wife in spite of all obstacles, and even if he were obliged, to secure her hand, by carrying her off without the paternal consent.

Had it been requisite, it is not certain whether Ramsay might not have been persuaded to have abandoned his party, so infatuated had he at last become with the really fascinating Wilhelmina.

But Ramsay was interrupted in the middle of one of his most favourite songs by old Koops, who informed him that the lieutenant of the cutter was waiting for him in his room. Apologising for the necessary absence, Ramsay quitted the music-room, and hastened to meet Vanslyperken.

Mr Vanslyperken had received his orders to return to the Hague a few days after the fright he had received from the nasal organ of the corporal. In pursuance of his instructions from Ramsay, he had not failed to open all the government despatches, and extract their contents. He had also brought over letters from Ramsay's adherents.

"You are sure these extracts are quite correct?" said Ramsay, after he had read them over.

"Quite so, sir," replied Vanslyperken.

"And you have been careful to seal the letters again, so as to avoid suspicion?"

"Does not my life depend upon it, Mr Ramsay?"

"Very true, and also upon your fidelity to us. Here's your money. Let me know when you sail, and come for orders."

Vanslyperken then took his bag of money, made his bow, and departed, and Ramsay commenced reading over the letters received from his friends. Mynheer Van Krause observed Vanslyperken as he was leaving the house, and immediately hastened to Ramsay's room to inquire the news. A portion of the contents of the despatches were made known to him, and the syndic was very soon afterwards seen to walk out, leaving his people to mark and tally the bales which were hoisting out from a vessel in the canal. The fact was, that Mynheer Van Krause was so anxious to get rid of his secret, that he could not contain himself any longer, and had set off to communicate to one of the authorities what he had obtained.

"But from whence did you receive this intelligence, Mynheer Krause," demanded the other. "The despatches have not yet been opened; we are waiting for Mynheer Van Wejen. I suppose we shall learn something there. You knew all before we did, when the cutter arrived last time. You must have some important friends at the English court, Mynheer Van Krause."

Here Mynheer Krause nodded his head, and looked very knowing, and shortly afterwards took his leave.

But this particular friend of Mynheer Krause was also his particular enemy. Krause had lately imparted secrets which were supposed to be known and entrusted to none but those in the entire confidence of the government. How could he have obtained them unless by the treachery of some one at home; and why should Mynheer Krause, who was not trusted by the government there, notwithstanding his high civil office, because he was known to be unsafe, be trusted by some one at home, unless it were for treacherous purposes? So argued Mr Krause's most particular friend, who thought it proper to make known his opinions on the subject, and to submit to the other authorities whether this was not a fair subject for representation in their next despatches to England; and in consequence of his suggestion, the representation was duly made. Mynheer Krause was not the first person whose tongue had got him into difficulties.

So soon as Vanslyperken had delivered his despatches to Ramsay, he proceeded to the widow Vandersloosh, when, as usual, he was received with every apparent mark of cordial welcome, was again installed on the little sofa, and again drank the beer of the widow's own brewing, and was permitted to take her fat hand. Babette inquired after the corporal, and, when rallied by the lieutenant, appeared to blush, and turned her head away. The widow also assisted in the play, and declared that it should be a match, and that Babette and herself should be married on the same day. As the evening drew nigh, Vanslyperken took his leave, and went on board, giving permission to the corporal to go on shore, and very soon the corporal was installed in his place.

This is a sad world of treachery and deceit.

Chapter XXXV

In which the agency of a red-herring is again introduced into our wonderful history.

WE are somewhat inclined to moralise. We did not intend to write this day. On the contrary, we had arranged for a party of pleasure and relaxation, in which the heels, and every other portion of the body upwards, except the brain, were to be employed, and that was to have a respite. The morning was fair, and we promised ourselves amusement, but we were deceived, and we returned to our task, as the rain poured down in torrents, washing the dirty face of mother earth. Yes, deceived; and here we cannot help observing, that this history of ours is a very true picture of human life—for what a complication of treachery does it not involve!

Smallbones is deceiving his master, Mr Vanslyperken —the corporal is deceiving Mr Vanslyperken—the widow is deceiving Mr Vanslyperken, so is Babette, and the whole crew of the *Yungfrau*. Ramsay is deceiving his host and his mistress. All the Jacobites, in a mass, are plotting against and deceiving the government, and as for Mr Vanslyperken; as it will soon appear, he is deceiving everybody, and will ultimately deceive himself. The only honest party in the whole history is the one most hated, as generally is the case in this world—I mean Snarleyyow. There is no deceit about him, and therefore, *par excellence*, he is fairly entitled to be the hero of, and to give his name to, the work. The next most honest party in the book is Wilhelmina; all the other women, except little Lilly, are cheats and impostors—and Lilly is too young; our readers may, therefore, be pleased to consider Snarleyyow and Wilhelmina as the hero and the heroine of the tale, and then it will leave one curious feature in it, the principals will not only not be united, but the tale will wind up without their ever seeing each other. *Allons en avant.*

But of all the treachery practised by all the parties, it certainly appears to us that the treachery of the widow was the most odious and diabolical. She was like a bloated spider, slowly entwining those threads for her victim which were to entrap him to his destruction, for she had vowed that she never would again be led to the hymeneal altar until Mr Vanslyperken was hanged. Perhaps, the widow Vandersloosh was in a hurry to be married, at least, by her activity, it would so appear—but let us not anticipate.

The little sofa was fortunately like its build, strong as a cob, or it never could have borne the weight of two such lovers as the widow Vandersloosh and the Corporal Van Spitter; there they sat, she radiant with love and beer, he with ditto; their sides met, for the sofa exactly took them both in, without an inch to spare; their hands met, their eyes met, and whenever one raised the glass, the other was on the alert, and their glasses met and jingled—a more practical specimen of hob and nob was never witnessed. There was but one thing wanting to complete their happiness, which, unlike other people's, did not hang upon a thread, but something much stronger, it hung upon a cord; the cord which was to hang Mr Vanslyperken.

And now the widow, like the three fates rolled into one, is weaving the woof, and, in good Dutch, is pouring into the attentive ear of the corporal her hopes and fears, her surmises, her wishes, her anticipations, and her desires—and he imbibes them all greedily, washing them down with the beer of the widow's own brewing.

"He has not been to the house opposite these two last arrivals," said the widow, "that is certain; for Babette and I have been on the watch. There was hanging matter there. Now I won't believe but that he must go somewhere; he carries his letters, and takes his gold as before, depend upon it. Yes, and I will find it out. Yes, yes, Mr Vanslyperken, we will see who is the 'cutest—you, or the widow Vandersloosh."

" Mein Gott, yes ! " replied the corporal.

"Now he landed a passenger last time, which he called a king's messenger, and I am as sure as I sit here that he was no king's messenger, unless he was one of King James's as was; for look you, Corporal Van Spitter, do you suppose that King William would employ an Englishman, as you say he was, for a messenger, when a Dutchman was to be had for love or money?

" No, no, we must find out where he goes to. I will have some one on the look out when you come again, and then set Babette on the watch; she shall track him up to the den of his treachery. Yes, yes, Mr Vanslyperken, we will see who gains the day, you or the widow Vandersloosh."

" Mein Gott ! yes," replied the corporal.

" And now, corporal, I've been thinking over all this ever since your absence, and all you have told me about his cowardly attempts upon that poor boy's life, and his still greater cowardice in believing such stuff as you have made him believe about the lad not being injured by mortal man. Stuff and nonsense ! the lad is but a lad."

" Mein Gott ! yes," said the corporal.

" And now, corporal, I'll tell you something else, which is, that you and the *Yungfraus* are just as great fools as Mynheer Vanslyperken, in believing all that stuff and nonsense about the dog. The dog is but a dog."

This was rather a trial to the corporal's politeness; to deny what the widow said, might displease, and, as he firmly believed otherwise, he was put to a nonplus; but the widow looked him full in the face, expecting assent, so at last the corporal drawled out, " Mein Gott ! yes— a tog is but a tog."

The widow was satisfied, and not perceiving the nice distinction, continued.

"Well, then, corporal, as a lad is but a lad, and a dog is but a dog, I have been setting my wits to work about getting the rascally traitor in my power. I mean to pretend to take every interest in him, and to get all his secrets, and then, when he tells me that Smallbones cannot be hurt by mortal man, I shall say he can by woman, at all events; and then I shall make a proposition, which he'll accept fast enough, and then I'll have more hanging matter for him, besides getting rid of the cur. Yes, yes, Mr Vanslyperken, match a woman if you can. We'll see if your dog is to take possession of my bedroom again."

"Mein Gott! yes," replied the corporal again.

"And now I'll tell you what I'll do, Mr Corporal; I will prepare it myself; and, then, Mr Vanslyperken shall have it grilled for his breakfast, and then he shall not eat it, but leave it for Smallbones, and then Smallbones shall pretend to eat it, but put it in his pocket, and then (for it won't do to do it on board, or he'll find out that the lad has given it to the dog) he shall bring it on shore, and give it to the dog here in the yard, so that he shall kill the dog himself, by wishing to kill others. Do you understand, corporal?"

"Mein Gott! yes, I understand what you say; but what is it that you are to prepare?"

"What? why, a red-herring to be sure."

"But how will a red-herring kill a body or a dog?"

"Lord, corporal, how stupid you are; I'm to put arsenic in."

"Yes; but you left that out till now."

"Did I? well, that was an oversight; but now, corporal, you understand it all?"

"Mein Gott! yes; but if the lad does not die, what will he think?"

"Think! that he can take poison like pea-soup, without injury, and that neither man nor woman can take his life; be afraid of the lad, and leave him alone."

"Mein Gott! yes," replied the rather obtuse corporal, who now understood the whole plot.

Such was the snare laid for Mr Vanslyperken by the treacherous widow; and before the cutter sailed, it was put in execution. She received the lieutenant now as an accepted lover, allowed him to talk of the day, wormed out of him all his secrets except that of his treason, abused Smallbones, and acknowledged that she had been too hasty about the dog, which she would be very happy to see on shore. Vanslyperken could hardly believe his senses—the widow forgive Snarleyyow, and all for his sake, he was delighted, enchanted, threw himself at her feet, and vowed eternal gratitude with his lips—but vengeance in his heart.

Oh! Mr Vanslyperken, you deserved to be deceived.

The dislike expressed by the widow against Smallbones was also very agreeable to the lieutenant, and he made her his confidant, stating what the corporal had told him relative to the appearance of Smallbones when he was adrift.

"Well then, lieutenant," said the widow, "if mortal man can't hurt him, mortal woman may; and for my love for you I will prepare what will rid you of him. But, Vanslyperken, recollect there's nothing I would not do for you; but if it were found out—O dear! O dear!"

The widow then informed him that she would prepare a red-herring with arsenic, which he should take on board, and order Smallbones to grill for his breakfast; that he was to pretend not to be well, and to allow it to be taken away by the lad, who would, of course, eat it fast enough.

"Excellent!" replied Vanslyperken, who felt not only that he should get rid of Smallbones, but have the widow in his power. "Dearest widow, how can I be sufficiently grateful? Oh! how kind, how amiable you are!" continued Vanslyperken, mumbling her fat fingers, which the widow abandoned to him without reserve.

Who would have believed that, between these two, there existed a deadly hatred? We might imagine such a thing to take place in the refinement and artificial air of a court, but not in a Dutch Lust Haus at Amsterdam. That evening, before his departure, did the widow present her swain with the fatal herring; and the swain received it with as many marks of gratitude and respect, as some knight in ancient times would have shown when presented with some magical gift by his favouring genius.

The red-herring itself was but a red-herring, but the charm consisted in the two-pennyworth of arsenic.

The next morning Vanslyperken did not fail to order the red-herring for his breakfast, but took good care not to eat it.

Smallbones, who had been duly apprised of the whole plan, asked his master, as he cleared away, whether he should keep the red-herring for the next day; but Mr Vanslyperken very graciously informed him that he might eat it himself. About an hour afterwards Mr Vanslyperken went on shore, taking with him, for the first time, Snarleyyow, and desiring Smallbones to come with him, with a bag of biscuit for the widow. This plan had been proposed by the widow, as Smallbones might be supposed to have eaten something on shore. Smallbones took as good care as his master not to eat the herring, but put it in his pocket as a *bonne bouche* for Snarleyyow. Mr Vanslyperken, as they pulled on shore, thought that the lad smelt very strong of herring, and this satisfied him that he had eaten it; but to make more sure, he exclaimed, " Confound it, how you smell of red-herring ! "

" That's all along of having eaten one, sir," replied Smallbones, grinning.

" You'll grin in another way before an hour is over," thought his master.

The lieutenant, the dog, and the biscuit were all graciously received.

" Has he eaten it ? " inquired the widow.

" Yes," replied Vanslyperken, with a nod. " Empty the bag, and I will send him on board again."

" Not yet, not yet—give him half an hour to saunter, it

will be better. That poor dog of yours must want a little grass," said the widow, "always being on board. Let him run a little in the yard, he will find plenty there."

The obedient lieutenant opened the back-door, and Snarleyyow, who had not forgotten either the widow or Babette, went out of his own accord. Mr Vanslyperken looked to ascertain if the yard-door, which led to the street, was fast, and then returned, shutting the back-door after him.

Smallbones was waiting at the porch as usual.

"Babette," cried the widow, "mind you don't open the yard-door and let Mr Vanslyperken's dog out. Do you hear?"

Smallbones, who understood this as the signal, immediately slipped round, opened the yard-door, took the herring out of his pocket, and threw it to Snarleyyow. The dog came to it, smelt it, seized it, and walked off, with his ears and tail up, to the sunny side of the yard, intending to have a good meal; and Smallbones, who was afraid of Mr Vanslyperken catching him in the act, came out of the yard, and hastened to his former post at the porch. He caught Babette's eye, coming down stairs, and winked and smiled. Babette walked into the room, caught the eye of the mistress, and winked and smiled. Upon which, the widow ordered Babette to empty the bread-bag and give it to Smallbones, to take on board,—an order repeated by Vanslyperken. Before he returned to the boat, Smallbones again passed round to the yard-door. Snarleyyow was there, but no signs of the red-herring. "He's a eaten it all, by gum," said Smallbones, grinning, and walking away to the boat, with the bread-bag over his shoulder. As soon as he had arrived on board, the lad communicated the fact to the crew of the *Yungfrau*, whose spirits were raised by the intelligence, with the exception still of old Coble, who shook his head, and declared, "It was twopence and a red-herring thrown away."

Mr Vanslyperken returned on board in the afternoon, fully expecting to hear of Smallbones being very ill. He was surprised that the man in the boat did not tell him, and he asked them carelessly if there was anything new on board, but received a reply in the negative. When he came on board, followed by Snarleyyow, the eyes of the crew were directed towards the dog, to see how he looked; but he appeared just as lively and as cross-grained as ever, and they all shook their heads.

Vanslyperken sent for Smallbones, and looked him hard in the face. " Ar'n't you well ? " inquired he.

"Well, sir!" replied Smallbones: "I'd a bit of a twinge in my stummick this morning, but it's all gone off now."

Mr Vanslyperken waited the whole day for Smallbones to die, but he did not. The crew of the vessel waited the whole day for the cur to die, but he did not. What inference could be drawn. The crew made up their minds that the dog was supernatural; and old Coble told them that he told them so. Mr Vanslyperken made up his mind that Smallbones was supernatural, and the corporal shook his head, and told him that he told him so.

The reason why Snarleyyow did not die was simply this, that he did not eat the red-herring. He had just laid it between his paws, and was about to commence, when Smallbones, having left the yard-door open in his hurry, the dog was perceived by a dog bigger than he, who happened to pass that way, and who pounced upon Snarleyyow, trampling him over and over, and walked off with the red-herring, which he had better have left alone, as he was found dead the next morning.

The widow heard, both from the corporal and Vanslyperken, the failure of both their projects. That Smallbones was not poisoned she was not surprised to hear, but she took care to agree with Vanslyperken that all attempts upon him were useless; but that the dog still lived was indeed a matter of surprise, and the widow became a convert to the corporal's opinion that the dog was not to be destroyed.

" A whole two-pennyworth of arsenic! Babette, only think what a cur it must be!" And Babette, as well as her mistress, lifted up her hands in amazement, exclaiming, " What a cur indeed ! "

Chapter XXXVI

In which Mr Vanslyperken, although at fault, comes in for the brush.

VANSLYPERKEN having obtained his despatches from the States General, called at the house of Mynheer Krause, and received the letters of Ramsay, then, once more, the cutter's head was turned towards England.

It may be as well to remind the reader, that it was in the month of January, sixteen hundred and ninety-nine, that we first introduced Mr Vanslyperken and his contemporaries to his notice, and that all the important events, which we have recorded, have taken place between that date and the month of May, which is now arrived. We think, indeed, that the peculiar merit of this work is its remarkable unity of time and place; for, be it observed, we intend to finish it long before the year is out, and our whole scene is, it may be said, laid in the channel, or between the channel and the Texel, which, considering it is an historical novel, is remarkable. Examine other productions of this nature, founded upon historical facts, like our own, and observe the difference. Read Scott, Bulwer, James, or Grattan, read their historical novels, and observe how they fly about from country to country, and from clime to clime. As the Scythians said to Alexander, their right arm extends to the east, and their left to the west, and the world can hardly contain them. And over how many years do they extend their pages ? while our bantling is produced in the regular nine months, being the exact period of time which is required for my three volumes. It must, therefore, be allowed that in unity of time, and place and design, and adherence to facts, our historical novel is unique.

We said that it was the month of May—not May coming in as she does sometimes in her caprice, pouting, and out of humour—but May all in smiles. The weather was warm, and the sea was smooth, and the men of the cutter had stowed away their pea-jackets, and had pulled off their fishermen's boots, and had substituted shoes. Mr Vanslyperken did not often appear on deck during the passage. He was very busy down below, and spread a piece of bunting across the skylight, so that no one could look down and see what he was about, and the cabin-door was almost always locked. What could Mr Vanslyperken be about? No one knew but Snarleyyow, and Snarleyyow could not or would not tell.

The cutter anchored in her old berth, and Vanslyperken, as usual, went on shore, with his double set of despatches, which were duly delivered; and then Mr Vanslyperken went up the main street, and turned into a jeweller's shop. What could Mr Vanslyperken do there? Surely it was to purchase something for the widow Vandersloosh—a necklace or pair of ear-rings. No, it was not with that intention; but nevertheless, Mr Vanslyperken remained there for a long while, and then was seen to depart. Seen by whom? By Moggy Salisbury, who had observed his entering, and who could not imagine why; she, however, said nothing, but she marked the shop, and walked away.

The next day, Mr Vanslyperken went on shore, to put into his mother's charge the money which he had received from Ramsay, and narrated all that had passed—how Smallbones had swallowed two-pennyworth of arsenic with no more effect upon him than one twinge in his stomach, and how he now fully believed that nothing would kill the boy.

"Pshaw! child—phut!—nonsense!—nothing kill him? —had he been in my hands, old as they are, and shaking as they do, he would not have lived; no, no—nobody escapes me when I am determined. We'll talk about that, but not now, Cornelius; the weather has turned warm at last, and there is no need of fire. Go, child, the money is locked up safe, and I have my mood upon me—I may even do you a mischief."

Vanslyperken, who knew that it was useless to remain after this hint, walked off and returned on board. As he pulled off, he passed a boat, apparently coming from the cutter, with Moggy Salisbury sitting in the stern-sheets. She waved her hand at him, and laughed ironically.

"Impudent hussy!" thought Vanslyperken, as she passed, but he dared not say a word. He turned pale with rage, and turned his head away; but little did he imagine, at the time, what great cause he had of indignation. Moggy had been three hours on board of the cutter talking with the men, but more particularly with Smallbones and the corporal, with which two she had been in earnest conference for the first hour that she was on board.

Moggy's animosity to Vanslyperken is well known, and she ridiculed the idea of Snarleyyow being anything more than an uncommon lucky dog in escaping so often. Smallbones was of her opinion, and again declared his intention of doing the dog a mischief as soon as he could. Moggy, after her conference with these two, mixed with the ship's company, with whom she had always been a favourite, and the corporal proceeded to superintend the cutting up and the distribution of the fresh beef which had that morning come on board.

The beef block was on the forecastle, where the major part of the crew, with Moggy, were assembled; Snarleyyow had always attended the corporal on these occasions, and was still the best of friends with him; for somehow or another, the dog had not seemed to consider the corporal a party to his brains being knocked out, but had put it all down to his natural enemy, Smallbones. The dog was, as usual, standing by the block close to the corporal, and picking up the fragments of beef which dropped from the chopper.

"I vowed by gum, that I'd have that ere dog's tail off," observed Smallbones; "and if no one will peach, off it shall go now. And who cares? If I can't a kill him dead, I'll get rid of him by bits. There's one eye out already, and now I've a mind for his tail. Corporal, lend me the cleaver."

"Bravo, Smallbones, we won't peach—not one of us."

"I'm not sure of that," replied Moggy; "some won't, I know; but there are others who may, and then Smallbones will be keel-hauled as sure as fate, and Vanslyperken will have right on his side. No, no, Smallbones—you must not do it. Give me the cleaver, corporal, I'll do it; and anyone may tell him who pleases, when he comes on board. I don't care for him—and he knows it, corporal. Hand me the cleaver."

"That's right, let Moggy do it," said the seamen.

The corporal turned the dog round, so as to leave his tail on the block, and fed him with small pieces of meat, to keep him in the same position.

"Are you all ready, Moggy?" said Smallbones.

"Back him a little more on the block, corporal, for I won't leave him an inch if I can help it," said Moggy; "and stand farther back, all of you."

Moggy raised the cleaver, took good aim—down it came upon the dog's tail, which was separated within an inch of its insertion, and was left bleeding on the block, while the dog sprang away aft, howling most terribly, and leaving a dotted line of blood to mark his course upon the deck.

"There's a nice skewer-piece for anyone who fancies it," observed Moggy, looking at the dog's tail, and throwing down the cleaver. "I think Mr Vanslyperken has had enough now for trying to flog my Jemmy—my own duck of a husband."

"Well," observed Coble, "seeing's believing; but, otherwise, I never should have thought it possible to have divided that ere dog's tail in that way."

"He can't be much of a devil now," observed Bill Spurey; "for what's a devil without a tail? A devil is like a sarpent, whose sting is in his tail."

"Yes," replied Short, who had looked on in silence.

"But, I say, Moggy, perhaps it's as well for him not to find you on board."

"What do I care?" replied Moggy. "He is more afraid of me than I of him; but, howsomever, it's just as well not to be here, as it may get others in trouble. Mind you say at once it was me—I defy him."

Moggy then wished them good-bye, and quitted the cutter, when she was met, as we have already observed, by Vanslyperken.

"Mein Gott! vat must be done now?" observed the corporal to those about him, looking at the mangy tail which still remained on the beef-block.

"Done, corporal," replied Smallbones, "why, you must come for to go for to complain on it, as he comes on board. You must take the tail, and tell the tale, and purtend to be as angry and as sorry as himself, and damn *her* up in heaps. That's what must be done."

This was not bad advice on the part of Smallbones—the ship's company agreed to it, and the corporal perceived the propriety of it.

In the meantime, the dog had retreated to the cabin, and his howlings had gradually ceased; but he had left a track of blood along the deck, and down the ladder, which Dick Short perceiving, pointed to it, and cried out "Swabs."

The men brought swabs aft, and had cleaned the deck and the ladder down to the cabin door, when Mr Vanslyperken came on board.

"Has that woman been here?" inquired Mr Vanslyperken, as he came on deck.

"Yes," replied Dick Short.

"Did not I give positive orders that she should not?" cried Vanslyperken.

"No," replied Dick Short.

"Then I do now," continued the lieutenant.

"Too late," observed Short, shrugging up his shoulders, and walking forward.

"Too late! what does he mean?" said Vanslyperken, turning to Coble.

"I knows nothing about it, sir," replied Coble. "She came for some of her husband's things that were left on board."

Vanslyperken turned round to look for the corporal for explanation.

There stood Corporal Van Spitter, perfectly erect, with a very melancholy face, one hand raised as usual to his cap, and the other occupied with the tail of Snarleyyow.

"What is it? what is the matter, corporal?"

"Mynheer Vanslyperken," replied the corporal, retaining his respectful attitude, "here is de tail."

"Tail! what tail?" exclaimed Vanslyperken, casting his eyes upon the contents of the corporal's left hand.

"Te tog's tail, mynheer," replied the corporal, gravely, "which de dam tog's wife—Moggy——"

Vanslyperken stared; he could scarcely credit his eyesight, but there it was. For a time he could not speak for agitation; at last, with a tremendous oath, he darted into the cabin.

What were his feelings when he beheld Snarleyyow lying in a corner tailless, with a puddle of blood behind him.

"My poor, poor dog!" exclaimed Vanslyperken, covering up his face.

His sorrow soon changed to rage—he invoked all the curses he could imagine upon Moggy's head—he vowed revenge—he stamped with rage—and then he patted Snarleyyow; and as the beast looked wistfully in his face, Vanslyperken shed tears. "My poor, poor dog! first your eye—and now your tail—what will your persecutors require next? Perdition seize them! may perdition be my portion if I am not revenged. Smallbones is at the bottom of all this; I can—I will be revenged on him."

Vanslyperken rang the bell, and the corporal made his appearance with the dog's tail still in his hand.

"Lay it down on the table, corporal," said Vanslyperken, mournfully, "and tell me how this happened."

The corporal then entered into a long detail of the way in which the dog had been *de*tailed—how he had been cutting up beef—and how while his back was turned, and Snarleyyow, as usual, was at the block, picking up the bits, Moggy Salisbury, who had been allowed to come on board by Mr Short, had caught up the cleaver and chopped off the dog's tail.

"Was Smallbones at the block?" inquired Vanslyperken.

"He was, mynheer," replied the corporal.

"Who held the dog while his tail was chopped off?" inquired Vanslyperken; "some one must have held him."

This was a home question; but the corporal replied, "Yes, mynheer, some one must have held the dog."

"You did not hear who it was, or if it were Smallbones?"

"I did not, mynheer," replied the corporal; "but," added he with a significant look, "I tink I could say."

"Yes, yes, corporal, I know who you mean. It was him —I am sure—and as sure as I sit here I'll be revenged. Bring a swab, corporal, and wipe up all this blood. Do you think the poor animal will recover?"

"Yes, mynheer; there be togs with tail and togs without tail."

"But the loss of blood—what must be done to stop the bleeding?"

"Dat d———n woman Moggy, when I say te tog die— tog bleed to death, she say, tell Mynheer Vanslyperken dat de best ting for cure de cur be de red hot poker."

Here Vanslyperken stamped his feet and swore horribly.

"She say, mynheer, it stop all de bleeding."

"I wish she had a hot poker down her body," exclaimed Vanslyperken, bitterly.

"Go for the swab, corporal, and send Smallbones here." Smallbones made his appearance.

"Did you come for—to want me, sir?"

"Yes, sir. I understand from the corporal that you held the dog while that woman cut off his tail."

"If so be as how as the corporal says that ere," cried

Smallbones, striking the palm of his left hand with his right fist, " why I am jiggered if he don't tell a lie as big as himself—that's all. That ere man is my mortal henemy; and if that ere dog gets into trouble I'm a sartain to be in trouble too. What should I cut the dog's tail off for, I should like for to know? I arn't so hungry as all that, any how."

The idea of eating his dog's tail increased the choler of Mr Vanslyperken. With looks of malignant vengeance he ordered Smallbones out of the cabin.

"Shall I shy this here overboard, sir?" said Smallbones, taking up the dog's tail, which lay on the table.

"Drop it, sir," roared Vanslyperken.

Smallbones walked away, grinning with delight, but his face was turned from Mr Vanslyperken.

The corporal returned, swabbed up the blood, and reported that the bleeding had stopped. Mr Vanslyperken had no further orders for him—he wished to be left alone. He leaned his head upon his hand, and remained for some time in a melancholy reverie, with his eyes fixed upon the tail, which lay before him—that tail, now a "bleeding piece of earth," which never was to welcome him with a wag again. What passed in Vanslyperken's mind during this time, it would be too difficult and too long to repeat, for the mind flies over time and space with the rapidity of the lightning's flash. At last he rose, took up the dog's tail, put it into his pocket, went on deck, ordered his boat, and pulled on shore.

Chapter XXXVII

In which Mr Vanslyperken drives a very hard bargain.

WE will be just and candid in our opinion relative to the historical facts which we are now narrating. Party spirit, and various other feelings, independent of misrepresentation, do, at the time, induce people to form their judgment, to say the best, harshly, and but too often, incorrectly. It is for posterity to calmly weigh the evidence handed down, and to examine into the merits of a case divested of party bias. Actuated by these feelings, we do not hesitate to assert, that, in the point at question, Mr Vanslyperken had great cause for being displeased; and that the conduct of Moggy Salisbury, in cutting off the tail of Snarleyyow was, in our opinion, not justifiable.

There is a respect for property, inculcated and protected by the laws, which should never be departed from; and, whatever may have been the aggressions on the part of Mr Vanslyperken, or of the dog, still a tail is a tail, and whether mangy or not, is *bonâ fide* a part of the living body; and this aggression must inevitably come under the head of the cutting and maiming act, which act, however, it must, with the same candour which will ever guide our pen, be acknowledged, was not passed until a much later period than that to the history of which our narrative refers.

Having thus, with all deference, offered our humble opinion, we shall revert to facts. Mr Vanslyperken went on shore, with the dog's tail in his pocket. He walked with rapid strides towards the half-way houses, in one of which was the room tenanted by his aged mother; for, to whom else could he apply for consolation in this case of severe distress? That it was Moggy Salisbury who gave the cruel blow, was a fact completely substantiated by evidence; but that it was Smallbones who held the dog, and who thereby became an active participator, and therefore equally culpable, was a surmise to which the insinuations of the corporal had given all the authority of direct evidence. And, as Mr Vanslyperken felt that Moggy was not only out of his power, but even if in his power, that he dare not retaliate upon her, for reasons which we have already explained to our readers; it was, therefore, clear to him, that Smallbones was the party upon whom his indignation could be the most safely vented: and, moreover, that in so doing, he was only paying off a long accumulating debt of hatred and ill-will. But, at the same time, Mr Vanslyperken had made up his mind that a lad who could be floated out to the Nab buoy and back again without sinking—who could have a bullet through his head without a mark remaining—and who could swallow a whole twopenny-worth of arsenic without feeling more than a twinge in his stomach, was not so very easy to be made away with. That the corporal's vision was no fiction, was evident—the lad was not to be hurt by mortal man; but although the widow's arsenic had failed, Mr Vanslyperken, in his superstition, accounted for it on the grounds that the woman was not the active agent on the occasion, having only prepared the herring, it not having been received from her hands by Smallbones. The reader may recollect that, in the last interview between Vanslyperken and his mother, the latter had thrown out hints that if she took Smallbones in hand he would not have such miraculous escapes as he had had, as, in all she undertook, she did her business thoroughly. Bearing this in mind, Mr Vanslyperken went to pour forth his sorrows, and to obtain the assistance of his much-to-be-respected and venerable mother.

"Well, child, what is it—is it money you bring?" cried the old woman, when Vanslyperken entered the room.

"No, mother," replied Vanslyperken, throwing himself on the only chair in the room, except the one with the legs cut off half-way up, upon which his mother was accustomed to rock herself before the grate.

"No, mother; but I have brought something—and I come to you for advice and assistance."

"Brought no money—yet brought something!—well, child, what have you brought?"

"This!" exclaimed Vanslyperken, throwing the dog's tail down upon the table.

"This!" repeated the old beldame, lifting up the tail, and examining it as well as she could, as the vibration of her palsied members were communicated to the article—"and pray, child, what is this?"

"Are you blind, old woman," replied Vanslyperken in wrath, "not to perceive that it is my poor dog's tail?"

"Blind old woman! and dog's tail, eh! Blind old woman, eh! Mr Cornelius, you dare to call me a blind old woman, and to bring here the mangy tail of a dog—and to lay it on my table! Is this your duty, sirrah? How dare you take such liberties? There, sir," cried the hag in a rage, catching hold of the tail, and sending it flying out of the casement, which was open—"there, sir—and now you may follow your tail. D'ye hear?—leave the room instantly, or I'll cleave your craven skull. Blind old woman, forsooth—undutiful child——"

Vanslyperken, in spite of his mother's indignation, could not prevent his eyes from following the tail of his dog, as it sailed through the ambient air surrounding the half-way houses, and was glad to observe it landed among some cabbage-leaves thrown into the road, without attracting notice. Satisfied that he should regain his treasure when he quitted the house, he now turned round to deprecate his mother's wrath, who had not yet completed the sentence which we have quoted above.

"I supplicate your pardon, my dear mother," said Vanslyperken, who felt that in her present humour he was not likely to gain the point with her that he had in contemplation. "I was so vexed—so irritated—that I knew not what I was saying."

"Blind old woman, indeed," repeated the beldame.

"I again beg you to forgive me, dearest mother," continued Vanslyperken.

"All about a dog's tail cut off. Better off than on—so much the less mange on the snarling cur."

This was touching up Vanslyperken on the raw; but he had a great object in view, and he restrained his feelings.

"I was wrong, mother—very wrong—but I have done all I can, I have begged your pardon. I came here for your advice and assistance."

"What advice or assistance can you expect from a blind old woman?" retorted the old hag. "And what advice or assistance does so undutiful a child deserve?"

It was some time before the ruffled temper of the beldame could be appeased: at last, Vanslyperken succeeded. He then entered into a detail of all that had passed, and concluded by observing, "that as Smallbones was not to be injured by mortal man, he had come to her for assistance."

"That is to say—you have come to me to ask me to knock the lad's brains out—to take away his life—to murder him, in fact. Say, Cornelius, is it not so?"

"It is exactly so, my dearest mother. I know your courage—your——"

"Yes, yes, I understand all that; but, now hear me, child. There are deeds which are done, and which I have done, but those deeds are only done upon strong impulses. Murder is one; but people murder for two reasons only—for revenge and for gold. People don't do such acts as are to torture their minds here, and perhaps be punished hereafter—that is, if there be one, child. I say, people don't do such deeds as these, merely because a graceless son comes to them, and says, 'if you please, mother.' Do you understand that, child? I've blood enough on my hands already—good blood too—they are not defiled with the scum of a parish boy, nor shall they be, without——"

"Without what, mother?"

"Have I not told you, Cornelius, that there are but two great excitements—revenge and gold? I have no revenge against the lad. If you have—if you consider that a dog's tail demands a human victim—well and good—do the deed yourself."

"I would," cried Vanslyperken, "but I have tried in vain. It must be done by woman."

"Then hear me, Cornelius; if it must be done by woman, you must find a woman to do it, and you must pay her for the deed. Murder is at a high price. You apply to me—I am content to do the deed; but I must have gold—and plenty too."

Vanslyperken paused before he replied. The old woman had charge of all his money—she was on the verge of the grave—for what could she require his gold?—could she be so foolish?—it was insanity. Vanslyperken was right—it was insanity, for avarice is no better.

"Do you mean, mother," replied Vanslyperken, "that you want gold from me?"

"From whom else?" demanded the old woman sharply.

"Take it, then, mother—take as many pieces as you please."

"I must have all that there is in that chest, Cornelius."

"All, mother?"

"Yes, all; and what is it, after all? What price is too high for blood which calls for retribution? Besides, Cornelius, it must be all yours again when I die; but I shall not die yet—no, no."

"Well, mother," replied Vanslyperken, "if it must be so, it shall all be yours—not that I can see what difference it makes, whether it is called yours or mine."

"Then why not give it freely? Why do you hesitate to give to your poor old mother what may be again yours before the leaf again falls? Ask yourself why, Cornelius, and then you have my answer. The gold is here in my charge, but it is not *my* gold—it is yours. You little think how often I've laid in bed and longed that it was all *mine*. Then I would count it—count it again and again—watch over it, not as I do now as a mere deposit in my charge, but as a mother would watch and smile upon her first-born child. There is a talisman in that word *mine*, that not approaching *death* can wean from *life*. It is our natures, child—say, then, is all that gold *mine*?"

Vanslyperken paused; he also felt the magic of the word; and although it was but a nominal and temporary divestment of the property, even that gave him a severe struggle; but his avarice was overcome by his feelings of revenge, and he answered solemnly, "As I hope for revenge, mother, *all* that gold is *yours*, provided that you do the deed."

Here the old hag burst into a sort of shrieking laugh. "Send him here, child;" and the almost unearthly cachinnation was continued—" send him here, child—I can't go to seek him—and it is done—only bring him here."

So soon as this compact had been completed, Vanslyperken and his mother had a consultation; and it was agreed, that it would be advisable not to attempt the deed until the day before the cutter sailed, as it would remove all suspicion, and be supposed that the boy had deserted. This arrangement having been made, Vanslyperken made rather a hasty retreat. The fact was, that he was anxious to recover the fragment of Snarleyyow, which his mother had so contemptuously thrown out of the casement.

Chapter XXXVIII

In which Mr Vanslyperken is taken for a witch.

Mr Vanslyperken hastened into the street, and walked towards the heap of cabbage-leaves, in which he observed the object of his wishes to have fallen; but there was some one there before him, an old sow, very busy groping among the refuse. Although Vanslyperken came on shore without even a stick in his hand, he had no fear of a pig, and walked up boldly to drive her away, fully convinced that, although she might like cabbage, not being exactly carnivorous, he should find the tail in *statu quo*. But it appeared that the sow not only would not stand being interfered with, but, moreover, was carnivorously inclined; for she was at that very moment routing the tail about with her nose, and received Vanslyperken's advance with a very irascible grunt, throwing her head up at him with a savage augh; and then again busied herself with the fragment of Snarleyyow. Vanslyperken, who had started back, perceived that the sow was engaged with the very article in question; and finding it was a service of more danger than he had expected, picked up one or two large stones, and threw them at the animal to drive her away. This mode of attack had the effect desired in one respect; the sow made a retreat, but at the same time she would not retreat without the *bonne bouche*, which she carried away in her mouth.

Vanslyperken followed; but the sow proved that she could fight as well as run, every minute turning round to bay, and chumping and grumbling in a very formidable manner. At last, after Vanslyperken had chased for a quarter of a mile, he received unexpected assistance from a large dog, who bounded from the side of the road, where he lay in the sun, and seizing the sow by the ear, made her drop the tail to save her own bacon.

Vanslyperken was delighted; he hastened up as fast as he could to regain his treasure, when, to his mortification, the great dog, who had left the sow, arrived at the spot before him, and after smelling at the not one bone, but many bones of contention, he took it in his mouth, and trotted off to his former berth in the sunshine, laid himself down, and the tail before him.

"Surely one dog won't eat another dog's tail," thought Vanslyperken, as he walked up to the animal; but an eye like fire, a deep growl, and exposure of a range of teeth equal to a hyena's, convinced Mr Vanslyperken that it would be wise to retreat—which he did, to a respectable distance, and attempted to coax the dog. "Poor doggy, there's a dog," cried Vanslyperken, snapping his fingers, and approaching gradually. To his horror, the dog did the same thing exactly: he rose, and approached Mr Vanslyperken gradually, and snapped his fingers: not content with that, he flew at him, and tore the skirt of his great-coat clean off, and also the hinder part of his trousers, for Mr Vanslyperken immediately turned tail, and the dog appeared resolved to have his tail as well as that of his darling cur. Satisfied with about half a yard of broadcloth as a trophy, the dog returned to his former situation, and remained with the tail of the coat and the tail of the cur before him, with his fierce eyes fixed upon Mr Vanslyperken, who had now retreated to a greater distance.

But this transaction was not unobserved by several of the people who inhabited the street of cottages. Many eyes were directed to where Mr Vanslyperken and the sow and dog had been at issue, and many were the conjectures thereon.

When the dog retreated with the skirt of the great-coat, many came out to ascertain what was the cause of the dispute, and among others, the man to whom the dog belonged, and who lived at the cottage opposite to where the dog had lain down. He observed Vanslyperken, looking very much like a vessel whose sails have been split in a gale, and very rueful at the same time, standing at a certain distance, quite undecided how to act, and he called out to him, "What is it you may want with my dog, man?"

Man! Vanslyperken thought this designation an affront; whereas, in our opinion, Vanslyperken was an affront to the name of man. "Man!" exclaimed Vanslyperken; "why your dog has taken my property!"

"Then take your property," replied the other, tossing to him the skirt of his coat, which he had taken from the dog.

By this time there was a crowd collected from out of the various surrounding tenements.

"That's not all," exclaimed Vanslyperken; "he has got my dog's tail there."

"Your dog's tail!" exclaimed the man, "what do you mean? Is it this ragged mangy thing you would have?" and the man took the tail of Snarleyyow, and held it up to the view of the assembled crowd.

"Yes," replied Vanslyperken, coming towards the man with eagerness; "that is what I want," and he held out his hand to receive it.

"And pray, may I ask," replied the other, looking very suspiciously at Vanslyperken, "what can you want with this piece of carrion?"

"To make soup of," replied another, laughing; "he can't afford ox-tail."

Vanslyperken made an eager snatch at his treasure; but the man lifted it up on the other side, out of his reach.

"Let us have a look at this chap," said the first, examining Vanslyperken, whose peaked nose and chin, small ferret eyes, and downcast look were certainly not in his favour; neither were his old and now tattered habiliments. Certainly no one would have taken Vanslyperken for a king's officer—unfortunately they took him for something else.

"Now tell me, fellow, what were you going to do with this?" inquired the man in a severe tone.

"I sha'n't tell you," replied Vanslyperken.

"Why that's the chap that I sees go in and out of the room where that old hell-fire witch lives, who curses all day long."

"I thought as much," observed the man, who still held up the cur's tail. "Now I appeal to you all, what can a fellow want with such as this—ay, my good people, and want it so much too, as to risk being torn to pieces for it—if he arn't inclined to evil practices?"

"That's sartain sure," replied another.

"A witch—a witch!" cried the whole crowd.

"Let's duck him—tie his thumbs—away with him—come along, my lads, away with him."

Although there were not, at the time we write about, regular witch-finders, as in the time of James I., still the feeling against witches, and the belief that they practised, still existed. They were no longer handed over to summary and capital punishment, but whenever suspected they were sure to meet with very rough treatment. Such was the fate of Mr Vanslyperken, who was now seized by the crowd, buffeted, and spit upon, and dragged to the parish pump, there being, fortunately for him, no horse-pond near. After having been well beaten, pelted with mud, his clothes torn off his back, his hat taken away and stamped upon, he was held under the pump and drenched for nearly half-an-hour, until he lay beneath the spout in a state of complete exhaustion. The crowd were then satisfied, and he was left to get away how he could, which he did, after a time, in a most deplorable plight, bare-headed, in his shirt and torn trousers. He contrived to walk as far as to the house where his mother resided, was admitted to her room, when he fell exhausted on the bed. The old woman was astonished; and having some gin in her cupboard, revived him by administering a small quantity, and, in the course of half-an-hour, Vanslyperken could tell his story; but all the consolation he received from the old beldame was, " Serve you right too, for being such an ass. I suppose you'll be bringing the stupid people about my ears soon—they've hooted me before now. Ah, well—I'll not be pumped upon for nothing—my knife is a sharp one."

Vanslyperken had clothes under his mother's charge, and he dressed himself in another suit, and then hastened away, much mortified and confounded with the latter events of the day. The result of his arrangements with his mother was, however, a balm to his wounded spirit, and he looked upon Smallbones as already dead. He hastened down into his cabin, as soon as he arrived on board, to ascertain the condition of Snarleyyow, whom he found as well as could be expected, and occasionally making unavailing attempts to lick the stump of his tail.

" My poor dog!" exclaimed Vanslyperken, " what have you suffered, and what have I suffered for you? Alas! if I am to suffer as I have to-day for only your tail, what shall I go through for your whole body?" And, as Vanslyperken recalled his misfortunes, so did his love increase for the animal who was the cause of them. Why so, we cannot tell, except that it has been so from the beginning, is so now, and always will be the case, for the best of all possible reasons—that it is *human nature.*

Chapter XXXIX

In which is recorded a most barbarous and bloody murder.

WE observed, in a previous chapter, that Mr Vanslyperken was observed by Moggy Salisbury to go into a jeweller's shop, and remain there some time, and that Moggy was very inquisitive to know what it was that could induce Mr Vanslyperken to go into so unusual a resort for him.

The next day she went into the shop upon a pretence of looking at some ear-rings, and attempted to enter into conversation with the jeweller; but the jeweller, not perhaps admiring Moggy's appearance, and not thinking her likely to be a customer, dismissed her with very short answers. Failing in her attempt, Moggy determined to wait till Nancy Corbett should come over, for she knew that Nancy could dress and assume the fine lady, and be more likely to succeed than herself. But although Moggy could not penetrate into the mystery, it is necessary the reader should be informed of the proceedings of Mr Vanslyperken.

When Ramsay had shown him how to open the government despatches, and had provided him with the false seals for the re-impressions, he forgot that he also was pointing out to Vanslyperken the means of also opening his own, and discovering his secrets, as well as those of government; but Vanslyperken, who hated Ramsay, on account of his behaviour towards him, and would with pleasure have seen the whole of his party, as well as himself, on the gibbet, thought that it might be just as well to have two strings to his bow; and he argued, that if he could open the letters of the conspirators, and obtain their secrets, they would prove valuable to him, and perhaps save his neck, if he were betrayed to the government. On his passage, therefore, to Amsterdam, he had carefully examined the seal of Ramsay, and also that on the letters forwarded to him; and, having made a drawing, and taken the impression in wax, as a further security, he had applied to the jeweller in question to get him seals cut out with these impressions, and of the exact form and size. The jeweller, who cared little what he did, provided that he was well paid, asked no questions, but a very high price, and Vanslyperken, knowing that they would be cheap to him at any price, closed with him on his own terms, provided that they were immediately forthcoming. In the week, according to the agreement, the seals were prepared. Mr Vanslyperken paid his money, and now was waiting for orders to sail.

The dog's stump was much better.

On the ninth day, a summons to the admiral's house was sent, and Vanslyperken was ordered to hold himself in readiness to sail the next morning at daylight. He immediately repaired to the Jew's, to give intimation, and from thence to his mother's to prepare her for the arrival of Smallbones that evening a little before dusk.

Vanslyperken had arranged that, as soon as the murder had been committed, he would go to the Jew's for letters, and then hasten on board, sailing the next morning at daylight; so that if there was any discovery, the whole onus might be on his mother, who, for all he cared, might be hung. It is a true saying, that a good mother makes a good son.

When Vanslyperken intimated to Smallbones that he was going on shore in the evening, and should take him with him, the lad did not forget the last walk that he had in company with his master, and, apprehensive that some mischief was intended, he said, "I hope it arn't for to fetch another walk in the country, sir?"

"No, no," replied Vanslyperken, "it's to take some biscuit up to a poor old woman close by. I don't want to be robbed, any more than you do, Smallbones."

But the very quick reply of his master only increased the apprehension of Smallbones, who left the cabin, and hastened to Corporal Van Spitter, to consult with him.

Corporal Van Spitter was of the same opinion as Smallbones, that mischief was intended him, and offered to provide him with a pistol; but Smallbones, who knew little about fire-arms, requested that he might have a bayonet instead, which he could use better. He was supplied with this, which he concealed within his shirt, and when ordered, he went into the boat with Vanslyperken. They landed, and it was dark before they arrived at the half-way houses. Vanslyperken ascended the stairs, and ordered Smallbones to follow him. As soon as they were in the room, Mr Vanslyperken said, "Here is the biscuit, good woman, and much good may it do you."

"It's very kind of you, sir, and many thanks. It's not often that people are charitable now-a-days, and this has been a hard winter for poor folk. Put the bag down there, my good little fellow," continued the old hypocrite, addressing Smallbones.

"And now, good woman, I shall leave my lad with you, till I come back. I have to call at a friend's, and I need not take him. Smallbones, stay here till I return; get the biscuit out of the bag, as we must take that on board again."

Smallbones had no objection to remain with a withered, palsied old woman. He could have no fear of her, and he really began to think that his master had been guilty of charity.

Mr Vanslyperken departed, leaving Smallbones in company with his mother.

"Come now, my lad, come to the chair, and sit down by the fire," for a fire had been lighted by the old woman expressly, "sit down, and I'll see if I can find you something in my cupboard; I have, I know, a drop of cordial left somewhere. Sit down, child; you have had the kindness to bring the bread up for me, and I am grateful."

The tones of the old beldame's voice were very different from those she usually indulged in; there was almost a sweetness about them, which proved what she might have effected at the period when she was fair and young. Smallbones felt not the least disquietude; he sat down in the chair by the fire, while the old woman looked in the cupboard behind him for the cordial, of which she poured him a good allowance in a tea-cup.

Smallbones sipped and sipped, he was not in a hurry to get rid of it, as it was good; the old woman went again to the cupboard, rattled the things about a little, and then, on a sudden, taking out a large hammer, as Smallbones unconsciously sipped, she raised it with both her hands, and down came the blow on his devoted head.

The poor lad dropped the cup, sprang up convulsively, staggered, and then fell. Once he rolled over, his leg quivered, and he then moved no more.

The beldame watched him with the hammer in her hand, ready to repeat the blow if necessary, indeed she would have repeated it had it not been that after he fell, in turning over, Smallbones' head had rolled under the low bedstead where she slept.

"My work is sure," muttered she, "and *all* the *gold* is *mine*."

Again she watched, but there was no motion—a stream of blood appeared from under the bed, and ran in a little rivulet towards the fire-place.

"I wish I could pull him out," said the old woman, lugging at the lad's legs; "another blow or two would make more sure." But the effort was above her strength, and she abandoned it. "It's no matter," muttered she; "he'll never tell tales again."

But there the old hag was mistaken; Smallbones had been stunned, but not killed; the blow of the hammer had fortunately started off, divided the flesh of the skull for three inches, with a gash which descended to his ear. At the very time that she uttered her last expressions, Smallbones was recovering his senses, but he was still confused, as if in a dream.

"Yes, yes," said the old woman, after some minutes' pause, "all the gold is mine."

The lad heard this sentence, and he now remembered where he was, and what had taken place. He was about to rise, when there was a knocking at the door, and he lay still. It was Vanslyperken. The door was opened by the old beldame.

"Is it done?" said he, in a loud whisper.

"Done!" cried the hag; "yes, and well done. Don't tell me of charmed life. My blows are sure—see there."

"Are you sure that he is dead?"

"Quite sure, child—and all the gold is mine."

Vanslyperken looked with horror at the stream of blood still flowing, and absorbed by the ashes in the grate.

"It was you did it, mother; recollect it was not I," cried he.

"I did it—and you paid for it—and all the gold is mine."

"But are you quite sure that he is dead?"

"Sure—yes, and in judgment now, if there is any."

Vanslyperken surveyed the body of Smallbones, who, although he had heard every word, lay without motion, for he knew his life depended on it. After a minute or two the lieutenant was satisfied.

"I must go on board now, mother; but what will you do with the body?"

"Leave that to me; who ever comes in here? Leave that to me, craven, and, as you say, go on board."

Vanslyperken opened the door, and went out of the room; the old hag made the door fast, and then sat down on the chair, which she replaced by the side of the fire, with her back to Smallbones.

The lad felt very faint from loss of blood, and was sick at the stomach, but his senses were in their full vigour. He now was assured that Vanslyperken was gone, and that he had only the old woman opposed to him. His courage was unsubdued, and he resolved to act in self-defence if required; and he softly drew the bayonet out of his breast, and then watched the murderous old hag, who was rocking herself in the chair.

"Yes, yes, the gold is mine," muttered she—"I've won it, and I'll count it. I won it dearly;—another murder—well, 'tis but one more. Let me see, what shall I do with the body? I must burn it, by bits and bits—and I'll count the gold—it's all mine, for he's dead."

Here the old woman turned round to look at the body, and her keen eyes immediately perceived that there was a slight change of position.

"Heh!" cried she, "not quite dead yet; we must have the hammer again," and she rose from her chair, and walked with an unsteady pace to pick up the hammer, which was at the other side of the fire-place. Smallbones, who felt that now was his time, immediately rose, but before he could recover his feet, she had turned round to him: with a sort of low yell, she darted at him with an agility not to be imagined in one of her years and decrepit appearance, and struck at him. Smallbones raised his left arm, and received the blow, and with his right plunged the bayonet deep into the wrinkled throat of the old woman. She grappled with him, and the struggle was dreadful; she caught his throat in one of her bony hands, and the nails pierced into it like the talons of a bird of prey—the fingers of the other she inserted into the jagged and gaping wound on his head, and forced the flesh still more asunder, exerting all her strength to force him on his back; but the bayonet was still in her throat, and with the point descending towards the body, and Smallbones forced and forced it down, till it was buried to the hilt. In a few seconds the old hag loosed her hold, quivered, and fell back dead; and the lad was so exhausted with the struggle, and his previous loss of blood, that he fell into a swoon at the side of the corpse.

When Smallbones recovered, the candle was flickering

in the socket. He rose up in a sitting posture, and tried to recollect all that had passed.

The alternating light of the candle flashed upon the body of the old woman, and he remembered all. After a few minutes he was able to rise, and he sat down upon the bed giddy and faint. It occurred to him that he would soon be in the dark, and he would require the light to follow up his intended movements, so he rose, and went to the cupboard to find one. He found a candle, and he also found the bottle of cordial, of which he drank all that was left, and felt himself revived, and capable of acting. Having put the other candle into the candlestick, he looked for water, washed himself, and bound up his head with his handkerchief. He then wiped up the blood from the floor, threw some sand over the part, and burnt the towel in the grate. His next task was one of more difficulty, to lift up the body of the old woman, put it into the bed, and cover it up with the clothes, previously drawing out the bayonet. No blood issued from the wound—the hemorrhage was all internal. He covered up the face, took the key of the door, and tried it in the lock, put the candle under the grate to burn out safely, took possession of the hammer; then having examined the door, he went out, locked it from the outside, slid the key in beneath the door, and hastened away as fast as he could. He was not met by anybody, and was soon safe in the street, with the bayonet, which he again concealed in his vest.

These precautions taken by Smallbones, proved that the lad had conduct as well as courage. He argued that it was not advisable that it should be known that this fatal affray had taken place between the old woman and himself. Satisfied with having preserved his life, he was unwilling to be embroiled in a case of murder, as he wished to prosecute his designs with his companions on board.

He knew that Vanslyperken was capable of swearing anything against him, and that his best safety lay in the affair not being found out, which it could not be until the cutter had sailed, and no one had seen him either enter or go out. There was another reason which induced Smallbones to act as he did—without appealing to the authorities—which was, that if he returned on board, it would create such a shock to Mr Vanslyperken, who had, as he supposed, seen him lying dead upon the floor. But there was one person to whom he determined to apply for advice before he decided how to proceed, and that was Moggy Salisbury, who had given her address to him when she had gone on board the *Yungfrau*. To her house he therefore repaired, and found her at home. It was then about nine o'clock in the evening.

Moggy was much surprised to see Smallbones enter in such a condition; but Smallbones' story was soon told, and Moggy sent for a surgeon, the services of whom the lad seriously required. While his wound was dressing, which was asserted by them to have been received in a fray, Moggy considered what would be the best method to proceed. The surgeon stated his intention of seeing Smallbones the next day, but he was requested to leave him sufficient dressing, as it was necessary that he should repair on board, as the vessel which he belonged to sailed on the following morning. The surgeon received his fee, recommended quiet and repose, and retired.

A consultation then took place. Smallbones expressed his determination to go on board; he did not fear Mr Vanslyperken, as the crew of the cutter would support him—and, moreover, it would frighten Mr Vanslyperken out of his wits. To this Moggy agreed, but she proposed that instead of making his appearance on the following morning, he should not appear to Mr Vanslyperken until the vessel was in the blue water; if possible, not till she was over on the other side. And Moggy determined to go on board, see the corporal, and make the arrangements with him and the crew, who were now unanimous, for the six marines were at the beck of the corporal, so that Mr Vanslyperken should be frightened out of his wits. Desiring Smallbones to lie down on her bed, and take the rest he so much needed, she put on her bonnet and cloak, and taking a boat, pulled gently alongside the cutter.

Vanslyperken had been on board for two hours, and was in his cabin; the lights, however, were still burning. The corporal was still up, anxiously waiting for the return of Smallbones, and he was very much alarmed when he heard Moggy come alongside. Moggy soon detailed to the corporal, Dick Short, and Coble, all that had taken place, and what it was proposed should be done. They assented willingly to the proposal, declaring that if Vanslyperken attempted to hurt the lad, they would rise, and throw Mr Vanslyperken overboard; and everything being arranged, Moggy was about to depart, when Vanslyperken, who was in a state of miserable anxiety and torture, and who had been drowning his conscience in scheedam, came on deck not a little the worse for what he had been imbibing.

"Who is that woman?" cried Vanslyperken.

"That woman is Moggy Salisbury," cried Moggy, walking up to Vanslyperken, while the corporal skulked forward without being detected.

"Have I not given positive orders that this woman does not come on board?" cried Vanslyperken, holding on by the skylight. "Who is that—Mr Short?"

"Yes," replied Short.

"Why did you allow her to come on board?"

"I came without leave," said Moggy. "I brought a message on board."

"A message! what message—to whom?"

"To you," replied Moggy.

"To me—from whom, you cockatrice?"

"I'll tell you," replied Moggy, walking close up to him; "from Lazarus the Jew. Will you hear it, or shall I leave it with Dick Short?"

"Silence—silence—not a word; come down into the cabin, good Moggy. Come down—I'll hear it then."

"With all my heart, Mr Vanslyperken, but none of your attacks on my vartue; recollect I am an honest woman."

"Don't be afraid, my good Moggy—I never hurt a child."

"I don't think you ever did," retorted Moggy, following Vanslyperken, who could hardly keep his feet.

"Well, there's Abacadabra there, anyhow," observed Coble to Short, as they went down.

"Why she turns him round her finger."

"Yes," quoth Short.

"I can't comprehend this not no how."

"No," quoth Short.

As soon as they were in the cabin, Moggy observed the bottle of scheedam on the table. "Come, Mr Vanslyperken, you'll treat me to-night, and drink my health again, won't you?"

"Yes, Moggy, yes—we're friends now, you know;" for Vanslyperken, like all others suffering under the stings of conscience, was glad to make friends with his bitterest enemy.

"Come, then, help me, Mr Vanslyperken, and then I'll give my message."

As soon as Moggy had taken her glass of scheedam, she began to think what she should say, for she had no message ready prepared; at last a thought struck her.

"I am desired to tell you, that when a passenger, or a person disguised as a sailor, either asks for a passage, or volunteers for the vessel, you are to take him on board immediately, even if you should know them in their disguise not to be what they pretend to be—do you understand?"

"Yes," replied Vanslyperken, who was quite muddled.

"Whether they apply from here, or from the other side of the channel, no consequence, you must take them—if not——"

"If not, what?" replied Vanslyperken.

"You'll swing, that's all, my buck. Good-night to you," replied Moggy, leaving the cabin.

"I'll swing," muttered Vanslyperken, rolling against

the bulkhead. "Well, if I do, others shall swing too. Who cares? damn the faggot!"

Here Mr Vanslyperken poured out another glass of scheedam, the contents of which overthrew the small remnant of his reasoning faculties. He then tumbled into his bed with his clothes on, saying, as he turned on his side, "Smallbones is dead and gone, at all events."

Moggy took leave of her friends on deck, and pushed on shore. She permitted Smallbones, whom she found fast asleep, to remain undisturbed until nearly three o'clock in the morning, during which time she watched by the bedside. She then roused him, and they sallied forth, took a boat, and dropped alongside of the cutter. Smallbones' hammock had been prepared for him by the corporal. He was put into it, and Moggy then left the vessel.

Mr Vanslyperken was in a state of torpor during this proceeding, and was, with great difficulty, awoke by the corporal, according to orders given, when it was daylight, and the cutter was to weigh anchor.

"Smallbones has not come off, sir, last night," reported the corporal.

"I suppose the scoundrel has deserted," replied Vanslyperken, "I fully expected that he would. However, he is no loss, for he was a useless, idle, lying rascal." And Mr Vanslyperken turned out; having all his clothes on, he had no occasion to dress. He went on deck, followed by the tail-less Snarleyyow, and in half an hour the cutter was standing out towards St Helen's.

Chapter XL

In which a most horrid spectre disturbs the equanimity of Mr Vanslyperken.

Two days was the cutter striving with light winds for the Texel, during which Mr Vanslyperken kept himself altogether in his cabin. He was occasionally haunted with the memory of the scene in his mother's room.—Smallbones dead, and the stream of blood running along the floor, and his mother's diabolical countenance, with the hammer raised in her palsied hands; but he had an instigator to his vengeance beside him, which appeared to relieve his mind whenever it was oppressed; it was the stump of Snarleyyow, and when he looked at that he no longer regretted, but congratulated himself on the deed being done. His time was fully occupied during the day, for with locked doors he was transcribing the letters sent to Ramsay, and confided to him.

He was not content with taking extracts, as he did of the government despatches for Ramsay; he copied every word, and he replaced the seals with great dexterity. At night his mind was troubled, and he dare not lie himself down to rest until he had fortified himself with several glasses of scheedam; even then his dreams frightened him; but he was to be more frightened yet.

Corporal Van Spitter came into the cabin on the third morning with a very anxious face.—"Mein Gott! Mynheer Vanslyperken, de whole crew be in de mutinys."

"Mutiny!" exclaimed Vanslyperken, "what's the matter?"

"They say, sir, dat dey see de ghost of Smallbones last night on de bowsprit, with one great cut on his head, and de blood all over de face."

"Saw what? who saw him?"

"Mein Gott, mynheer! it all true, I really think I see it myself at de taffrail, he sit there and have great wound from here down to," said the corporal, pointing to his own head, and describing the wound exactly. "The people say that he must have been murdered, and dey kick up de mutiny."

"I did not do it, corporal, at all events," replied Vanslyperken, pale and trembling.

"So Smallbones tell Dick Short, when he speak to him on bowsprit."

"Did it speak to Short?" inquired Vanslyperken, catching the corporal's arm.

"Yes, mynheer; Mynheer Short speak first, and den the ghost say dat you not do it, but dat you give gold to old woman to do it, and she knock him brain out vid de hammer."

To portray Vanslyperken's dismay at this intelligence would be impossible. He could not but be certain that there had been a supernatural communication. His knees knocked and trembled, and he turned sick and faint.

"O Lord, O Lord! corporal, I am a great sinner," cried he at last, quite unaware of what he was saying. "Some water, corporal." Corporal Van Spitter handed some water, and Vanslyperken waved his hand to be left alone; and Mr Vanslyperken attempted to pray, but it ended in blaspheming.

"It's a lie, all a lie," exclaimed he, at last, pouring out a tumbler of scheedam. "They have frightened the corporal. But—no—he must have seen him, or how could they know how he was murdered. He must have told them; and him I saw dead and stiff, with these own eyes. Well, I did not do the deed," continued Vanslyperken, attempting to palliate his crime to himself; but it would not do, and Mr Vanslyperken paced the little cabin racked by fear and guilt.

Remorse he felt none, for there was before his eyes the unhealed stump of Snarleyyow. In the evening Mr Vanslyperken went on deck; the weather was now very warm, for it was the beginning of July; and Mr Vanslyperken, followed by Snarleyyow, was in a deep reverie, and he turned and turned again.

The sun had set, and Mr Vanslyperken still continued his walk, but his steps were agitated and uneven, and his face was haggard. It was rather the rapid and angry pacing of a tiger in his den, who has just been captured, than that of a person in deep contemplation. Still Mr Vanslyperken continued to tread the deck, and it was quite light with a bright and pale moon.

The men were standing here and there about the forecastle and near the booms in silence and speaking in low whispers, and Vanslyperken's eye was often directed towards them, for he had not forgotten the report of the corporal, that they were in a state of mutiny.

Of a sudden, Mr Vanslyperken was roused by a loud cry from forward, and a rush of all the men aft. He thought that the crew had risen, and that they were about to seize him; but, on the contrary, they passed him and hastened to the taffrail with exclamations of horror.

"What! what is it?" exclaimed Vanslyperken, fully prepared for the reply by his own fears.

"O Lord! have mercy upon us," cried Bill Spurey.

"Good God, deliver us!" exclaimed another.

"Ah, Mein Gott!" screamed Jansen, rushing against Vanslyperken and knocking him down on the deck.

"Well, well, murder will out!—that's sartain," said Coble, who stood by Vanslyperken when he had recovered his legs.

"What, what!" exclaimed Vanslyperken, breathless.

"There, sir,—look there," said Coble, breathless, pointing to the figure of Smallbones, who now appeared from the shade in the broad moonshine.

His head was not bound up, and his face appeared pale and streaked with blood. He was in the same clothes in which he had gone on shore, and in his hand he held the hammer which had done the deed.

The figure slowly advanced to the quarter-deck, Vanslyperken attempted to retreat, but his legs failed him, he dropped down on his knees, uttered a loud yell of despair, and then threw himself flat on the deck face downwards.

Certainly, the pantomime was inimitably got up, but it had all been arranged by Moggy, the corporal, and the others. There was not one man of the crew who had not been sworn to secrecy, and whose life would not have been endangered if, by undeceiving Vanslyperken, they had been deprived of such just and legitimate revenges.

Smallbones disappeared as soon as Vanslyperken had fallen down.

He was allowed to remain there for some time to ascertain if he would say anything, but as he still continued silent, they raised him up and found that he was insensible. He was consequently taken down into the cabin and put into his bed.

The effect produced by this trial of Mr Vanslyperken's nerves, was most serious. Already too much heated with the use of ardent spirits, it brought on convulsions, in which he continued during the major part of the night. Towards the morning, he sank into a perturbed slumber.

It was not till eleven o'clock in the forenoon that he awoke and perceived his *faithful* corporal standing by the side of the bed.

"Have I not been ill, corporal?" said Mr Vanslyperken, whose memory was impaired for the time.

"Mein Gott! yes, mynheer."

"There was something happened, was not there?"

"Mein Gott! yes, mynheer."

"I've had a fit; have I not?"

"Mein Gott! yes, mynheer."

"My head swims now; what was it, corporal?"

"It was de ghost of de poy," replied the corporal.

"Yes, yes," replied Vanslyperken, falling back on his pillow.

It had been intended by the conspirators, that Smallbones should make his appearance in the cabin, as the bell struck one o'clock; but the effect had already been so serious that it was thought advisable to defer any further attempts. As for Smallbones being concealed in the vessel for any length of time there was no difficulty in that; for allowing that Vanslyperken should go forward on the lower deck of the vessel, which he never did, Smallbones had only to retreat into the eyes of her, and it was there so dark that he could not be seen. They therefore regulated their conduct much in the same way as the members of the inquisition used to do in former days; they allowed their patient to recover, that he might be subjected to more torture.

It was not until the fourth day, that the cutter arrived at the port of Amsterdam, and Mr Vanslyperken had kept his bed ever since he had been put into it; but this he could do no longer, he rose weak and emaciated, dressed himself, and went on shore with the despatches which he first delivered, and then bent his steps to the syndic's house, where he delivered his letters to Ramsay.

The arrival of the cutter had been duly notified to the widow Vandersloosh, before she had dropped her anchor, and in pursuance with her resolution she immediately despatched Babette to track Mr Vanslyperken, and watch his motions. Babette took care not to be seen by Mr Vanslyperken, but shrouding herself close in her cotton print cloak, she followed him to the Stadt House, and from the Stadt House to the mansion of Mynheer Van Krause, at a short distance from the gates of which she remained till he came out. Wishing to ascertain whether he went to any other place, she did not discover herself until she perceived that he was proceeding to the widow's—she then quickened her pace so as to come up with him.

"Oh! Mynheer Vanslyperken, is this you? I heard you had come in and so did my mistress, and she has been expecting you this last half-hour."

"I have made all the haste I can, Babette. But I was obliged to deliver my despatches first," replied Vanslyperken.

"But I thought you always took your despatches to the Stadt House?"

"Well, so I do, Babette; I have just come from thence."

This was enough for Babette, it proved that his visit to the syndic's was intended to be concealed; she was too prudent to let him know that she had traced him.

"Why, Mr Vanslyperken, you look very ill. What has been the matter with you? My mistress will be quite frightened."

"I have not been well, Babette," replied Vanslyperken.

"I really must run home as fast as I can. I will tell my mistress you have been unwell, for otherwise she will be in such a quandary;" and Babette hastened ahead of Mr Vanslyperken, who was in too weak a state to walk fast.

"The syndic's house—heh!"—said the widow, "Mynheer Van Krause. Why he is thorough king's man, by all report," continued she. "I don't understand it. But there is no trusting any man now-a-days.

"Babette, you must go there by-and-bye and see if you can find out whether that person he brought over, and he called a king's messenger, is living at the syndic's house. I think he must be, or why would Vanslyperken go there? and if he is, there's treason going on—that's all! and I'll find it out, or my name is not Vandersloosh."

Shortly after, Mr Vanslyperken arrived at the house and was received with the usual treacherous cordiality; but he had not remained more than an hour when Coble came to him (having been despatched by Short), to inform Mr Vanslyperken that a frigate was coming in with the royal standard at the main, indicating that King William was on board of her.

This intelligence obliged Mr Vanslyperken to hasten on board, as it was necessary to salute, and also to pay his respects on board of the frigate.

The frigate was within a mile when Mr Vanslyperken arrived on board of the cutter, and when the batteries saluted, the cutter did the same. Shortly afterwards the frigate dropped her anchor and returned the salute. Mr Vanslyperken, attired in his full uniform, ordered his boat to be manned and pulled on board.

On his arrival on the quarter-deck Vanslyperken was received by the captain of the frigate, and then presented to King William of Nassau, who was standing on the other side of the deck, attended by the Duke of Portland, Lord Albemarle, and several others of his courtiers, not all of them quite as faithful as the two whom we have named.

When Mr Vanslyperken was brought forward to the presence of his Majesty, he trembled almost as much as when he had beheld the supposed spirit of Smallbones, and well he might, for his conscience told him as he bowed his knee that he was a traitor. His agitation was, however, ascribed to his being daunted by the unusual presence of royalty. And Albemarle, as Vanslyperken retreated with a cold sweat on his forehead, observed to the king with a smile,

"That worthy lieutenant would show a little more courage, I doubt not, your Majesty, if he were in the presence of your enemies."

"It is to be hoped so," replied the king, with a smile. "I agree with you, Keppel."

But his Majesty and Lord Albemarle did not know Mr Vanslyperken, as the reader will acknowledge.

Chapter XLI

In which is shown how dangerous it is to tell a secret.

MR VANSLYPERKEN received orders to attend with his boat upon his Majesty's landing, which took place in about a quarter of an hour afterwards, amidst another war of cannon.

King William was received by the authorities at the landing-stairs, and from thence he stepped into the carriage, awaiting him, and drove off to his palace at the Hague; much to the relief of Mr Vanslyperken, who felt ill at ease in the presence of his sovereign. When his Majesty put his foot on shore, the foremost to receive him, in virtue of his office, was the syndic Mynheer Van Krause, who, in full costume of gown, chains, and periwig, bowed low, as his Majesty advanced, expecting as usual the gracious smile and friendly nod of his sovereign; but to his mortification, his reverence was returned with a grave, if not stern air, and the king passed him without further notice. All the courtiers also, who had been accustomed to salute, and to exchange a few words with him, to his astonishment turned their heads another way. At first, Mynheer Van Krause could hardly believe his senses, he who had always been so graciously received, who had been considered most truly as such a staunch supporter of his king, to be neglected, mortified in this way, and without cause. Instead of following his Majesty to his carriage, with the rest of the authorities, he stood still and transfixed, the carriage drove off, and the syndic hardly replying to some questions put to him, hurried back to his own house in a state of confusion and vexation almost indescribable. He hastened upstairs and entered the room of Ramsay, who was very busy with the despatches which he had received. "Well, Mynheer Van Krause, how is his Majesty looking," inquired Ramsay, who knew that the syndic had been down to receive him on his landing.

Mynheer Krause threw himself down in a chair, threw open his gown, and uttered a deep sigh.

"What is the matter, my dear sir, you appear ruffled," continued Ramsay, who from the extracts made by Vanslyperken from the despatches, was aware that suspicions had been lodged against his host.

"Such treatment—to one of his most devoted followers," exclaimed Krause, at last, who then entered into a detail of what had occurred.

"Such is the sweet aspect, the smile, we would aspire to of kings, Mynheer Krause."

"But there must be some occasion for all this," observed the syndic.

"No doubt of it," replied Ramsay—"some reason—but not a just one."

"That is certain," replied the syndic, "some one must have maligned me to his Majesty."

"It may be," replied Ramsay, "but there may be other

causes, kings are suspicious, and subjects may be too rich and too powerful. There are many paupers among the favourites of his Majesty, who would be very glad to see your property confiscated, and you cast into prison."

"But, my dear sir,—"

"You forget also, that the Jacobites are plotting, and have been plotting for years; that conspiracy is formed upon conspiracy, and that when so surrounded and opposed, kings will be suspicious."

"But his Majesty, King William,—"

"Firmly attached, and loyal as I am to my sovereign, Mynheer Krause, I do not think that King William is more to be relied upon than King James. Kings are but kings, they will repay the most important services by smiles, and the least doubtful act with the gibbet. I agree with you that some one must have maligned you, but allow me to make a remark that if once suspicion or dislike enters into a royal breast, there is no effacing it, a complete verdict of innocence will not do it; it is like the sapping of one of the dams of this country, Mynheer Krause, the admission of water is but small at first, but it increases and increases, till it ends in a general inundation."

"But I must demand an audience of his Majesty and explain."

"Explain—the very attempt will be considered as a proof of your guilt; no, no, as a sincere friend I should advise you to be quiet, and to take such steps as the case requires. That frown, that treatment of you in public, is sufficient to tell me that you must prepare for the event. Can you expect a king to publicly retract?"

"Retract! no—I do not require a public apology from my sovereign."

"But if having frowned upon you publicly, he again smiles upon you publicly, he does retract. He acknowledges that he was in error, and it becomes a public apology."

"God in heaven! then I am lost," replied the syndic,

throwing himself back in his chair. "Do you really think so, Mynheer Ramsay?"

"I do not say that you are lost. At present, you have only lost the favour of the king; but you can do without that, Mynheer Krause."

"Do without that—but you do not know that without that I am lost. Am I not Syndic of this town of Amsterdam, and can I expect to hold such an important situation if I am out of favour?"

"Very true, Mynheer Krause; but what can be done? you are assailed in the dark, you do not know the charges brought against you, and therefore cannot refute or parry with them."

"But what charges can they bring against me?"

"There can be but one charge against a person in your high situation, that of disaffection."

"Disaffection! I who am and have always been so devoted."

"The most disaffected generally appear the most devoted, Mynheer Krause, that will not help you."

"My God! then," exclaimed Krause, with animation, "what will, if loyalty is to be construed into a sign of disaffection?"

"Nothing," replied Ramsay, coolly. "Suspicion in the heart of a king is never to be effaced, and disaffection may soon be magnified into high treason."

"Bless me!" exclaimed Van Krause, crossing his hands on his heart in utter despair. "My dear Mynheer Ramsay, will you give me your opinion how I should act?"

"There is no saying how far you may be right in your conjectures, Mynheer Krause," replied Ramsay: "you may have been mistaken."

"No, no, he frowned—looked cross—I see his face now."

"Yes, but a little thing will sour the face of royalty, his corn may have pinched him, at the time he might have had a twinge in the bowels—his voyage may have affected him."

"He smiled upon others, upon my friend, Engelback, very graciously."

This was the very party who had prepared the charges against Krause—his own very particular friend.

"Did he?" replied Ramsay. "Then depend upon it, that's the very man who has belied you."

"What, Engelback? my particular friend?"

"Yes, I should imagine so. Tell me, Mynheer Krause, I trust you have never entrusted to him the important secrets which I have made you acquainted with, for if you have, your knowledge of them would be quite sufficient."

"My knowledge of them. I really cannot understand that. How can my knowledge of what is going on among the king's friends and councillors be a cause of suspicion?"

"Why, Mynheer Krause, because the king is surrounded by many who are retained from policy and fear of them. If these secrets are made known contrary to oath, is it not clear that the parties so revealing them must be no sincere friends of his Majesty's, and will it not be naturally concluded that those who have possession of them, are equally his open or secret enemies."

"But then, Mynheer Ramsay, by that rule you must be his Majesty's enemy."

"That does not follow, Mynheer Krause, I may obtain the secrets from those who are not so partial to his Majesty as they are to me, but that does not disprove my loyalty. To expose them would of course render me liable to suspicion—but I guard them carefully. I have not told a word to a soul, but to you, my dear Mynheer Krause, and I have felt assured that you were much too loyal to make known to anyone, what it was your duty to your king to keep secret; surely, Mynheer Krause, you have not trusted that man?"

"I may have given a hint or so—I'm afraid that I did; but he is my most particular friend."

"If that is the case," replied Ramsay, "I am not at all surprised at the king's frowning on you: Engelback having intelligence from you, supposed to be known only to the highest authorities, has thought it his duty to communicate it to government, and you are now suspected."

"God in heaven! I wish I never had your secrets, Mynheer Ramsay. It appears then that I have committed treason without knowing it."

"At all events, you have incurred suspicion. It is a pity that you mentioned what I confided to you, but what's done cannot be helped, you must now be active."

"What must I do, my dear friend?"

"Expect the worst and be prepared for it—you are wealthy, Mr Van Krause, and that will not be in your favour, it will only hasten the explosion, which sooner or later will take place. Remit as much of your money as you can to where it will be secure from the spoilers. Convert all that you can into gold, that you may take advantage of the first opportunity, if necessary, of flying from their vengeance. Do all this very quietly. Go on, as usual, as if nothing had occurred—talk with your friend Engelback—perform your duties as syndic. It may blow over, although I am afraid not. At all events you will have, in all probability, some warning, as they will displace you as syndic before they proceed further. I have only one thing to add. I am your guest, and depend upon it, shall share your fortune whatever it may be; if you are thrown into prison, I am certain to be sent there also. You may therefore command me as you please. I will not desert you, you may depend upon it."

"My dear young man, you are indeed a friend, and your advice is good. My poor Wilhelmina, what would become of her."

"Yes, indeed, used to luxury—her father in prison, perhaps his head at the gates—his whole property confiscated, and all because he had the earliest intelligence. Such is the reward of loyalty."

"Yes, indeed," repeated the syndic, "'put not your trust in princes,' says the psalmist. If such is to be the return for my loyalty—but there is no time to lose. I must send this post, to Hamburgh and Frankfort. Many thanks, my dear friend for your kind council, which I shall follow," so saying, Mynheer Krause went to his room, threw off his gown and chains in a passion, and hastened to his counting-house to write his important letters.

We may now take this opportunity of informing the reader of what had occurred in the house of the syndic. Ramsay had, as may be supposed, gained the affections of Wilhelmina; had told his love, and received her acknowledgment in return; he had also gained such a power over her, that she had agreed to conceal their attachment from her father; as Ramsay wished first, he asserted, to be possessed of a certain property which he daily expected would fall to him, and, until that, he did not think that he had any right to aspire to the hand of Wilhelmina.

That Ramsay was most seriously in love there was no doubt; he would have wedded Wilhelmina, even if she had not a sixpence; but at the same time, he was too well aware of the advantages of wealth not to fully appreciate it, and he felt the necessity and the justice to Wilhelmina, that she should not be deprived, by his means, of those luxuries to which she had been brought up. But here there was a difficulty, arising from his espousing the very opposite cause to that espoused by Mynheer Krause, for the difference of religion he very rightly considered as a mere trifle compared with the difference in political feelings. He had already weaned Wilhelmina from the political bias, imbibed from her father and his connections, without acquainting her with his belonging to the opposite party, for the present. It had been his intention as soon as his services were required elsewhere, to have demanded Wilhelmina's hand from her father, still leaving him in error as to his politics; and by taking her with him, after the marriage, to the court of St Germains, to have allowed Mynheer Krause to think what he pleased, but not to enter into any explanation; but, as Ramsay truly observed, Mynheer Krause had, by his not retaining the secrets confided to him, rendered himself suspected, and once suspected with King William, his disgrace, if not ruin, was sure to follow. This fact, so important to Ramsay's plans, had been communicated in the extracts made by Vanslyperken from the last despatches, and Ramsay had been calculating the consequences when Mynheer Krause returned discomfited from the presence of the king.

That Ramsay played a very diplomatic game in the conversation which we have repeated is true; but still it was the best game for Krause as well as for his own interests, as the events will show. We must, however, remind the reader that Ramsay had no idea whatever of the double treachery on the part of Vanslyperken, in copying all the letters sent by and to him, as well as extracting from the government despatches.

"My dearest Edward, what has detained you so long from me this morning," inquired Wilhelmina when he entered the music-room, about an hour after his conversation with the syndic.

Ramsay then entered into the detail of what had occurred, and wove in such remarks of his own as were calculated to disgust Wilhelmina with the conduct of King William, and to make her consider her father as an injured man. He informed her of the advice he had given him, and then pointed out to her the propriety of her enforcing his following it with all the arguments of persuasion in her power.

Wilhelmina's indignation was roused, and she did not fail, when speaking with her father, to rail in no measured tones against the king, and to press him to quit a country where he had been so ill-used. Mynheer Krause felt the same, his pride had been severely wounded; and it may be truly said, that one of the staunchest adherents of the Protestant king was lost by a combination of circumstances as peculiar as they were unexpected.

In the meantime, the corporal had gone on shore as usual and made the widow acquainted with the last attempt upon Smallbones, and the revenge of the ship's company. Babette had also done her part.

She had found out that Ramsay lived in the house of the syndic, and that he was the passenger brought over by Vanslyperken in the cutter.

The widow, who had now almost arranged her plans, received Vanslyperken more amicably than ever; anathematised the—supposed defunct Smallbones; shed tears over the stump of Snarleyyow, and asked Vanslyperken when he intended to give up the nasty cutter and live quietly on shore.

Chapter XLII

In which is shown the imprudence of sleeping in the open air, even in a summer's night.

THE *Yungfrau* was not permitted to remain more than two days at her anchorage. On the third morning Mr Vanslyperken's signal was made to prepare to weigh. He immediately answered it, and giving his orders to Short, hastened, as fast as he could, up to the syndic's house to inform Ramsay, stating, that he must immediately return on board again, and that the letters must be sent to him: Ramsay perceived the necessity of this, and consented. On his return to the boat, Mr Vanslyperken found that his signal to repair on board the frigate had been hoisted, and he hastened on board to put on his uniform and obey this order. He received his despatches from the captain of the frigate, with orders to proceed to sea immediately. Mr Vanslyperken, under the eye of his superior officer, could not dally or delay: he hove short, hoisted his mainsail, and fired a gun as a signal for sailing; anxiously looking out for Ramsay's boat with his letters, and afraid to go without them; but no boat made its appearance, and Mr Vanslyperken was forced to heave up his anchor. Still he did not like to make sail, and he remained a few minutes more, when he at last perceived a small boat coming off. At the same time he observed a boat coming from the frigate, and they arrived alongside the cutter about the same time, fortunately Ramsay's boat the first, and Mr Vanslyperken had time to carry the letters down below.

"The commandant wishes to know why you do not proceed to sea, sir, in obedience to your orders," said the officer.

"I only waited for that boat to come on board, sir," replied Vanslyperken to the lieutenant.

"And pray, sir, from whom does that boat come?" inquired the officer.

"From the syndic's, Mynheer Van Krause," replied Vanslyperken, not knowing what else to say, and thinking that the name of the syndic would be sufficient.

"And what did the boat bring off, to occasion the delay, sir?"

"A letter or two for England," replied Vanslyperken.

"Very well, sir, I wish you a good morning," said the lieutenant, who then went into his boat, and Vanslyperken made sail.

The delay of the cutter to receive the syndic's letters was fully reported the same evening to the commandant, who, knowing that the syndic was suspected, reported the same to the authorities, and this trifling circumstance only increased the suspicions against the unfortunate Mynheer Van Krause; but we must follow the cutter and those on board of her. Smallbones had remained concealed on board, his wounds had been nearly healed, and it was now again proposed that he should, as soon as they were out at sea, make his appearance to frighten Vanslyperken; and that, immediately they arrived at Portsmouth, he should go on shore and desert from the cutter, as Mr Vanslyperken would, of course, find out that his mother was killed, and the consequences to Smallbones must be dangerous, as he had no evidence, if Vanslyperken swore that he had murdered his mother; but this arrangement was overthrown by events which we shall now narrate. It was on the third morning after they sailed, that Vanslyperken walked the deck: there was no one but the man at the helm abaft. The weather was extremely sultry, for the cutter had run with a fair wind for the first eight-and-forty hours, and had then been becalmed for the last twenty-four, and had drifted to the back of the Isle of Wight, when she was not three leagues from St Helen's. The consequence was, that the ebb-tide had now drifted her down very nearly opposite to that part of the island where the cave was situated of which we have made mention. Vanslyperken heard the people talking below, and, as usual, anxious to overhear what was said, had stopped to listen. He heard the name of Smallbones repeated several times, but could not make out what was said.

Anxious to know, he went down the ladder, and, instead of going into his cabin, crept softly forward on the lower deck, when he overheard Coble, Short, and Spurey in consultation.

"We shall be in to-morrow," said Spurey, "if a breeze springs up, and then it will be too late: Smallbones must frighten him again to-night."

"Yes," replied Short.

"He shall go into his cabin at twelve o'clock, that will be the best way."

"But the corporal."

"Hush!—there is someone there," said Spurey, who, attracted by a slight noise made by Vanslyperken's boots, turned short round.

Vanslyperken retreated and gained the deck by the ladder; he had hardly been up when he observed a face at the hatchway, who was evidently looking to ascertain if he was on deck.

These few words overheard, satisfied Vanslyperken that Smallbones was alive and on board the cutter; and he perceived how he had been played with. His rage was excessive, but he did not know how to act. If Smallbones was alive, and that he appeared to be, he must have escaped from his mother, and, of course, the ship's company must know that his life had been attempted. That he did not care much about; he had not done the deed; but how the lad could have come on board! did he not see him lying dead? It was very strange, and the life of the boy must be charmed. At all events, it was a mystery which Mr Vanslyperken could not solve; at first, he thought that he would allow Smallbones to come into the cabin, and get a loaded pistol ready for him. The words, "But the corporal," which were cut short, proved to him that the corporal was no party to the affair; yet it was strange that the ship's company could have concealed the lad without the corporal's knowledge. Vanslyperken walked and walked, and thought and thought; at last he resolved to go down into his cabin, pretend to go to bed, lock his door, which was not his custom, and see if they would attempt to come in. He did so, the corporal was dismissed, and at twelve o'clock his door was tried and tried again; but being fast, the party retreated. Vanslyperken waited till two bells to ascertain if any more attempts would be made; but none were, so he rose from his bed, where he had thrown himself with his clothes on, and, opening the door softly, crept upon deck. The night was very warm, but there was a light and increasing breeze, and the cutter was standing in and close to the shore to make a long board upon next tack. Vanslyperken passed the man at the helm, and walked aft to the taffrail; he stood up on the choak to ascertain what way she was making through the water, and he was meditating upon the best method of proceeding. Had he known where Smallbones' hammock was hung, he would have gone down with the view of ascertaining the fact; but with a crew so evidently opposed to him, he could not see how even the ascertaining that Smallbones was on board, would be productive of any good consequences. The more Vanslyperken thought, the more he was puzzled. The fact is, that he was between the horns of a dilemma; but the devil, who always helps his favourites, came to the aid of Mr Vanslyperken. The small boat was, as usual, hoisted up astern, and Mr Vanslyperken's eyes were accidentally cast upon it. He perceived a black mass lying on the thwarts, and he examined it more closely: he heard snoring; it was one of the ship's company sleeping there against orders. He leant over the taffrail, and putting aside the great-coat which covered the party, he looked attentively on the face—there was no doubt it was Smallbones himself. From a knowledge of the premises, Vanslyperken knew at once that the lad was in his power.

The boat, after being hauled up with tackles, was hung by a single rope at each davit. It was very broad in proportion to its length, and was secured from motion by a single gripe, which confined it in its place, bowsing it close to the stern of the cutter, and preventing it from turning over bottom up, which, upon the least weight upon one gunnel or the other, would be inevitably the case. Smallbones was lying close to the gunnel next to the stern of the cutter. By letting go the gripe, therefore, the boat would immediately turn bottom up, and Smallbones would be dropped into the sea. Vanslyperken carefully examined the fastenings of the gripe, found that they were to be cast off by one movement, and that his success was certain; but still he was cautious. The man at the helm must hear the boat go over; he might hear Smallbones' cry for assistance. So Vanslyperken went forward to the man at the helm, and desired him to go down and to order Corporal Van Spitter to mix a glass of brandy-and-water, and send it up by him, and that he would steer the vessel till he came up again. The man went down to execute the order, and Vanslyperken steered the cutter for half a minute, during which he looked forward to ascertain if any one was moving. All was safe, the watch was all asleep forward, and Vanslyperken, leaving the cutter to steer itself, hastened aft, cast off the gripe, the boat, as he calculated, immediately turning over, and the sleeping Smallbones fell into the sea. Vanslyperken hastened back to the helm, and put the cutter's head right. He heard the cry of Smallbones, but it was not loud, for the cutter had already left him astern, and it was fainter and fainter, and at last it was heard no more, and not one of the watch had been disturbed.

"If ever you haunt me again," muttered Vanslyperken, "may I be hanged."

We particularly call the reader's attention to these words of Mr Vanslyperken.

The man returned with the brandy-and-water, with which Vanslyperken drank *bon voyage* to poor Smallbones. He then ordered the cutter to be put about, and as soon as she was round, he went down into his cabin and turned in with greater satisfaction than he had for a long time.

"We shall have got rid of him at last, my poor dog," said he, patting Snarleyyow's head. "Your enemy is gone for ever."

And Mr Vanslyperken slept soundly, because, although he had committed a murder, there was no chance of his being found out. We soon get accustomed to crime: before, he started at the idea of murder; now, all that he cared for was detection.

"Good-night to you, Mr Vanslyperken."

Chapter XLIII

In which Smallbones changes from a king's man into a smuggler, and also changes his sex.

IF we adhered to the usual plans of historical novel writers, we should, in this instance, leave Smallbones to what must appear to have been his inevitable fate, and then bring him on the stage again with a *coup de théâtre*, when least expected by the reader. But that is not our intention; we consider that the interest of this our narration of by-gone events is quite sufficient, without condescending to what is called claptrap; and there are so many people in our narrative continually labouring under deception of one kind or another, that we need not add to it by attempting to mystify our readers; who, on the contrary, we shall take with us familiarly by the hand, and, like a faithful historian, lead them through the events in the order in which they occurred, and point out to them how they all lead to one common end. With this intention in view, we shall now follow the fortunes of Smallbones, whom we left floundering in about seven fathoms water.

The weather was warm, even sultry, as we said before; but notwithstanding which, and notwithstanding he was a very tolerable swimmer, considering that he was so thin, Smallbones did not like it. To be awoke out of a profound sleep, and all of a sudden to find yourself floundering out of your depth about half a mile from the nearest land, is anything but agreeable; the transition is too rapid. Smallbones descended a few feet before he could divest himself of the folds of the Flustering coat which he had wrapped himself up in. It belonged to Coble, he had purchased it at a sale-shop on the Point for seventeen shillings and sixpence, and, moreover, it was as good as new. In consequence of this delay below water-mark, Smallbones had very little breath left in his body when he rose to the surface, and he could not inflate his lungs so as to call loud until the cutter had walked away from him at least one hundred yards, for she was slipping fast through the water, and another minute plainly proved to Smallbones that he was left to his own resources.

At first, the lad had imagined that it was an accident, and that the rope had given way with his weight; but when he found that no attention was paid to his cries, he then was convinced that it was the work of Mr Vanslyperken.

"By *gum*, he's a done for me at last. Well, I don't care, I can die but once, that's sartin sure; and he'll go to the devil, that's sartin sure."

And Smallbones, with this comfortable assurance, continued to strike out for the land, which, indeed, he had but little prospect of ever making.

"A shame for to come for to go to murder a poor lad three or four times over," sputtered Smallbones, after a time, feeling his strength fail him. He then turned on his back, to ease his arms.

"I can't do it no how, I sees that," said Smallbones, "so I may just as well go down like a dipsey lead."

But, as he muttered this, and was making up his mind to discontinue further exertions,—not a very easy thing to do, when you are about to go into another world, still floating on his back, with his eyes fixed on the starry heavens, thinking, as Smallbones afterwards narrated himself, that there wa'n't much to live for in this here world, and considering what there could be in that 'ere, his head struck against something hard. Smallbones immediately turned round in the water to see what it was, and found that it was one of the large corks which supported a heavy net laid out across the tide for the taking of shoal-fish. The cork was barely sufficient to support his weight, but it gave him a certain relief, and time to look about him, as the saying is. The lad ran under the net and cork with his hands until he arrived at the nearest shoal, for it was three or four hundred yards long. When he arrived there, he contrived to bring some of the corks together, until he had quite sufficient for his support, and then Smallbones voted himself pretty comfortable after all, for the water was very warm, and now quite smooth.

Smallbones, as the reader may have observed during the narration, was a lad of most indisputable courage and of good principles. Had it been his fortune to have been born among the higher classes, and to have had all the advantages of education, he might have turned out a hero; as it was, he did his duty well in that state of life to which he had been called, and as he said in his speech to the men on the forecastle, he feared God, honoured the king, and was the natural enemy to the devil.

The Chevalier Bayard was nothing more, only he had a wider field for his exertions and his talents; but the armed and accoutred Bayard did not show more courage and conduct when leading armies to victory, than did the unarmed Smallbones against Vanslyperken and his dog. We consider that *in his way*, Smallbones was quite as great a hero as the Chevalier, for no man can do more than his best · indeed, it is unreasonable to expect it.

While Smallbones hung on to the corks, he was calculating his chances of being saved.

"If so be as how they comes to take up the nets in the morning, why then I think I may hold on; but if so be they waits, why they'll then find me dead as a fish," said Smallbones, who seldom ventured above a monosyllable, and whose language if not considered as pure English, was certainly amazingly Saxon; and then Smallbones began to reflect, whether it was not necessary that he should forgive Mr Vanslyperken before he died, and his pros and cons ended with his thinking he could, for it was his duty; however he would not be in a hurry about it, he thought that was the last thing that he need do; but as for the dog, he wa'n't obliged to forgive him that was certain—as certain as that his tail was off; and Smallbones, up to his chin in the water, grinned so at the remembrance, that he took in more salt water than was pleasant.

He spit it out again, and then looked up to the stars, which were twinkling above him.

I wonder what o'clock it is, thought Smallbones, when he thought he heard a distant sound. Smallbones pricked up his ears and listened;—yes, it was in regular cadence, and became louder and louder. It was a boat pulling.

"Well, I am sure," thought Smallbones, "they'll think they have caught a queer fish anyhow:" and he waited very patiently for the fisherman to come up. At last he perceived the boat, which was very long and pulled many oars. "They be the smuglars," thought Smallbones.

"I wonder whether they'll pick up a poor lad? Boat ahoy!"

The boat continued to pass towards the coast, impelled at the speed of seven or eight miles an hour, and was now nearly abreast of Smallbones, and not fifty yards from him.

"I say, boat ahoy!" screamed Smallbones, to the extent of his voice.

He was heard this time, and there was a pause in the pulling, the boat still driving through the water with the impulse which had been given her, as if she required no propelling power.

"I say you arn't a going for to come for to leave a poor lad here to be drowned, are you?"

"That's Smallbones, I'll swear," cried Jemmy Ducks, who was steering the boat, and who immediately shifted the helm.

But Sir Robert Barclay paused; there was too much at stake to run any risk, even to save the life of a fellow-creature.

"You takes time for to think on it anyhow," cried Smallbones—"you are going for to leave a fellow-christian stuck like a herring in a fishing net, are you? you would not like it yourself, anyhow."

"It is Smallbones, sir," repeated Jemmy Ducks, "and I'll vouch for him as a lad that's good and true."

Sir Barclay no longer hesitated: "Give way, my lads, and pick him up."

In a few minutes, Smallbones was hauled in over the gunnel, and was seated on the stern-sheets opposite to Sir Robert.

"It's a great deal colder out of the water than in, that's sartain," observed Smallbones, shivering.

"Give way, my lads, we've no time to stay," cried Sir Robert.

"Take this, Smallbones," said Jemmy.

"Why, so it is, Jemmy Ducks!" replied Smallbones, with astonishment—"why, how did you come here?"

"Sarcumstances," replied Jemmy; "how did you come there?"

"Sarcumstances too, Jemmy," replied Smallbones.

"Keep silence," said Sir Robert, and nothing more was said until the lugger dashed into the cave.

The cargo was landed, and Smallbones who was very cold was not sorry to assist. He carried up his load with the rest, and as usual the women came halfway down to receive it.

"Why, who have we here?" said one of the women to whom Smallbones was delivering his load, "why, it's Smallbones."

"Yes," replied Smallbones, it is me; "but how came you here, Nancy?"

"That's tellings, but how came you, my lad?" replied Nancy.

"I came by water anyhow."

"Well, you are one of us now, you know there's no going back."

"I'm sure I don't want to go back, Nancy; but what is to be done? nothing unchristianlike I hope."

"We're all good Christians here, Smallbones; we don't bow down to idols and pay duty to them as other people do."

"Do you fear God, and honour the king?"

"We do; the first as much as the other people, and as for the king, we love him and serve him faithfully."

"Well, then I suppose that's all right," replied Smallbones; "but where do you live?"

"Come with me, take your load up, and I will show you, for the sooner you are there the better; the boat will be off again in half-an-hour, if I mistake not."

"Off, where?"

"To France, with a message to the king."

"Why, the king's in Holland! we left him there when we sailed."

"Pooh! nonsense! come along."

When Sir Robert arrived at the cave, he found an old friend anxiously awaiting his arrival; it was Graham, who had been despatched by the Jacobites to the court of St Germains, with intelligence of great importance, which was the death of the young Duke of Gloucester, the only surviving son of King William. He had, it was said, died of a malignant fever; but if the reader will call to mind the address of one of the Jesuits on the meeting at Cherbourg, he may have some surmises as to the cause of the duke's decease. As this event rendered the succession uncertain, the hopes of the Jacobites were raised to the highest pitch: the more so as the country was in a state of anxiety and confusion, and King William was absent at the Hague. Graham had, therefore, been despatched to the exiled James, with the propositions from his friends in England, and to press the necessity of an invasion of the country. As Nancy had supposed, Sir Robert decided upon immediately crossing over to Cherbourg, the crew were allowed a short time to repose and refresh themselves, and once more returned to their laborious employment; Jemmy Ducks satisfied Sir Robert that Smallbones might be trusted and be useful, and Nancy corroborated his assertions. He was, therefore, allowed to remain in the cave with the women, and Sir Robert and his crew, long before Smallbones' garments were dry, were again crossing the English Channel.

Now, it must be observed, that Smallbones was never well off for clothes, and, on this occasion, when he fell overboard, he had nothing on but an old pair of thin linen trousers and a shirt which, from dint of long washing, from check had turned to a light cerulean blue: what with his struggles at the net and the force used to pull him into the boat, the shirt had more than one-half disappeared—that is to say, one sleeve and the back were wholly gone, and the other sleeve was well prepared to follow its fellow, on the first capful of wind. His trousers also were in almost as bad a state. In hauling him in, when his head was over the gunnel, one of the men had seized him by the seat of his trousers to lift him into the boat, and the consequence was, that the seat of his trousers having been too long set upon, was also left in his muscular gripe. All these items put together, the reader may infer, that, although Smallbones might appear merely ragged in front, that in his rear he could not be considered as decent, especially as he was the only one of the masculine sex among a body of females. No notice was taken of this by others, nor did Smallbones observe it himself, during the confusion and bustle previous to the departure of the smugglers; but now they were gone, Smallbones perceived his deficiencies, and was very much at a loss what to do, as he was aware that daylight would discover them to others as well as to himself: so he fixed his back up against one of the rocks, and remained idle while the women were busily employed storing away the cargo in the various compartments of the cave.

Nancy, who had not forgotten that he was with them, came up to him.

"Why do you stay there, Smallbones? you must be hungry and cold, come in with me, and I will find you something to eat."

"I can't, Mistress Nancy, I want your advice first. Has any of the men left any of their duds in this here cavern?"

"Duds, men! No, they keep them all on the other side. We have nothing but petticoats here and shimmeys."

"Then what must I do?" exclaimed Smallbones.

"Oh, I see, your shirt is torn off your back. Well, never mind, I'll lend you a shimmey."

"Yes, Mistress Nancy, but it be more worse than that, I an't got no behind to my trousers, they pulled it out when they pulled me into the boat. I sticks to this here rock for decency's sake. What must I do?"

Nancy burst into a laugh. "Do, why if you can't have men's clothes, you must put on the women's, and then you'll be in the regular uniform of the cave."

"I do suppose that I must, but I can't say that I like the idea much, anyhow," replied Smallbones.

"Why, you don't mean to stick to that rock like a

limpit all your life, do you? there's plenty of work for you."

"If so be, I must, I must," replied Smallbones.

"You can't appear before Mistress Alice in that state," replied Nancy. "She's a lady bred and born, and very particular too, and then there's Miss Lilly, you will turn her as red as a rose, if she sees you."

"Well then, I suppose I must, Mistress Nancy, for I shall catch my death of cold here, I'm all wet and shivery, from being so long in the water, and my back against the rock, feels just as ice."

"No wonder, I'll run and fetch you something," replied Nancy, who was delighted at the idea of dressing up Smallbones as a woman.

Nancy soon returned with a chemise, a short flannel petticoat, and a shawl, which she gave to Smallbones, desiring him to take off his wet clothes, and substitute them. She would return to him as soon as he had put them on, and see that they were put tidy and right.

Smallbones retired behind one of the rocks, and soon shifted his clothes, he put everything on the hind part before, and Nancy had to alter them when she came. She adjusted the shawl, and then led him into the cave where he found Mistress Alice, and some of the women who were not busy with the cargo.

"Here's the poor lad who was thrown overboard, madam," said Nancy, retaining her gravity. "All his clothes were torn off his back, and I have been obliged to give him these to put on."

Lady Barclay could hardly repress a smile. Smallbones' appearance was that of a tall gaunt creature, pale enough, and smooth enough to be a woman certainly, but cutting a most ridiculous figure. His long thin arms were bare, his neck was like a crane's, and the petticoats were so short as to reach almost above his knees. Shoes and stockings he had none. His long hair was platted and matted with the salt water, and one side of his head was shaved, and exhibited a monstrous half-healed scar.

Lady Barclay asked him a few questions, and then desired Nancy to give him some refreshment, and find him something to lie down upon in the division of the cave which was used as a kitchen.

But we must now leave Smallbones to entertain the inhabitants of the cave with the history of his adventures, which he did at intervals, during his stay there. He retained his women's clothes, for Nancy would not let him wear any other, and was a source of great amusement not only to the smugglers' wives, but also to little Lilly, who would listen to his conversation and remarks which were almost as naive and unsophisticated as her own.

Chapter XLIV

In which Mr Vanslyperken meets with a double defeat.

It was late in the evening of the day after Smallbones had been so satisfactorily disposed of that the cutter arrived at Portsmouth; but from daylight until the time that the cutter anchored, there was no small confusion and bustle on board of the *Yungfrau*. When Vanslyperken's cabin door was found to be locked, it was determined that Smallbones should not appear as a supernatural visitant that night, but wait till the one following; consequently the parties retired to bed, and Smallbones, who found the heat between decks very oppressive, had crept up the ladder and taken a berth in the small boat that he might sleep cool and comfortable, intending to be down below again long before Mr Vanslyperken was up; but, as the reader knows, Mr Vanslyperken was up before him, and the consequence was that Smallbones went down into the sea instead of the lower deck as he had intended.

The next morning it was soon ascertained that Smallbones was not to be found, and the ship's company were in a state of dismay. The boat, as soon as Smallbones had been turned out, had resumed her upright position, and one of the men when busy washing the decks, had made fast the gripe again, which he supposed had been cast off by accident when the ropes had been coiled up for washing, Smallbones not being at that time missed. When, therefore, the decks had been searched everywhere and the lad was discovered not to be in the ship, the suspicion was very great. No one had seen him go aft to sleep in the boat. The man who was at the wheel stated that Mr Vanslyperken had sent him down for a glass of grog, and had taken the helm for the time; but this proved nothing. His disappearance was a mystery not to be unravelled. An appeal to Mr Vanslyperken was, of course, impossible, for he did not know that the lad was on board. The whole day was spent in surmises and suppositions; but things all ended in the simple fact, that somehow or another Smallbones had fallen overboard, and there was an end of the poor fellow.

So soon as the cutter was at anchor, Mr Vanslyperken hastened to perform his official duties, and anxious to learn how Smallbones had contrived to escape the clutches of his mother, bent his steps towards the half-way houses. He arrived at the door of his mother's room, and knocked as usual, but there was no reply. It was now the latter end of July, and although it was past seven o'clock it was full daylight. Vanslyperken knocked again and again. His mother must be out, he thought; and if so, she always took the key with her. He had nothing to do but to wait for her return. The passage and staircase was dark, but there was a broad light in the room from the casement, and this light streamed from under the door of the room. A shade crossing the light attracted Vanslyperken's attention, and to while away the tediousness of waiting he was curious to see what it was; he knelt down, looked under the door, and perceived the key which Smallbones had placed there; he inserted his finger and drew it forth, imagining that his mother had slid it beneath till her return.

He fitted it to the lock and opened the door, when his olfactory nerves were offended with a dreadful stench, which surprised him the more as the casement was open. Vanslyperken surveyed the room, he perceived that the blood had been washed from the floor and sand strewed over it. Had he not known that Smallbones had been on board of the cutter the day before, he would have thought that it had been the smell of the dead body not yet removed. This thought crossing his imagination, immediately made the truth flash upon him, and, as if instinctively, he went up to the bed and pulled down the clothes, when he recoiled back with horror at uncovering the face of his mother, now of a livid blue and in the last stage of putrefaction.

Overcome with the horrid sight, and the dreadful stench which accompanied it, he reeled to the casement and gasped for breath. A sickness came over him, and for some time he was incapable of acting and barely capable of reflection.

"She is gone then," thought he at last, and he shuddered when he asked himself *where*. "She must have fallen by the hands of the lad," continued he, and immediately the whole that had happened appeared to be revealed to him. "Yes, yes, he has recovered from the blow—killed her and locked the door—all is clear now, but I have revenged her death."

Vanslyperken, who had now recovered himself, went softly to the door, took out the key and locked himself in. He had been debating in his mind whether he should call in the neighbours; but, on reflection, as no one had seen him enter, he determined that he would not. He would take his gold and leave the door locked and the key under it, as he found it before her death was discovered: it would be supposed that she died a natural death, for the state of the body would render it impossible to prove the contrary. But there was one act necessary to be performed at which Vanslyperken's heart recoiled. The key of the oak chest was about his mother's person and he must obtain it, he must search for it in corruption and death, amongst creeping worms and noisome stench. It was half an hour before he could make up his mind to the task! but what will avarice not accomplish!

He covered up the face, and with a trembling hand turned over the bedclothes. But we must not disgust our readers, it will suffice to say, that the key was obtained, and the chest opened.

Vanslyperken found all his own gold, and much more than he had ever expected belonging to his mother. There were other articles belonging to him, but he thought it prudent not to touch them. He loaded himself with the treasure, and when he felt that it was all secure, for he was obliged to divide it in different parcels and stow it in various manners about his person, he re-locked the chest, placed the key in the cupboard, and quitting the room made fast the door, and like a dutiful son, left the remains of his mother to be inhumed at the expense of the parish.

As he left the house without being observed, and gained the town of Portsmouth, never was Mr Vanslyperken's body so heavily loaded, or his heart lighter. He had got rid of Smallbones and of his mother, both in a way perfectly satisfactory to himself.

He had recovered his own gold, and had also been enriched beyond his hopes by his mother's savings. He felt not the weight which he carried about his person, he wished it had been heavier. All he felt was, very anxious to be on board and have his property secured. His boat waited for him, and one of the men informed him his presence was required at the admiral's immediately; but Mr Vanslyperken first went on board, and having safely locked up all his treasures, then complied with the admiral's wishes. They were to sail immediately, for the intelligence of the Duke of Gloucester's death had just arrived with the despatches, announcing the same to be taken to King William, who was still at the Hague. Vanslyperken sent the boat on board with orders to Short, to heave short and loose sails, and then hastened up to the house of Lazarus, the Jew, aware that the cutter would, in all probability, be despatched immediately to the Hague. The Jew had the letters for Ramsay all prepared. Vanslyperken once more touched his liberal fee, and, in an hour, he was again under way for the Texel.

During the passage, which was very quick, Mr Vanslyperken amused himself as usual, in copying the letters to Ramsay, which contained the most important intelligence of the projects of the Jacobites, and, from the various communications between Ramsay and the conspirators, Vanslyperken had also been made acquainted with the circumstance hitherto unknown to him, of the existence of the caves above the cove, where he had been taken to by the informer, as mentioned in the early part of this work, and also of the names of the parties who visited it.

Of this intelligence Vanslyperken determined to avail himself by-and-bye. It was evident that there were only women in the cave, and Mr Vanslyperken counted his gold, patted the head of Snarleyyow, and indulged in anticipations of further wealth, and the hand of the widow Vandersloosh.

All dreams! Mr Vanslyperken.

The cutter arrived, and he landed with his despatches for the government; and his letters to Ramsay being all delivered, Vanslyperken hastened to the widow's, who, as usual, received him, all smiles. He now confided to her the death of his mother, and astonished her by representing the amount of his wealth, which he had the precaution to state, that the major part of it was left him by his mother.

"Where have you put it all, Mr Vanslyperken?" inquired the widow. And Vanslyperken replied that he had come to ask her advice on the subject, as it was at present all on board of the cutter. The widow, who was not indifferent to money, was more gracious than ever. She had a scheme in her head of persuading him to leave the money under her charge; but Vanslyperken was anxious to go on board again, for he discovered that the key was not in his pocket, and he was fearful that he might have left it on the cabin table; so he quitted rather abruptly, and the widow had not time to bring the battery to bear. As soon as Mr Vanslyperken arrived on board, Corporal Van Spitter, without asking leave, for he felt it was not necessary, went on shore, and was soon in the arms of his enamoured widow Vandersloosh. In the meantime, Mr Vanslyperken discovered the key in the pocket of the waistcoat he had thrown off, and having locked his door, he again opened his drawer, and delighted himself for an hour or two in re-arranging his treasure; after which, feeling himself in want of occupation, it occurred to him, that he might as well dedicate a little more time to the widow, so he manned his boat and went on shore again.

It is all very well to have a morning and afternoon lover if ladies are so inclined, just as they have a morning and afternoon dress, but they should be worn separately. Now, as it never entered the head of Mr Vanslyperken that the corporal was playing him false, so did it never enter the idea of the widow, that Mr Vanslyperken would make his appearance in the evening, and leave the cutter and Snarleyyow, without the corporal being on board to watch over them.

But Mr Vanslyperken did leave the cutter and Snarleyyow, did come on shore, did walk to the widow's house, and did most unexpectedly enter it, and what was the consequence?—that he was not perceived when he entered it, and the door of the parlour as well as the front door being open to admit the air, for the widow and the corporal found that making love in the dog days was rather warm work for people of their calibre—to his mortification and rage the lieutenant beheld the corporal seated in his berth, on the little fubsy sofa, with one arm round the widow's waist, his other hand joined in hers, and, *proh pudor!*

sucking at her dewy lips like some huge carp under the water-lilies on a midsummer's afternoon.

Mr Vanslyperken was transfixed—the parties were too busy with their amorous interchange to perceive his presence; at last the corporal thought that his lips required moistening with a little of the beer of the widow's own brewing, for the honey of her lips had rather glued them together—he turned towards the table to take up his tumbler, and he beheld Mr Vanslyperken.

The corporal, for a moment, was equally transfixed, but on these occasions people act mechanically because they don't know what to do. The corporal had been well drilled, he rose from the sofa, held himself perfectly upright, and raised the back of his right hand to his forehead, there he stood like a statue saluting at the presence of his superior officer.

The widow had also perceived the presence of Vanslyperken almost as soon as the corporal, but a woman's wits are more at their command on these occasions than a man's. She felt that all concealment was now useless, and she prepared for action. At the same time, although ready to discharge a volley of abuse upon Vanslyperken, she paused, to ascertain how she should proceed. Assuming an indifferent air, she said—" Well, Mr Vanslyperken?"

"Well!" exclaimed Vanslyperken, but he could not speak for passion.

"Eaves-dropping, as usual, Mr Vanslyperken?"

"May the roof of this house drop on you, you infernal——."

"No indelicate language, if you please, sir," interrupted the widow, "I won't put up with it in my house, I can tell you—ho, ho, Mr Vanslyperken," continued the widow, working herself into a rage, "that won't do here, Mr Vanslyperken."

"Why, you audacious—you double-faced——"

"Double-faced!—it's a pity you wer'n't double-faced, as you call it, with that snivelling nose and crooked chin of yours. Double-faced, heh!—oh! oh! Mr Vanslyperken—we shall see—wait a little—we shall see who's double-faced. Yes, yes, Mr Vanslyperken—that for you, Mr Vanslyperken—I can hang you when I please, Mr Vanslyperken. Corporal, how many guineas did you see counted out to him at the house opposite?"

During all this the corporal remained fixed and immovable with his hand up to the salute; but on being questioned by his mistress, he replied, remaining in the same respectful attitude.

"Fifty golden guineas, Mistress Vandersloosh."

"A lie! an infamous lie!" cried Vanslyperken, drawing his sword. "Traitor, that you are," continued he to the corporal, "take your reward." This was a very critical moment. The corporal did not attempt the defensive, but remained in the same attitude, and Vanslyperken's rage at the falsehood of the widow, and the discovery of his treason was so great, that he had lost all command of himself. Had not a third party come in just as Vanslyperken drew his sword, it might have gone hard with the corporal; but fortunately Babette came in from the yard, and perceiving the sword fly out of the scabbard, she put her hand behind the door, and snatched two long-handled brooms, one of which she put into the hands of her mistress, and retained the other herself.

"Take your reward!" cried Vanslyperken, running furiously to cut down the corporal. But his career was stopped by the two brooms, one of which took him in the face, and the other in the chest. The widow and Babette now ranged side by side, holding their brooms as soldiers do their arms in charge of bayonets.

How did the corporal act? He retained his former respectful position, leaving the defensive or offensive in the hands of the widow and Babette.

This check on the part of Vanslyperken only added to his rage. Again he flew with his sword at the corporal, and again he was met with the besoms in his face. He caught one with his hand, and he was knocked back with the other. He attempted to cut them in two with his sword, but in vain.

"Out of my house, you villain!—you traitor—out of my house," cried the widow, pushing at him with such force as to drive him against the wall, and pinning him there while Babette charged him in his face which was now streaming with blood. The attack was now followed up with such vigour, that Vanslyperken was first obliged to retreat to the door, then out of the door into the street, followed into the street he took to his heels, and the widow and Babette returned victorious into the parlour to the corporal. Mr Vanslyperken could not accuse him of want of respect to his superior officer; he had saluted him on entering, and he was still saluting him when he made his exit.

The widow threw herself on the sofa—Corporal Van Spitter then took his seat beside her. The widow overcome by her rage and exertion, burst into tears and sobbed in his arms.

The corporal poured out a glass of beer, and persuaded her to drink it.

"I'll have him hanged to-morrow, at all events. I'll go to the Hague myself," cried the widow. "Yes, yes, Mr Vanslyperken, we shall see who will gain the day," continued the widow, sobbing.

"You can prove it, corporal?"

"Mein Gott, yes," replied the corporal.

"As soon as he's hung, corporal, we'll marry."

"Mein Gott, yes."

"Traitorous villain!—sell his king and his country for gold!"

"Mein Gott, yes."

"You're sure it was fifty guineas, corporal?"

"Mein Gott, yes."

"Ah, well, Mr Vanslyperken, we shall see," said the widow, drying her eyes. "Yes, yes, Mr Vanslyperken, you shall be hanged, and your cur with you, or my name's not Vandersloosh."

"Mein Gott, yes," replied the corporal.

Chapter XLV

In which Mr Vanslyperken proves his loyalty and his fidelity to King William.

MR VANSLYPERKEN hastened from his inglorious conflict, maddened with rage and disappointment. He returned on board, went down into his cabin, and threw himself on his bed. His hopes and calculations had been so brilliant—rid of his enemy Smallbones—with gold in possession, and more in prospect, to be so cruelly deceived by the widow —the cockatrice! Then by one to whom he fully confided, and who knew too many of his secrets already—Corporal Van Spitter—he too!—and to dare to aspire to the widow —it was madness—and then their knowledge of his treason —the corporal having witnessed his receiving the gold— with such bitter enemies what could he expect but a halter —he felt it even now round his neck, and Vanslyperken groaned in the bitterness of his spirit.

In the meantime, there was a consultation between the widow and the corporal as to the best method of proceeding That the corporal could expect nothing but the most determined hostility from Vanslyperken was certain; but for this the corporal cared little, as he had all the crew of the cutter on his side, and he was in his own person too high in rank to be at the mercy of Vanslyperken.

After many pros and cons, and at least a dozen bottles of beer—for the excitement on the part of the corporal, and the exertion of the widow, had made them both dry— it was resolved that the Frau Vandersloosh should demand an audience at the Hague the next morning, and should communicate the treasonable practices of Mr Vanslyperken, calling upon the corporal as a witness to the receipt of the money from the Jesuit.

"Mein Gott! exclaimed the corporal, striking his bull forehead as if a new thought had required being forced out, " but they will ask me how I came there myself, and what shall I say?"

"Say that the Jesuit father had sent for you to try and seduce you to do his treason, but that you would not consent."

" Mein Gott, yes—that will do."

The corporal then returned on board, but did not think it worth while to report himself to Mr Vanslyperken.

Mr Vanslyperken had also been thinking over the matter, and in what way he should be able to escape from the toils prepared for him. That the widow would immediately inform the authorities he was convinced. How was he to get out of his scrape?

Upon mature reflection, he decided that it was to be done. He had copies of all Ramsay's letters, and those addressed to Ramsay, and the last delivered were very important. Now, his best plan would be to set off for the Hague early the next morning—demand an interview with one of the ministers, or even his Majesty himself—state that he had been offered money from the Jacobite party to carry their letters, and that, with a view to serve his Majesty by finding out their secrets, he had consented to do it, and had taken the money to satisfy them that he was sincere. That he had opened the letters and copied them, and that now as the contents were important, he had thought it right to make them immediately known to the government, and at the same time to bring the money received for the service, to be placed at his Majesty's disposal.

" Whether she is before or after me," thought Vanslyperken, "it will then be little matter, all I shall have to fear will be from Ramsay and his party, but the government will be bound to protect me."

There certainly was much wisdom in this plan of Vanslyperken, it was the only one which could have been attended with success, or with any chance of it.

Mr Vanslyperken was up at daylight, and dressed in his best uniform; he put in his pocket all the copies of the Jacobite correspondence, and went on shore—hired a calash, for he did not know how to ride, and set off for the Hague, where he arrived about ten o'clock. He sent up his name, and requested an audience with the Duke of Portland, as an officer commanding one of his Majesty's vessels: he was immediately admitted.

"What is your pleasure, Mr Vanslyperken?" said the duke, who was standing at the table, in company with Lord Albemarle.

Vanslyperken was a little confused—he muttered, and stammered about anxiety, and loyalty, and fidelity, and excess of zeal, &c.—

No wonder he stammered, for he was talking of what he knew nothing about—but these two noblemen recollecting his confusion when presented to his sovereign on board of the frigate, made allowances.

"I have at last," cried Vanslyperken, with more confidence, "been able to discover the plots of the Jacobites, your grace."

"Indeed! Mr Vanslyperken," replied the duke, smiling incredulously, "and pray what may they be? you must be as expeditious as possible, for his Majesty is waiting for us."

"These letters will take some time to read," replied Vanslyperken; "but their contents are most important."

"Indeed, letters—how have you possession of their letters?"

"It will be rather a long story, sir—my lord! I mean," replied Vanslyperken; "but they will amply repay an hour of your time, if you can spare it."

At this moment, the door opened and his Majesty entered the room. At the sight of the king, Vanslyperken's confidence was again taking French leave.

"My lords, I am waiting for you," said the king, with a little asperity of manner.

"May it please your Majesty, here is Lieutenant Vanslyperken, commanding one of your Majesty's vessels, who states that he has important intelligence, and that he has possession of Jacobite papers."

"Indeed!" replied King William, who was always alive to Jacobite plotting, from which he had already run so much risk.

"What is it, Mr Vanslyperken? speak boldly what you have to communicate."

"Your Majesty, I beg your gracious pardon, but here are copies of the correspondence carried on by the traitors in England and this country. If your Majesty will deign to have it read, you will then perceive how important it is—after your Majesty has read it, I will have the honour to explain to you by what means it came into my possession."

King William was a man of business, and Vanslyperken had done wisely in making this proposal. His Majesty at once sat down, with the Duke of Portland on the one side and Lord Albemarle on the other: the latter took the letters which were arranged according to their dates, and read them in a clear distinct voice.

As the reading went on, his Majesty made memorandums and notes with his pencil on a sheet of paper, but did not interrupt during the whole progress of the lecture. When the last and most important was finished, the two noblemen looked at his Majesty with countenances full of meaning. For a few moments his Majesty drummed with the second and third finger of his left hand upon the table, and then said—

"Pray, Mr Vanslyperken, how did you obtain possession of these papers and letters, or make copies of these letters?"

Vanslyperken, who had been standing at the other side of the table during the time of the reading, had anxiously watched the countenance of his Majesty and the two noblemen, and perceived that the intelligence which the letters contained, had created a strong feeling, as he expected. With a certain degree of confidence, he commenced his explanation.

He stated that the crew of the cutter had been accustomed to frequent the Lust Haus of a certain widow

Vandersloosh, and that he had made her acquaintance, by several times going there to look after his seamen.

That this widow had often hinted to him, and at last proposed to him, that he should take letters for some friends of hers—at last she had told him plainly that it was for the Jacobite party, and he pretended to consent.

That he had been taken by her to the house of a Jesuit, 169, in the Bur street, nearly opposite to her Lust Haus, and that the Jesuit had given him some letters and fifty guineas for his trouble.

He then stated, that he had opened, copied, and resealed them; further, that he had brought over one of the confederates, who was now residing in the house of the syndic, Van Krause. That he should have made all this known before, only that he waited till it was more important. That the last letters appeared of such consequence, that he deemed it his duty no longer to delay.

"You have done well, Mr Vanslyperken," replied his Majesty.

"And played a bold game," observed Lord Albemarle, fixing his eyes upon Vanslyperken. "Suppose you had been found out co-operating with traitors, before you made this discovery!"

"I might have forfeited my life in my zeal," replied Mr Vanslyperken, with adroitness; "but that is the duty of a king's officer."

"That is well said," observed the Duke of Portland.

"I have a few questions to put to you, Mr Vanslyperken," observed his Majesty.

"What is the cave they mention so often?"

"It is on the bank of the Isle of Wight, your Majesty. I did not know of its existence, but from the letters—but I once laid a whole night in the cove underneath it, to intercept the smugglers, upon information that I had received, but the alarm was given, and they escaped."

"Who is their agent at Portsmouth?"

"A Jew of the name of Lazarus, residing in little Orange Street, at the back of the Point, your Majesty!"

"Do you know of any of the names of the conspirators?"

"I do not, your Majesty, except a woman, who is very active, one Moggy Salisbury—her husband not a month back, was the boatswain of the cutter, but by some interest or another, he has obtained his discharge."

"My Lord of Portland, take a memorandum to inquire who it was applied for the discharge of that man. Mr Vanslyperken you may retire—we will call you in by-and-bye—you will be secret as to what has passed."

"I have one more duty to perform," replied Vanslyperken, taking some rouleaus of gold out of his pocket; "this is the money received from the traitors—it is not for a king's officer to have it in his possession."

"You are right, Mr Vanslyperken, but the gold of traitors is forfeited to the crown, and it is now mine, you will accept it as a present from your king."

Mr Vanslyperken took the gold from the table, made a bow, and retired from the royal presence.

The reader will acknowledge that it was impossible to play his cards better than Mr Vanslyperken had done in this interview, and that he deserved great credit for his astute conduct. With such diplomatic talents, he would have made a great prime minister.

"The council was ordered at twelve o'clock, my lords. These letters must be produced. That they are genuine appears to me beyond a doubt."

"That they are faithful copies, I doubt not," replied Lord Albemarle, "but——"

"But what, my Lord Albemarle?"

"I very much suspect the fidelity of the copier—there is something more that has not been told, depend upon it."

"Why do you think so, my lord?"

"Because, your Majesty, allowing that a man would act the part that Mr Vanslyperken says that he has done to discover the conspiracy, still, would he not naturally, to avoid any risk to himself, have furnished government with the first correspondence, and obtained their sanction for prosecuting his plans? This officer has been employed for the last two years or more in carrying the despatches to the Hague, and it must at once strike your Majesty, that a person who can, with such dexterity, open the letters of others can also open those of his own government."

"That is true, my lord," replied his Majesty, musing.

"Your Majesty is well aware that suspicions were entertained of the fidelity of the syndic, suspicions which the evidence of this officer have verified. But why were these suspicions raised? Because he knew of the government secrets, and it was supposed he obtained them from some one who is in our trust, but inimical to us and unworthy of the confidence reposed in him.

"Your Majesty's acuteness will at once perceive that the secrets may have been obtained by Mynheer Krause, by the same means as have been resorted to, to obtain the secrets of the conspirators. I may be in error, and if I do this officer wrong by my suspicions, may God forgive me, but there is something in his looks which tells me——"

"What, my lord?"

"That he is a traitor to both parties. May it please your Majesty."

"By the Lord, Albermarle, I think you have hit upon the truth," replied the Duke of Portland.

"Of that we shall soon have proof—at present, we have to decide whether it be advisable to employ him to discover more, or at once to seize upon the parties he has denounced. But that had better be canvassed in the council-chamber. Come, my lords, they be waiting for us."

The affair was of too great importance not to absorb all other business, and it was decided that the house of Mynheer Krause, and of the Jesuit, and the widow Vandersloosh should be entered by the peace-officers, at midnight, and that they and any of the conspirators who might be found should be thrown into prison. That the cutter should be despatched immediately to England, with orders to seize all the other parties informed against by Vanslyperken, and that a force should be sent to attack the cave, and secure those who might be found there, with directions to the admiral, that Mr Vanslyperken should be employed both as a guide, and to give the assistance of the cutter and his crew.

These arrangements having been made, the council broke up, King William had a conference with his two favourites, and Vanslyperken was sent for.

"Lieutenant Vanslyperken, we feel much indebted to you for your important communications, and we shall not forget, in due time, to reward your zeal and loyalty as it deserves. At present, it is necessary that you sail for England as soon as our despatches are ready, which will be before midnight; you will then receive your orders from the admiral, at Portsmouth, and I have no doubt you will take the opportunity of affording us fresh proofs of your fidelity and attachment."

Mr Vanslyperken bowed humbly and retired, delighted with the successful result of his manœuvre, and, with a gay heart he leaped into his calash, and drove off.

"Yes, yes," thought he, "Madam Vandersloosh, you would betray me. We shall see. Yes, yes, we shall see, Madam Vandersloosh."

And sure enough he did see Madam Vandersloosh, who in another calash was driving to the palace, and who met him face to face.

Vanslyperken turned up his nose at her as he passed by, and the widow astonished at his presumption, thought as she went on her way, "Well, well, Mr Vanslyperken, we shall see, you may turn up your snivelling nose, but stop till your head's in the halter—yes, Mr Vanslyperken, stop till your head's in the halter."

We must leave Mr Vanslyperken to drive, and the widow Vandersloosh to drive, while we drive on ourselves.

The subsequent events of this eventful day we will narrate in the following chapter.

Chapter XLVI

In which there is much bustle and confusion, plot and counter-plot.

ABOUT two hours after the council had broken up, the following communication was delivered into the hands of Ramsay by an old woman, who immediately took her departure.

"The lieutenant of the cutter has taken copies of all your correspondence and betrayed you. You must fly immediately, as at midnight you and all of you will be seized. In justice to Mynheer Krause, leave documents to clear him.

"The cutter will sail this evening—with orders to secure your friends at Portsmouth and the cave."

"Now, by the holy cross of our Saviour! I will have revenge upon that dastard; there is no time to lose; five minutes for reflection, and then to act," thought Ramsay, as he twisted up this timely notice, which, it must be evident to the reader, must have been sent by one who had been summoned to the council. Ramsay's plans were soon formed, he despatched a trusty messenger to the Jesuit's, desiring him to communicate immediately with the others, and upon what plan to proceed. He then wrote a note to Vanslyperken, requesting his immediate presence, and hastened to the morning apartment of Wilhelmina. In a few words, he told her that he had received timely notice that it was the intention of the government to seize her father and him as suspected traitors, and throw them that very night in prison.

Wilhelmina made no reply.

"For your father, my dearest girl, there is no fear: he will be fully acquitted; but I, Wilhelmina, must depart immediately, or my life is forfeited."

"Leave me, Edward?" replied Wilhelmina.

"No, you must go with me, Wilhelmina, for more than one reason; the government have ordered the seizure of the persons to be made in the night, to avoid a disturbance; but that they will not be able to prevent; the mob are but too happy to prove their loyalty, when they can do so by rapine and plunder, and depend upon it that this house will be sacked and levelled to the ground before to-morrow evening. You cannot go to prison with your father; you cannot remain here, to be at the mercy of an infuriated and lawless mob. You must go with me, Wilhelmina; trust to me, not only for my sake, but for your father's."

" My father's, Edward, it is that only I am thinking of; how can I leave my father at such a time?"

" You will save your father by so doing. Your departure with me will substantiate his innocence; decide, my dearest girl; decide at once; you must either fly with me, or we must part for ever."

" Oh no, that must not be, Edward," cried Wilhelmina, bursting into tears.

After some further persuasions on the part of Ramsay, and fresh tears from the attached maiden, it was agreed that she should act upon his suggestions, and with a throbbing heart, she went to her chamber to make the necessary preparations, while Ramsay requested that Mynheer Krause would give him a few minutes of his company in his room above.

The syndic soon made his appearance; " Well, Mynheer Ramsay, you have some news to tell me, I am sure;" for Mynheer Krause, notwithstanding his rebuff from the king, could not divest himself of his failing of fetching and carrying reports. Ramsay went to the door and turned the key.

" I have, indeed, most important news, Mynheer Krause, and, I am sorry to say, very unpleasant also."

" Indeed," replied the syndic, with alarm.

" Yes; I find from a notice given me by one of his Majesty's council, assembled this morning at the Hague, that you are suspected of treasonable practices."

" God in heaven!" exclaimed the syndic.

"And that this very night you are to be seized and thrown into prison."

"I, the syndic of the town! I, who put everybody else into prison!"

"Even so; such is the gratitude of King William for your long and faithful services, Mynheer Krause! I have now sent for you, that we may consult as to what had best be done. Will you fly? I have the means for your escape."

"Fly, Mynheer Ramsay; the syndic of Amsterdam fly? Never! they may accuse me falsely; they may condemn me and take off my head before the Stadt House, but I will not fly."

"I expected this answer; and you are right, Mynheer Krause; but there are other considerations worthy of your attention. When the populace know you are in prison for treason, they will level this house to the ground."

"Well, and so they ought, if they suppose me guilty; I care little for that."

"I am aware of that; but still your property will be lost; but it will be but a matter of prudence to save all you can: you have already a large sum of gold collected."

"I have four thousand guilders, at least."

"You must think of your daughter, Mynheer Krause. This gold must not find its way into the pockets of the mob. Now, observe, the king's cutter sails to-night, and I propose that your gold be embarked, and I will take it over for you and keep it safe. Then, let what will happen, your daughter will not be left to beggary."

"True, true, my dear sir, there is no saying how this will end: it may end well; but, as you say, if the house is plundered, the gold is gone for ever. Your advice is good, and I will give you, before you go, orders for all the monies in the hands of my agents at Hamburgh and Frankfort and other places. I have taken your advice my young friend, and, though I have property to the amount of some hundred thousand guilders, with the exception of this house they will hold little of it which belongs to

Mynheer Krause. And my poor daughter, Mynheer Ramsay!"

"Should any accident happen to you, you may trust to me, I swear it to you, Mynheer Krause, on my hope of salvation."

Here the old man sat down much affected, and covered his face.

"Oh! my dear young friend, what a world is this, where they cannot distinguish a true and a loyal subject from a traitor. But why could you not stay here,—protect my house from the mob,—demand the civic guard."

"I stay here, my dear sir, why I am included in the warrant of treason."

"You?"

"Yes; and there would be no chance of my escaping from my enemies, they detest me too much. But cheer up, sir, I think that, by my means, you may be cleared of all suspicions."

"By your means?"

"Yes; but I must not explain; my departure is necessary for your safety: I will take the whole upon myself, and you shall be saved."

"I really cannot understand you, my dear friend; but it appears to me, as if you were going to make some great sacrifice for my sake."

"I will not be questioned, Mynheer Krause; only this I say, that I am resolved that you shall be proved innocent. It is my duty. But we have no time to lose. Let your gold be ready at sunset: I will have everything prepared."

"But my daughter must not remain here; she will be by herself, at the mercy of the mob."

"Be satisfied, Mynheer Krause, that is also cared for, your daughter must leave this house, and be in a safe retreat before the officers come in to seize you: I have arranged everything."

"Where do you propose sending her?"

"Not to any of your friends' houses, Mynheer Krause, no—no, but I'll see her in safety before I leave, do not be afraid; it must depend upon circumstances, but of that hereafter, you have no time to lose."

"God in heaven!" exclaimed Mynheer Krause, unlocking the door, "that I, the syndic, the most loyal subject!—well, well, you may truly say, 'put not your trust in princes.'"

"Trust in me, Mynheer Krause," replied Ramsay, taking his hand.

"I do, I will, my good friend, and I will go to prison proudly, and like an innocent and injured man."

And Mynheer Krause hastened down to his connting-house, to make the proposed arrangements, Ramsay returning to Wilhelmina, to whom he imparted what had taken place between him and her father, and which had the effect of conforming her resolution.

We must now return to the widow Vandersloosh, who has arrived safely, but melting with the heat of her journey, at the Palace of the Hague. She immediately informed one of the domestics that she wished to speak with his Majesty upon important business.

"I cannot take your name into his Majesty, but if you will give it me, I will speak to Lord Albemarle."

The widow wrote her name down upon a slip of paper; with which the servant went away, and then the widow sat down upon a bench in the hall, and cooled herself with her fan.

"Frau Vandersloosh," said Lord Albemarle, on reading the name.

"Let her come up,—why this," continued he, turning to the Duke of Portland, who was sitting by him, "is the woman who is ordered to be arrested this night, upon the evidence of Lieutenant Vanslyperken; we shall learn something now, depend upon it."

The Frau Vandersloosh made her appearance, sailing in the room like a Dutch man-of-war of that period, under full sail, high pooped and broad sterned. Never having stood in the presence of great men, she was not a little confused, so she fanned herself most furiously.

"You wish to speak with me," said Lord Albemarle.

"Yes, your honour's honour, I've come to expose a snivelling traitor to his Majesty's crown. Yes, yes, Mr Vanslyperken, we shall see now," continued the widow, talking to herself, and fanning away.

"We are all attentive, madam."

Mistress Vandersloosh then began, out of breath, and continued out of breath till she had told the whole of her story, which, as the reader must be aware, only corroborated all Vanslyperken had already stated, with the exception that he had denounced the widow. Lord Albemarle allowed her to proceed without interruption, he had a great insight into character, and the story of the widow confirmed him in his opinion of Vanslyperken.

"But my good woman," said Lord Albemarle, "are you aware that Mr Vanslyperken has already been here?"

"Yes, your honour, I met him going back, and he turned his nose up at me, and I then said, 'Well, well, Mr Vanslyperken, we shall see; wait a little, Mr Vanslyperken.'"

"And," continued Lord Albemarle, "that he has denounced you as being a party to all these treasonable practices."

"Me—denounced me—he—O Lord, O Lord, only let me meet him face to face—let him say it then if he dares, the snivelling—cowardly—murdering wretch."

Thereupon Mrs Vandersloosh commenced the history of Vanslyperken's wooing, of his cur Snarleyyow, of her fancy for the corporal, of his finding her with the corporal the day before, of her beating him off with the brooms, and of her threats to expose his treason. "And so, now, when he finds that he was to be exposed, he comes up first himself; that's now the truth of it, or my name's not Vandersloosh, your honour," and the widow walked up and down with the march of an elephant, fanning herself violently, her bosom heaving with agitation, and her face as red as a boiled lobster.

"Mistress Vandersloosh," said Lord Albemarle, "let

the affair rest as it is for the present, but I shall not forget what you have told me. I think now that you had better go home."

At this dismissal the widow turned round.

"Thank your worship kindly," said she, "I'm ready to come whenever I'm wanted. Yes, yes, Mr Vanslyperken," resumed the widow, as she walked to the door, quite forgetting the respect due to the two noblemen, "we shall see; yes, yes, we shall see."

"Well, my lord, what think you of this?" said Lord Albemarle to the duke, as the widow closed the door.

"Upon my soul I think she is honest; she is too fat for a traitor."

"I am of your opinion. The episode of the corporal was delightful, and has thrown much light upon the lieutenant's conduct, who is a traitor in my opinion, if ever there was one; but he must be allowed to fulfil his task, and then we will soon find out the traitor; but if I mistake not, that man was born to be hung."

We must now return to Mr Vanslyperken, who received the note from Ramsay, just as he was going down to the boat. As he did not know what steps were to be taken by government, he determined to go up to Ramsay, and inform him of his order for immediately sailing.

He might gain further information from his letters, and also remove the suspicion of his having betrayed him. Ramsay received Mr Vanslyperken with an air of confidence.

"Sit down, Mr Vanslyperken, I wish to know whether there is any chance of your sailing."

"I was about to come up to you to state that I have orders to sail this evening."

"That is fortunate, as I intended to take a passage with you, and what is more, Mr Vanslyperken, I have a large sum in specie, which we must contrive to get on board. Cannot we contrive it, I cannot go without it."

"A large sum in specie?" Vanslyperken reflected. "Yes, he would secure Ramsay as a prisoner, and possess himself of the specie if he could. His entrapping Ramsay on board would be another proof of his fidelity and dexterity. But then Vanslyperken thought of the defection of the corporal, but that was of no great consequence. The crew of the cutter dare not disobey him, when they were ordered to seize a traitor."

While Vanslyperken was meditating this, Ramsay fixed his eyes upon him waiting for his reply.

"It will be difficult," observed Vanslyperken, "to get the specie on board without being seen."

"I'm afraid so too, but I have a proposition to make. Suppose you get under way, and—heave to a mile outside, I will then come off in the syndic's barge. I can have the use of it. Then nothing will be discovered."

Vanslyperken appeared to reflect again.

"I shall still run a great risk, Mr Ramsay."

"You will run some little perhaps, but you will be well paid for it, I promise you."

"Well, sir, I consent," replied Vanslyperken. "At what hour do you propose to embark?"

"About eleven or a little earlier. You will have a light over the stern; hail the boat when you see it coming, and I shall answer, 'King's messenger, with despatches;' that will be a blind to your crew—they supposed me a king's messenger before."

"Yes, that will be prudent," replied Vanslyperken, who then took his leave with great apparent cordiality.

"Villain," muttered Ramsay, as Vanslyperken shut the door, "I know your thoughts."

We must pass over the remainder of this eventful day. Wilhelmina had procured the dress of a boy, in which disguise she proposed to elope with Ramsay, and all her preparations were made long before the time. Mynheer Krause was also occupied in getting his specie ready for embarkation, and Ramsay in writing letters. The despatches from the Hague came down about nine o'clock, and Vanslyperken received them on board. About ten, he weighed and made sail, and hove-to about a mile outside, with a light shown as agreed. About the time arranged, a large boat appeared pulling up to the cutter. "Boat, ahoy!" "King's messenger with despatches," was the reply. "All's right," said Vanslyperken, "get a rope there from forward."

The boat darted alongside of the cutter. She pulled ten oars, but, as soon as she was alongside, a number of armed men sprang from her on the decks, and beat the crew below, while Ramsay, with pistols in his belt, and his sword in his hand, went aft to Vanslyperken.

"What is all this?" exclaimed the terrified lieutenant.

"Nothing, sir, but common prudence on my part," replied Ramsay. "I have an account to settle with you."

Vanslyperken perceived that his treachery was discovered, and he fell upon his knees. Ramsay turned away to give orders, and Vanslyperken darted down the hatchway, and gained the lower deck.

"Never mind," said Ramsay, "he'll not escape me; come, my lads, hand up the boxes as fast as you can."

Ramsay then went to the boat, and brought up Wilhelmina, who had remained there, and conducted her down into the cabin. The boxes were also handed down, the boat made fast, and the conspirators remained in possession of the deck. The helm was taken by one of them; sail again made on the cutter, and the boat with a boat-keeper towed astern.

Chapter XLVII

Which is rather interesting.

MR VANSLYPERKEN's retreat was not known to the crew, they thought him still on deck, and he hastened forward to secrete himself, even from his own crew, who were not a little astonished at this unexpected attack which they could not account for. The major part of the arms on board were always kept in Mr Vanslyperken's cabin, and that was not only in possession of the assailants, but there was a strong guard in the passage outside which led to the lower deck.

"Well, this beats my comprehension entirely," said Bill Spurey.

"Yes," replied Short.

"And mine too," added Obadiah Coble, "being as we are, as you know, at peace with all nations, to be boarded and carried in this way."

"Why, what, and who can they be?"

"I've a notion that Vanslyperken's at the bottom of it," replied Spurey.

"Yes," said Short.

"But it's a bottom that I can't fathom," continued Spurey.

"My dipsey line arn't long enough either," replied Coble.

"Gott for dam, what it can be!" exclaimed Jansen. "It must be the treason."

"Mein Gott! yes," replied Corporal Van Spitter. "It is all treason, and the traitor be Vanslyperken." But although the corporal had some confused ideas, yet he could not yet arrange them.

"Well, I've no notion of being boxed up here," observed Coble, "they can't be so many as we are, even if they were stowed away in the boat, like pilchards in a cask. Can't we get at the arms, corporal, and make a rush for it."

"Mein Gott! de arms are all in the cabin, all but three pair pistols and the bayonets."

"Well, but we've handspikes," observed Spurey.

"Got for dam, gif me de handspike," cried Jansen.

"We had better wait till daylight, at all events," observed Coble, "we shall see our work better."

"Yes," replied Short.

"And, in the meantime, get everything to hand that we can."

"Yes," replied Short.

"Well, I can't understand the manœuvre. It beats my comprehension, what they have done with Vanslyperken."

"I don't know, but they've kicked the cur out of the cabin."

"Then they've kicked him out too, depend upon it."

Thus did the crew continue to surmise during the whole night, but, as Bill Spurey said, the manœuvre beat their comprehension.

One thing was agreed upon, that they should make an attempt to recover the vessel as soon as they could.

In the meantime, Ramsay with Wilhelmina, and the Jesuits, had taken possession of the cabin, and had opened all the despatches which acquainted them with the directions in detail, given for the taking of the conspirators at Portsmouth, and in the cave. Had it not been to save his friends, Ramsay would, at once, have taken the cutter to Cherbourg, and have there landed Wilhelmina and the treasure; but his anxiety for his friends, determined him to run at once for the cave, and send overland to Portsmouth. The wind was fair and the water smooth, and, before morning, the cutter was on her way.

In the meantime, the crew of the cutter had not been idle; the ladders had been taken up and hatches closed. The only chance of success was an attack upon the guard, who was stationed outside of the cabin.

They had six pistols, about two hundred pounds of ammunition, but with the exception of half-a-dozen bayonets, no other weapons. But they were resolute men, and as soon as they had made their arrangements, which consisted of piling up their hammocks, so as to make a barricade to fire over, they then commenced operations, the first signal of which, was a pistol-shot discharged at the men who were on guard in the passage, and which wounded one of them. Ramsay darted out of the cabin, at the report of the pistol, another and another was discharged, and Ramsay then gave the order to fire in return. This was done, but without injury to the seamen of the cutter, who were protected by the hammocks, and Ramsay having already three of his men wounded, found that the post below was no longer tenable. A consultation took place, and it was determined that the passage on the lower deck and the cabin should be abandoned, as the upper deck it would be easy to retain.

The cabin's skylight was taken off, and the boxes of gold handed up, while the party outside the cabin door maintained the conflict with the crew of the *Yungfrau*. When all the boxes were up, Wilhelmina was lifted on deck, the skylight was shipped on again, and, as soon as the after hatches were ready to put on, Ramsay's men retreated to the ladder, which they drew up after them, and then put on the hatches.

Had not the barricade of hammocks prevented them, the crew of the *Yungfrau* might have made a rush, and followed the others on deck; but, before they could beat down the barricades, which they did as soon as they perceived their opponents' retreat, the ladder was up, and the hatches placed over the hatchways.

The *Yungfraus* had gained the whole of the lower deck, but they could do no more; and Ramsay perceived that if he could maintain possession of the upper deck, it was as much as he could expect with such determined assailants. This warfare had been continued during the whole morning, and it was twelve o'clock before the cabin and lower deck had been abandoned by Ramsay's associates. During the whole day the skirmishes continued, the crew of the *Yungfrau* climbing on the table of the cabin, and firing through the skylight, but in so doing, they exposed themselves to the fire of the other party who sat like cats watching for their appearance, and discharging their pieces the moment that a head presented itself. In the meantime, the cutter darted on before a strong favourable breeze, and thus passed the first day. Many attempts were made during the night by the seamen of the cutter to force their way on deck, but they were all prevented by the vigilance of Ramsay; and the next morning the Isle of Wight was in sight. Wilhelmina had passed the night on the forecastle, covered up with a sail; none of his people had had anything to eat during the time that they were on board, and Ramsay was most anxious to arrive at his destination.

About noon, the cutter was abreast of the Black Gang Chine: Ramsay had calculated upon retaining possession of the cutter, and taking the whole of the occupants of the cave over to Cherbourg, but this was now impossible. He had five of his men wounded, and he could not row the boat to the cave without leaving so few men on board, that they would be overpowered, for his ammunition was expended, with the exception of one or two charges, which were retained for an emergency. All that he could do now, was, therefore, to put his treasure in the boat, and with Wilhelmina and his whole party make for the cave, when he could send notice to Portsmouth for the others to join them, and they must be content to await the meditated attack upon the cave, and defend it till they could make their escape to France. The wind being foul for the cutter's return to Portsmouth, would enable him to give notice at Portsmouth, over land, before she could arrive.

There was a great oversight committed when the lower deck was abandoned, the despatches had been left on Mr Vanslyperken's bed. Had they been taken away or destroyed, there would have been ample time for the whole of his party to have made their escape from England, before duplicates could arrive. As it was, he could do no more than what we have already mentioned.

The boat was hauled up, the boxes of specie put in, the wounded men laid at the bottom of the boat, and having, at the suggestion of one of the men, cut the lower riggings, halyards, &c., of the cutter to retard its progress to Portsmouth, Ramsay and his associates stepped into the boat, and pulled for the cave.

Their departure was soon ascertained by the crew of the *Yungfrau* who now forced the skylight, and gained the deck, but not before the boat had entered the cave.

"What's to be done now?" said Coble. "Smash my timbers, but they've played old Harry with the rigging. We must knot and splice."

"Yes," replied Short.

"What the devil have they done with Vanslyperken?" cried Bill Spurey.

"Either shoved him overboard, or taken him with them, I suppose," cried Coble.

"Well, it's a nice job altogether," observed Spurey.

"Mein Gott! yes," replied the corporal; "we will have a pretty story to tell de admiral."

"Well, they've rid us of him at all events; I only hope they'll hang him."

"Mein Gott! yes."

"He'll have his desarts," replied Coble.

"Got for tam! I like to see him swing."

"Now he's gone, let's send his dog after him. Hurrah, my lads! get a rope up on the yard, and let us hang Snarleyyow."

"Mein Gott! I'll go fetch him," cried the corporal.

"You will—will you?" roared a voice.

The corporal turned round, so did the others, and there, with his drawn sword, stood Mr Vanslyperken.

"You d——d mutinous scoundrel," cried Vanslyperken, "touch my dog, if you dare."

The corporal put his hand up to the salute, and Vanslyperken shook his head with a diabolical expression of countenance.

"Now where the devil could he come from?" whispered Spurey.

Coble shrugged up his shoulders, and Short gave a long whistle expending more breath than usual.

However, there was no more to be said; and as soon as the rigging was knotted and spliced, sail was made in the cutter; but the wind being dead in their teeth, they did not arrive until late the next evening, and the admiral did not see despatches till the next morning, for the best of all possible reasons, that Vanslyperken did not take them on shore. He had a long story to tell, and he thought it prudent not to disturb the admiral after dinner, as great men are apt to be very choleric during the progress of digestion.

The consequence was, that when, the next morning, Mr Vanslyperken called upon the admiral, the intelligence had been received from the cave, and all the parties had absconded. Mr Vanslyperken told his own tale, how he had been hailed by a boat purporting to have a messenger on board, how they had boarded him and beat down himself and his crew, how he and his crew had fought under hatches and beat them on deck, and how they had been forced to abandon the cutter. All this was very plausible, and then Vanslyperken gave the despatches opened by Ramsay.

The admiral read them in haste, gave immediate orders for surrounding and breaking into the house of the Jew Lazarus, in which the military found nobody but an old tom-cat, and then desired Mr Vanslyperken to hold the cutter in readiness to embark troops and sail that afternoon; but troops do not move so fast as people think, and before one hundred men had been told off by the sergeant with their accoutrements, knapsacks, and sixty pounds of ammunition, it was too late to embark them that night, so they waited until the next morning. Moreover, Mr Vanslyperken had orders to draw from the dock-yard three large boats for the debarkation of the said troops; but the boats were not quite ready, one required a new gunnel, another three planks in the bottom, and the third having her stern out, it required all the carpenters in the yard to finish it by the next morning. Mr Vanslyperken's orders were to proceed to the cave, and land the troops, to march up to the cave, and to cover the advance of the troops, rendering them all the assistance in his power in co-operating with the major commanding the detachment; but where the cave was, no one knew, except that it was thereabouts.

The next morning, at eight o'clock, the detachment, consisting of one hundred men, were embarked on board of the cutter, but the major commandant finding that the decks were excessively crowded, and that he could hardly breathe, ordered section first, section second, and section third, of twenty-five men each, to go into the boats and be towed. After which there was more room, and the cutter stood out for St Helen's.

Chapter XLVIII

In which there is a great deal of correspondence, and the widow is called up very early in the morning.

WE must now return to Mynheer Krause, who, after he had delivered over his gold, locked up his counting-house and went up to the saloon, determining to meet his fate with all the dignity of a Roman senator. He sent for his daughter, who sent word back that she was packing up her wardrobe, and this answer appeared but reasonable to the syndic, who, therefore, continued in his chair, reflecting upon his approaching incarceration, conning speeches, and anticipating a glorious acquittal, until the bell of the cathedral chimed the half-hour after ten. He then sent another message to his daughter, and the reply was that she was not in the room, upon which he despatched old Koop to Ramsay, requesting his attendance. The reply to this second message was a letter presented to the syndic, who broke the seal and read as follows:

"MY DEAR AND HONOURED SIR,
"I have sought a proper asylum for your daughter during the impending troubles, and could not find one which pleased, and in consequence I have taken the bold step, aware that I might not have received your sanction if applied for, of taking her on board the cutter with me; she will there be safe, and as her character might be, to a certain degree, impeached by being in company with a man of my age, I intend, as soon as we arrive in port, to unite myself to her, for which act, I trust, you will grant me your pardon. As for yourself, be under

no apprehension, I have saved you. Treat the accusation with scorn, and if you are admitted into the presence of his Majesty, accuse him of the ingratitude which he has been guilty of; I trust that we shall soon meet again, that I may return to you the securities and specie of which I have charge, as well as your daughter, who is anxious once more to receive your blessing.

"Yours ever, till death,
"EDWARD RAMSAY."

Mynheer Krause read this letter over and over again, it was very mystifying. Much depends in this world upon the humour people are in at the time; Mynheer Krause was, at that time, full of Cato-like devotion and Roman virtue, and he took the contents of the letter in true Catonic style.

"Excellent young man—to preserve my honour he has taken her away with him! and, to preserve her reputation he intends to marry her! Now, I can go to prison without a sigh. He tells me that he has saved me—saved me!—why, he has saved everything; me, my daughter, and my property! Well, they shall see how I behave! They shall witness the calmness of a stoic; I shall express no emotion or surprise at the arrest, as they will naturally expect, because I know it is to take place—no fear—no agitation when in prison, because I know that I am to be saved. I shall desire them to bear in mind that I am the syndic of this town, and must receive that respect which is due to my exalted situation," and Mynheer Van Krause lifted his pipe and ordered Koop to bring him a stone jug of beer, and thus doubly-armed like Cato, he awaited the arrival of the officer with all the stoicism of beer and tobacco.

About the same hour of night that the letter was put into the hands of Mynheer Krause, a packet was brought up to Lord Albemarle, who was playing a game of put with his Grace the Duke of Portland; at that time put was a most fashionable game; but games are like garments, as they become old they are cast off, and handed down to the servants. The outside of the despatch was marked "To Lord Albemarle's own hands. Immediate and most important." It appeared, however, as if the two noble lords considered the game of put as more important and immediate, for they finished it without looking at the packet in question, and it was midnight before they threw up the cards. After which, Lord Albemarle went to a side table, apart from the rest of the company, and broke the seals. It was a letter with enclosures, and ran as follows:

"MY LORD ALBEMARLE,

"Although your political enemy, I do justice to your merits, and to prove my opinion of you, address to you this letter, the object of which is to save your government from the disgrace of injuring a worthy man, and a staunch supporter, to expose the villany of a coward and a scoundrel. When I state that my name is Ramsay, you may at once be satisfied that, before this comes to your hands, I am out of your reach. I came here in the king's cutter, commanded by Mr Vanslyperken, with letters of recommendation to Mynheer Krause, which represented me as a staunch adherent of William of Orange and a Protestant, and, with that impression, I was well received, and took up my abode in his house. My object you may imagine, but fortune favoured me still more, in having in my power Lieutenant Vanslyperken. I opened the government despatches in his presence, and supplied him with false seals to enable him to do the same, and give me the extracts which were of importance, for which I hardly need say he was most liberally rewarded; this has been carried on for some time, but it appears, that in showing him how to obtain your secrets, I also showed him how to possess himself of ours, and the consequence has been that he has turned double traitor, and I have now narrowly escaped.

"The information possessed by Mynheer Krause was

given by me, to win his favour for one simple reason, that I fell in love with his daughter, who has now quitted the country with me. He never was undeceived as to my real position, nor is he even now. Let me do an honest man justice. I enclose you the extracts from your duplicates made by Mr Vanslyperken, written in his own hand, which I trust will satisfy you as to his perfidy, and induce you to believe in the innocence of the worthy syndic from the assurance of a man, who, although a Catholic, a Jacobite, and if you please an attainted traitor, is incapable of telling you a falsehood. I am, my lord, with every respect for your noble character.

"Yours most obediently,
"EDWARD RAMSAY."

"This is corroborative of my suspicions," said Lord Albemarle, putting down the papers before the Duke of Portland.

The duke read the letter and examined the enclosures.

"Shall we see the king to-night?"

"No, he is retired, and it is of no use, they are in prison by this time; we will wait the report to-morrow morning—ascertain how many have been secured—and then lay these documents before his Majesty."

Leaving the two noble lords to go to bed, we shall now return to Amsterdam at twelve o'clock at night precisely; as the bell tolled, a loud knock was heard at the syndic's house. Koop, who had been ordered by his master to remain up, immediately opened the door, and a *posse comitatus* of civil power filled the yard.

"Where is Mynheer Krause?" inquired the chief in authority.

"Mynheer, the syndic, is upstairs in the saloon."

Without sending up his name, the officer went up, followed by three or four others, and found Mynheer Krause smoking his pipe.

"Ah, my very particular friend, Mynheer Engelback,

what brings you here at this late hour with all your people? Is there a fire in the town?"

"No, Mynheer Syndic. It is an order I am very sorry to say to arrest you, and conduct you to prison."

"Arrest and conduct me to prison—me the syndic of the town—that is strange—will you allow me to see your warrant—yes, it is all true and countersigned by his Majesty; I have no more to say, Mynheer Engelback. As syndic of this town, and administrator of the laws, it is my duty to set the example of obedience to them, at the same time protesting my entire innocence. Koop, get me my mantle. Mynheer Engelback, I claim to be treated with the respect due to me, as syndic of this town."

The officers were not a little staggered at the coolness and *sang froid* of Mynheer Krause, he had never appeared to so much advantage; they bowed respectfully as he finished his speech.

"I believe, Mynheer Krause, that you have some friends staying with you?"

"I have no friend in the house except my very particular friend, Mynheer Engelback," replied the syndic.

"You must excuse us, but we must search the house."

"You have his Majesty's warrant so to do, and no excuse is necessary."

After a diligent search of half an hour, nobody was found in the house, and the officers began to suspect that the government had been imposed upon. Mynheer Krause, with every mark of attention and respect, was then walked off to the Hotel de Ville, where he remained in custody, for it was not considered right by the authorities, that the syndic should be thrown into the common prison upon suspicion only. When he arrived there, Mynheer Krause surprised them all by the philosophy with which he smoked his pipe.

But, although there was nobody to be found, except the syndic in the syndic's house, and not a soul at the house inhabited by the Jesuit, there was one more person included in the warrant, which was the widow Vandersloosh; for Lord Albemarle, although convinced in his own mind of her innocence, could not take upon himself to interfere with the decisions of the council; so, about one o'clock, there was a loud knocking at the widow's door, which was repeated again and again before it awoke the widow, who was fatigued with her long and hot journey to the Hague. As for Babette, she made a rule never to wake at anything, but the magical No. 6, sounded by the church clock, or by her mistress's voice.

"Babette," cried the widow Vandersloosh, "Babette."

"Yes, ma'am."

"There's a knock at the door, Babette."

"Only some drunken sailors, ma'am—they go away when they find they cannot get in."

Here the peals were redoubled.

"Babette, get up, Babette—and threaten them with the watch."

"Yes, ma'am," replied Babette, with a terrible yawn.

Knocking and thumping with strokes louder than before.

"Babette, Babette!"

"I must put something on, ma'am," replied Babette, rather crossly.

"Speak to them out of the window, Babette."

Here poor Babette came down to the first floor, and opening the window at the landing-place on the stairs, put her head out and cried,

"If you don't go away, you drunken fellows, my mistress will send for the watch."

"If you don't come down and open the door, we shall break it open," replied the officer sent to the duty.

"Tell them it's no inn, Babette, we won't let people in after hours," cried the widow, turning in her bed and anxious to resume her sound sleep.

Babette gave the message and shut down the window.

"Break open the door," cried the officer to his attendants. In a minute or two the door was burst open, and the party ascended the staircase.

"Mercy on me! Babette, if they arn't come in," cried the widow, who jumped out of her bed, and nearly shutting her door, which had been left open for ventilation, she peeped out to see who were the bold intruders; she perceived a man in black with a white staff.

"What do you want?" screamed the widow, terrified.

"We want Mistress Vandersloosh. Are you that person?" said the officer.

"To be be sure I am. But what do you want here?"

"I must request you to dress and come along with me directly to the Stadt House," replied the officer, very civilly.

"Gott in himmel! what's the matter?"

"It's on a charge of treasonable practices, madam."

"Oh, ho! I see: Mr Vanslyperken. Very well, good sir; I'll put on my clothes directly. I'll get up any hour in the night, with pleasure, to bring that villain——. Yes, yes, Mr Vanslyperken, we shall see. Babette, take the gentleman down in the parlour, and give them some bottled beer. You'll find it very good, sirs; it's of my own brewing. And Babette, you must come up and help me."

The officer did not think it necessary to undeceive the widow, who imagined that she was to give evidence against Vanslyperken, not that she was a prisoner herself. Still, the widow Vandersloosh did not like being called up at such an unseasonable hour, and thus expressed herself to Babette as she was dressing herself.

"Well, we shall see the ending of this, Babette.—My under petticoat is on the chair.—I told the lords the whole truth, every word of it; and I am convinced that they believed me, too.—Don't pull tight all at once, Babette; how often do I tell you that. I do believe you missed a hole.—The cunning villain goes there and says that I—yes, Babette—that I was a traitor myself; and I said to the lords, 'Do I look like a traitor?'—My petticoats, Babette; how stupid you are, why, your eyes are half shut now; you know I always wear the blue first, then the green, and the red last, and yet you will give me the first which comes.—He's a handsome lord, that Duke of Portland; he was one of the *bon* —— before King William went over and conquered England, and he was made a lord for his valour.—My ruff, Babette. The Dutch are a brave nation.—My bustle now.—How much beer did you give the officers? Mind you take care of everything while I am gone. I shall be home by nine, I dare say. I suppose they are going to try him now, that he may be hanged at sunrise. I knew how it would be. Yes, yes, Mr Vanslyperken, every dog has his day; and there's an end of you, and of your cur also, I've a notion."

The widow being now duly equipped, walked down stairs to them, and proceeded with the officers to the Stadt House. She was brought into the presence of Mynheer Engelback, who held the office of provost.

"Here is the widow Vandersloosh, mynheer."

"Very well," replied Engelback, who was in a very bad humour at the unsuccessful search after the conspirators, "away with her."

"Away! where?" exclaimed the widow.

Engelback did not condescend to make a reply. The officers were mute; but one stout man on either side seized her arm and led her away, notwithstanding expostulation, and some resistance on her part.

"Where am I going? what is all this?" exclaimed the widow, terrified; but there was no answer.

At last they came to a door, held open already by another man with a bunch of keys. The terrified woman perceived that it was a paved stone cell, with a brick arch over it; in short, a dungeon. The truth flashed upon her, for the first time. It was she who had been arrested for treason. But before she could shriek she was shoved in, and the door closed and locked upon her; and the widow sank down into a sitting posture on the ground, overcome with astonishment and indignation. "Was it possible? Had the villain prevailed?" was the question, which she asked herself over and over again, changing alternately from sorrow to indignation: at one time wringing her hands, and at others exclaiming, "Well, well, Mr Vanslyperken, we shall see."

Chapter XLIX

In which is related much appertaining to the "pomp and glorious circumstance" of war.

THE arrival of Ramsay and his party was so unexpected, that, at first, Lady Barclay imagined they had been betrayed, and that the boat was filled with armed men from the king's cutter, who had come on shore with a view of forcing an entrance into the cave. In a minute every preparation was made for defence; for it had long been arranged, that, in case of an unexpected attack, the women should make all the resistance in their power, and which the nature of the place enabled them to do.

But, as many observed, the party, although coming from the cutter, and not badly armed, did not appear to advance in a hostile manner. After waiting some time near the boat, they advanced, each with a box on his shoulder; but what those boxes might be was a puzzle; they might be hand-grenades for throwing into the cave. However, they were soon down to the rock at which the ladder was let down, and then Smallbones stood up with a musket in his hands, with his straddling legs and short petticoat, and bawled out, "Who comes there?"

Ramsay, who was assisting Wilhelmina, looked up surprised at this singular addition to the occupants of the cave. And Wilhelmina also looked at him, and said, "Can that be a woman, Ramsay?"

"At all events, I've not the honour of her acquaintance. But she is pointing her musket,—we are friends," cried Ramsay. "Tell Mistress Alice it is Ramsay."

Smallbones turned round and reported the answer; and

then, in obedience to his orders from Mistress Alice, he cried out, in imitation of the sentinels, "Pass, Ramsay, and all's well!" presented his arms, and made a flying leap off the rock where he stood, down on the platform, that he might lower the ladder as soon as Ramsay was up, who desired everybody might be sent down to secure the boxes of specie as fast as they could, lest the cutter's people, releasing themselves, should attempt an attack. Now, there was no more concealment necessary, and the women as well as the men went down the precipitous path and brought up the treasure, while Ramsay introduced Wilhelmina to Lady Barclay, and, in a brief, but clear narrative, told her all that had passed, and what they had now to expect. There was not a moment for delay; the cutter's people might send the despatches over land if they thought of it, and be there as soon, if not sooner than themselves. Nancy Corbett was summoned immediately, and her instructions given. The whole of the confederates at Portsmouth were to come over to the cave with what they could collect and carry about their persons; and, in case of the cutter sending over land, with the precaution of being in disguise. Of arms and ammunition there was sufficient in the cave, which Ramsay now felt was to be defended to the last, until they could make a retreat over to the other side of the channel. In half an hour, Nancy was gone, and that very night had arrived at Portsmouth, and given notice to the whole of the confederates. Upon consultation, it was considered that the best disguise would be that of females; and, in consequence, they were all so attired, and before morning had all passed over, two or three in a boat, and landed at Ryde, where they were collected by Moggy Salisbury, who alone, of the party, knew the way to the retreat. They walked across the island by two and three, one party just keeping sight of the next ahead of them, and arrived without suspicion or interruption, conducted by Moggy Salisbury, Lazarus the Jew, and sixteen stout and desperate men, who had remained secreted in the Jew's house, ready to obey any order, however desperate the risk might be, of their employers.

When they were all assembled at the brow of the precipice, with the exception of Lazarus, who looked like a little old woman, a more gigantic race of females was never seen; for, determined upon a desperate resistance if discovered, they had their buff jerkins under their female garments. They were soon in the cave, and very busy, under Ramsay's directions, preparing against the expected attack. Sir Robert Barclay, with his boat, had been over two days before, and it was not known when he would return. That his presence was most anxiously looked for may be readily conceived, as his boat's crew would double their force if obliged to remain there; and his boat would enable them, with the one brought by Ramsay, to make their escape without leaving one behind, before the attack could be made.

Nancy Corbett, as the reader may have observed, did not return to the cave with the conspirators. As she was not suspected, she determined to remain at Portsmouth till the last, and watch the motions of the authorities.

The cutter did not arrive till the evening of the second day, and the despatches were not delivered to the admiral till the third morning, when all was bustle and preparation. Nancy Corbett was everywhere, she found out what troops were ordered to embark on the expedition, and she was acquainted with some of the officers, as well as the sergeants and corporals; an idea struck her which she thought she could turn to advantage. She slipped into the barrack-yard, and to where the men were being selected, and was soon close to a sergeant whom she was acquainted with.

"So, you've an expedition on hand, Sergeant Tanner."

"Yes, Mistress Corbett, and I'm one of the party."

"I wish you joy," replied Nancy, sarcastically.

"Oh, it's nothing, Mistress Corbett, nothing at all, only some smugglers in a cave; we'll soon rout them out."

"I've heard a different account from the admiral's clerk."

"Why, what have you heard?"

"First, tell me how many men are ordered out."

"A hundred rank and file—eight non-commissioned officers—two lieutenants—one captain—and one major."

"Bravo, sergeant, you'll carry all before you."

"Why, I hope so, Mistress Corbett, especially as we are to have the assistance of the cutter's crew."

"Better and better still," replied Nancy, ironically. "I wish you joy of your laurels, sergeant, ha, ha, ha."

"Why do you laugh, Mistress Corbett, and what is that you have heard at the admiral's office?"

"What you may hear yourself, and what I know to be true; there is not a single smuggler in the cave."

"No!" exclaimed the sergeant. "What, nobody there?"

"Yes, there is somebody there, the cave has been chosen by the smugglers to land their goods in."

"But some of them must be there in charge of the goods."

"Yes, so there are, but they are all women, the smugglers' wives, who live there; what an expedition! Let me see:—one gallant major, one gallant captain, two gallant lieutenants, eight gallant non-commissioned officers, and a hundred gallant soldiers of the Buffs, all going to attack, and rout, and defeat a score of old women."

"But you're joking, Mistress Nancy."

"Upon my life I'm not, sergeant, you'll find it true; the admiral's ashamed of the whole affair, and the cutter's crew swear they won't fire a single shot."

"By the god of war!" exclaimed the sergeant, "but this is cursed bad news you bring, Mistress Corbett."

"Not at all; your regiment will become quite the fancy, you'll go by the name of the lady-killers, ha, ha, ha. I wish you joy, sergeant, ha, ha, ha."

Nancy Corbett knew well the power of ridicule, she left the sergeant, and was accosted by one of the lieutenants; she rallied him in the same way.

"But are you really in earnest, Nancy?" said Lieutenant Dillon, at last.

"Upon my soul I am; but, at the same time I hear, that they will fight hard, for they are well-armed and desperate, like their husbands, and they swear that they'll all die to a woman, before they yield; so now we shall see who fights best, the women or the men. I'll back my own sex for a gold Jacobus, lieutenant: will you take the bet?"

"Good God, how very annoying! I can't, I won't order the men to fire at women; I could not do so if they were devils incarnate; a woman is a woman still."

"And never the worse for being brave, Lieutenant Dillon; as I said to Sergeant Tanner, your regiment, after this, will always go by the name of the lady-killers."

"D—n!" exclaimed the lieutenant; "but now I recollect there must be more there; those who had possession of the cutter and who landed in her boat."

"Yes, with forty boxes of gold they say; but do you think they would be such fools as to remain there and allow you to take their money—that boat started for France yesterday night with all the treasure, and are now safe at Cherbourg. I know it for a fact, for one of the men's wives who lives here, showed me a letter to that effect, from her husband, in which he requests her to follow him. But I must go now, good-bye, Mr Lady-killer."

The lieutenant repeated what Nancy had told him to the officers, and the major was so much annoyed, that he went up to the admiral and stated what the report was, and that there were only women to contend with.

"It is mentioned in the despatches, I believe," observed the admiral, "that there are only women supposed to be in the cave; but the smugglers who were on board the cutter——"

"Have left with their specie yesternight, admiral; so that we shall gain neither honour nor profit."

"At all events, you will have the merit of obeying your orders, Major Lincoln."

The major made no reply, but went away very much dissatisfied. In the meantime, the sergeant had communicated with his non-commissioned officers and the privates ordered on the duty, and the discontent was universal. Most of the men swore that they would not pull a trigger against women, if they were shot for it, and the disaffection almost amounted to mutiny. Nancy, in the meantime, had not been idle, she had found means to speak with the boats' crews of the *Yungfrau*, stated the departure of the smugglers with their gold, and the fact that they were to fight with nothing but women, that the soldiers had vowed that they would not fire a shot, and that Moggy Salisbury, who was with them, swore that she would hoist up her smock as a flag, and fight to the last. This was soon known on board of the *Yungfrau*, and gave great disgust to every one of the crew, who declared to a man, that they would not act against petticoats, much less fire a shot at Moggy Salisbury.

What a mountain of mischief can be heaped up by the insidious tongue of one woman!

After this explanation, it may be supposed that the zeal of the party despatched was not very great. The fact is, they were all sulky, from the major downwards, among the military, and from Vanslyperken downwards, among the naval portion of the detachment. Nancy Corbett, satisfied with having effected her object, had crossed over the night before, and joined her companions in the cave, and what was extremely fortunate, on the same night Sir Robert Barclay came over in the lugger, and finding how matters stood, immediately hoisted both the boats up on the rocks, and taking up all the men, prepared with his followers for a vigorous resistance, naturally to be expected from those whose lives depended upon the issue of the conflict.

Next morning the cutter was seen coming down with the boats in tow, hardly stemming the flood, from the lightness of the breeze, when Nancy Corbett requested to speak with Sir Robert Barclay. She stated to him what she had done, and the dissatisfaction among the troops and seamen in consequence, and submitted to him the propriety of all the smugglers being dressed as women, as it would operate more in their favour than if they had fifty more men to defend the cave. Sir Robert perceived the good sense of this suggestion, and consulted with Ramsay, who strongly urged the suggestion being acted upon. The men were summoned, and the affair explained to them, and the consequence was, that there was a scene of mirth and laughter, which ended with every man being fitted with woman's attire. The only one who remained in the dress of a man was a woman, Wilhelmina Krause, but she was to remain in the cave with the other women, and take no part in the coming fray.

Chapter L

In which the officers, non-commissioned officers, and rank and file, are all sent to the right about.

ABOUT noon the *Yungfrau* hove-to off the cave, and the troops were told off into the boats.

About half-past twelve the troops were in the boats all ready.

About one Mr Vanslyperken had hoisted out his own boats, and they were manned. Mr Vanslyperken, with his pistols in his belt, and his sword drawn, told Major Lincoln that he was all ready. Major Lincoln, with his spy-glass in his hand, stepped into the boat with Mr Vanslyperken, and the whole detachment pulled for the shore, and landed in the small cove, where they found the smugglers' boats hoisted up on the rocks, at which the men appeared to be rejoiced, as they took it for granted that they would find some men to fight with instead of women. The major headed his men, and they commenced a scramble up the rocks and arrived at the foot of the high rock which formed the platform above at the mouth of the cave, when the major cried "Halt!"—a very judicious order, considering that it was impossible to go any further. The soldiers looked about everywhere, but could find no cave, and after an hour's strict search, Major Lincoln and his officers, glad to be rid of the affair, held a consultation, and it was agreed that the troops should be re-embarked. The men were marched down again very hot from their exertions, and thus the expedition would have ended without bloodshed, had it not been for the incautious behaviour of a woman. That woman was Moggy Salisbury, who, having observed that the troops were re-embarking, took the opportunity, while Sir Robert and all the men were keeping close, to hoist up a certain under-garment to a pole, as if in derision, thus betraying the locality of the cave, and running the risk of sacrificing the whole party in it. This, as it was going up, caught the eye of one of the seamen in the boat, who cried out, "There goes the ensign up to the peak at last."

"Where?" exclaimed the major, pulling out his telescope, "Yes, by heavens! there it is—and there then must be the cave."

Neither Sir Robert nor any of the conspirators were aware of this manœuvre of Moggy's; for Smallbones, perceiving what she had done, hauled it down again in a minute afterwards. But it had been hoisted, and the major considered it his duty to return, so once more the troop ascended the precipitous path.

Moggy then went into the cave. "They have found us out, sir," said she, "they point to us, and are coming up again. I will stand as sentry. The men won't fire at me, and if they do I don't care."

Sir Robert and Ramsay were in close consultation. It appeared to them that by a bold manœuvre they would be able to get out of their scrape. The wind had gone down altogether, the sea was as smooth as glass, and there was every appearance of a continued calm.

"If we could manage it—and I think we may—then the sooner the affair is brought to an issue the better."

Moggy had now taken a musket on her shoulder, and was pacing up and down the edge of the flat in imitation of a sentry. She was soon pointed out, and a titter ran through the whole line: at last, as the major approached, she called out,

"I say, soger, what are you doing here? keep off, or I'll put a bullet in your jacket."

"My good woman," replied the major, while his men laughed, "we do not want to hurt you, but you must surrender."

"Surrender!" cried Moggy, "who talks of surrender? —hoist the colours there."

Up went the chemise to the end of the pole, and Smallbones grinned as he hoisted it.

"My good woman, we must obey our orders."

"And I must obey mine," retorted Moggy. "Turn out the guard there."

All the women now made their appearance, as had been arranged, with muskets on their shoulders, headed by little Lilly, with her drawn sword.

The sight of the child commanding the detachment was hailed with loud cheers and laughter.

"That will do, that will do," cried Sir Robert, fearful for Lilly, "let them come in again."

"They'll not fire first at all events," cried Moggy, "never fear, sir. Guard, turn in," continued she; upon which, Lilly and her squadron then disappeared.

"Upon my honour this is too ridiculous," said Lieutenant Dillon.

"Upon my soul I don't know what is to be done," rejoined the major.

"Moggy, we must commence hostilities somehow or another," cried Sir Robert from within. Smallbones here came out with his musket to release Moggy, and Moggy retired into the cave.

The major, who imagined that there must be a path to the cave on the other side, now advanced with the determination of finding it out, and somehow or another putting an end to this unusual warfare.

"If you please you'll keep back, or I'll fire," cried Smallbones, levelling his musket.

The major went on, heedless of the threat. Smallbones discharged his piece, and the major fell.

"Confound that she-devil!—Are you hurt, major?" cried Lieutenant Dillon.

"Yes, I am—I can't move."

Another shot was now fired, and the sergeant fell.

"Hell and flames! what must we do?"

But now the whole party of smugglers poured out of the cave as women with bonnets on, and commenced a murderous fire upon the troops who fell in all directions. The captain who had assumed the command, now attempted to find his way to the other side of the cave, where he had no doubt he should find the entrance, but in so doing the soldiers were exposed to a most galling fire, without being able to return it.

At first, the troops refused to fire again, for that they had to deal with the smugglers' wives, they made certain of: even in the thickest of the smoke there was nothing masculine to be seen; and those troops who were at a greater distance, and who could return the fire, did not. They were rather amused at the character of the women, and not being aware that their comrades were falling so fast, remained inactive. But there is a limit to even gallantry, and as the wounded men were carried past them, their indignation was roused, and, at last, the fire was as warmly returned, but before that took place, one half of the detachment were *hors de combat*.

All the assistance which they might have received from the covering party of sailors on the beach, was neutralised; they did not know how much the soldiers had suffered, and although they fired in pursuance of orders, they would not take any aim.

For some time the soldiers were forced on to the eastern side of the rock, which, as the reader may recollect, was much more precipitous than the western side, where it was descended from by the ladder. Here they were at the mercy of the conspirators, who, concealed below the masses of the rock on the platform, took unerring aim. The captain had fallen, Lieutenant Dillon was badly wounded and led back to the boats, and the command had devolved upon a young man who had but just joined the regiment, and who was ignorant of anything like military tactics, even if they could have been brought into play upon the service.

"Do you call this fighting with women, Sergeant Tanner?" said one of the men. "I've seen service, but such a murderous fire I was never in. Why, we've lost two-thirds of our men."

"And shall lose them all before we find out the mouth of this cursed cave. The regiment has lost its character for ever, and I don't care how soon a bullet settles my business."

Ramsay now detached a party of the men to fire at the covering party of seamen who were standing by the boats in the cove and who were unprotected, while his men were concealed behind the masses of rocks. Many fell, wounded or killed; and Vanslyperken, after shifting about from one position to another, ordered the wounded men to be put into his boat, and with two hands he pulled off as he said to procure more ammunition, leaving the remainder of his detachment on shore, to do as well as they could.

"I thought as how this work would be too warm for him," observed Bill Spurey.

"Yes," replied Short, who, at the moment received a bullet in his thigh, and fell down among the rocks.

The fire upon the seamen continued to be effective. Move from their post they did not, but one after another they sank wounded on the ground. The soldiers who were now without any one to command them, for those who had forced their way to the western side of the rock, finding that advance or retreat was alike impossible, crawled under the sides of the precipice to retreat from a murderous fire which they could not return. The others were scattered here and there, protecting themselves as well as they could below the masses of stone, and returning the fire of the conspirators surely and desperately. But of the hundred men sent on the expedition, there were not twenty who were not killed or wounded, and nearly the whole detachment of seamen had fallen where they stood.

It was then four o'clock, the few men who remained unhurt were suffering from the extreme heat and exertion, and devoured with thirst. The wounded cried for water. The sea was still, calm, and smooth as a mirror; not a breath of wind blew to cool the fevered brows of the wounded men, and the cutter, with her sails hanging listless, floated about on the glassy water, about a quarter of a mile from the beach.

"Now is our time, Sir Robert."

"Yes, Ramsay—now for one bold dash—off with this woman's gear, my men—buckle on your swords and put pistols in your belts."

In a very short time this order was complied with, and, notwithstanding some of the men were wounded in this day's affair, as well as in the struggle for the deck of the cutter, the three bands from Amsterdam, Portsmouth, and Cherbourg mustered forty resolute and powerful men.

The ladder was lowered down, and they descended. Sir Robert ordered Jemmy Ducks and Smallbones to remain and haul up the ladder again, and the whole body hastened down to the cove, headed by Sir Robert and Ramsay, seized the boats, and shoved off for the cutter.

Chapter LI

In which the Jacobite cause is triumphant by sea as well as by land.

THE great difficulty which Sir Robert Barclay had to surmount, was to find the means of transport over the channel for their numerous friends, male and female, then collected in the cave: now that their retreat was known, it was certain that some effective measures would be taken by government, by which, if not otherwise reduced, they would be surrounded and starved into submission.

The two boats which they had were not sufficient for the transport of so numerous a body, consisting now of nearly one hundred and fifty individuals, and their means of subsistence were limited to a few days.

The arrival of the cutter with the detachments was no source of regret to Sir Robert, who hoped, by the defeat of the troops, to obtain their boats, and thus make his escape; but this would have been difficult, if not impossible, if the cutter had been under command, as she carried four guns, and could have prevented their escape, even if she did not destroy the boats; but when Sir Robert observed that it had fallen calm, it at once struck him, that if, after defeating the troops, they could board and carry the cutter, that all their difficulties were over: then they could embark the whole of their people, and run her over to Cherbourg.

This was the plan proposed by Sir Robert, and agreed to by Ramsay, and to accomplish this, now that the troops were put to the rout, they had made a rush for, and obtained the boats. As for the women left in the cave, they were perfectly secure for the time, as, without scaling-ladders, there was no possibility of the remaining troops, even if they were rallied, being able to effect anything.

That part of the crew of the *Yungfrau* who had perceived them rush down to the beach, reported it to Mr

Vanslyperken, who had gone down to his cabin, not choosing to take any further part in the affray, or to risk his valuable life. Vanslyperken came on deck, where he witnessed the manning of the boats, and their pushing out of the cove.

"They are coming to attack us, sir," said Coble, who had been left in charge of the cutter when Mr Vanslyperken went on shore.

Mr Vanslyperken turned pale as a sheet; his eyes were fixed upon the form of Ramsay, standing up on the stern-sheets of the first boat, with his sabre raised in the air—he immediately recognised him, panted for breath, and could make no reply.

The crew of the cutter, weakened as they were by the loss of most of their best men, flew to their arms; Coble, Cornelius, and Jansen, and Corporal Van Spitter were to be seen in the advance, encouraging them.

"Gott for dam—let us have one slap for it," cried Jansen.

"Mein Gott, yes," shouted the corporal.

Vanslyperken started up. "It's no use, my men—it's madness—useless sacrifice of life; they are two to one—we must surrender. Go down below, all of you—do you hear, obey my orders?"

"Yes, and report them, too, to the admiral," replied Coble; "I never heard such an order given in my born days, and fifty odd years I have served in the king's fleet."

"Corporal Van Spitter, I order you below—all of you below," cried Vanslyperken; "I command here—will you obey, sir?"

"Mein Gott, yes," replied the corporal, walking away, and coolly descending the ladder.

The boats were now within ten yards of the cutter, and the men stood irresolute; the corporal obeying orders had disheartened them: some of them followed the corporal.

"It's no use," said Coble, "I sees now it's of no use; it's only being cut to pieces for nothing, my men; but

I won't leave the deck." Coble threw away his cutlass, and walked aft; the other men did the same, all but Jansen, who still hesitated. Coble caught the cutlass out of his hand, and threw it overboard, just as the boats dashed alongside.

"Gott for dam," muttered Jansen, folding his arms and facing the men who jumped on the cutter's decks. Ramsay, who was first on board when he perceived that the men were standing on the decks without making any opposition, turned and threw up the points of the swords of some of his men who were rushing blindly on, and, in a minute all was quiet on the decks of the *Yungfrau*. Mr Vanslyperken was not to be seen. At the near approach of the boats he had hastened into his cabin and locked himself in; his only feeling being, that Ramsay's wrath must cool, and his life be spared.

"My lads," said Sir Robert to the crew of the cutter, "I am very glad that you made no resistance to a force which you could not resist, as I should have been sorry if one of you had lost his life; but you must now go down below and leave the cutter's deck in our possession. Perhaps it would be better if some of you took one of your boats and went on shore to pick up your messmates who are wounded."

"If you please, sir, we will," said Coble, coming forward, "and the cutter is yours, as far as we are concerned. We will make no attempts to retake her, at all events, for your kindness in thinking of our poor fellows lying there on the beach. I think you will promise that, my lads," continued Coble, turning to the men.

"Yes, we promise that," said the men.

Coble then took the crew with him and pulled on shore to the cove, on the margin of which they found all their men lying either killed or wounded. Dick Short, Spurey, and nine others were taken on board: those that were quite dead were left upon the sand. Leaving only ten men on board the cutter, which, however, was sufficient to cope with the few of the *Yungfrau* remaining on board, had they been inclined to forfeit their word, Sir Robert and Ramsay then returned with the rest of the party to the boats, and pulled on shore, for the rest of their assailants were not subdued; about twenty of the soldiers still remained unhurt and were sitting down on the rocks.

Ramsay, as soon as he landed, showed a white handkerchief on a bayonet fixed to the muzzle of a musket.

"Sergeant Tanner," said one of the men, "there's a flag of truce."

"Is there? I'm not sorry for it,—they are two to one even now. I'll go forward to meet it."

The sergeant advanced to meet Ramsay.

"We might, if we pleased, oblige you to surrender or cut you to pieces—that you must own; but we have no wish to hurt you—there are too many good men dead already."

"That's true," replied the sergeant, "but it's one comfort you have turned out at last to be men and not women."

"We have; but to the terms. You were sent to take possession of the cave,—you shall have possession as soon as we are gone, if you will draw off your party higher up this cliff and allow us to embark without molestation. If you do not immediately accept these terms, we shall certainly attack you, or you may do better if you please—pile your muskets, collect your wounded men, bring them down to the beach all ready to put into the boats, which, as soon as we are safe, we will give you possession of—now is it a truce or not?—you must be immediate."

"Yes, then, it is a truce, for I see no chance of better terms. I am commanding officer, and you have the faith of Sergeant Tanner."

The sergeant then returned, and when half way, called to his men:

"Party fall in—pile arms." The soldiers, worn out by the long conflict, and aware that they had no chance against such superior numbers, gladly obeyed, and were now divided in sections of three and four, collecting the wounded and carrying them down to the cove.

Sir Robert and his men hastened to the rock—the ladder was lowered, and all was on the alert for embarkation—Lady Barclay and Lilly flew into his arms, while Wilhelmina hung on Ramsay; but they allowed but a short time for endearment—time was too precious. The luggage had all been prepared and the chests of specie were lowered, the bundles thrown down, and, in a quarter of an hour, the cave was cleared of all that they could take away with them.

The women then descended, and all hands were employed carrying away the specie and luggage down to the boats. As soon as one boat was loaded with the boxes of money, Lady Ramsay, Lilly, and Wilhelmina were put in it, and one half of the men went with them on board of the cutter where Coble had already arrived with the wounded seamen. Ramsay remained with the other boat to embark the women and luggage; when all was in, he called the sergeant, pointed out to him the ladder, and told him that he might find something worth his trouble in the cave.

"Is there a drop of anything to drink, sir? for we who are whole are dying with thirst, and it's cruel to hear the poor wounded fellows beg for water."

"You will find both water and spirits in plenty there, sergeant, and you may tell your own story when you arrive at Portsmouth, we shall never contradict you."

"The list of killed, wounded, and missing, will tell the story fast enough," replied the sergeant; "but run up there, my lads, and get some water for these poor fellows. Good-bye, sir, and many thanks."

"Good-bye to you, Sergeant Tanner," said one of the women in the boat.

"Nancy Corbett, by all that's wonderful!" cried the sergeant.

"I told you so, sergeant—you'll never lose the name of lady-killer."

"Pretty lady killing," muttered the sergeant, turning away in a rage. Ramsay took the boats on board, and, as soon as they were cleared, they were towed on shore to the cove by some of the *Yungfrau's* men.

During this time the ladies, as well as the women, had remained aft on deck, Vanslyperken having locked himself up in his cabin; but Sir Robert now ordered his men to force the cabin door, and take Mr Vanslyperken forward on the lower deck. When the door was opened, Vanslyperken was found in his bed more dead than alive: he was pulled out and dragged forward. The ladies were then handed below, and, as soon as the specie had been put down, and the luggage cleared from the upper deck, the women were ordered to go down on the lower deck, and Mr Vanslyperken ordered to be brought up.

Chapter LII

In which a great deal of loyalty is shown to counterbalance the treason of Vanslyperken.

WE must not, however, forget the syndic and the widow Vandersloosh, whom we left in confinement at Amsterdam. We left Mynheer Krause smoking his pipe, and showing to those about him how great a great man always proves himself when under adversity. The widow also, had she performed in public, would have been acknowledged to have been a great woman. She could not but lament the present, for she was on the floor of a dungeon, so she occasionally wrung her hands; but she looked forward to the future, and to better times, not abandoning herself to despair, but comforting herself with hope, as might have been clearly proved by her constant repetition of these words: "Well, well, Mr Vanslyperken, we shall see."

That the night appeared long to both parties is not to be denied, but the longest night will have its end, so long as the world continues to turn round; the consequence was, that the morning came as usual to the syndic, although the widow from the peculiarity of her situation, had not the same advantage.

After morning, comes breakfast, in the natural order of mundane affairs, and kings, being but men, and subject to the same wants as other mortals, his Majesty, King William, sat down, and despatched a very hasty meal, in company with his Grace the Duke of Portland, and the Right Honourable the Lord Albemarle. History does not record, as it sometimes does in works of this description, by what viands his Majesty's appetite was stimulated; we must therefore pass it over, and as his Majesty did on that occasion, as soon as breakfast was over, proceed to business.

"Have you received information, my Lord Albemarle, how many of the conspirators have been seized?"

"May it please your Majesty, I am sorry to inform you, that all who were innocent have been imprisoned, and all who were guilty, have escaped."

Upon this intelligence his Majesty looked very grave.

"How do you mean, my lord?" said he, after a pause.

"The conspirators have all received some friendly notice, and the only two who are in custody are the syndic, Mynheer Krause, and the woman who keeps the Lust Haus."

"And you put the syndic down as an innocent person, my lord?"

"If your Majesty will be pleased to read this communication," replied Lord Albemarle, presenting Ramsay's letter and enclosures, "you will then be of my opinion."

King William took the letter and read it. "What Ramsay—he who was attainted with Sir Robert Barclay?"

"The same, your Majesty."

"So near us, and escaped—but what credence would you place in him?"

"Every credence, may it please your Majesty. I believe him to be incapable of a lie."

"A traitor, like him!"

"A traitor to your Majesty, but most true to his Catholic Majesty, King James that was. But if I venture to point out to your Majesty, the enclosures prove that Lieutenant Vanslyperken's word is not of much value. He, at least, is a double traitor."

"Yes, a little hanging will do him no harm—you are sure this is his writing?"

"There can be no doubt of it, your Majesty, I have compared it."

"You will see to this, my lord: and now to the syndic."

"He has, as your Majesty will perceive, been grossly deceived, and suspected without reason."

"And the woman?——"

"Was here yesterday, and fully convinced me that Vanslyperken was a traitor, and that she was innocent. His Grace of Portland was present."

"Well, my lord, you may give orders for their release; of course a little surveillance will be advisable. You will justify the proceedings to the council, this afternoon."

"But may I presume to submit to your Majesty, that the public affront offered to the syndic should be repaired."

"Certainly—send for him," replied his Majesty, carelessly. "I will receive him to-morrow morning," and his Majesty left the room.

Lord Albemarle immediately despatched a courier with an order for the release of the syndic and the Frau Vandersloosh, with a note to the former, stating that his Majesty would receive him on the following day at noon. But while this act of justice had been preparing at the palace of the Hague, there were other acts, not quite so justifiable performing at the town of Amsterdam.

The sun made its appearance more than an hour, before the troops of the royal Guard. Mobs were collected in knots in the street, and in front of the Hotel de Ville, or

Stadt House, and the object of their meeting, was to canvas the treason and imprisonment of the syndic, Mynheer Van Krause. "Shame—shame,"—"Death to the traitor,"—"Tear him to pieces,"—and "Long life to King William," were the first solitary remarks made—the noise and hubbub increased. The small knots of people gradually joined together, until they formed a large mob, all burning with loyalty, and each individual wishing to give a practical evidence of it—again were the cries of "Long live the King!" and "Death to traitors!" to be heard, with loud huzzas. A confused din followed, and the mob appeared, as if simultaneously, to be all impelled in one direction. At last the word was given, which they all waited for. "To his house—to his house—down with it—death to the traitor!" and the loyal mob hastened on, each individual eager to be first to prove his loyalty, by helping himself to Mynheer Krause's goods and chattels.

In the low countries, this species of loyalty always has been, and is now very much the fashion. In ten minutes, the gates were forced open—old Koop knocked down, and trod under foot till he was dead—every article of value that was portable, was secured; chairs, tables, glasses, not portable, were thrown out of the window; Wilhelmina's harp and pianoforte battered to fragments; beds, bedding, everything flew about in the air, and then the fragments of the furniture were set fire to, and in less than an hour Mynheer Krause's splendid house was burning furiously, while the mob cheered and cried, "Long live King William!"

Before the courier could arrive from the Hague, all that was left of Mr Krause's property was the bare walls. Merchandises, everything was consumed, and part of the building had fallen into the canal and choked it up, while fifteen schuyts waiting to be discharged of their cargoes had been obliged to retreat from the fury of the flames, the phlegmatic skippers looking on with their pipes in their mouths, and their hands in their wide breeches-pockets.

The loyal mob having effected their object, gradually retired. It is singular, that popular feeling is always expressed in the same way. Had the mob collected for disloyal purposes, they would have shown their disloyalty just in the like manner, only it would have been the Stadt House instead of that of Mynheer Krause.

But now there was a fresh impetus given to the feelings of the mob. The news had been spread like wildfire, that Mynheer the syndic had been proved innocent, and ordered to be immediately liberated, and was sent for by his Majesty; upon which, the mob were undecided, whether they should prove their indignation, at this unjust imprisonment of their worthy magistrate, by setting fire to some public building, or by carrying him in triumph to his own house, which they forgot they had burnt down. Fortunately they decided upon the latter, they surrounded the Stadt House with cries of "Long life to our worthy syndic—prosperity to Mynheer Krause," and rushing up stairs, they caught him in their arms, and carried him triumphantly through the streets bringing him at last to the smoking ruins of his own house, and there they left him; they had done all they could, they had carried him there in triumph, but, as for building the house up again, that was impossible; so, as Mynheer Krause looked with dismay at the wreck of all his property, the loyal mob dispersed, each feeling that he had been a little too hasty in possessing himself of a small share of it. What a fine thing is loyalty! Mynheer Krause found himself alone; he looked with scorn and indignation upon the scene of violence, and then walked away to an hotel, particularly disgusted with the loyal cry of "Long live King William."

In the meantime, the door of the dungeon where the widow Vandersloosh was incarcerated was thrown open, and she was informed that she was no longer a prisoner. The widow indignant that she should have been confined for her loyalty, raved and walked majestically out of the Stadt House, not deigning to answer to the compliments offered to her by some of the inferior officers. Her bosom swelled with indignation, and she was determined to tell his Majesty a bit of her mind, if she should obtain access to him; and the next day she took the trouble to go all the way to the Hague, again to see his Majesty, but his Majesty wasn't at home, and Lord Albemarle to whom she sent in, was indisposed, and his Grace the Duke of Portland was particularly engaged; so the widow had the journey for nothing, and she declared to Babette, that she never would put her foot under the palace roof again as long as she lived.

But, although Madam Vandersloosh was not received at court that day, the syndic Mynheer Krause was; when he sent in his name, Lord Albemarle led the syndic by the hand to his Majesty.

"We have been too hasty, Mynheer Krause," said his Majesty, with a gracious smile.

Mynheer bowed low.

"I regret to hear that the populace in their loyalty have burnt down your house, Mr Krause—they were too hasty."

Mynheer Krause made another low bow.

"You will continue your office of syndic of the town of Amsterdam."

"Pardon me, your Majesty," replied Mynheer Krause respectfully, but firmly, "I have obeyed your summons to appear in your presence, but will request that your Majesty will release me from the burden. I have come to lay my chain and staff of office at your Majesty's feet, it being my intention to quit the town."

"You are too hasty, Mynheer Krause," replied his Majesty with displeasure.

"May it please your Majesty," replied Krause. "He who has been confined as a prisoner in the Stadt House, is not fit to exercise his duties there as a judge; I have served your Majesty many years with the utmost zeal and fidelity. In return, I have been imprisoned and my property destroyed, I must now return to a station more suitable to my present condition, and once more with every assurance of loyalty, I beg to be permitted to lay my insignia of office at your Majesty's feet."

Mynheer Krause suited the action to the word. The king frowned and turned away to the window, and Mynheer Krause perceiving that his Majesty's back was turned upon him, walked out of the door.

"Too hasty," thought Mynheer Krause, "I am loyal and thrown into prison, and am expected to be satisfied with the plea of being too hasty. My house is burnt down, and the plundering mob have been too hasty. Well—well—it is fortunate I took Ramsay's advice, my house and what was in it was a trifle; but if all my gold at Hamburgh and Frankfort, and in the charge of Ramsay had been there, and I had been made a beggar, all the satisfaction I should have received would have been a smile, and the excuse of being too hasty. I wonder where my daughter and Ramsay are? I long to join them."

From which mental soliloquy, it will be evident to the reader, that Mynheer Krause's loyalty had been considerably diminished, perhaps thinking that he had paid too dear for the commodity.

Upon his return, Mynheer Krause publicly announced that he had resigned the office of syndic, much to the astonishment of those who heard of it, and much to the delight of his very particular friend Engelback, who, the next morning set off for the Hague, and had an interview with his Grace the Duke of Portland, the result of which was, that upon grounds best known to the parties; for history will not reveal everything, Mynheer Engelback was recommended to fill the office of syndic of the town of Amsterdam, vacant by the resignation of Mynheer Krause; and that in consequence of this, all those who took off their hats to Mynheer Krause but two days before, and kept them on when they met Mynheer Engelback, now kept them on when they met Mynheer Krause, and pulled them off very politely to Mynheer Krause's very particular friend, Mynheer Engelback.

Chapter LIII

Trial and execution of two of the principal personages in our history.

We left Sir Robert Barclay on the deck of the cutter, the ladies and women sent down below, and Mr Vanslyperken on the point of being dragged aft by two of Sir Robert's men. The crew of the *Yungfrau*, at the time, were on the lower deck, some assisting the wounded men, others talking with Jemmy Salisbury and his wife, whom they were astonished to find among the assailants.

"Why, Jemmy, how did you get a berth among those chaps?"

"I'll tell you," said Moggy, interrupting: "when he was last at Portsmouth, they heard him playing his fiddle and singing, and they took such a fancy to him, that they were determined to have him to amuse them in the cave. So one evening, they *kidnapped* him, took him away by main force, and kept him a prisoner ever since."

"That's carrying the joke rather too far," observed one of the men.

"Mein Gott! yes," replied the corporal.

"But I am at liberty again now at all events," replied Jemmy, taking the cue from his wife; "and if that chap, Vanslyperken, don't command the cutter any more, which I've a notion he will not, I shall enter as boatswain—heh, Dick."

"Yes," replied Short, who was swinging in his hammock.

"Well—when I found that Jemmy couldn't be found, that my dear darling duck of a husband—my jewel, a box of diamonds (arn't you my Jemmy), didn't I tear my hair, and run about the streets, like a mad woman," continued Moggy. "At last I met with Nancy Corbett, whose husband is one of the gang, and she told me where he was, fiddle and all, and I persuaded her to let me go to him, and that's why we both are here."

This was a good invention of Moggy's, and as there was nobody who took the trouble to disprove it, it was received as not the least apocryphal. But now Mr Vanslyperken was dragged past them by two of the conspirators, and all the men of the *Yungfrau* followed on deck, to see what was to take place.

When Mr Vanslyperken had been brought aft, his legs tottered, and he could hardly stand. His face was livid, and his lips white with fear, and he knew too well that he had little mercy to expect.

"Now, sir," said Sir Robert, with a stern air, "hear the accusation against you, for although we may be lawless, we will still be just. You voluntarily entered into our service, and received our pay. You were one of us, with only this difference, that we have taken up the cause from principle and loyalty, and you joined us from mercenary motives. Still we kept our faith with you; for every service performed, you were well and honourably paid. But you received our money and turned against us; revealed our secrets, and gave information to your government, by which that gentleman" (pointing to Ramsay) "and many others, had not they fortunately received timely notice, would have perished by the gibbet. Now, sir, I wish to know, what you can bring forward in your defence, what have you to urge that you should not die the death which you so traitorously prepared for others."

"Die!" exclaimed Vanslyperken, "no—no—mercy, sir —mercy. I am not fit to die."

"Few are—but this is certain—that a villain like you is not fit to live."

"On my knees, I ask mercy," cried the frightened wretch, dropping down. "Mr Ramsay, speak for me."

"I will speak," replied Ramsay, "but not for you, I will show you, that even if you were to escape us, you would still be hung; for all your extracts of the despatches, I have, with full explanation, put into the hands of the

English government. Do you expect mercy from them—they have not showed much as yet."

"O God—O God!" exclaimed Vanslyperken, throwing himself down on the deck in despair.

"Now, my lads, you have heard the charges against this man, and also that he has no defence to offer, what is your sentence?"

"Death!" exclaimed the conspirators.

"You men, belonging to the cutter, you have heard that this man has betrayed the present government of England, in whose pay and service he was at the time—what is your opinion?"

Hereupon, Obadiah Coble hitched up his trousers, and said, "Why, as a matter of opinion, I agrees with you, sir, whomsoever you may be."

"Mein Gott! yes, sir," exclaimed the corporal.

And all the crew cried out together, "Death—death!" which, by-the-bye, was very mutinous.

"You perceive that you are doubly condemned as a double traitor," said Sir Robert. "So prepare to die; the religion you profess I know not, but the time you will be allowed to make your peace with your God is fifteen minutes."

"Oh!" groaned Vanslyperken, with his face to the deck.

"Up there, my lads, and get a whip on the yard-arm," said Ramsay.

Some of his party went to obey the order, and they were assisted by the seamen of the *Yungfrau*. But while they were getting the whip ready on the starboard, Jemmy Ducks was very quietly employed getting another on the larboard yard-arm, which nobody took notice of.

As soon as the whip, and the cord with the hangman's noose made fast to it, were all ready, it was reported to Sir Robert by Corporal Van Spitter, who stepped up to him with his usual military salute. Sir Robert took off his hat in return. His watch had been held in his hand, from the time that he had passed sentence upon Vanslyperken, who still remained prostrate on the deck.

"It is my duty to inform you, sir, that but five minutes are left of the time awarded to you," said Sir Robert to Vanslyperken.

"Five minutes!" exclaimed Vanslyperken, jumping up from the deck, "but five minutes—to die in five minutes," continued he, looking up with horror at the rope at the yard-arm, and the fatal noose at the end of it, held in the hand of Corporal Van Spitter. "Stop, I have gold—plenty of gold—I can purchase my life."

"Kingdoms would not purchase it," said Sir Robert, scornfully.

"Oh!" exclaimed Vanslyperken, wringing his hands, "must I leave all my gold?"

"You have but two minutes, sir," observed Sir Robert. "Let the rope be put round his neck."

This office was performed by Corporal Van Spitter. The corporal was quite an amateur.

"Mercy, mercy," cried Vanslyperken, again falling on his knees, and holding up his hands.

"Call upon Heaven for mercy, you have but one minute left."

But here an interruption took place.

A female made her appearance on the other side of the deck, dragging, by a cord, the hero of our novel, Snarleyyow, who held back with all his power, jerking his head to the right and to the left, but it was of no use, he was dragged opposite to where Vanslyperken knelt. As the reader may guess, this person was Smallbones, who had tied on a bonnet, and muffled up his face, so as not to be observed when he first went on board. Jemmy Ducks now assisted, and the whip on the larboard yard-arm was made fast to a cord with a running noose, for the hanging of the cur.

The sight roused Vanslyperken. "My dog!" exclaimed he, "woman, leave that dog alone—who are you that dare touch my dog?"

The female turned round, threw off her bonnet and handkerchief and exhibited to the terrified lieutenant, the face of the supposed departed Smallbones.

"Smallbones!" exclaimed the crew of the *Yungfrau* in a breath.

"God of mercy—help me, God of mercy!" cried Vanslyperken, aghast.

"I suppose that you do come for to go to know me now, anyhow," said Smallbones.

"Hath the sea given up its dead?" replied Vanslyperken, in a hollow voice.

"No, it arn't, 'cause why? I never was a drowned," replied Smallbones; "no thanks to you, though; but if so be as I supposes, you be a going to be hung—as I'm a good Christian, I'll forgive you—that is, if you be hung, you know."

Vanslyperken, who now perceived that Smallbones had been by some miracle preserved, recovered himself.

"If you forgive me," replied Vanslyperken, "then pray do not ill-treat my dog."

"I'se not forgiven him, anyhow—I owes him enough, and now I'll have his account settled, by gum. When you goes up there, he goes up here, as sure as I'm Peter Smallbones."

"Be merciful!" exclaimed Vanslyperken, who, strange to say, forgot his own miseries in pleading for his darling cur.

"He be a convicted traitor, and he shall die, by gum!" cried Smallbones, smacking his fist into the palm of his hand.

During the conversation, the time allotted to Vanslyperken had long expired, but the interest occasioned by it had inclined Sir Robert to wait till it was over.

"Enough," cried Sir Robert, "your time is too long expired. Commend your soul to God—let the rope be manned."

"Now Jemmy, stand by to toddle forward," cried Smallbones.

"One moment—I ask but one moment," cried Vanslyperken, much agitated, "only one moment, sir."

"For what?"

"To kiss my poor dog," replied Vanslyperken, bursting into tears; strange and almost ridiculous as was the appeal, there was a seriousness and a pathos in Vanslyperken's words and manner, which affected those who were present like a gleam of sunshine, this one feeling which was unalloyed with baser metal shone upon the close of a worthless and wicked life, Sir Robert nodded his head, and Vanslyperken walked with his rope round his neck over to where the dog was held by Smallbones, bent over the cur and kissed it again and again.

"Enough," cried Sir Robert, "bring him back."

Corporal Van Spitter took hold of Vanslyperken by the arm, and dragged him to the other side of the deck. The unfortunate wretch was wholly absorbed in the fate of his cur, who had endeavoured to follow his master. His eyes were fixed upon Snarleyyow, and Snarleyyow's were fixed upon his master, thus they were permitted to remain for a few seconds, when Sir Robert gave the signal. Away went the line of men who had manned the starboard whip, and away went Jemmy Ducks on the larboard side, and, at the yard-arms of the cutter were suspended the bodies of Vanslyperken and Snarleyyow.

Thus perished one of the greatest scoundrels, and one of the vilest curs, which ever existed. They were damnable in their lives, and in their deaths they were not divided.

By the manuscript records, found in the Jacobite papers, it appears that the double execution took place on the 3rd of August in the year of our Lord, 1700.

Chapter LIV

In which affairs begin to wind up.

THERE are few people whose vindictive feelings are not satisfied with the death of the party against whom those feelings have been excited. The eyes of all on deck (that is all except one) were at first directed to the struggling Vanslyperken, and then, as if sickened at the sight of his sufferings, were turned away with a feeling very near akin to compassion.

One only looked or never thought of Vanslyperken, and that one was Smallbones, who watched the kicking and plunging of his natural enemy, Snarleyyow. Gradually, the dog relaxed his exertions, and Smallbones watched, somewhat doubtful, whether a dog who had defied every other kind of death, would condescend to be hanged. At last, Snarleyyow was quite still. He appeared nearly to have gone to—" Where the wicked cease from troubling, and the weary are at rest."

"He won't a cum to life any more this time," said Smallbones; "but I'll not let you out of my hands yet. They say a cat have nine lives, but, by gum, some dogs have ninety."

There was a dead silence on the deck of the cutter for a quarter of an hour, during which the bodies remained suspended. A breeze then came sweeping along and ruffled the surface of the water. This was of too great importance to allow of further delay. Sir Robert desired the seamen of the *Yungfrau* to come aft, told them he should take their cutter to Cherbourg, to land the women and his own people, and that then they would be free to return to Portsmouth; all that he requested of them was to be quiet and submissive during the short time that he and his party were on board. Coble replied for the ship's company—" As for the matter of that 'ere—there was no fear of their being quiet enough when there were more than two to one against them; but that, in fact, they had no animosity: for even if they did feel a little sore at what had happened, and their messmates being wounded, what was swinging at the yard-arm made them all friends again. The gentleman might take the cutter where he pleased, and might use her as long as he liked, and when he had done with her it was quite time enough to take her back to Portsmouth."

"Well, then, as we understand one another, we had now better make sail," said Sir Robert. "Cut away that rope," continued he, pointing to the whip by which Vanslyperken's body was suspended.

Jansen stepped forward with his snickasee, the rope was divided at once, and the body of the departed Vanslyperken plunged into the wave and disappeared.

"They mayn't cut this tho'!" cried Smallbones. "I'll not trust him—Jemmy, my boy, get up a pig of ballast. I'll sink him fifty fathoms deep, and then if so be he cum up again, why then I give it up for a bad job."

Jemmy brought up the pig of ballast, the body of Snarleyyow was lowered on board, and, after having been secured with divers turns of the rope to the piece of iron, was plunged by Smallbones into the wave.

"There," said Smallbones, "I don't a think that he will ever bite me any more, anyhow; there's no knowing though. Now I'll just go down and see if my bag be to be found, and then I'll dress myself like a Christian."

The cutter flew before the breeze which was on her quarter, and now that the hanging was over the females came on deck. One of the Jesuit priests was a good surgeon, and attended to the wounded men, who all promised to do well, and as Bill Spurey said,

"They'd all dance yet at the corporal's wedding."

"I say corporal, if we only could go to Amsterdam instead of going to Portsmouth."

"Mein Gott, yes;" replied the corporal, and acting upon this idea, he went aft and entered into conversation with Ramsay, giving him a detail of the affair with the widow and of her having gone to the Hague to accuse Vanslyperken, ending with expressing his wish of himself and the crew that they might go to the Hague instead of going to Portsmouth. Nothing could please Ramsay better. He was most anxious to send a letter to Mynheer Krause to inform him of the safety of his daughter, and he immediately answered that they might go if they pleased.

"Mein Gott—but how, mynheer—we no have the excuse."

"But I'll give you one," replied Ramsay—"you shall go to the Hague."

The corporal touched his hat with the greatest respect, and walked forward to communicate this good news. The crew of the *Yungfrau* and the conspirators or smugglers were soon on the best of terms, and as there was no one to check the wasteful expenditure of stores and no one accountable, the liquor was hoisted up on the forecastle, and the night passed in carousing.

"Well, he did love his dog after all," said Jemmy Ducks.

"And he's got his love with him," replied one of the smugglers.

"Now, Jemmy, let's have a song."

"It must be without the fiddle then," replied Jemmy, "for that's jammed up with the baggage—so here goes,"

I've often heard the chaplain say, when Davey Jones is nigh,
That we must call for help in need, to Providence on high,
But then he said, most plainly too, that we must do our best,
Our own exertions failing, leave to Providence the rest.

I never thought of this much till one day there came on board,
A chap who ventur'd to join as *seaman* by the Lord !
His hair hung down like reef points, and his phiz was very queer,
For his mouth was like a shark's, and turn'd down from ear to ear.

He hadn't stow'd his hammock, not much longer than a week,
When he swore he had a call, and the Lord he was to seek.
Now where he went to seek the Lord, I can't at all suppose,
'Twas not on deck for there I'm sure, he never show'd his nose.

He would not read the Bible, it warn't good enough for him,
The course we steered by that he said, would lead us all to sin ;
That we were damn'd and hell would gape, he often would us tell,
I know that when I heard his jaw, it made me gape like hell.

A storm came on, we sprung a leak, and sorely were we tired,
We plied the pumps, 'twas spell and spell, with lots of work beside ;
And what d'ye think this beggar did, the trick I do declare,
He called us all to leave the pumps and join with him in prayer

At last our boatswain Billy, who was a thund'ring Turk,
Goes up to him and says, "My man, why don't you do your work?"
"Avaunt you worst of sinners, I must save my soul," he cried,
"Confound your soul," says Billy, "then you shall not save your hide."

Acquaintance then he made soon with the end of the fore-brace,
It would have made you laugh to see his methodisty face;
He grinn'd like a roast monkey, and he howl'd like a baboon,
He had a dose from Billy, that he didn't forget soon.

"Take that," said Billy, when he'd done, "and now you'll please to work,
I read the Bible often—but I don't my duty shirk,
The pumps they are not choked yet, nor do we yet despair,
When all is up or we are saved, we'll join with you in prayer."

"And now we'll have one from the other side of the house," said Moggy, as soon as the plaudits were over.

"Come then, Anthony, you shall speak for us, and prove that we can sing a stave as well as honester men."

"With all my heart, William;—here's my very best."

The smuggler then sang as follows:

    Fill, lads, fill;
    Fill, lads, fill.
   Here we have a cure
    For every ill.
   If fortune's unkind
   As the north-east wind,
   Still we must endure,
   Trusting to our cure,
    In better luck still.

    Drink, boys, drink;
    Drink, boys, drink.
   The bowl let us drain
    With right good will.
   If women deceive
   Why should we grieve?
   Forgetting our pain,
   Love make again,
    With better luck still.

    Sing, lads, sing;
    Sing, lads, sing.
   Our voices we'll raise;
    Be merry still;
   If dead to-morrow,
   We brave all sorrow.
   Life's a weary maze—
   When we end our days,
    'Tis better luck still.

As the wounded men occupied the major part of the lower deck, and there was no accommodation for the numerous party of men and women on board, the carousing was kept up until the next morning, when, at daylight, the cutter was run into Cherbourg. The officers who came on board, went on shore with the report that the cutter belonged to the English government, and had been occupied by Sir Robert and his men, who were well known. The consequence was, an order for the cutter to leave the port immediately, as receiving her would be tantamount to an aggression on the part of France. But this order, although given, was not intended to be rigidly enforced, and there was plenty of time allowed for Sir Robert and his people to land with their specie and baggage.

Ramsay did not forget his promise to the corporal. He went to the French authorities, stated the great importance of his forwarding a letter to Amsterdam immediately, and that the way it might be effected would be very satisfactory. That, aware that King William was at the Hague, they should write a letter informing him of the arrival of the cutter; and that his Majesty might not imagine that the French government could sanction such outrages, they had sent her immediately on to him, under the charge of one of their officers, to wait upon his Majesty, and express their sentiments of regret that such a circumstance should have occurred. The authorities were aware that, to obey Sir Robert would not be displeasing to the court of Versailles, and that the excuse for so doing could only be taken as a compliment to the English court, therefore acted upon this suggestion. A French officer was sent on board of the cutter with the despatch, and Ramsay's letter to Mynheer Krause was committed to the charge of the corporal.

Before the sun had set, the *Yungfrau* was again at sea, and, on the third morning, anchored in her usual berth off the town of Amsterdam.

Chapter LV

In which we trust that everything will be arranged to the satisfaction of our readers.

THE French officer who was sent to explain what had occasioned the arrival of the cutter in the port of Cherbourg, immediately set off for the Hague, and was received by Lord Albemarle.

As soon as his credentials had been examined, he was introduced to his Majesty, King William.

"It appears," said his Majesty to Lord Albemarle, after the introduction, " that these Jacobite conspirators have saved us one trouble by hanging this traitor, Vanslyperken."

"Yes, your Majesty, he has met with his deserved punishment," replied Lord Albemarle.

Then addressing himself to the officer, "We will return our acknowledgments for this proof of good will on the part of the French government," said his Majesty, bowing. "My Lord Albemarle, you will see that this gentleman is suitably entertained."

The officer bowed low and retired.

"This is an over politeness which I do not admire," observed his Majesty to Lord Albemarle. "Let that person be well watched, depend upon it the letter is all a pretext, there is more plotting going on."

"I am of your Majesty's opinion, and shall be careful that your Majesty's commands are put in force," replied his lordship, as King William retired into his private apartments.

The cutter had not been half-an-hour at anchor, before Obadiah Coble went on shore with the corporal. Their first object was to apply to the authorities, that the wounded men might be sent to the hospital, which they were before the night; the next was to deliver the letter to Mynheer Krause. They thought it advisable to go first to the widow Vandersloosh, who was surprised at the sight of her dear corporal, and much more enraptured when she heard that Mr Vanslyperken and his cur had been hanged.

"I'll keep my word, corporal," cried the widow, "I told you I would not marry until he was hung, I don't care if I marry you to-morrow."

"Mein Gott, yes, to-day."

"No, no, not to-day, corporal, or to-morrow either, we must wait till the poor fellows are out of the hospital, for I must have them all to the wedding."

"Mein Gott, yes," replied the corporal.

The widow then proceeded to state how she had been thrown into a dungeon, and how she and Mynheer Krause, the syndic, had been released the next day, how Mynheer Krause's house had been burnt to the ground, and all the other particulars with which the reader is already acquainted.

This reminded the corporal of the letters to the Mynheer Krause, which he had for a time forgotten, and he inquired where he was to be found; but the widow was too prudent to allow the corporal to go himself—she sent Babette, who executed her commission without exciting any suspicion, and made Mynheer Krause very happy. He soon made his arrangements, and joined his daughter and Ramsay, who had not, however, awaited his arrival, but had been married the day after they landed at Cherbourg. Mynheer Krause was not a little surprised to find that his son-in-law was a Jacobite, but his incarceration and loss of his property had very much cooled his loyalty. He settled at Hamburgh, and became perfectly indifferent whether England was ruled by King William or King James.

Ramsay's marriage made him also less warm in the good cause; he had gained a pretty wife and a good fortune, and to be very loyal a person should be very poor. The death of King James in the year following, released him from his engagements, and, as he resided at

Hamburgh, he was soon forgotten, and was never called upon to embark in the subsequent fruitless attempts on the part of the Jacobites.

As it was necessary to write to the Admiralty in England, acquainting them with the fate of Mr Vanslyperken, and demanding that another officer should be sent out to take the command of the *Yungfrau*, a delay of three or four weeks took place, during which the cutter remained at Amsterdam; for Dick Short and Coble were no navigators, if they had wished to send her back; and, moreover, she had so many of her crew at the hospital, that she was weak-handed.

It was about a month after her arrival at Amsterdam, that every soul belonging to the cutter had gone on shore, and she was left to swing to the tide and foul her hawse, or go adrift if she pleased, for she had to take care of herself. This unusual disregard to naval instructions arose from the simple fact, that on that day was to be celebrated the marriage of widow Vandersloosh and Corporal Van Spitter.

Great, indeed, had been the preparations; all the ingenuity and talent of Jemmy Ducks, and Moggy, and Bill Spurey, for he and all the others were now discharged from the hospital, had been summoned to the assistance of the widow and Babette, in preparing and decorating the Lust Haus for the important ceremony, which the widow declared King William himself should hear of, cost what it might. Festoons of flowers, wreaths of laurel garlands from the ceiling, extra chandeliers, extra musicians, all were dressed out and collected in honour of this auspicious day.

The whole of the crew of the cutter were invited, not, however, to feast at the widow's expense; neither she nor the corporal would stand treat;—but to spend their money in honour of the occasion. And it must be observed, that since their arrival in port, the *Yungfrau* had spent a great deal of money at the widow's; which was considered strange, as they had not, for some time, received any pay.

And it was further observed, that none appeared so wealthy as Smallbones and Corporal Van Spitter. Some had asserted that it was the gold of Mr Vanslyperken, which had been appropriated by the crew to their own wants, considering themselves as his legitimate heirs. Whether this be true or not, it is impossible to say; certain it is, that there was no gold found in Mr Vanslyperken's cabin when his successor took possession of it. And equally certain it was, that all the *Yung fraus* had their pockets full of gold, and that the major part of this gold did ultimately fall into the possession of the widow Vandersloosh, who was heard to say, that Mr Vanslyperken had paid the expenses of her wedding. From these facts collected, we must leave the reader to draw what inference he may please.

The widow beautifully dressed;—a white kersey petticoat, deep blue stockings, silver buckles in her shoes, a scarlet velvet jacket, with long flaps before and behind, a golden cross six inches long, suspended to a velvet ribbon, to which was attached, half-way between the cross and her neck, a large gold heart, gold ear-rings, and on her head an ornament, which, in Holland and Germany, is called a *zitternabel*, shook and trembled as she walked along to church, hanging on the arm of her dear corporal. Some of the bridges were too narrow to admit the happy pair to pass abreast. The knot was tied. The name Vandersloosh was abandoned without regret, for the sharper one of Van Spitter; and flushed with joy, and the thermometer at ninety-six, the cavalcade returned home, and refreshed themselves with some beer of the Frau Van Spitter's own brewing.

Let it not, however, be supposed, that they dined *tête-à-tête*; no, no—the corporal and his wife were not so churlish as that. The dinner party consisted of a chosen set, the most particular friends of the corporal. Mr Short, first officer and boatswain, Mr William Spurey, Mr and Mrs Salisbury; and last, although not the least important person in this history, Peter Smallbones, Esquire, who having obtained money somehow, was now remarkable for the neatness of his apparel. The fair widow, assisted by

Moggy and Babette, cooked the dinner, and when it was ready came in from the kitchen as red as a fury and announced it: and then it was served up, and they all sat down to table in the little parlour. It was very close, the gentlemen took off their jackets, and the widow and Moggy fanned themselves, and the enormous demand by evaporation was supplied with foaming beer. None could have done the honours of the table better than the corporal and his lady who sat melting and stuck together on the little fubsy sofa, which had been the witness of so much pretended and so much real love.

But the Lust Haus is now lighted up, the company are assembling fast; Babette is waddling and trotting like an armadillo from corner to corner: Babette here, and Babette there, it is Babette everywhere. The room is full, and the musicians have commenced tuning their instruments; the party run from the table to join the rest. A general cheer greets the widow as she is led into the room by the corporal—for she had asked many of her friends as well as the crew of the *Yungfrau*, and many others came who were not invited; so that the wedding day, instead of disbursement, produced one of large receipt to the happy pair.

"Now then, corporal, you must open the ball with your lady," cried Bill Spurey.

"Mein Gott, yes."

"What shall it be, Madam Van Spitter?"

"A waltz, if you please."

The musicians struck up a waltz, and Corporal Van Spitter, who had no notion of waltzing, further than having seen the dance performed by others, seized his wife by the waist, who, with an amorous glance, dropped her fat arm upon the corporal's shoulder. This was the signal for the rest—the corporal had made but one turn before a hundred couple more were turning also—the whole room seemed turning. The corporal could not waltz, but he could turn—he held on fast by the widow, and with such a firm piece of resistance he kept a centrifugal balance, and without regard to time or space, he increased his velocity at a prodigious rate. Round they went, with the dangerous force of the two iron balls suspended to the fly-wheel which regulate the power of some stupendous steam-engine.

The corporal would not, and his better half could not, stop. The first couple they came in contact with were hurled to the other side of the room; a second and a third fell, and still the corporal wheeled on; two chairs and a table were swept away in a moment. Three young women, with baskets of cakes and nuts, were thrown down together, and the contents of all their baskets scattered on the floor; and "Bravo, corporal!" resounded from the crew of the *Yungfrau*—Babette and two bottles of ginger beer were next demolished; Jemmy Ducks received a hoist, and Smallbones was flatted to a pancake. Every one fled from the orbit of these revolving spheres, and they were left to wheel by themselves. At last, Mrs Van Spitter finding that nothing else would stop her husband, who, like all heavy bodies, once put in motion, returned it in proportion to his weight, dropped down, and left him to support her whole weight. This was more than the corporal could stand, and it brought him up all standing—he stopped, dropped his wife, and reeled to a chair, for he was so giddy that he could not keep his legs, and so out of breath that he had lost his wind.

"Bravo, corporal!" was shouted throughout the room, while his spouse hardly knew whether she should laugh, or scold him well; but, it being the wedding night, she deferred the scolding for that night only, and she gained a chair, and fanned and wiped, and fanned and wiped again. The corporal, shortly afterwards, would have danced again, but Mrs Van Spitter having had quite enough for that evening, she thanked him for the offer, was satisfied with his prowess, but declined on the score of the extreme sultriness of the weather; to which observation, the corporal replied, as usual,

"Mein Gott, yes."

The major part of the evening was passed in dancing and drinking. The corporal and his wife, with Babette, now attending to the wants of their customers, who, what with the exercise, the heat of the weather, and the fumes of tobacco, were more than usually thirsty, and as they became satisfied with dancing, so did they call for refreshments.

But we cannot find space to dwell upon the quantity of beer, the variety of liquors which were consumed at this eventful wedding, with which we wind up our eventful history; nor even to pity the breathless, flushed, and overheated Babette, who was so ill the next day, as to be unable to quit her bed; nor can we detail the jokes, the merriment, and the songs which went round, the peals of laughter, the loud choruses, the antic feats performed by the company; still more impossible would it be to give an idea of the three tremendous cheers, which shook the Lust Haus to its foundations, when Corporal and Mistress Van Spitter, upon their retiring, bade farewell to the company assembled.

The observation of Jemmy Salisbury, as he waddled out, was as correct as it was emphatic:

"Well, Dick, this *has been* a spree!"

"Yes," replied Dick Short.

THE END.

www.ingramcontent.com/pod-product-compliance
Lightning Source LLC
Chambersburg PA
CBHW022148300426
44115CB00006B/396